The New Race Question

The New Race Question

How the Census Counts
Multiracial Individuals

JOEL PERLMANN AND MARY C. WATERS
EDITORS

Russell Sage Foundation
New York, New York

The Levy Economics Institute of Bard College
Annandale-on-Hudson, New York

The Levy Economics Institute of Bard College

The Levy Economics Institute of Bard College, founded in 1986, is a nonprofit, nonpartisan research organization devoted to public service. Through scholarship and economic research it generates viable, effective public policy responses to important economic problems that profoundly affect the quality of life in the United States and abroad.

Library of Congress Cataloging-in-Publication Data

The new race question : how the census counts multiracial individuals / Joel Perlmann and Mary C. Waters, editors.
p. cm.
Includes bibliographical references and index.
ISBN 0-87154-657-4
1. Racially mixed people—United States—Census—Methodology. 2. Racially mixed people—United States—Statistics. 3. Minorities—United States—Statistics. 4. United States—Census—Methodology. I. Perlmann, Joel. II. Waters, Mary

E184.A1 M568 2002
305.8′04′073—dc21   2002066750

Text design by Suzanne Nichols

RUSSELL SAGE FOUNDATION
112 East 64th Street, New York, New York 10021
10 9 8 7 6 5 4 3 2 1

In memory of Hugh Davis Graham

Contents

Contributors   ix

Acknowledgments   xiii

Introduction   1

PART I   **WHAT DO WE KNOW FROM COUNTING MULTIRACIALS?**

Chapter 1   RACIAL IDENTITIES IN 2000: THE RESPONSE TO THE
                MULTIPLE-RACE RESPONSE OPTION   33
                Reynolds Farley

Chapter 2   DOES IT MATTER HOW WE MEASURE? RACIAL
                CLASSIFICATION AND THE CHARACTERISTICS
                OF MULTIRACIAL YOUTH   62
                David R. Harris

Chapter 3   MIXED RACE AND ETHNICITY IN CALIFORNIA   102
                Sonya M. Tafoya

PART II   **HOW MUCH WILL IT MATTER?**

Chapter 4   BACK IN THE BOX: THE DILEMMA OF USING
                MULTIPLE-RACE DATA FOR SINGLE-RACE LAWS   119
                Joshua R. Goldstein and Ann J. Morning

Chapter 5   INADEQUACIES OF MULTIPLE-RESPONSE RACE DATA
                IN THE FEDERAL STATISTICAL SYSTEM   137
                Roderick J. Harrison

Chapter 6   THE LEGAL IMPLICATIONS OF A MULTIRACIAL CENSUS   161
                Nathaniel Persily

PART III   **A MULTIRACIAL FUTURE?**

Chapter 7   AMERICAN INDIANS: CLUES TO THE FUTURE OF OTHER
                RACIAL GROUPS   189
                C. Matthew Snipp

Chapter 8   CENSUS BUREAU LONG-TERM RACIAL PROJECTIONS:
             INTERPRETING THEIR RESULTS AND SEEKING THEIR
             RATIONALE   215
             Joel Perlmann

Chapter 9   RECENT TRENDS IN INTERMARRIAGE AND IMMIGRATION
             AND THEIR EFFECTS ON THE FUTURE RACIAL
             COMPOSITION OF THE U.S. POPULATION   227
             Barry Edmonston, Sharon M. Lee, and Jeffrey S. Passel

PART IV   **THE POLITICS OF RACE NUMBERS**

Chapter 10   HISTORY, HISTORICITY, AND THE CENSUS COUNT BY
             RACE   259
             Matthew Frye Jacobson

Chapter 11   WHAT RACE ARE YOU?   263
             Werner Sollors

Chapter 12   COUNTING BY RACE: THE ANTEBELLUM LEGACY   269
             Margo J. Anderson

Chapter 13   THE ORIGINS OF OFFICIAL MINORITY DESIGNATION   288
             Hugh Davis Graham

Chapter 14   LESSONS FROM BRAZIL: THE IDEATIONAL AND
             POLITICAL DIMENSIONS OF MULTIRACIALITY   300
             Melissa Nobles

Chapter 15   REFLECTIONS ON RACE, HISPANICITY, AND ANCESTRY
             IN THE U.S. CENSUS   318
             Nathan Glazer

Chapter 16   MULTIRACIALISM AND THE ADMINISTRATIVE STATE   327
             Peter Skerry

Chapter 17   MULTIPLE RACIAL IDENTIFIERS IN THE 2000 CENSUS,
             AND THEN WHAT?   340
             Jennifer L. Hochschild

Chapter 18   RACE IN THE 2000 CENSUS: A TURNING POINT   354
             Kenneth Prewitt

Appendix   BRIDGING FROM OLD TO NEW   363

Chapter 19   COMPARING CENSUS RACE DATA UNDER THE OLD AND
             THE NEW STANDARDS   365
             Clyde Tucker, Steve Miller, and Jennifer Parker

Index   391

Contributors

Joel Perlmann is a senior scholar at the Levy Economics Institute of Bard College and the Levy Economics Institute Research Professor at the college.

Mary C. Waters is the Harvard College Professor and chair of the Sociology Department at Harvard University.

Margo J. Anderson is professor of history and director of the Urban Studies Programs at the University of Wisconsin at Milwaukee.

Barry Edmonston is professor of urban studies and planning and director of the Population Research Center at Portland State University.

Reynolds Farley is a research scientist at the Population Studies Center at the University of Michigan's Institute for Social Research and professor of sociology.

Nathan Glazer is professor emeritus of education and sociology at Harvard University.

Joshua R. Goldstein is associate professor in the Department of Sociology and the Woodrow Wilson School of Public and International Affairs at Princeton University.

Hugh Davis Graham was Holland N. McTyeire Professor of History and professor of political science at Vanderbilt University.

David R. Harris is assistant professor of sociology at the University of Michigan and assistant research scientist at the Institute for Social Research.

Roderick J. Harrison is associate professor of sociology at Howard University. He was chief of racial statistics at the Census Bureau from 1990 to 1997.

Jennifer L. Hochschild is professor of government at Harvard University, with a joint appointment in the Afro-American Studies Department.

Matthew Frye Jacobson is professor of American studies, history, and African American studies at Yale University.

Sharon M. Lee is professor of sociology at Portland State University.

Steve Miller is a mathematical statistician in the Office of Survey Methods Research at the U.S. Bureau of Labor Statistics.

Ann J. Morning is a doctoral candidate in the Department of Sociology at Princeton University.

Melissa Nobles is associate professor of political science at the Massachusetts Institute of Technology.

Jennifer Parker is acting chief of the Population Epidemiology Branch at the National Center for Health Statistics.

Jeffrey S. Passel is principal research associate at the Population Studies Center of the Urban Institute.

Nathaniel Persily is assistant professor at the University of Pennsylvania Law School.

Kenneth Prewitt is the Carnegie Professor of Public Affairs at Columbia University and was director of the Census Bureau from 1998 to 2001.

Peter Skerry is professor of government at Claremont McKenna College and senior fellow at the Brookings Institution.

C. Matthew Snipp is professor of sociology at Stanford University.

Werner Sollors is the Henry B. and Anne M. Cabot Professor of English Literature and professor of Afro-American studies at Harvard University.

Sonya M. Tafoya is a research associate at the Public Policy Institute of California.

Clyde Tucker is senior survey methodologist in the Office of Survey Methods Research at the U.S. Bureau of Labor Statistics.

Acknowledgments

It is difficult to imagine how editing a volume of essays could have been smoother or simpler. The two editors enjoyed working together throughout. Our authors were excited by the topic, interested in each other's work, grateful for suggestions about revision, and even attentive to them.

All of the intellectual excitement that this project engendered, first at a conference and since in the creation of this volume, has rested on an earlier decision taken by Dimitri B. Papadimitriou, president of the Levy Economics Institute of Bard College, that the topic was indeed important—both generally to the conceptualization of key features of American social life, and to public policy issues in particular. The Levy Institute undertook the cost and effort of bringing several dozen scholars and government officials together to its splendid accommodations and encouraging the production of excellent papers; the Institute staff, under the leadership of Francis Spring and Susan Howard, has been tireless, efficient, and patient from first to last. We are glad to have an opportunity to thank everyone connected with the Institute for all manner of support over an extended period.

The Russell Sage Foundation showed an interest in the manuscript from the first, and rounded up thoughtful and helpful anonymous reviewers who read and commented with dispatch. The staff at Russell Sage then shepherded the manuscript through to publication carefully and with an absolute minimum of attention from us. We are grateful to them, and especially to Production Editor Emily Chang and Director of Publications Suzanne Nichols. We are most grateful to Eric Wanner, president of the Foundation, for his support of this volume, and for the program of high-quality research on the census that the foundation has supported for many years.

Many more people attended the conference and contributed observations during discussions than our list of authors would imply. We are especially grateful to those others who accepted a role in the conference program. Listed by their affiliation at the time, they are: Arthur Cresce, Jorge del Pinal, Nampeo Mckenny and John Thompson (Census Bureau); Susan Schechter (Office of Management and Budget); Jennifer Madans and Jacqueline Wilson Lucas (National Center for Health Statistics); Anita S. Hodgkiss (Justice Department), David McMillen (U. S. House Committee on Government Reform); Charles Hirschman (University of Washington); Nancy Krieger (Harvard University); and Naomi Mezey (Georgetown University).

Finally, we are grateful to TerriAnn Lowenthal (Census 2000 Initiative) and to Heather Gerken (Harvard University); neither could make it to the conference but each patiently fielded many questions while also offering encouragement.

We dedicate the volume to the memory of a fellow contributor to this volume. An important historian of the recent past, he will be sorely missed. He did not expect to see the published copy, but made sure to leave his revised draft the way he wanted it read.

Joel Perlmann
Mary C. Waters

INTRODUCTION

Joel Perlmann and Mary C. Waters

B ITTERLY fought controversies surrounded the late-twentieth century censuses in the United States, and in particular the 1990 census, over the issue of population undercounts and possible adjustments. Such controversies drew attention again in connection with Census 2000. Yet Kenneth Prewitt, the director of the Census Bureau during the 2000 enumeration, writes in this volume that when historians look back on the history of the census, the debates over the undercount will get only a footnote; the change in the race question will get a chapter. Indeed, the 2000 census race question has opened the door to a new way of measuring and thinking about race. By allowing individuals to report identification with more than one race, the census challenges long-held fictions and strongly defended beliefs about the very nature and definition of race in our society. This volume examines these monumental changes from a multidisciplinary perspective.

Under the old formulation of the race question, the respondent was instructed to select his or her race from a list and to mark one category only; under the new formulation, which was introduced in Census 2000 and will be used by all federal agencies by 2003, the respondent may mark one or more races. The Census Bureau (and other government data collectors) must now decide how people who mark more than one race will be counted and how the counts of races will be aggregated from the raw data.

At first sight the issue seems technical and marginal; but behind it lie at least two important features of American life and American thinking about race. The first is the growing prevalence and recognition of racial intermarriage. Not so long ago, according to the typical pattern, interracial sex and marriage were officially forbidden, and offspring of unions that violated these norms were ignored or defined away. The mechanism by which this was usually accomplished was the "one-drop rule," which defined anyone with any African ancestors as black. Under these circumstances, "race" distinguished social groups in important ways.

By contrast, if members of different "races" are allowed to inter-mingle and their mixed status is not ignored (no one-drop rule placing them in one race category only), and if racial groups do in fact intermingle to a great extent, then racial origins begin to look like ethnic origins—that is, as origins that are often mixed. Tens, if not hundreds, of millions of Americans have ancestors from three or more places, such as England, Germany, and Italy.

Second, the development of the strong antidiscrimination and voting rights laws of the 1960s, and affirmative action policies, came at great social and political costs, first for African Americans and later for other groups as well. These laws need simple and clear race categories into which to place individuals for the purposes of documenting and redressing discrimination. Yet the social reality of racial intermarriage is increasingly at odds with this requirement for simplicity.

Race counts are used in connection with legislative and judicial actions involving civil rights and voting rights, as well as in educational and health statistics. They are also the basis for Census Bureau projections about the future racial composition of the U.S. population. In addition, researchers across the social sciences use race data to analyze the experiences of racial and ethnic groups. How, then, will racial combinations be aggregated under the new race question? Who will decide, for example, whether a respondent who self-identifies as black and white, or an Asian category and white, will be counted as a member of the minority or as a white? At present, the Office of Management and Budget (OMB) has been handed the politically hot potato. That agency has ruled that, for purposes of civil rights enforcement, people who identify themselves as members of more than one race should be counted in the minority category. For all other purposes guidelines have been slower to emerge and are looser.

As many of the chapters in this volume make clear, there is more than one reasonable way in which these classificatory decisions might be made. This is the context for the conference held at the Levy Economics Institute on September 22 and 23, 2000, which considered these issues under several rubrics. The conference brought together scholars from sociology, demography, political science, history, and American studies and government officials from several important federal agencies—the Office of Management and Budget, the Department of Justice, the Bureau of Labor Statistics, and the National Center for Health Statistics, as well as the Census Bureau. These experts came together to debate the past and future of counting and classifying Americans by race and to assess the implications of the new question that allows more than one race to be reported.

This volume brings to light the many ways in which a seemingly small change in the way race data is solicited and reported can have far-reaching effects and expose deep fissures in our society. Before turning to the individual contributions, however, we want to bring a broader background into view—on the American experience with ethnic and racial blending and on the ways in which American data collection have related, on the one hand, to that experience of blending and, on the other hand, to the data collection needs of a government that monitors racial discrimination and the nature of racial inequality.

Interethnic Union in American History

American history would be unrecognizable without ethnic blending among the descendants of immigrants, especially (though not exclusively) immigrants from Europe. From colonial times to the present, immigrants typically married their own; the second generation did so much less consistently; and the third generation still less so, with probably a majority by then marrying members of other ethnic groups. By the fourth and fifth generations, few kept track of all the origins. Although we have many sociological studies of intermarriage among the first and second generations, studies examining intermarriage in later generations have been few, no doubt because of the limitations of evidence. Nevertheless, the basic pattern is clear enough. Ethnic intermarriage is about as overwhelming and unambiguous as any generalization about the American population. From Michel (J. Hector St. John) de Crèvecoeur's eighteenth-century observations on "the American, this new man," arising out of various European immigrant stocks to the data from census after census in the twentieth century, intermarriage among the descendants of European groups has been crucial to the making of "Americans" out of the descendants of "hyphenated Americans" (Heer 1980, 512–21; Lieberson and Waters 1988).

Even among Europeans, the immigrant generation often drew firm lines of division between groups. Arguments for immigration restriction—in congressional debate and across the land—turned, in part, on the notion that the "racial composition" of the immigrant pool was changing. As late as 1920, the suggestion that members of all these "races" were "white" would have elicited amused or heated rejoinders from many influential Americans that the statement was untrue or that it missed crucial "inherent" divisions among whites (Higham 1994 [1955], chapters 6–11).

Ethnic groupings can be loosely thought of as classifications relating people's origins in the different countries or local areas of the world from which they or their ancestors came (including American Indians, who trace their ancestries to pre-Columbian America). The meanings of "race" are painfully woven into the texture of American life. We need not try to exhaust either past or present meanings to make a simple observation. Races are usually discussed, in demographic terms, as a special subset of ethnicity, in that race relates to classifications of ancestral origins for groups treated in especially distinct ways in the American past. Typically, when we use the term "race" we mean to denote a group that is still treated in some specially distinct ways. For example, a concern with racial classification arises from such legacies as slavery, the near extermination of the American Indian groups, and state laws forbidding interracial marriage—laws that survived in various states until 1967, when the U.S. Supreme Court finally ruled them unconstitutional.

Moreover, even if none of these forces are directly operating today, the groups in question remain distinct in American life for a host of reasons, suggesting the need to monitor their well-being by collecting evidence about them.[1] Since 1978 the federal government has officially designated certain racial and ethnic groups—whites, African Americans, American Indians, Asians, and Hispanics. The OMB's Directive 15 codified American ideas about race into statistical categories that every federal agency was to use in its record keeping. However, the directive gave special status to Hispanics, designating them as a group but stating that they could be of any race.

How much racial blending, then, has there been in America, and how much is occurring now? In some sense, everyone is the product of mixed racial origins. In terms of one or another of the differing definitions of race that have operated in this country since 1900, most Americans are of mixed racial origin; at the turn of the century, "Nordic," "alpine," and "Mediterranean" groups were often classified as races. However, the situation is similar even if we restrict ourselves to the current common meanings of race—black, white, Native American, Asian, and the added "ethnic minority group," Hispanic. Never mind that all humanity appears to have emerged from African ancestors; a shorter "long view" will suffice to make the point, especially for blacks, Native Americans, and Hispanics.[2]

The importance of a clear-cut difference between free and slave, and later between subjugated blacks and subordinating whites, meant that the black-white color line was sharply and unambiguously drawn. From early colonial times, for example, black-white marriages were illegal. However, notwithstanding the law and the ideology of race, black-white sexual unions occurred in a wide variety of social circumstances, often, of course, involving the sexual exploitation of the enslaved. An extensive mulatto population was documented when the census of 1850 first explored their prevalence nationally. Over the long course of slavery, these mixed-race people came to be defined as black in law and custom, according to the "one-drop" rule, by which membership in the white race was limited to those without any black ancestors. Not all societies built around a racial divide have been organized in this way; South Africa, for example, recognized the "colored" population of mixed-race descent as a separate legal status. Melissa Nobles, in her contribution to this volume, traces the differences in classification of mixed black-white people in Brazil and the United States. In the United States, those in the middle were moved over the line to the black category.

Because a substantial mulatto population intermarried into the rest of the black population, demographers estimate that extraordinarily high proportions of "black Americans" in the United States in fact have some white ancestry (quite apart from any recent trends in interracial marriage). Moreover, some fraction of those mulattoes fair-skinned enough to "pass for white" did so; and because these people typically married into white America, a nontrivial proportion of "white Americans"—amounting to tens of millions of "white" people—have some black ancestry. Thus until recently, the black-white line was preserved in law and race theory, and in much of popular culture, but not in the true genealogical legacies of the population.[3]

Among Native Americans, a somewhat different pattern emerged; there are many reasons for the difference, but certainly a crucial one is the absence of institutionalized slavery for the Native American. In general, as Matthew Snipp notes in chapter 7, by the early twentieth century many people who said they were Native Americans by race also noted that they were of mixed descent, with some white or black ancestors as well. Consequently, when government dealt with tribal communities in the twentieth century for numerous purposes, tribal membership was defined in terms of the proportion of an individual's ancestors who had been tribal members. The required proportion differed from tribe to tribe: a quarter, an eighth, or less. In addition, the individual had to be recognized by the tribe as a part of the community. That is, the criteria of membership include both a "blood quantum" (a specific fraction of Native American ancestry) and a subjective element of communal recognition; there was no "one-drop rule" for them.

Hispanic Americans present a third variant. The intermingling of Africans, Europeans, and native peoples in the societies of Latin America occurred under a variety of circumstances, but the upshot was that many Hispanic immigrants arrive in this country knowing that they have origins in two or more of these different peoples. At the same time, they also learn that in the United States black and white are sharply divided. The treatment of Hispanics in the statistical system was shaped by early attempts to measure this population in the Southwest. In 1930, the Census Bureau added "Mexican" to the list of "races" or colors on the census schedule. The Mexican government responded with an official protest to the effect that all Mexicans are white. Since that time the census has gathered data on the Hispanic population separately from that of other races—since 1970 through the use of a separate Spanish-origin question. Officially, the OMB states that Hispanics can be of any race. However, even in 2000 the Census Bureau and the federal government did not recognize intermixing among Hispanics. The national origin question still does not allow multiple responses.

Thus a person who is Cuban and Mexican cannot report both but must choose just one identity.

Against this historical background, consider the present-day intermarriage patterns of the groups we commonly designate as races. Two of these groups, Asians and Hispanics, dominate the great wave of contemporary American immigration; and conversely, contemporary immigrants dominate the populations of these two groups. Consequently, it should not be surprising that the intermarriage patterns among these groups are similar to those noted among other descendants of immigrant groups: the first generation have tended to marry their own (many, indeed, arrived as married couples); but their children have been more likely to intermarry. We do not yet sense the full impact of these intermarried couples and their children in social patterns and social statistics because the second generation of the post-1965 immigration is only now reaching marriageable age. Yet as these groups age generationally, intermarriage is sure to increase from already high levels. A high rate of intermarriage also occurs among American Indians (although the numbers involved are relatively small compared with Asians, Hispanics, or African Americans).[4] By contrast, the black intermarriage rate is very low.

Consider for example, native-born, young (between twenty-four and thirty-five years of age) married people in 1990. Some two-fifths of this cohort of Hispanics and more than half of these Asians and American Indians married members of other groups.[5] Yet more than nine out of ten blacks in the group married other blacks. Nevertheless, even blacks have been out-marrying more than before; the rate for better-educated young black men rose from about 6 percent in 1980 to more than 9 percent in 1990 (Qian 1997; Besharov and Sullivan 1996, 19–21).[6] So there are really two patterns of interracial marriage today: it is still relatively uncommon among blacks and increasingly common among other nonwhites.

Both of these patterns involve huge numbers of nonwhite Americans. Race in America has always meant first and foremost the black-white divide—hardly a surprise given that that divide once distinguished slave from master and that by far the greatest numbers of nonwhites have in the past been blacks. Thus until recently racial intermarriage meant first and foremost black-white intermarriage. However, that way of thinking about interracial marriage has been rendered inadequate by the rising number of Asians and Hispanics and their rising proportion among all nonwhite groups.

The proportion of blacks in this nonwhite population is dropping sharply. If one met a nonwhite American before 1970, he or she was very likely to have been black; today the chances are better than even that the nonwhite American will not be black. The percentage of blacks among all nonwhites stood at 66 percent in 1970, 48 percent in 1990, and 43 percent in 2000 and can be expected to continue declining in coming decades (Harrison and

Bennett 1995, 142; Farley 1996, 213; U.S. Census Bureau 2001, 8, 10).[7] The high intermarriage rates among the other nonwhites (those who are not blacks) is therefore crucial.

Will black intermarriage be much more prevalent in the future? We cannot judge with any certainty today. One source of change is the children of today's black-white marriages; these children may be more likely to intermarry than children of two black parents. Moreover, the impact of relatively small increases in black intermarriage generally should be appreciated: if over the next generation, for example, the out-marriage rate for blacks rose from roughly 6 percent overall to roughly 10 percent overall, that would be glacial progress by any standard except the black-white standard of the past. Yet even at a 6 percent out-marriage rate, the proportion of new interracial *marriages* amounts to 11 percent of all new marriages involving a black member—because each intraracial marriage involving a black includes two blacks, and each interracial marriage involving a black includes only one black; and a 10 percent out-marriage rate for individuals implies that the proportion of new interracial marriages would rise to 18 percent of all marriages involving a black member. Generally, it is the rate of new interracial marriages, not the rate of out-marrying individuals, that determines the rate of interracial offspring.[8] In any case, whatever the future of black out-marriage, interracial marriage among the native born in the other legally designated nonwhite groups is common today.

Government Data Collection and Ethnic Blending

First, how does the U.S. Census Bureau gather information on ethnicity generally, and second, how does the bureau handle the offspring of ethnic intermarriages? Researchers and government bureaucrats have identified groups through the question on birthplace and birthplace of parents asked from 1850 to 1970, through a "native tongue" or language question, and, in the case of Hispanic Americans, through a classification based on having a Spanish surname and, after 1970, a separate Spanish-origin question. We stress the birthplace and birthplace of parents question in the discussion that follows. Birthplace has been the criteria used most continuously over the years for collecting ethnic information, and also the focus on birthplaces will allow us to highlight certain contrasts with the procedure for collecting race information.

Between 1850 and 1970, the Census Bureau collected information on the individual's birthplace. The parental birthplace question was added in 1880 and was included in every census through 1970. The parental birthplace question does not appear in the 1980, 1990, or 2000 decennial censuses—much to the chagrin of social scientists concerned with ethnicity.

The parental birthplace questions have, however, appeared fairly regularly during the past twenty years on the bureau's Current Population Survey (typically, of some fifty thousand sampled households) and on other census instruments. Insofar as birthplace is one criterion of ethnic origin, the issue of mixed ethnic origins arises in connection with the parental birthplace questions: each parent can be born in only one country, but of course it need not be the same country for each parent. Both parents born in Italy? One born in Italy, one in Poland? One in Italy, one in the United States? All acceptable responses. Thus parental birthplace is recognized as requiring two questions, each limited by definition to one country.[9]

In the censuses conducted from 1980 to 2000, the Census Bureau replaced the parental birthplace questions with a question inquiring into ethnic origins that could extend much further back in time than merely the two generations of information captured by respondent's and parents' birthplaces. This question was a response to claims from European ethnic groups that the first- and second-generation birthplace questions did not capture their membership (which was increasingly third and later generation in nature). The ancestry question asked each individual to state the ancestry or ancestries with which he or she identified.

The Census Bureau also added a Hispanic-origin question on the long form to a sample of respondents in 1970 and, in 1980, on the short form to the entire population. The Hispanic-origin question replaced the Spanish-origin question; the new question was designed to identify the Hispanic population of the country, including those who no longer spoke Spanish, and thus could not be identified through the language question, and those who did not have a Spanish surname. The Hispanic-origin question asks whether or not the respondent is of Hispanic origin, and if so from which of several specific countries of origin. Because the answer to the Hispanic origin question can be cross-classified with the race question, we often see the categories "non-Hispanic whites" "non-Hispanic blacks" and "Hispanics" (the last with the footnote that "Hispanics may be of any race"). Groups representing the Hispanic population strongly support inclusion of the Hispanic-origin question because asking specifically about Hispanic origin increases the number of people identifying as Hispanic (as compared with just counting those who give a Hispanic response to the ancestry question or who write in a Hispanic response to the race question). The ancestry question, by contrast, appears only on the census long form, reaching a huge sample but not most households.

Although both the ancestry question and the Hispanic-origin question ask respondents to report their ethnic origins, the two questions were stimulated by different political forces and are administered and coded separately at the bureau. They also have different purposes, because counts from the Hispanic-origin question can be used in legal cases involving civil and voting rights of Hispanics. In the other major government survey—the Current Population Survey (the CPS, administered by the Bureau of Labor Statistics and the Census Bureau), the origin question reveals a strange outcome of the historical processes we have been discussing. For the past quarter century, CPS interviewers have asked, "What is the origin or descent of each person in this household?" The interviewers then show respondents a flashcard with some twenty ethnic categories; seven of these categories apply to Hispanic origin: Mexican American, Chicano, Mexican, Puerto Rican, Cuban, Central or South American, and Other Hispanic. The rest of the categories apply to other major American origin groups: German, Italian, Irish, Dutch, French, Swedish, Polish, Hungarian, Russian, English, Scottish, Afro-American (as well as "another group" and "don't know"). However, though all this information is duly coded, for some two decades the CPS reports have published the counts only for the Hispanic-origin responses, and they have included only those counts in the data sets released to researchers.[10]

Three features of the ancestry question are crucially relevant to understanding racial classification. First, the ancestry question asks people to declare the ancestry or ancestries with which they most closely identify. Thus a strong subjective element is built into the question. Unlike questions such as "Where were you born?" or "How many years of schooling have you had?" it does not ask for what might be called an objective answer; rather, it explicitly encourages a statement of preferences. The rationale for this formulation leads us back to intermarriage. Many people are able to trace their origins to numerous ancestries (too many to list) or may not even know about all of their ancestries. So they are asked to list the ancestries they consider most meaningful.[11]

The second relevant feature of the ancestry question is that the Census Bureau instructs Americans explicitly that they can identify themselves with more than one ethnic ancestry. Many millions of Americans have taken the trouble to list two ethnic ancestries, and millions more list three. The Census Bureau has taken the trouble to code first- and second-ancestry responses and, in 1980, even to detail the most prevalent combinations of three responses.

The third relevant feature is how much the ancestry responses have varied among the same people over time. The question calls for a subjective response about loyalties that for many appear to be very weak. In 1980, "English" was given as one example in the question wording, whereas "German" was not. In 1990, "German" was present but "English" was not. As a result of this seemingly trivial change, the percentage listing English ancestry declined by a large fraction, and the percentage claiming German ancestry rose by a comparable amount. Moreover, as a result, in 1980, English was reported as the largest ancestry group in the United States, and in 1990, Germans took the lead. Other ancestry groups also fluctuated widely depending on whether they were represented in the list of examples. This confusion in the responses tells us something important about the long-term results of population mixing and the attenuation of connections with the origins of relatively remote ancestors. Keeping track of American ancestries at the Census Bureau eventually gets messy because of intermarriage patterns; and that is as it should be. A simple answer would be a false answer. It would imply that people did not intermarry much in American history, or that Americans keep careful track of the ethnic origin of distant ancestors whom they never knew (Alba 1995, 5).

The Old Race Question and Racial Blending

In sum, for the most important questions that have traditionally defined ethnicity—parental birthplace and ancestry—the Census Bureau allows for the possibility that the respondent is of multiple ethnic origins and often tabulates the results of these ethnic intermarriages (we return to Hispanic origins after considering the race question). On the race question, by contrast, there was an explicit instruction to mark only one category. What if a person demurred and marked two or more? Using certain rules (such as which race is listed first), the bureau recoded the response so that only one race was counted.[12]

For our purposes, this instruction to mark one race only is the most striking peculiarity of the census race question. However, there are others. A second is that in some years the question is labeled on the census form as a question about race and in other years it is not. In 1990 it was labeled, but in 1980 respondents were simply asked to complete the sentence, "This person is . . ." There followed the four specific racial designations— white, black, Native American, and Asian or Pacific Islander—and the designation "other." Later, the bureau tabulated the answers under a heading of races. A third peculiarity is that the list of races includes heterogeneous subgroupings of peoples—for example, the countries of birth or origin in Asia or specific Native American tribes. The bureau's description of the race question reveals the subjective nature of the racial data it was collecting and the general ambivalence, and touchiness, about the intellectual standing of the material. As described by the Census Bureau, "The concept of race as used by the Census Bureau reflects self-identification; it does not denote any clear-cut scientific definition of biological stock. The data for race represent self-classification by people according to the race with which they most closely identify. Furthermore, it is recognized that the categories of the race item include both racial and national origin or sociocultural groups" (U.S. Census Bureau 1992, B-30).

This statement unequivocally rules out any need for government officials to believe that racial classification has a meaningful basis in biology or to define any objective meaning for a racial category at all: "race" is a term in popular usage and whatever it may mean, a person belongs to whatever category of race that person believes he or she belongs. However, if the answer is based on subjective identification, as in the ancestry question, why can't respondents chose two or more races with which to identify, as they can with ancestry? The answer is clear when one appreciates the current use and origin of the race categories. They emerge from the OMB Directive 15—used to classify people for federal statistical purposes into counts that lie at the heart of a great deal of civil rights legislation.

Civil Rights Legislation, Government Directives, and the Debate over Changing the "Old" Race Question

The great irony is that the American government gathers data on people's race through a more or less slippery and subjective procedure of self-identification and then must use these counts as the basis of legal status in an important domain of law and administrative regulation—namely, civil rights. That domain requires legal statuses that are, in the words of the original mandate to the OMB, "complete and non-overlapping." In order to square this circle, the government, while relying on a subjective definition of race, also placed an unrealistic restriction on that subjectivity—only one race could be chosen (even as it routinely accepted multiple parental birthplaces and ethnic ancestries). In order to have clear-cut racial categories for legal purposes we have created a system of counting that ignores an increasingly widespread reality. Denying that members of different races marry is like treating them as members of different biological species. All the while, the Census Bureau is acknowledging the stunningly high rates of intermarriage among those ethnic groups not designated as racial groups, through its allowing and coding of multiple responses to the ancestry question. If we mean to break down racial barriers, we have an interest in seeing to it that racial intermarriage is treated in the same matter-of-fact way that any other form of ethnic intermarriage is treated. Yet we also have an interest in ensuring that civil rights legislation, which rests on clear counts of racial membership, is not hobbled by ambiguities. In this context, multiracial interest groups demanded that they not be obliged to mark themselves or their offspring as members of only one race. The success of this pressure group—in forcing the issue out of technical committees and into the broader public domain—helped trigger, during the late 1990s, a full review of the federal government's 1970s efforts (in Directive 15) to specify a straight-forward racial classification scheme, with complete and unambiguous racial allocations.

In the context of this contrast between traditional measures of ethnicity, on the one hand, and the old race question, on the other, it is fascinating to consider, if only as an aside, the current nature of the Hispanic-origin question. The Hispanic-origin question is also a subjective one. How is a respondent with one Mexican-origin great-grandmother, no other Hispanic ancestors, and no knowledge of Spanish to answer this question? However he or she chooses. In this light the Hispanic question is more like the ancestry than the birthplace question; it calls for a subjective decision about identity—although the Hispanic question, unlike the ancestry question, does not explicitly appeal to subjective identity but, rather, implies that "Hispanic origin" is a more objectively definable category, like birthplace, age, or gender. On the other hand, the Hispanic-origin question also contains within it a more restrictive demand. If one responds to it in the affirmative, there is a follow-up question: to which particular Hispanic country does the respondent trace origins? Here, one must mark one country only: an individual whose mother is Cuban and father Puerto Rican must choose only one.[13] This feature of forced choice again reflects the legal and administrative purposes of the Hispanic-origin question: it may be important to detect specific origins for civil and voting rights cases, and the goal has been to keep categories for such purposes complete and non-overlapping.

Because there are now three questions on the census dealing with race and ethnicity—race, ancestry, and Hispanic origin—one can report multiple origins by reporting different things on these questions. Thus one can claim Puerto Rican identity in the Hispanic question, black identity in the race question, and write in Jamaican and Puerto Rican ancestry in the ancestry question. Researchers can then combine all three questions to learn about multiple-ancestry people. Indeed Joshua Goldstein and Ann Morning do exactly that in chapter 4 of this volume. Yet to the respondent faced with forced-choice questions, it looks as though one is being forced to deny one's heritage in the race and Hispanic-origin questions. Moreover, only one out of five people receive the long form with the ancestry question, but everyone receives the long from with the race and Hispanic-origin questions.

On purely intellectual grounds, one might imagine that a movement might have arisen to change the Hispanic question so that it no longer forced respondents with origins in two Hispanic countries to "mark one Hispanic country only." However, the emotional and political forces that called forth the demand not to force respondents with origins in two or more races to "mark one race only" are simply not the same in the Hispanic case, and no such movement seems to have been considered.

In any case, the debate about the classification of the mixed-race person inspired interest groups lined up on two sides (see U.S. House of Representatives 1994; OMB 1995, 44673–93). On one side are organizations claiming to represent the American multiracial population; these include among them articulate parents in mixed marriages who are concerned about the way they are asked to identify their children. These organizations demanded equal recognition for multiracials in the government's racial classification system; they asked that the category "multiracial" be added to the specific racial categories—white, black, Native American and Asian–Pacific Islander—that currently appear on the census form. People who select the multiracial category would then indicate from which two, three, or four of these racial groups they are descended The demand seems to have been more for recognition of multiraciality than for any specific political or economic advantage for multiracials. The advocates simply do not want to deny a part of their own or their children's origins.[14]

The other side in this debate opposes adding a multiracial category and permitting people to list more than one race. This group includes civil rights organizations and representatives of African Americans, Hispanics, Native Americans, and Asians and Pacific Islanders. At the core of their opposition is the concern that if individuals are allowed to indicate origins in more than one racial group, the counting of races that undergirds so much civil rights legislation will be muddled and enforcement of civil rights thereby weakened. If, for example, a person who is black can be counted in various ways, it will be much harder to enforce laws promoting racial equality—antidiscrimination efforts, affirmative action, and voting rights could all be affected.

Extensive review and hearings by interagency governmental committees and by congressional committees followed. Eventually, the Office of Management and Budget concluded that a change in the form of the race question was required, such that the social reality of racial blending could not be ignored. The upshot was the present "mark one or more" form of the racial-origin question. With this historic change, the big issue shifted to the use of the responses, both for understanding American social patterns and for the enforcement of civil rights legislation.

Another important theme raised in the debates over the reform of the "old" race question involved Hispanic respondents. Here the issue was not the parallels between the "mark one only" features of the race and Hispanic-origin questions. Rather, the issue involved how Hispanics respond to the race question itself. They had not found it easy to place themselves within the American racial categories provided on the form—being asked, in essence, to choose identification as either white or black, neither of which seemed to apply in a straightforward way. Consequently, large proportions of Hispanics had been marking "some other race"; and huge proportions of those marking "some other race" turned out to be Hispanics. Consequently, an additional group interested in changing the format of the race question was the Census Bureau demographers, and some Hispanics, who felt that a better arrangement would produce clearer responses. However, the "better arrangement" proved hard to find: could "Hispanic" be listed as a race, or could "the race question" be called something else? In the end, the Hispanic question was presented before the race question, in hopes that Hispanics would then view the race question as a cross-cutting inquiry. The results did not confirm these expectations, however; as the proportion of Hispanics marking "some other race" seems to have increased, despite these changes in format.

Finally, another issue, reflective of America's long and complex history of race mingling, floated in the background of the discussions over multiraciality, census counts, and civil rights laws. Would respondents have in mind their parents or their distant ancestors in responding? Preliminary evidence suggested that they generally had the recent past in mind. For example, the ancestry data from the censuses of 1980 and 1990 show us that (as just mentioned) whites rarely identify with an African ancestry and blacks rarely identify with a European ancestry (Farley 1990).[15] Moreover, surveys conducted by the Census Bureau in connection with the OMB review of the late 1990s seemed to indicate small changes in group size when the multiple race responses were allowed. To put it differently, the subjective element in the way Americans have been determining racial membership allows demographers to bypass the complexity that is inherent in the long genealogical record; what we get, for the most part, is information about recent family history.[16] Nevertheless, as awareness of multiracial origins grows, and discussion of it becomes more acceptable, there is no guarantee that the subjective element in this response pattern will remain unchanged.

Civil Rights Legislation and the "New" Race Question: The Issue of Tabulation

As already noted, the tension involved in the multirace issue is that American civil rights law requires clear and nonoverlapping categories of race, but self-identification produces complexity that erodes clear and nonoverlapping categories—when people select two or more races.[17] Because the "new" race question allows individuals to select more than one race, the distinctive feature in the present moment is that this tension involved in the multirace issue has moved to the tabulation procedures. There are now a set of procedures, created by President Bill Clinton's executive branch and published by the Office of Management and Budget, that specify how mixed race individuals are to be counted for purposes of civil rights monitoring and enforcement. These procedures are discussed in detail in chapters 4, 5, and 6 of this volume; in effect, they specify that in most cases in which a person reports two races, of which one is white and the other is nonwhite, the respondent is counted for civil rights purposes as a member of the nonwhite race. The President's Office of Management and Budget has issued a "Guidance" covering the legal and voting rights contexts: "Federal agencies will use the following rules to allocate multiple race responses for use in civil rights monitoring and enforcement . . . Responses that combine one minority race and white are allocated to the minority race" (OMB 2000, Sect. II). A guidance does not offer a justification for its rules, and none has been provided.[18]

In some ways the situation was more explosive when the old race question was in use, because the tension involved in the multirace issue was presented to the entire population: everyone faced the old instruction to mark only one race. By contrast, the tabulation procedures are buried (for the moment anyway) deep within an OMB bulletin. On the other hand, the shift in the locus of the tension to the tabulation procedure means that the executive branch must state its tabulation rules explicitly—rather than (as before) allowing each of a quarter-billion respondents to "make the rule" about racial classification for themselves—without explanation and without possibility of review. Moreover, because the data needed to recalculate the tabulations using some set of tabulation rules other than the OMB rules are now available, there is an enormous potential for public scrutiny and debate about any tabulation procedure. The three branches of the federal government will be forced to confront the tension on this new terrain of debatable tabulation procedures.[19]

What is new today is not the effort to decide the legal standing of the mixed-race individual; that effort is as old as British North America. It was a staple of racist laws and court decisions from the colonial era until well into this century. More recently, the status of the mixed-race person has arisen at least implicitly in civil rights legislation since the 1960s; discrimination cases often concerned people of mixed black and white origins, for example. When it could be shown that the discriminator's perceptions operated to place the mixed-race person in the group discriminated against, presumably civil rights law applied.

What is new today, then, is how to determine the count of an entire protected group when the size of the group is a factor in a decision about discrimination—in counting for voting rights, or the size of a relevant pool of minority group applicants, for example. Can the status of mixed-race individuals under civil rights legislation provide a clear guide for determining whom to include in the count of a protected group? One way of making this connection from the legal treatment of the individual to the count of the legally protected group has often been voiced, and it is bound to carry weight in the future. According to this argument, in the racist legal past, individuals with "one drop" of black blood (or some other very low fraction of black origins) were defined as black; therefore, means of redress in the civil rights era should tabulate by the same principle. Thus, individuals who select both black and white races today should be counted, for legal determinations of group size, as black.

Yet this argument will not carry the day unopposed. One problem with it is that it may appear to take unfair advantage of the single-race black. It may seem an advantage in voting rights legislation to include the mixed-race individual in the black column; but what are the implications for affirmative action counts and procedures? Does a person with one black parent and one white parent have the same claim to redress of past racial oppression as the person with two black parents? And what of the person with one black and three white grandparents?

A more general reason that this argument from the racist one-drop legal past will not carry the day unopposed is that it also seems to perpetuate rather than erode thinking in terms of the racist divisions: the law must continue to invoke the notion that someone with one drop of black blood is black and only black. The danger of perpetuation in this context may seem slight to many, compared with the claims for redress; but many others will not see it that way.

Of course, it is possible that the proportion of individuals who select more than one race will be too small to affect many contested outcomes. Nevertheless, the tabulation procedures could still cause debate if their impact is misperceived to be larger than it is or if litigants expect larger impacts in the future. In any case, if the impact is large even in a single congressional district, for example, it is far from improbable that the interested parties would take the issue to court and force legislators, the press, and the judiciary to confront the implications of procedures for the voting rights of all. The scholars who examine this issue in the pages that follow disagree about the impact of this formulation of the tabulation procedures. Roderick Harrison argues that it could undermine the entire federal statistical system on race, while Nathaniel Persily and Reynolds Farley speculate that it might not have much impact at all on legal cases.

We imagine that the impact of the tabulation procedure will vary—along several dimensions. First, differences in procedures are bound to have a greater impact on some groups than others. Present-day intermarriage between native-born Hispanics or Asians or American Indians and whites is much more common than between blacks and whites. Second, the individuals who mark both the black and white race categories may be distributed very thinly across many voting districts and constitute a significant proportion of the voters in only a few districts or in none. Third, some branches of civil rights law are more likely to be affected than others in the short run. Because voting redistricting involves so many conflictual decisions soon after Census 2000 data are released, and because many such cases can work their way quickly to the Supreme Court, redistricting is probably the first front to watch.

Perhaps, however, the issue will not generate much conflict—either because differences in tabulation procedures will not matter much to outcomes or because all concerned find it in their interest to avoid the issue, and find ways to do so. The OMB's guidance was issued in March 2000; it drew precious little public attention during the remainder of the presidential term; and a year into the Bush presidency, there has been no public call for that guidance to be revoked, nor (so far as we know) any active reformulation of policy by the Bush team. This was true as of September 10, and since then public attention has been focused elsewhere. One reason the Bush team may not have acted before that date is that election law was a sore point with them, following the contested election results in Florida; the first uses of any reformulation would very likely have been in connection with election districts (we note later other reasons for not acting).

Federal officials are likely to insist that interested parties may tabulate the data however they want for any number of important purposes (for example, research on education, health or income levels); only for purposes of civil and voting rights law is the tabulation procedure fixed by the guidance. However, the emerging tabulations used for other topics have the potential to threaten the legitimacy of tabulation procedures used for civil and voting rights law; for this reason, federal authorities might be tempted to try to restrict the machine-readable raw data necessary to test various tabulation procedures or to be vague about tabulation procedures for civil and voting rights law. It is not likely, however, given the precedents for release of census data in recent years and given the directives and guidances on defining race and ethnicity, that it will be possible for officials to act on such temptations.

We leave to others the detailed analysis of political calculations made by various Washington players as the race question was being changed and as the guidance for its use was being formulated. However, we offer three observations. The first pertains to the period in which multiracial groups were calling for the right to mark more than one race; how is it that these parents and their supporters were able to put their concerns on the public agenda? It is certainly true that multiraciality is becoming more prevalent in America; but not every rising trend gets attention in Washington. Were these multiracial advocacy groups and the Republican right in Congress able to exploit a joint interest—to dilute the strength of black political interest groups—albeit for very different goals? Second, once the decision had been taken to review the OMB's Directive 15, was it simply "the logic of the situation" that produced the federal statisticians' decision to recognize that one may be of more than one racial origin? The same forces that had produced the pressure to consider multiraciality in the first place had not disappeared. The solution (the new race question) may have been intellectually balanced partly because the forces were politically balanced. In any case, the decision, taken late in the Clinton years, may well have appeared not merely inescapable but also acceptable—precisely because it left the big issues for the tabulation phase.

And so our last observation concerns this phase of the process. Clearly Republicans and Democrats had short-term and long-term interests in the process of determining tabulation procedures for voting rights cases; but the crucial calculation may not have been about the impact of tabulation procedures on outcomes in a few electoral districts—opaque at this stage anyway (we do not know how such people vote relative to blacks, for example). Rather, the crucial consideration may have been the self-interest, and even more the identity politics, of the Congressional Black Caucus. The guidance directing that black-white multiracials will be counted as blacks may have little effect, and its impact on elections may be difficult to gauge; but it clearly means that the Congressional Black Caucus speaks for more rather than fewer people. The caucus, then, has a clear-cut interest in the guidance, and it is not impossible that neither party will find any countervailing interest great enough to antagonize the caucus with an alternative guidance. If so, the role of challenger will fall to interested parties in court cases.

The change to allowing respondents to check as many races as they wanted to on the census race question had appeared on the 2000 census, conducted in April of that year, and a few months before the conference of scholars and government officials that joined us at the Levy Institute in late September. At the time of the conference, and now at the time of publication, we sense that we are living though an important change in the statistical system and perhaps in the way ordinary Americans think about the meaning of race and their own racial identities. Yet much remains uncertain. The conference participants discussed and debated some large questions occasioned by this change in statistical policy. How did we come to measure race at all in the census and in our statistical systems? How was it decided which categories were identified as races and which ones were eligible for government protections and special legal statuses? What impact would allowing individuals to check more than one race have for the statistical system itself, for legal cases that use racial statistics, for other important research and policy development, and for average Americans' understandings of race and the government's role in measuring it? There were also important speculations about the future. What models, both from our own history and from other countries, might we look to in order to understand what recognizing multiracial responses might mean for our society? What might the future look like with increasing intermarriage and growing identification with more than one race? Some debates centered on normative questions: Should we as a society continue to collect data on race, and if so, which races should we be concerned with? If, as some argue, the recognition of multiracials that began in Census 2000 marks the beginning of the end of federal recognition and use of race data, is that a good thing or a bad thing for our society?

We have arranged the chapters into four groups, although these groups are not, to use the OMB's language, "complete and non-overlapping." The first three explore directly what the efforts to count multiracials have shown. Reynolds Farley reviews the way in which the census has measured race, Hispanic ethnicity, and ancestry and the ways in which the multiracial "movement" effectively changed the way in which race is measured. He shows that almost half of the multiracial population identified by the new question are not combinations of groups we think of as races but the result of a census coding decision that classifies people who write in a Hispanic ancestry to the race question and then check both the "other" racial category and another specific race, for example, white or black. In addition, using newly available 2000 census data, Farley shows the wide geographic variability in the difference made by the new race question. Although the numbers of people choosing more than one race are not very high at the national level, they can make a real difference in population totals at the county level, especially for some groups like American Indians, Asians, and Hawaiians.

David Harris uses data from a recent survey on adolescent health behaviors that asked a variety of innovative racial questions and allowed for multiracial responses. He shows that the manner in which the question is asked makes a large difference in the types of responses elicited. The subjective and volatile nature of multiracial reporting means, for instance, that an individual will report one race when asked at home but multiple races when asked at school. Harris also finds some significant socioeconomic differences in the characteristics of monoracial as opposed to multiracial respondents. The implications of his study for the wider question of interpreting census data are strong. Harris shows that individuals switch between monoracial and multiracial identities depending on the context and mode of the question. The differences, then, in income or education between subjectively defined monoracial and multiracial groups that he finds are hard to interpret. Are they a function of real differences in the underlying populations or momentary and volatile differences in who reports a multiple as opposed to a single race?

Using state-level birth records, Sonya Tafoya provides an analysis of the potential and the reality of mixed-race youth in California. The largest state, California is also at the forefront of the trends that have led to the growth in the mixed-race population. It is a state with large numbers of Asian and Hispanic immigrants and with high intermarriage rates for all racial groups. Tafoya shows the huge potential for further growth in the mixed-race population in the future, given the large numbers of mixed-race births recorded in recent decades.

In the second group of chapters, scholars debate how much this change in measurement will matter in the contexts that have used race counts—especially in civil rights law but also for understanding health, education, income, and other crucial topics on which public race counts have been common. Joshua Goldstein and Ann Morning conduct a number of simulations using 1990 ancestry and race data along with preliminary 2000 data to assess whether the OMB tabulation rule would conform to the possible choices multiracial people themselves would make if they had to put themselves "back in the box" of only one race. They find that the so-called one-drop rule of allocation that OMB has adopted for cases involving civil rights enforcement runs counter to the way multiracial people themselves would choose to self-identify. They also find that racial reallocation changes the socioeconomic profile of some groups—whites and American Indians and, to a much lesser extent, Asians—and has little impact on the profile of African Americans.

Roderick Harrison points to three aspects of the change to the multiracial reporting that he believes could undermine the entire federal racial statistical system and open it to both public disenchantment and legal challenge. First, he points to the geographic variability in multirace reporting and the impact it has on the size of some groups such as Asians and American Indians. Harrison argues that the whole system could be challenged by a single case in which the discrepancy between the overall monoracial and multiracial counts was sufficient to make a difference in a court case or a voting rights case. He points out that there are counties and small areas in which the manner in which multiple-race people are allocated makes a big difference in the overall population counts. In addition, he argues that the subjectivity and selectivity of multiple-race reporting means that the category of combined races does not signify any recognized population group. Because only 50 percent of the offspring of interracial couples actually report more than one race, Harrison notes, these subjectively defined categories (those choosing to say they are white and black) differ so greatly from an objectively defined category (those having a black parent and a white parent) that the data are in some sense meaningless. Finally, he argues that without good bridging techniques the ability of the federal statistical system to track changes in the welfare of racial groups in our society will be severely challenged as statisticians will be unable to tell whether the changes are attributable to real changes in the world or simply to a new way of measuring the group.

Nathaniel Persily disagrees with Harrison about the probable impact of these changes on the use of the data in civil rights enforcement, although he acknowledges the possibility that at least it could open the door to legal challenges to the system. Persily provides for the layman a useful review of the place of race counts in current civil rights laws; in each domain of the law, he also considers how the change in race data might matter to the ways in which the counts are used. He makes the important point that most racial discrimination cases hinge not on population counts at the census level but rather on institutional data, such as the number of employees of a particular race. Of course, as the new question filters down into institutional record keeping the same issues that now arise with census data might arise in school and employment data. Persily also examines the importance of the change in measurement for voting rights cases. He argues that the requirements of the law operate in a way that may blunt the impact of the changes. Although counting multiple-race people as members of a minority race might increase the size of the group, it might also dilute the voting records of the group; thus the change in the data measurement would not have obvious effects on a voting rights case.

As we ask how the option of multiple-race responses will influence the use of race data, we also call attention to the chapter by Clyde Tucker, Steve Miller, and Jennifer Parker, which we have placed in a technical appendix to this volume. One crucial problem involved in the new race counts involves linking them to the old race counts. If, for example, Asians or Native Americans now have a smaller population base because some people formerly classified in that category are being placed instead in multiracial categories, how do we relate the incidence of poverty or diphtheria— or fertility and college graduation—in 2000 to the rates in 1990 (which were calculated under the old race question)? Tucker and his colleagues provide a detailed comparison of different methods of "bridging" between the old and new data, evaluating gains and losses of using any given method. It is a reflective "how-to" manual, focused on principles.

In the third group of three chapters, authors examine possible scenarios for the future in a country, such as ours, in which the rates of intermarriage among racial groups are high and mixed-race people are recognized. Matthew Snipp examines the particular case of American Indians as an example of what issues might affect all racial groups in the future. American Indians have had a long history of high intermarriage rates, relatively large numbers of multiple-ancestry people, and long-standing debates about who should be included as an Indian. Snipp examines the ways in which American Indians have dealt with mixed-race people and the ways in which the decisions about whom to include could have implications for other groups.

The other two chapters in this section examine the interesting case of population projections. The Census Bureau has published many projections of the future of racial and ethnic composition of the United States, and those published during the past decade have received much public attention (usually the news comes in the form, "In the year 2050, the proportion of nonwhites in the U.S. population will be . . . ."). None of these bureau projections have taken intermarriage into account; rather, the bureau's methodology has assumed that there would be no future intermarriage and that all population groups would grow or decline only through births, deaths, and immigration. Joel Perlmann first explores how the federal government got into the business of making racial projections. He then highlights the problems of ignoring intermarriage in projections by presenting data on the descendants of early-twentieth-century Italian immigrants across four generations. Barry Edmonston, Sharon Lee, and Jeffrey Passel, building on their years of earlier work, now present an alternative projection methodology that includes intermarriage, nativity, and generational status as well as the parameters that the Census Bureau's current projections include. They project rapid growth in the multiple-race proportion in most groups in the future; how multiracial people identify themselves will be crucial to the future size and composition of America's racial groups.

The final section of this book takes up the politics of race numbers. It begins with four historical pieces on race counting in the United States. Matthew Jacobson stresses that counting by race is intricately bound up in the long history of race relations; and the change being made in the 2000 census is also historically and socially situated and reflects the socially constructed reality of our time. Thus, for example, even when we realize that we "defend race and racialized data" we cannot escape the need to do so, given that "the vital protections that are the legacies of the civil rights struggle" rely on them; similarly, even if we speak of the social construction of races, and the fluidity of the system of classification over time, we cannot ignore that race "is a construction that has, in fact, translated into social realities." Jacobson also points to the important role of the state and of science in defining race. This by its very nature combines scientific concerns about measurement with political concerns about measuring for political and administrative purposes.

Werner Sollors, it might be said, stresses the other edge of the same sword; he insists on the dangers that continue to accrue from "the combination of state power, census, and race . . . even [when combined] for well-intentioned policies"; and so "we may . . . still be operating on a set of assumptions that go back to the very core of racism." For related reasons, Sollors offers a survey of the etymology of "race" and a history of the actual provisions of the "one-drop" laws for defining races in earlier centuries. Most readers will be surprised to learn that these provisions were not, in fact, based on a single drop; we add that the parallels between the criteria here and the "blood quantum" criterion that Snipp describes in connection with American Indians—although used for vastly different ends—are important to appreciate as an indication of the dilemmas involved in keeping track of origins for institutional purposes.

Margo Anderson describes how race came into the census and its evolving role before the Civil War. At several crucial moments, from the framing of the constitution to the eve of the war, how to count races and how to use racial statistics were at the center of national political debate, each time in a different way.

Hugh Davis Graham examines more recent history to ask the fascinating question of why some groups were determined to be worthy of special government protections and programs, and others were not—and how the "ethnoracial pentagon" that we now take so much for granted, was formed in the first place. Graham shows how political and administrative concerns combined in federal agencies to create the categories we now use.

The fifth chapter in this section, by Melissa Nobles, contrasts the experiences of the statistical systems of Brazil and the United States (in both countries there have been recent popular movements concerned with the issue). Brazil has long recognized the multiracial nature of its population, and its census has developed many categories for measuring that population. Nobles cautions, however, that the mere existence of data does not change the reality, and in fact the ways in which multiracial data are interpreted are as important as the ways in which they are collected. She points out that as the United States is moving toward a greater recognition of the multiracial nature of our population, Brazil has been debating a move in the opposite direction—toward greater recognition of the contrast between white and black.

The final four chapters offer observations on the political processes that have brought us this far and some strategies for proceeding, as well. Nathan Glazer recognizes the political nature of the decisions about what data we collect and how we use it, and so he offers his further reflections with little belief that they will be embraced. Yet, he argues, the high levels of racial intermarriage, except for blacks, that has consumed so much of our attention is emblematic of the fact that these other "races" no longer need concern the state as races—as groups separated from one another, and especially from "whites," by impermeable divides. What the state should continue to concern itself with, Glazer argues, is recognizing and counting blacks and monitoring the evolution of black-white inequalities.

The final three chapters on political processes all argue, or at least recognize the possibility, that the arrival of the multiple-race option will have profound effects on American social and political life. Peter Skerry predicts that this change will promote more public scrutiny to the messy and inherently political nature of race data in the federal statistical system. He worries that though the perception will be accurate, it may bring down race counts or race-based policies like affirmative action without bringing down the persisting racial inequalities.

Jennifer Hochschild, too, considers the possibility that the change in race counts will spell the end of government's gathering of racial statistics. She confesses uncertainty as to how she would appraise such an eventuality. Would it be a good or a bad thing if the government stopped collecting race data? How should such a question be decided? Who would win and lose in such a scenario?

Finally, Kenneth Prewitt asserts that the change in the race question is indeed an important turning point that will have far-reaching, if as yet unknowable, effects on the ways in which our society treats race. The very complexity of the data will make it more difficult for those who use it to make policy or legal findings based on it; and it will lead to greater public discomfort with the whole enterprise of collecting race data.

We have emphasized repeatedly in this overview that the present moment in the long history of racial counts involves the clash of two competing needs. One is the need to acknowledge the increasing population of the offspring of interracial marriage and to recognize that these interracial offspring, at least among the native born, seem to be following patterns quite like the patterns of American ethnic groups that we do not classify as races. The second is the need for simplicity, clarity, and the absence of ambiguity in the system for counting that underlies civil and voting rights law and programs such as affirmative action. This is a clash between a need for an accurate interpretation of social patterns, on the one hand, and the need for procedures—rules of action—on the other. In the best light, each need, taken by itself, is unimpeachable and indeed highly praiseworthy; each individually can be seen as advancing the cause of American racial equality—by highlighting how some old divides have been eroded or by working directly to attack the divides that yet remain high. Moreover, because these laudable aims clash with each other, from either vantage point the claims of the opposing need is likely to been seen not "in its best light" but rather in its worst—the demands for recognition of multiraciality as defeating the progress of civil and voting rights legislation, and the insistence on staying with procedures based on single races as defeating the progress of actual racial integration by rigidly supporting divides that, in fact, seem to be eroding.

Most of the chapters in this book also discuss aspects of this clash—not only the historical and reflective pieces but also the seemingly empirical or legal scholarship of Farley, Goldstein and Morning, Persily, and Harrison, for example. What, then, are we to make of such a clash? Several attempts to step back and think about this sort of problem as a historical process are represented here. Graham's chapter highlights how the early stages of a process that later became an explosive issue—racial classification for legal redress—were undertaken by bureaucrats without any attention from the public or much understanding on the part of those involved of what the future would hold for such categories. (Perlmann's contribution speculates about a similar historical process at work.) In a somewhat similar way, our own discussion here of the various "origins" questions suggests that these questions may have developed in response to different needs within different offices of the same large census bureaucracy, operating largely independently of one another. On the other hand, the essays by Anderson and Nobles, and some of the discussion by Jacobson and Sollors, describe other times and places in which racial counts became central to the political struggles of a time. Indeed, Anderson's chapter shows several instances of this kind of pattern over the long period from the Constitutional Convention to the Civil War: for different reasons, arguments over how races should be counted became very public and highly charged at particular moments. Evolving cultural vulnerabilities or political interests sometimes force a policy or procedure from a quiet, unexamined corner onto center stage.

We appear to be living through one of those moments in which the issue of the count—and the right to check more than one box on a federal form—has intertwined with national interests in contradictory ways and has thereby moved to center stage. One challenge is to specify more clearly how this process of movement occurred. Farley narrates some of this process of mobilization (as Nobles and others have done elsewhere); in Skerry's observations the issue of mobilization comes up as well, but in two ways that are not so easily reconciled: On the one hand, he notes that the success of the multiracial lobby seems to confirm the responsiveness of the Census Bureau to public pressures (which on the whole he sees as a good thing). Skerry also notes, however, the darker interpretation: that the mobilization succeeded because it played into the agenda of Newt Gingrich's congressional right, who seized on it out of no great concern with the goals of the multiracial groups themselves but as a way of weakening some of their opponents—namely, black interest groups whom they perceived to be pressing for illegitimate ends with the arguments of another era's civil rights movement and overblown legal procedures that have developed since. Of course, both of the forces Skerry notes were surely operative, largely independently of one another and for different ends. However, in evaluating why a movement won (a partial) success, it makes a difference whether we think the credit goes to institutional responsiveness in the face of a popular mobilization or to the support of a powerful group in Congress, manipulating the cause for their own ends. More work on this theme will be useful.

Is the moment of public scrutiny and bitter struggle significant as a reflection of wider cultural themes only, or will it have important consequences in its own right? There is some clear division among the authors on this point; Goldstein and Morning stress the procrustean efforts to put the "multi" back in the "single" box; Harrison argues that an understanding of how the changes will degrade the quality of evidence on racial disparities has been lacking; Edmonston, Lee, and Passel, as well as Perlmann, stress the impossibility of continuing in the old way with racial projections; Glazer believes the extent of racial intermarriage indicates that we would do well to forget about all the racial divides except the one that has resisted mingling—the black-white divide. On the other hand, Farley and Persily are skeptical about whether the changes that the new race question brings in its wake will be those that have been expected. Farley points out that many were expecting a barrage of court cases to deal with challenges to the use of race data, notably, in creating voting districts; yet apparently none has emerged to date; moreover there seems to have been more attention paid to the dangers or advantages of collecting the data than to the data themselves, at least the data released to date. Was this a social movement that succeeded, then, Farley asks, only to be irrelevant? Persily approaches a similar issue as a legal scholar; he recognizes, first, the inherent arbitrariness of any race classification and, second, the fact that multiraciality may well change American culture and affect patterns of discrimination and the racial divide generally; but all that does not mean that the legal system will be much affected for the foreseeable future. He considers, in connection with each domain of the law, how the multiracial option is likely to affect the legal situation. The court cases, Persily stresses, most typically involve blacks, among whom the proportion of multiracials is likely to be small, and Hispanics, who are not directly affected by the race definitions because their numbers are established by another question. So the likelihood of a case being swayed by great numerical shifts owing to the multiracial option are negligible. The challenge for the legal system that Persily does take seriously for the short run involves the greater complexity or delays that could result from some challenges to the way relevant races in a case are being construed or numbers in a voting district are being defined. Yet the courts have dealt with increasing complexity before; the challenges to a way of counting, or even a case being tossed out, will not bring down the system of civil rights law.

Our inclination is to come down on the other side, but not because we disagree with Persily on the specifics of where the challenges will land or on the short-term magnitude of relevant demographic shifts. Like Persily, we think that the likely outcome of legal challenges will be greater complexity, with cases being tossed back for further review as a result of shifting perceptions of what is an acceptable way to count for a given purpose. It is important to stress that the numerical impact need not be immense to impress a judge that the counting issues could significantly affect some people's rights in some situations. Once the principle of how to count is raised and recognized as affecting these rights, it may indeed lead to greater complexity and cases being tossed back for reformulation. This is precisely the sort of occurrence that has bedeviled, for example, the evolution of voting rights cases; "all" Sandra Day O'Connor did was to challenge principles of counting and to toss a case back for revision. The Justice Department under Clinton, by the informal accounts we have heard, hardly thought it moot whether one box or many could be checked off.

Finally, as Persily notes, the major threats may arise not directly in court cases but in shifting public perceptions of what legitimately is to be counted as membership in a race when racial lines shift. This kind of process, however, creates an environment in which closely decided court issues may be pushed over the line. In an era of a sharply divided Supreme Court, this is an especially relevant consideration.

Notes

1. A variant of the ancestry question could eventually do away with the race question, but that does not seem to be in the works any time soon.

2. The historical discussion in the following paragraphs is based heavily upon Williamson 1995 [1980], Davis 1991, and Snipp 1989, chapter 2; see also Nash 1995, 941–64.

3. Until very recently indeed: laws against intermarriage were not ruled unconstitutional by the Supreme Court until 1967, and such laws were on the books in many states in the 1950s.

4. The reference is to those who consider themselves Native American by race, not to the much larger group, nearly all of whom consider themselves white, who indicate that they have some Native American ancestry. On the 1990 intermarriage rates for individuals between the ages of twenty-three and thirty-five years, see Farley 1996, 264–65.

5. Of course, even a Hispanic or an Asian marrying within his or her own "racial" group might well be marrying someone with origins in a different country (a descendant of Chinese immigrants might marry a descendant of Asian Indians, for example).

6. The reference here is to native-born black males, aged twenty to twenty-nine years of age; reported by Qian 1997; see also Besharov and Sullivan 1996, 19–21.

7. The 43 percent figure for 2000 is calculated roughly from U.S. Census Bureau 2001. In 1960, the Census Bureau did not take account of "Hispanics" in discussing race at all; among those it did count as nonwhite, some 90 percent were black. The "chances of meeting" a black or other nonwhite obviously vary dramatically across the country; the example in the paragraph should be thought of as referring to randomly chosen nonwhites selected from the American population.

8. Barring, that is, improbably large countervailing differences in fertility across intraracial and interracial unions. The calculation of the cited proportions is as follows: with 6 percent out-marrying, $6 / (6 + 94/2) = 11$ percent; and with 10 percent out-marrying, $10 / (10 + 90/2) = 18$ percent. Note, however, that the calculation applies only to the matter of actual, "genealogical" origins; how these children will identify—as blacks, whites, or both—is a more subtle question, affected by the changing rates, surely, but not fully determined by them.

9. This is not to say that the question cannot be simplified; indeed, it has been in the presentation of tables or even the coding of public-use samples in some years. In the latter, for example, individuals were coded in 1960 and 1970 in terms of father's place of birth only, with a second (shorter) field listing whether or not the respondent's mother was foreign or native born and whether (if foreign born) she was from the same country as the father or from a different one (but that different one was not reported). See, for example, the code books at the convenient IPUMS (Integrated Public Use Microdata Series) website, at *www.ipums.umn.edu.* For a convenient compendium of the census questions prior to 1990, see U.S. Bureau of the Census 1979.

10. From 1971 to 1975, virtually identical categories were fully coded (the question for those years is known as the "ethnic-origin" question). Since 1976, with the collapsed coding, the question has been known as the "Spanish-ethnicity" question. See Unicon Research Corporation 1998.

11. Another rationale was thought to be that it would tap into putative ethnic loyalties related to the "white ethnic revival" of the late 1970s.

12. Similarly, in direct interviews (as opposed to the mail-in forms most people filled out), "if a person could not provide a single race response, the race of the mother was used. If a single race response could not be provided for the person's mother, the first race reported by the person was used" (U.S. Census Bureau 1992, B-30).

13. On ancestry and the Hispanic-origin question, see, for example, Lieberson and Waters 1988, 16–18.

14. Though the demand may be for recognition, it is worth noting that should the multiracial population be defined as a distinct racial group, it might then become eligible for various benefits.

15. The picture is more mixed with regard to Native Americans. In 1980, for example, in addition to the large number of whites claiming some Native American ancestry, about 22 percent of those claiming Native American racial status also claimed some European ancestry (Snipp 1989, 51). However,

the crucial point is that the counts of Native Americans do not change in statistically significant ways when the instructions to the race question change.

16. In another test, the Census Bureau asked people who said that they were multiracial whether they said so because their parents were of different races, because more distant ancestors were of different races, or because the nature of their group was multiracial. Some three-quarters chose the first reason (Tucker et al. 1996). With regard to the second response, which concerns us here, the real point is that only a tiny fraction of those who could conceivably have declared a multiracial legacy did so. For example, in the black population alone a substantial majority would have had some rational basis for marking more than one category if they were inclined to do so; had they done so, the number of multiracials would have been many times greater than it was. Similarly, Hispanics may be confused about whether to mark black, white, or "other," but the confusion is not based on a desire to resolve their problem by marking two or three of the available race choices instead of one; rather, they appear to be uncomfortable being labeled in any of the available race groups.

17. When we speak of civil rights law, we use the term as short-hand for anti-discrimination, civil rights, and voting rights law as well as for court cases related to policies of affirmative action. When we speak of the OMB guidelines we have in mind the *Guidance on Aggregation and Allocation of Data on Race for Use in Civil Rights Monitoring and Enforcement* (OMB 2000).

18. Our point here is not to argue against any particular OMB decision; quite the contrary, any OMB guideline on how to allocate individuals who select two or more races would generate challenges from groups whose interests are better served by some other method of tabulation.

19. That race data are no longer justified by reference to natural, biological, or anthropological divisions among people, but rather because they are required for legal and administrative purposes, is not the new element in our situation; that feature of the race question goes back at least to Directive 15. The fluidity of relevant racial classification and the handling of mixed-race individuals also are not new elements (as scholars have shown in discussing U.S. censuses from 1790 to 1970).

References

Alba, Richard. 1995. "Assimilation's Quiet Tide." *Public Interest* 119(spring): 1–18.

Besharov, Douglas J., and Timothy S. Sullivan. 1996. "One Flesh: America is Experiencing an Unprecedented Increase in Black-White Intermarriage." *The New Democrat* (July/August): 19–21.

Davis, F. James. 1991. *Who Is Black? One Nation's Definition.* University Park: Pennsylvania State University Press.

Farley, Reynolds. 1990. *Race and Ethnicity in the U.S. Census: An Evaluation of the 1980 Ancestry Question.* Ann Arbor, Mich.: Population Studies Center.

———. 1996. *The New American Reality: Who We Are, How We Got There, Where We Are Going.* New York: Russell Sage Foundation.

Harrison, Roderick J., and Claudette Bennett. 1995. "Racial and Ethnic Diversity." In *State of the Union: America in the 1990s.* Vol. 2: *Social Trends,* edited by Reynolds Farley. New York: Russell Sage Foundation.

Heer, David M. 1980. "Intermarriage." In *Harvard Encyclopedia of American Ethnic Groups,* edited by Stephan Thernstrom. Cambridge, Mass.: Belknap Press of Harvard University.

Higham, John. 1994 [1955]. *Strangers in the Land: Patterns of American Nativism, 1860–1925.* New Brunswick, N.J.: Rutgers University Press.

Lieberson, Stanley, and Mary Waters. 1988. *From Many Strands: Ethnic and Racial Groups in Contemporary America.* New York: Russell Sage Foundation.

Nash, Gary B. 1995. "The Hidden History of Mestizo America." *Journal of American History* 82(3): 941–64.

Office of Management and Budget (OMB), Executive Office of the President. 1995. "Standards for the Classification of Federal Data on Race and Ethnicity; Notice." *Federal Register* 60(166): 44673–44693.

———. 2000. *Guidance on Aggregation and Allocation of Data on Race for Use in Civil Rights Monitoring and Enforcement.* Bulletin 00–02. Washington (March 9).

Qian, Zhenchao. 1997. "Breaking the Racial Barriers: Variations in Interracial Marriage Between 1980 and 1990. *Demography* 34(2): 263–76.

Snipp, C. Matthew. 1989. *American Indians: The First of This Land.* New York: Russell Sage Foundation.

Tucker, Clyde, Ruth McKay, Brian Kohjetin, Roderick Harrison, Manuel de la Puente, Linda Stinson and Ed Robison. 1996. *Testing Methods of Collecting Racial and Ethnic Information: Results of the Current Population Survey Supplement on Race and Ethnicity.* Bureau of Labor Statistics, Statistical Note no. 40. Washington: Bureau of Labor Statistics.

U.S. Bureau of the Census. 1979. "Twenty Censuses: Population and Housing Questions, 1790–1980." Washington: U.S. Government Printing Office.

———. 1992. Census of Population and Housing.1990. "Race." Public Use Microdata Sample, U.S. Technical Documentation, 1992, Appendix B, Definition of Subject Characteristics, B-30. Washington: U.S. Government Printing Office.

———. 2001. "Overview of Race and Hispanic Origin, 2000." Census 2000 Brief, March. Washington: U.S. Government Printing Office.

U.S. Congress. House. 1994. *Review of Federal Measurements of Race and Ethnicity Hearings before the Subcommittee on Census, Statistics, and Postal Personnel of the Committee on Post Office and Civil Service.* House of Representatives, 103d Cong., 1st sess., April 14, June 30, July 20, November 3, 1993. Washington: U.S. Government Printing Office.

Unicon Research Corporation. 1998. *CPS Utilities: Annual Demographic and Income Supplement (March 1970–1997).* Manual, Section 4. Santa Monica, Calif. Available at: *www.unicon.com.*

Williamson, Joe. 1995 [1980]. *New People: Miscegenation and Mulattoes in the United States.* Baton Rouge: Louisiana State University Press.

Part I

WHAT DO WE KNOW FROM
COUNTING MULTIRACIALS?

1

RACIAL IDENTITIES IN 2000: THE RESPONSE TO THE MULTIPLE-RACE RESPONSE OPTION

Reynolds Farley

T HE GREATEST change in the measurement of race in the history of the United States occurred in the census of 2000. For more than two centuries, the federal statistical system had classified each respondent into a single race. That is no longer the case. According to the new rules, anyone may now identity with as many races as he or she desires.

Classifying the population by race has been controversial since the Constitution was first drafted. The past century and a half have seen spirited debates in Congress preceding each census, debates focused on how race questions will be asked and which racial terms will appear on the enumeration schedule (Anderson 1988, chapter 3). In the mid-nineteenth century, Southern representatives in Congress added "mulatto" to the list of races, believing that these persons were biologically different from—and inferior to—both whites and blacks. The Social Darwinist ideology prevalent at the end of the century led Congress to add "quadroon" and "octoroon" in 1890. Congress also insisted that in areas with high concentrations of American Indians, census takers report what fraction of a respondent's blood was Indian, white, or Negro (Snipp 1989, chapter 2).

Only three racial terms—white, Chinese, and Japanese—have appeared on the enumeration forms for every census in the twentieth century. "Black" was used in 1900 and 1910 but was replaced by "Negro" for the 1920 to 1960 span, after which the option "Negro or Black" appeared on the census. In 2000, the census form used "Black, African American, or Negro" as a racial category. "Mexican" was listed as a race only once—in 1930—and, because of protests from the Mexican government, the Census Bureau provided few tabulations about the Mexican race (Cortes 1980). "Hindu" appeared in 1930 and 1940 but has not been used since. In the

1960s, following the liberalization of immigration laws, newcomers arrived from many Asian nations, and this led to demands that specific terms identifying specific groups be listed on the census form (Petersen 1987), presumably because the appearance of a term on the form increases the count of a group. Racial designations including Asian Indian, Guamanian, Korean, Samoan, and Vietnamese were added in 1980 and 1990 (U.S. Bureau of the Census 1973). Beginning with the census of 1970, forms were filled out by respondents themselves, not enumerators. The change to self-identification of a respondent's race further altered the racial count, leading to an unexpectedly large increase in the number of American Indians—who had previously been identified by census takers as white (Harris 1994, table 3).

Identifying with Multiple Races: The Social Movement That Is Changing the Nation's Racial Classification System

Through 1990, congressional discussions and federal court rulings never challenged the idea that each American could readily be classified into one and only one race. The Census Bureau's long but futile history of trying to count mulattoes, quadroons, and octoroons had been forgotten. Just eight years later, however, the one-race-only principle had disappeared from the federal statistical system. How did this happen so quickly?

As early as the 1950s, married interracial couples had organized clubs in Detroit, Los Angeles, and New York to support one another and their mixed-race children (Spencer 1997, chapter 1). In 1988, Susan Graham, who resided in the Atlanta suburbs, developed an umbrella organization for groups representing the interests of mixed-race couples and their children. Graham is a white woman married to a black anchorman for CNN. She knew that the Georgia public school system automatically classified her children and the children of other mixed-race couples into the minority race, regardless of the preferences of the child or the parents. Hence she chose Reclassify All Children Equally (Project RACE) as the name for this organization. The arrival of her census questionnaire in March 1990 propelled her to a leadership position in the small but effective multiple-race movement. Examining her form, she found that each household member could identify with only one race, and so she called the Census Bureau. Graham claims that she was told that she must mark her own race for all of her children because only the mother's race could be known with certainty.

Carlos Fernandez, an attorney in San Francisco of white and Mexican ancestry, was similarly upset by the federal requirement that each person identify with just one race. In response, he founded the Association of MultiEthnic Americans (AMEA). He considered filing suits about the 1990 census but could not locate qualified plaintiffs. Shortly thereafter, a variety of local groups emerged to represent the interests of mixed-race persons, including A Place for Us (APFU), a national advocacy group founded by a white man in Los Angeles who sought to marry an African American woman but had been turned down by his minister; the Brick by Brick Church organized by Pastor Kenneth Simpson in Lexington, Kentucky, to minister to the special spiritual needs of mixed-race individuals; the Interracial Family Alliance, founded by parishioners of an Episcopal church in Augusta, Georgia; and the Interracial Lifestyle Connection, created as a correspondence network for persons who wished to maintain friendships across racial lines (Skrentny 1999, chapter 2). The interracial movement may have been among the first social movements to capitalize upon the resources of e-mail and, a little later, the Internet. Rather than incur the costs of publishing bulletins, buying mailing lists, and postage, many in this new movement used the new low-cost electronic media.

To give national visibility to this emerging movement, the AMEA called a Loving Conference for June 1992 in Washington to commemorate the quarter-century anniversary of the Supreme Court's Loving v. Virginia decision (87 S. Ct. 1817 [1967]), which overturned those state laws that prohibited interracial marriages. This conference was a key event for the multiracial movement, drawing public attention to its cause. The AMEA invited government officials and succeeded in getting responses from Ohio representative Thomas Sawyer, who at the time headed the House subcommittee that oversaw the census, and from Nampeo McKinney, the Census Bureau official responsible for compiling racial statistics. The next year Representative Sawyer held hearings about the census of 2000. He invited representatives of the multiracial movement to speak, thereby giving them a prominent and important platform from which to promote their idea that multiracial Americans should not be forced by their government to identify with only one race. Susan Graham and her associates in Project RACE worked at the state level, informing legislatures of the psychological damage presumably suffered by multiracial children forced to identify with the race of only one parent. Her efforts persuaded legislatures in Georgia, Illinois, and Ohio to enact laws mandating the use of "multiracial" as a category in state statistical systems. It is important to stress that this social movement did not call for respondents to "check all races that apply." Rather, they demanded that the term "mixed race" or "multiracial" be added to the list of options.

By the summer of 1993, the traditional civil rights organizations realized they had a crucial stake in the issues raised by the multiracial movement. If "multiracial" were listed as a race on the census form and many marked it, the demographic foundation for advocacy groups would shrink, perhaps by a substantial amount. Billy Tidwell, the research director of the

Urban League, relied upon Roderick Harrison of the Census Bureau's Racial Statistics Branch to argue that black civil rights organization might find themselves representing a much smaller population if "multiracial" or "mixed race" were a racial choice in the 2000 census (Williams 2000, chapter 6).

Since 1977, federal policy on the collection of racial information has followed the Office of Management and Budget's (OMB) Directive 15. That directive mandated that all federal agencies collecting racial data must use the following four racial categories: white, black, Asian or Pacific Islander, and American Indian or Alaskan native. In addition, all agencies were required to collect data about the Hispanic origin of every individual. This might be accomplished with a distinct question about Hispanic origin—the approach used by the Census Bureau in 1980 and 1990—or by combining race and Hispanic-origin queries. In 1994, OMB officials announced that, because the old racial categories specified in Directive 15 were of decreasing value, it would consider revising them in time for the 2000 census (OMB 1994). Spokespersons for multiracial organizations and other advocacy groups were invited to submit their recommendations—a tremendous accomplishment for the multiracial movement. Similarly, all federal agencies were asked to prepare statements about how they measured race, how they used racial statistics, and what changes, if any, they would recommend.

As the leading statistical agency, the Census Bureau quickly got involved. It immediately commissioned three large national studies to determine how many people might identify themselves as "mixed race" or "multiple race" and how people would respond to different orderings of the race and Hispanic-origin questions. In 1995 a supplement on race and ethnicity was added to the Current Population Survey, and in 1996 the Census Bureau conducted a content test that pretested questions for the 2000 census and a race- and ethnicity-targeted test (REATT) that oversampled areas where minorities lived (Hirschman, Alba, and Farley 2000; U.S. Bureau of the Census 1996, 1997).

While OMB officials gathered data and took comments from the public, advocacy organizations succeeded in bringing more attention to their cause. As it happened, Susan Graham lived in Representative New Gingrich's district. Following the Republican victory in the mid-term election, House Speaker Gingrich endorsed her cause. It is possible that Gingrich and other Republicans thought that the multiracial question would minimize the count of specific minorities in the census, thereby aiding Republicans in reapportionment. The AMEA publicized the large number of prominent Americans who were often considered black but were really multiracial individuals, including W. E. B. Du Bois, Langston Hughes, Alex Haley, Malcolm X, and General Colin Powell. A Multiracial Solidarity March on

Washington was called for July 1996, with the specific aim of adding a "multiracial" option to the 2000 census questionnaire (Williams 2000, chapter 6). Tiger Woods, on the Oprah Winfrey show, declared that his race was neither black nor Thai but rather Cablinasian, reflecting his white, black, Indian, and Asian ancestry. Representative Thomas Petri from Wisconsin introduced House Bill 830, popularly known as the Tiger Woods Bill, which mandated the addition of "multiracial" or "multiethnic" as categories on federal forms. Though the bill was never enacted, it helped to bring the issue more forcefully into the public view. President William Clinton announced that he, too, was a multiracial American since some of his ancestors were American Indians.

Katherine Wallman, the chief author of the 1977 Directive 15, again served as the key OMB official responsible for federal racial statistics. By 1997, she let it be known that the OMB was considering allowing individuals to identify with as many races as they wished—a suggestion that was significantly different from the demands of the multiracial movement for a simple option for persons with mixed-race heritage. Some in the AMEA argued that the United States would quickly move past its racial divisiveness once large numbers of Americans realized they were not specifically white, black, or Indian but rather were descendants of multiple races. In the 1997 congressional hearings, most spokespersons for the multiracial movement were unenthusiastic about the "check all that apply" option. Though they recognized it as a major change, they felt that it would not readily identify the mixed-race population and would produce cumbersome data. Demographers and statisticians with high-power computers could analyze the data, but most users might be confused by the flood of new data.

By 1997, the most powerful civil rights lobbyists, especially the Leadership Conference on Civil Rights representing the interests of African Americans, came to endorse the recommendations of the OMB. They had two reasons. First, according to analysis of the three Census Bureau tests, only a small percentage of the population—perhaps 1.5 percent—would identify themselves as mixed by race, so it seemed unlikely that the count of blacks would drop sharply in the 2000 census because of the change in wording of the race question. Second, if respondents were allowed to check all races that apply, it was probable that the count of minority races would increase a bit because of the addition of people who primarily identify themselves as white but also knew that they had black, Asian, or Indian ancestors.

On October 30, 1997, the OMB announced its authoritative guidelines, just in time to get the 2000 census under way (OMB 1997). It prohibited the use of "multiracial" as a racial category but allowed respondents to identify with more than one race.

Interracial Marriage and the Growth of the Multiracial Population

The efforts to change the one-race-only classification system came from individuals who believed that many Americans shared multiple racial origins, but information about the size or growth of this population was seldom presented. Indeed, no reliable data existed before the Census Bureau pretested queries for the census of 2000. Although a small number of studies attempted to estimate changes over time in the frequency of interracial marriages (Kalmijn 1993, 1998), few data sets lend themselves to the measurement of rare events; until 1967, some states prohibited marriages across racial lines, and so there are few data on the mixed-race offspring of interracial unions. However, public-use files from census data may be used to ascertain the percentage of married couples in which the husband and wife reported different races. As a result, studies of interracial marriage have become numerous (Fu 2001; Gilbertston, Fitzpatrick, and Yang 1996; Heer 1974; Hwang, Saenz, and Aguirre 1995; Model and Fisher 2001; Qian 1997; Rosenfield 2001; Sandefur and McKinnell 1986; Schoen and Thomas 1989). Presumably, as the proportion of interracial marriages increases, so too will the percentage of children who think of themselves as multiple by race.

Table 1.1 reports data about interracial marriage compiled from the 1990 census and the March 2000 Current Population Survey. Spouses were classified into one of five mutually exclusive and exhaustive categories: Hispanic, non-Hispanic white, non-Hispanic black or African American, non-Hispanic Asian or Pacific Islander, and non-Hispanic American Indian. For these tabulations, Hispanic origin is treated as if it were equivalent to a race.

According to the table, the percentage of married couples in which the races of the spouses differ rose from 4.5 percent at the start of the 1990s to 5.4 percent at the end—an increase from 2.4 million interracial couples to about 3.0 million. This finding is consistent with previous studies that reported a secular trend toward increasing interracial marriage, especially among blacks and whites (Farley 1999, figures 5.7 and 5.8). Presumably, a growing but still small minority of children have parents of different races.

The primary reason for change through the 1990s was that white and black men and women increasingly married persons from races other than their own. The percentage of black men with nonblack wives rose from 6.3 to 8.4 percent, while that of white men with nonwhite wives went from 2.7 to 3.4 percent. Interestingly, the percentage of Hispanic and Asian spouses marrying outside their race decreased. Migration from abroad has produced rapid growth for these groups. Immigrant enclaves are getting much larger, and this presumably promotes greater racial homogamy for Hispanics and

TABLE 1.1   *Estimates of Racial Intermarriage, 1990 and 2000, by Race and Sex (Thousands)*

Racial Group	Men		Women	
	1990	2000	1990	2000
White				
Number	43,710	43,809	43,546	43,590
Percentage married out	2.7	3.4	2.2	2.9
Black				
Number (000)	3,566	4,089	3,383	3,872
Percentage married out	6.3	8.4	2.4	3.3
Hispanic				
Number (000)	3,489	5,181	3,562	5,318
Percentage married out	18.7	15.0	19.9	17.2
Asian				
Number (000)	1,299	1,922	1,543	2,201
Percentage married out	11.3	9.9	24.1	21.3
American Indian				
Number (000)	300	351	330	371
Percentage married out	57.8	52.3	61.5	53.9
Total				
Number (000)	52.364	55,352	52,364	55,352
Percentage married out	4.5	5.4	4.5	5.4

Source: U.S. Bureau of the Census, Public Use Microdata Files from the 5 Percent Sample of the Census of 1990 and from the March 2000 Current Population Survey.
Note: These data tabulate the race of spouses for persons married and living with a spouse. Five mutually exclusive races were used: Hispanic, non-Hispanic white, non-Hispanic black, non-Hispanic Asian (including Pacific Islanders), and non-Hispanic American Indian.

Asians who marry, especially among immigrants. When complete data from the 2000 census are released, we may find that native-born Hispanics and Asians increasingly married outside their own races and that the rise in racial homogamy for these groups shown in table 1.1 results from immigration.

Subsequent analyses with micro-level data from the 2000 enumeration will also provide local-area estimates of the number of children living in married-couple families in which the races of the spouses differ. These may then be compared with the racial reports of children to determine whether the interracial marriages explain the frequency of the reporting of multiple race for children (Smith and Jones 2001a, 2001b; Jones and Smith 2001).

The Official Governmental Decision About Measuring Race

Because these 1997 OMB guidelines will have consequences for decades to come, it is important to summarize them carefully. They include the following:

- When self-identification is used to identify race in the federal statistical system, respondents should be given the opportunity to identify with more than one race, but the term "multiracial" is not to be used. Rather, the names of specific races are to be presented as choices for the respondent.
- When self-identification is the method of data collection, separate questions should be asked to determine race and Hispanic ethnicity.
- The Hispanic-ethnicity question should precede the race question (an important change from the 1990 census procedure).
- "Arab" and "Cape Verdean" should not be used as races. (Spokespersons for these groups had advocated the addition of these terms as races.)
- The term "American Indian" should not be replaced by "Native American," but the term "Hawaiian" should be replaced by "Native Hawaiian."
- The term "Alaskan Native" should replace "Aleut" or "Eskimo."
- Asian races should be distinguished from Pacific Islander races. A broad racial category called "Native Hawaiian or Other Pacific Islander" (NHOPI or NHPI) should be used.
- The five major racial categories to be used are white, black or African American, American Indian, Asian, and Native Hawaiian or other Pacific Islander.

The radical shift away from the assumption that each person had only one racial identity did not occur because powerful civil rights organization or professional associations advocated a change nor because federal enforcement agencies demanded improved data to carry out the responsibilities mandated by Congress and the courts. Rather, a small number of persistent advocates who were greatly upset by the status quo effectively challenged the traditional system. They found a sympathetic hearing in Congress and in the Clinton administration: elected and appointed officials did not want to be in the untenable position of insisting that a person had one and only racial identity when he or she wished to identify with two or more races. The idea that every individual can be classified as a member of a single race may gradually disappear in the United States, just as the idea that people were either Angles or Saxons disappeared in England.

How the OMB Guidelines Were Put into Operation for the 2000 Enumeration

The OMB recommendations were published less than two years before the Census Bureau began printing questionnaires for the 2000 count. That agency had neither the time nor the resources to conduct a major new survey pretesting racial and Hispanic-origin questions entirely consistent with the new OMB rules, although they could draw upon findings from earlier surveys. Bureau officials faced the challenge of writing census questions that would:

- satisfy the explicit recommendations of OMB;
- be clear and understandable to the 105 million householders who would receive the census questionnaire in their mail boxes,[1] and then fill them out without detailed instructions and without consulting a Census Bureau employee; and
- satisfy congressional pressures and those of potent advocacy groups that wanted specific racial and Spanish-origin terms listed on the census enumeration form to make certain that their groups would be completely counted.

Figure 1.1 presents the questions about race and Hispanic ethnicity used in the 1990 and 2000 enumerations. On the 2000 census form, the query on Hispanic origin preceded the race question, and the "Spanish-Hispanic" option became "Latino-Spanish-Hispanic." This is consistent with the Census Bureau practice of using many terms for a group so as to maximize the count. This question was also reformatted, and in an important change, the six examples of Spanish or Hispanic origins listed in 1990 to suggest how the blank space might be filled out—Argentinean, Colombian, Dominican, Nicaraguan, Salvadoran, and Spaniard—were removed. It is still too early to know whether the elimination of these examples led to an increase in the number of people who simply checked the "other Spanish-Hispanic-Latino box" on the 2000 form and left empty the space for type of Hispanic ethnicity. Presumably, the removal of those six nouns from the census questionnaire led to a decrease in the number or proportion who wrote Argentinean, Colombian, Dominican, Nicaraguan, Salvadoran, or Spaniard.

The race question in 2000 listed the five major races appearing in the OMB guidelines, but not in the manner a reader of those guidelines might expect. Since 1980, Representative Robert Matsui from California has used his considerable influence to ensure that a substantial list of Asian and Pacific Islander origins is presented to the American public on the census schedule. As a result, both the 1990 and 2000 race questions listed six specific Asian and three Pacific Islander races. Unlike the 1990 query, the race question in 2000 had one open space in which American Indians and Alaska Natives were asked to print their tribe, another open space in which Asian and Pacific Islanders were asked to enter a racial or national origin term if none of the nine given on the census questionnaire were deemed appropriate, and yet another open space in which a respondent could write

FIGURE 1.1   *Questions About Hispanic Origin and Race Asked on the Census, 1990 and 2000*

Census of 2000
(Asked of Everyone)

⟶ **NOTE: Please answer BOTH Questions 7 and 8.**

7. Is Person 1 Spanish/Hispanic/Latino? *Mark* [X] *the "No" box if not* Spanish/Hispanic/Latino.

☐ No, not Spanish/Hispanic/Latino   ☐ Yes, Puerto Rican
☐ Yes, Mexican, Mexican Am., Chicano ☐ Yes, Cuban
☐ Yes, other Spanish/Hispanic/Latino -- *Print group.*

[| | | | | | | | | | | | | | | | | | | |]

8. What is Person 1's race? *Mark* [X] *one or more races to indicate what this person considers himself/herself to be.*

☐ White
☐ Black, African Am., or Negro
☐ American Indian or Alaska Native -- *Print name of enrolled or principal tribe.*

[| | | | | | | | | | | | | | | | | | | |]

☐ Asian Indian ☐ Japanese   ☐ Native Hawaiian
☐ Chinese   ☐ Korean   ☐ Guamanian or Chamorro
☐ Filipino   ☐ Vietnamese   ☐ Samoan
☐ Other Asian -- *Print race.*   ☐ Other Pacific Islander -- *Print race.*

[| | | | | | | | | | | | | | | | | | | |]

☐ Some other race -- *Print race.*

[| | | | | | | | | | | | | | | | | | | |]

⟶ **If more people live here, continue with Person 2.**

Source: U.S. Bureau of the Census, enumeration forms for the censuses of 1990 and 2000 (available at: *www.census.gov.*).

Census of 1990
(Asked of Everyone)

4. Race Fill ONE circle for the race that the person considers himself/herself to be. 　**If Indian (Amer.),** print the name of the enrolled or principal tribe. ——→ 　If **Other Asian or Pacific Islander (API)** print one group, for example: Hmong, Fijian, Laotian,Thai, Tongan, Pakistani, Cambodian, and so on. ————→ 　If **Other race,** print race.————→	○ White ○ Black or Negro ○ Indian (Amer.) (Print the name of the 　enrolled or principal tribe ⇾ ┌─────────────────────────┐ └─────────────────────────┘ ○ Eskimo ○ Aleut 　　　Asian or Pacific Islander (API) ○ Chinese　　　　○ Japanese ○ Filipino　■　　○ Asian Indian ○ Hawaiian　　　○ Samoan ○ Korean　　　　○ Guamanian ○ Vietnamese　　○ Other API⇾ ┌─────────────────────────┐ └─────────────────────────┘ ○ Other race (Print race)⟋
5. Age and year of birth 　a. Print each person's age at last birthday. Fill in the matching circle below each box. 　b. Print each person's year of birth and fill the matching circle below each box.	a. Age　　　　b. Year of birth ｜ ｜ ｜ ｜　*1*｜ ｜ ｜ ｜ 0○ 0○0○　1● 8○ 0○0○ 1○ 1○1○　　　9○ 1○1○ 　2○2○　　　　　2○ 2○ 　3○3○　　　　　3○ 3○ 　4○4○　■　　　4○ 4○ 　5○5○　　　　　5○ 5○ 　6○6○　　　　　6○ 6○ 　7○7○　　　　　7○ 7○ 　8○8○　　　　　8○ 8○ 　9○9○　　　　　9○ 9○
6. Marital status 　Fill ONE circle for each person.	○ Now married　○ Separated ○ Widowed　　　○ Never married ○ Divorced
7. Is this person of Spanish/Hispanic origin? 　Fill ONE circle for each person. 　**If Yes, other Spanish/Hispanic,** print one group. ————→	○ No (not Spanish/Hispanic) ○ Yes, Mexican, Mexican-Am., Chicano ○ Yes, Puerto Rican　■ ○ Yes, Cuban ○ Yes, Other Spanish/Hispanic 　　(Print one group, for example, 　　Argentinean, Colombian, 　　Dominican, Nicaraguan, 　　Salvadoran, Spaniard, and so on.) ┌─────────────────────────┐⟋ └─────────────────────────┘

in a race if none of the twelve listed races applied. Please note that though respondents were told to mark one or more races, there were no explicit instructions telling respondents what they had to do to be counted as identifying with two or more races, although the census questionnaire did provide several opportunities for a respondent to enter a term for his or her "other" race. Census Bureau pretests also led to the retention of the common and readily understood term Negro, though it was not on the OMB recommendation list.

After data were gathered in 2000, the Census Bureau developed coding rules to process the results. These rules increased the number of major races by adding a sixth option, "some other race." Persons who identified with a single race—those who either checked only one box or checked no box but wrote a term directly denoting race, such as white, black, or African American, in the "some other race" space or anywhere near the race question on the census questionnaire—were classified into one major race.

Other respondents presented challenges, and the Census Bureau devised new procedures for their classification. A person who marked two Asian races, such as Chinese and Vietnamese, or two Pacific Islander races, such as Guamanian and Samoan, was classified as identifying with a single major race—Asian or NHOPI, respectively.

Although not consistent with OMB recommendations, the Census 2000 enumeration form included a "some other race" box where a respondent could write a word or phrase. The size of the multiple race population depended greatly upon the coding procedures the Census Bureau developed for coding entries written in the "some other race" box.

If a person wrote any term indicating a Hispanic origin, he or she was automatically considered to be "other" by race. For example, a person who wrote Castilian, Cuban, or Argentinean was classified into the "other" race category. If the respondent had already checked a box for his or her and then wrote a Hispanic term, he or she was multiple by race. Thus persons who marked white or black for their race and then went on to write Dominican or Puerto Rican in the "some other race" box were classified as multiracial. This explains why two of the most frequently reported combinations were white and "some other race" and black and "some other race."

If a person wrote a term in the "some other race" box indicating an origin other than Hispanic, the Census Bureau may or may not have classified that individual into the "other" race category. The agency considered the word or phrase written on the 2000 Census form and then examined data for persons who wrote that same word or phrase for their ancestry in the enumeration of 1990. If 70 percent or more of the persons reporting that ancestry in 1990 identified with a specific race, that race was assigned to the 2000 respondent. If less than 70 percent of those reporting that ancestry in 1990 had identified with a race, then the person was considered "other" by race in 2000. Several examples illustrate this procedure. Those who wrote French or Irish in the "some other race" box on the Census 2000 form were classified as white since more than 70 percent of those reporting French or Irish as their ancestry in 1990 had marked white for their race. Those who wrote South African in the "some other race" box in Census 2000 were considered to be "other" by race since, in the 1990 census, those writing South African for their ancestry reported a variety of races: white, black, and Asian Indian. These coding rules mean that if a person marked white in 2000 and then went on to write "Spanish" in the "some other race" box, he or she was multiracial just as was a person who checked black and then wrote "Dominican" in the "some other race" box. However, a person who checked white on the Census 2000 and then wrote "French" or "Italian" in the "some other race" box was not multiple by race.

Identifying with Multiple Races: How Many Used This Option?

When this chapter was revised—in March 2002—only selected data had been released from the Census 2000. The data give us information about the frequency with which multiple races were reported, the most popular combinations of races, and geographic patterns of multiple reporting, but they do not allow investigations of which personal, household, or local geographic factors—if any—influenced a respondent's identification with one or several races. I stress that there were no instructions on the census form telling a respondent what to do to be tabulated as multiracial. Thus, the reported size of the multiracial population largely results from Census Bureau coding rules.

As table 1.2 indicates, 6.8 million of the 281.4 million Americans counted in 2000 marked two or more boxes or wrote a Hispanic-origin term for their second race, such that they were classified as identifying with two or more of the six major races used in the census. Approximately one American in forty identified with two races, whereas about one in one thousand marked boxes to identify with three or more races. Fewer than one thousand persons checked sufficient numbers of boxes to identify with all six major races.

Table 1.3 lists the racial combinations reported by at least one hundred thousand in 2000; the pie chart in figure 1.2 illustrates the distribution of the multirace population. The most popular combination—reported by one-third of those who identified with two or more races—was white and "some other race." Typically, these were people who marked both the box for white and the box for "some other race" and then wrote in a term denoting Hispanic origin. White and American Indian was the next most popular

TABLE 1.2   *Population by Number of Races Reported, 2000 Census*

Number of Races Reported	Number	Percentage of Total Population
One only	274,595,678	97.4
Two	6,368,075	2.3
Three	410,285	0.1
Four	38,408	< 0.1
Five	8,637	< 0.1
Six	823	< 0.1
Total	281,421,906	100.0

Source: U.S. Bureau of the Census 2001, table 1.

TABLE 1.3   *Frequency of Report of Multiple-Race Ancestry,*
            2000 Census

Racial Combination	Number Reported	Share of the Total Multiple-Race Population (Percentage)
Most Frequently Reported		
White and some other race	2,206,251	32.3
White and American Indian	1,082,683	15.9
White and Asian	868,395	12.7
White and black	784,764	11.5
Black and some other race	417,249	6.1
Asian and some other race	249,108	3.6
Black and American Indian	182,494	2.7
Asian and NHOPI	138,802	2.0
White and NHOPI	112,964	1.7
White, black, and American Indian	112,207	1.6
Black and Asian	106,782	1.6
All other combinations	564,529	8.3
Least Frequently Reported		
White-Black-Indian–NHOPI–some other race	68	< 0.1
Black-Indian-NHOPI–some other race	111	< 0.1
Indian-Asian-NHOPI–some other race	207	< 0.1
Black-Indian-Asian-NHOPI–some other race	216	< 0.1
White-Indian-NHOPI–some other race	309	< 0.1
White-black-NHOPI–some other race	325	< 0.1
Black-Indian-Asian–some other race	334	< 0.1
White-black-Asian-NHOPI–some other race	379	< 0.1
Indian-NHOPI–some other race	586	< 0.1
White-Indian-Asian-NHOPI–some other race	639	< 0.1
Total	6,826,228	100.0

Source: U.S. Bureau of the Census 2001.
Note: NHOPI refers to the major racial group of Native Hawaiians and other Pacific Islanders. Ninety-seven percent of those who marked "Some other race" as their only race went on to identify with a Spanish-Hispanic-Latino origin on the separate Hispanic-origin inquiry. Fifty-eight percent of those who marked "Some other race" in combination with one or more other major races went on to identify with a Spanish-Hispanic-Latino origin.

FIGURE 1.2   *Distribution of the Multiple-Race Population, 2000*

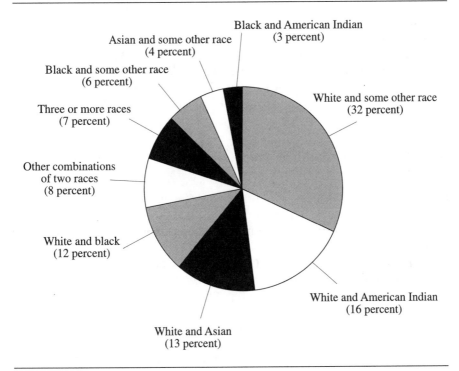

Source: U.S. Bureau of the Census 2001.

combination, followed by white and Asian. The most commonly reported second race for those who marked the box for black was also "some other race," just as it was for whites. Subsequent data from the census will allow us to confirm the hypothesis that many of the individuals who identified themselves as black and "some other race" were Caribbeans or Central Americans who identified with their African origin and then wrote a Spanish term, such as Dominican. The only three-race combination marked by one hundred thousand or more respondents was white, black, and American Indian—reflecting, undoubtedly, the high rates at which American Indians have married outside their own race since the arrival of the first Europeans.

The Census of 2000 provides counts for 6 major race designations (including "some other") and for all possible combinations of multiple reporting. There are 57 such possible combinations of 2 to 6 races—implying that this enumeration gives us counts for 63 distinct races or combinations of races down to the lowest level of census geography, the city block. When these 63 races are tabulated according to reported Hispanic ethnicity, data are available for 126 different groups.

Table 1.3 also lists the ten least frequently reported races. Some people identified with every one of the combinations, but fewer than ten thousand persons identified with 35 of the 57 possible multiple race groups, and fewer than one thousand persons checked boxes to identify with 14 of the combinations. As this table shows, the combination white-black–American Indian–NHOPI–some other race was chosen least frequently, with a national count of just sixty-eight persons. Most of the 57 multiple-race combinations were reported so infrequently that the groups will not be subject to scholarly analysis.

Maximum and Minimum Counts of the Race in 2000

The 2000 census data generate thirty-two different estimates of the size of each of the major races; that is, it provides a count of those who identified with each race only, five different counts for the two-race combination involving each race, ten different counts for both three-race and four-race combinations, five different counts for five-race combinations, and, finally, the count that includes persons who claimed all six major races. No longer is there an unambiguous answer to the question, how many whites, or how many American Indians, did the census count.

Figure 1.3 presents a comparison of the minimum and maximum counts of each of the six major race categories. There are substantial differences between these counts. Among those who marked a box to report they were white by race, for example, few went on to identify with a second race, and so the minimum count of whites is close to the maximum count. Among Native Hawaiians and other Pacific Islanders, however, there were many more who identified with a second or third race than who identified as NHOPI only.

Whites and African Americans differed from the other major races in that those who identified as white or black were relatively unlikely to identify with a second race—thus the minimum and maximum counts are fairly similar. Although 5.2 million Americans marked both white and a second race, 97.4 percent of those who marked white claimed white as their only race. Among those who marked black, 95.2 percent marked only black–African American–Negro.

The "some other race" group presented in figure 1.3 is largely—but not entirely—made up of Latinos; 90.4 percent of those who checked the "some other race" box went on to claim a Spanish-Hispanic-Latino identity on the distinct Hispanic-ethnicity question. Of those who checked only the "some other race" box, 97 percent marked themselves as Hispanic in origin.

American Indians and the NHOPI races were distinguished by the

FIGURE 1.3 *Minimum Counts of Census Race Groups Races as Percentage of Maximum Counts, 2000*

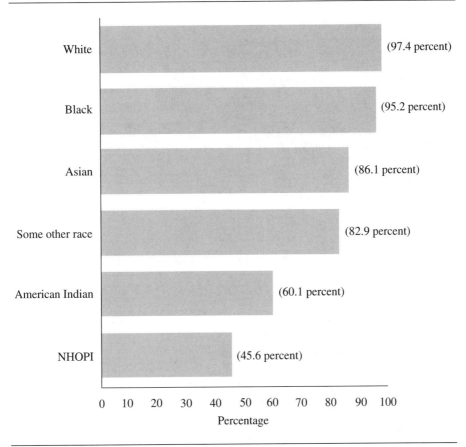

Source: U.S. Bureau of the Census 2001.

frequency with which they were reported in combination with other races. The estimates of the American Indian population are spread across a broad range in the census of 2000: from 2.5 million who identified uniquely with this race to a maximum of 4.1 million, if those who marked Indian along with a second or third race are included in the count. When data from the long-form census questionnaire are released, several additional estimates of the Native American population will be available, because there will also be counts of those who did not mark American Indian for their race but identified American Indian or a particular Indian tribe as their first or second ancestry.

The Geography of the Multiple Race Population in 2000

Information on the areas with relatively high or low concentrations of multiracial residents is presented in figures 1.4, 1.5, and 1.6. Included in the multiple-race population are those who wrote in a Hispanic term for their second race. Locations in each map are sorted into quintiles, the darkest areas showing the greatest frequency of multiple-race reporting and the lightest indicating the lowest frequency.

Two states often associated with great racial diversity, Hawaii and Alaska, are at the top of the rank as illustrated in figure 1.4. Indeed, Hawaii is "off the scale," with more than one in five persons enumerated there having reported more than one race. In that state, Asian-NHOPI, Asian-white, and white-NHOPI were the most frequently reported combinations. Not surprisingly, Hawaii also leads the nation in the density of triracial people: 7 percent of Hawaiians reported three or more races. Hawaii comprises just 0.4 percent of the national population, but it is home to 18 percent of the triracial population. The most common triplet in Hawaii was Asian-white-NHOPI. Although multiple-race reporting was high in California, as would be expected, it was even more frequent in Alaska, with its history of Aleuts, American Indians, Eskimos, Russian settlers, Filipino and Mexican cannery workers, and the many white and black Americans who were sent to military bases throughout that state during World War II and the cold war. White–American Indian or Alaska Native was the most frequently reported race combinations in Alaska, accounting for one-half of all multiple-race persons in that state. Although heterogeneous by race, just one-third of 1 percent of Alaskan residents identified with three or more races.

Given the large Hispanic-origin population in California, it is no surprise that white and "some other race" was the statistically dominant multiple race there. Oklahoma, the geographic area designated for Indians until 1889, also ranked high in multiple-race reporting. More than two-thirds of the multiple-race people in that state reported white and American Indian, undoubtedly reflecting the traditionally high rate of interracial marriages among the nation's Native American population.

At the other extreme were states that either never had many minority residents—West Virginia and Maine—or have heterogeneous populations but ones restricted to whites and African Americans. Indeed, two of the states with the lowest frequencies of multiple-race reporting—Mississippi and South Carolina—are two of the four states in which racial minorities have outnumbered whites. In the Deep South, presumably, a firm color line has been drawn for more than a century, so most residents are clearly aware of their racial identification and did not use the census to report they had both black and white forebears.

FIGURE 1.4   *Concentration of Multiple-Race Reporting, 2000, by State (As Percentage of State's Population)*

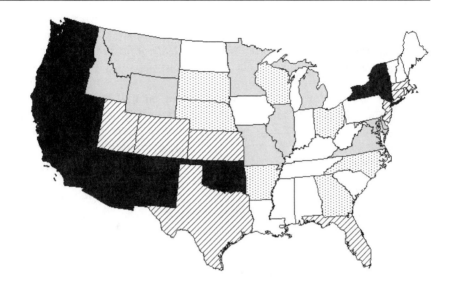

0.7 to 1.2 percent

1.2 to 1.4 percent

1.4 to 2.0 percent

2.0 to 2.8 percent

2.8 to 21.4 percent

Highest Concentration		Lowest Concentration	
Nevada	3.8 percent	Mississippi	0.7 percent
Oklahoma	4.5 percent	West Virginia	0.8 percent
California	4.8 percent	Maine	0.9 percent
Alaska	5.4 percent	Alabama	0.9 percent
Hawaii	21.4 percent	South Carolina	1.0 percent

United States: 2.4 percent

Source: U.S. Bureau of the Census 2001.

Figure 1.5, which shows the percentage reporting more than one race for the 315 metropolitan statistical areas (MSAs) in the United States, illustrates a substantial range in the concentration of multiracial residents. Honolulu, Anchorage, and the racially heterogeneous California metropolises reported the highest densities of multiple-race residents. In five of California's metropolitan areas, more than one resident in twenty was multiracial—an unusually high rate. The major metropolises now serving as ports of entry for international immigrants—Los Angeles, Houston, New York, Chicago, and Miami—ranked toward the top in multiple-race population. At the other extreme, in most smaller metropolises in Appalachia, the Deep South, and the Midwest, few respondents went on to identify with more than one race on the 2000 census form. Three metropolises in the mountains of Pennsylvania reported the smallest representation of multiracials. In only thirteen of the nation's metropolises did the percentage multiracial exceed 4.5 percent, but in thirty-eight of them fewer than one person in one hundred identified with two or more races.

Figure 1.6 presents similar information at the county level. Hawaii and Oklahoma led the nation in the number of counties with high rates of multiracial identification. Hawaii County—the largest island in the archipelago, where Hilo is situated—had the highest rate of multiple-race reporting in the nation, followed by four other Hawaii counties. Craig County, in the northeast corner of Oklahoma, was the mainland county with the highest occurrence of multiple-race reporting. In that small county, 68 percent identified themselves as white only and 16 percent as Indian only; 10 percent said they were both white and American Indian.

In a great swath of counties extending from the Indian homelands in Oklahoma through the Hispanic-populated sections of Texas, New Mexico, Colorado, Arizona, and into California, the reporting of multiple races was far above the national average. At the opposite end of the distribution, there is a great band of several hundred counties—beginning in the Pennsylvania Appalachians, extending into and through the traditional Black Belt of the South, and then swinging up into the wheat-growing areas of the northern Great Plains—in which few individuals used the census of 2000 to report that they identified with a second race. In Nebraska, the Dakotas, and Iowa are several dozen counties in which fewer than one person in five hundred checked a box for a second or third race.

Using and Analyzing Multiple-Race Data from the Census of 2000

Puzzlement is a common reaction to the confusing array of racial data now flowing from Census 2000. Many people think a simple solution would be to code all respondents back into their "primary," "preferred," or "real"

FIGURE 1.5   *Concentration of Multiple-Race Reporting, 2000, by Metropolitan Statistical Area (As Percentage of MSA's Population)*

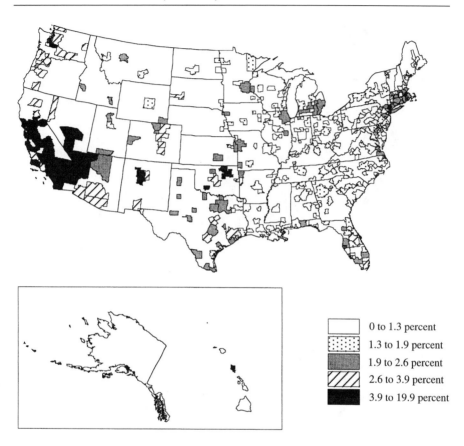

0 to 1.3 percent
1.3 to 1.9 percent
1.9 to 2.6 percent
2.6 to 3.9 percent
3.9 to 19.9 percent

Highest Concentration		Lowest Concentration	
Merced, California, MSA	5.7 percent	Altoona, Pennsylvania, MSA	0.6 percent
Vallejo-Fairfield-Napa,		Johnstown, Pennsylvania, MSA	0.6 percent
California, Primary MSA	5.8 percent	Scranton–Wilkes-Barre–	
Stockton-Lodi, California, MSA	6.1 percent	Hazleton, Pennsylvania, MSA	0.6 percent
Anchorage, Alaska, MSA	6.0 percent	Jackson, Missouri, MSA	0.6 percent
Honolulu, Hawaii, MSA	19.9 percent	Monroe, Louisiana, MSA	0.7 percent

United States: 2.4 percent

Source: U.S. Bureau of the Census 2001.

FIGURE 1.6   Concentration of Multiple-Race Reporting, 2000, by
County (As Percentage of County's Population)

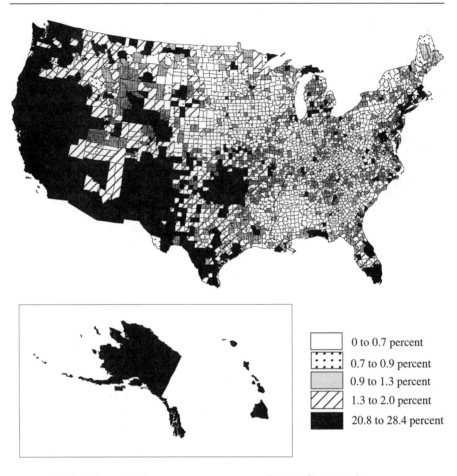

	0 to 0.7 percent
	0.7 to 0.9 percent
	0.9 to 1.3 percent
	1.3 to 2.0 percent
	20.8 to 28.4 percent

Highest Concentration		Lowest Concentration	
Craig, Oklahoma	11.4 percent	Wheeler, Nebraska	0.1 percent
Honolulu, Hawaii	19.9 percent	Emons, North Dakota	0.1 percent
Maui, Hawaii	22.2 percent	Slope, North Dakota	0.1 percent
Kauai, Hawaii	23.8 percent	Kidder, North Dakota	0.2 percent
Hawaii, Hawaii	28.4 percent	Griggs, North Dakota	0.2 percent

United States: 2.4 percent

Source: U.S. Bureau of the Census 2001.

race and thereby produce data resembling those from the twenty-one previous censuses. There is a commonly shared idea that everyone has some preferred or dominant race and that, had the census form only asked the right question, it would have generated orderly data rather than the complex and seemingly inconsistent data we now have. Most people understand the meaning of mixed ancestry or ethnicity, but that conceptualization does not currently extend to race. The Census Bureau's use of "some other race" is especially confusing. More than 90 percent of the 18.5 million census respondents who checked the "some other race" box were Hispanic, but those who did so made up less than half of the "real" Hispanic-origin population as identified by the separate question on Hispanic ethnicity.

Federal law required the Census Bureau to release racial and Hispanic-origin data down to the city-block level before April 1, 2001. The agency complied by posting on its website a table for every geographic area showing the counts for each of the major single-race categories and 57 combinations of races classified by Hispanic-origin—that is, 126 cells of racial information for every geographic area, including the 8.4 million city blocks. Interestingly, city blocks average only thirty-six residents, so most cells of racial data are blank when the city block, the block group, or the census tract is the geographic unit.

Recognizing the challenge of making these complex racial data sensible for users who need data for redistricting purposes or for enforcement of civil rights statutes, the OMB devoted a major effort—though, I believe, a futile one—to determining the most useful way to present data. They issued their recommendation in December 2000 in a ponderous document of more than two hundred pages. These suggestions were issued before racial data from the census were available (OMB 2000). They have not been updated or altered by the administration of President Bush.

Several dozen recommendations were made for the presentation of racial data tailored to the needs of different users, such as those responsible for redistricting, for monitoring employment for the Equal Employment Opportunity Commission, and for computing vital rates for race. One of the first recommendations suggests that the following racial categories be shown:

- each of the five major races: white, black, American Indian, Asian, and NHOPI;
- each of the four most common combinations of two races. The enumeration found these were: white-other, white-Indian, white-Asian, and white-black;
- any other combinations of major races that included 1 percent or more of the population (the census found no other combination that accounted for 1 percent of the population);

- the remainder of the population reporting two or more of the five major races.

This array would not sum to the total population, however, because it omits those who wrote in a term denoting Hispanic origin for their race.

At a later point, the OMB suggested using each of the six major races used in the census, the total multiple-race population, the Hispanic-origin population, and the non-Hispanic white population. In this case, the total would exceed 100 percent because Hispanic-origin individuals and whites would be included twice.

The constitutional justification for a census is reapportionment of seats in the U.S. Congress. State legislatures also use census data to draw congressional and legislative districts. The OMB recommended that, for redistricting purpose, a person who identified as white and one minority race should be included with the minority race. OMB officials correctly presumed that few individuals would identify with two of the four major minority races. However, those redrawing electoral districts were encouraged to examine the population reporting two minority races to see what difference their inclusion in one or the other race would make.

Data from the census of 2000 have been released in a way that is consistent with the OMB recommendations, but with many substantial alterations. The Census Bureau adopted the following:

- The complete array of data for 126 distinct race and Hispanic-origin groups is available for all levels of geography down to the city block.
- For geographic units down to the census-tract level, the Census Bureau produced a tabulation of the minimum counts of each of the six major race categories—that is, those who reported only one race—and the total multiple-race population tabulated by Hispanic origin. This is a useful fourteen-race classification that sums to the total population of an area, but it reveals nothing about the components of the multiple-race population.
- For geographic units down to the census-tract level, the Census Bureau released a tabulation of the maximum counts of each of the six races and the multiple-race population tabulated by Hispanic origin. This is also a fourteen-race classification, but it sums to more than the total population, a result that is likely to confuse users. This tabulation also provides a count of the total number of major races reported by the residents of an area, a number that obviously exceeds the population count.

Summary File 2 provides iterations of demographic characteristics for 249 racial and Hispanic-origin groups down to the census-tract level. Following an OMB recommendation, data are shown for geographic units only if a specific racial or Hispanic-origin group includes one hundred or more residents. This large number of potential racial groups, 249, includes the following:

- One hundred thirty-two racial groups: This includes the specific races, such as Chinese, Taiwanese, Filipino, and Sri Lankan, that are components of the major race termed Asian. Data are shown for sixteen component races of the Asian and NHOPI population.
- Seventy-eight American Indian and Alaska Native tribes: This provides data for the minimum counts of thirty-nine different tribes—that is, persons who wrote in that tribe as their only race—and then the maximum counts of the same thirty-nine tribes.
- Hispanic-origin groups: This includes information for specific groups, such as those who wrote in Chilean, Colombian, or Nicaraguan as their Hispanic origin. Nineteen different Hispanic origins are identified. The total population in the 249 groups will exceed the total population of the area because a single person might be classified into more than one of the different racial groups. For most geographic areas, data are shown for few of the 249 groups since a minimum count of one hundred was required.

Conclusion

In the 1990s, a small but highly effective social movement challenged the traditional idea that each person could be classified into only one race. Congress and those superintending the federal statistical system responded and fundamentally changed the system of racial classification. The census of 2000 allowed individuals to identify simultaneously with as many as six races. By 2003, all federal agencies collecting data about race will give respondents this option.

Putting this new conceptualization of race into practice on the self-administered census form presented a formidable challenge to the Census Bureau. Their decision was to classify all persons into one or more of six race categories: white, black, American Indian, Asian, Native Hawaiian and other Pacific Islander, and "some other race."

Current regulations of the Office of Management and Budget strongly recommend that the Hispanic-origin question be asked, in addition to the mandatory race question. This may confuse respondents and certainly adds a burden for users of data: approximately 40 percent of those who identified with a Hispanic origin in both the 1990 and 2000 censuses did not mark a box for any one of the major races. Instead, they wrote a term denoting a Hispanic origin for their race and were thereby classified by the Census Bureau as "some other race."

In the census of 2000, approximately 2.4 percent of the total population—one person in forty—identified with two or more races. This number is misleading, however, because it includes those who wrote in a term denoting Hispanic origin for their second race. If those who wrote in a Hispanic-origin term are excluded, approximately 1.6 percent of the population identified with two or more of the five major races—that is, about one person in sixty-five.

Multiple-race reporting was more common among the young, reflecting the demographic consequences of increasing interracial marriage. Among those under the age of eighteen, 4.4 percent identified with two or more races; among those eighteen years and older, that figure fell to 1.9 percent. If those who were counted as multiple in race because they wrote in a Hispanic-origin term for their second race are excluded, then the multiple-race population accounted for 3.2 percent of the population under the age of eighteen and 1.4 percent for their elders. Stated differently, about one American child in thirty-one was reported to be multiracial, compared with one in seventy-one for the population eighteen and older.

The reporting of multiple races displays strong geographic patterns. It is most common in Hawaii, Alaska, and California. Given the large black and white populations, the history of miscegenation, and a significant literature describing generations of mulattoes, one might expect multiple-race reporting to be high in the southern states. Instead, such reporting was lowest in the Deep South. Data that would allow a determination of how a person's demographic characteristics or those of a person's family or neighborhood influenced identification with more than one race are not yet available.

The reporting of multiple races has not, apparently, had a significant consequence for the drawing of congressional or legislative districts. By early 2002, states had completed redistricting for the November elections. Although many census issues have been debated and some are being litigated, the reporting of multiple races has not been a central one. Presumably, persons who marked both white and a minority race were classified into the minority race for purposes of drawing districts. In most areas, so few identified with two minority races that their numbers had no impact.

The social movement that led to the change in racial identification has not been active in the years since census data were collected. It has faded. Because of apparent increases in marriages across racial lines, however, there will inevitably be a growing population of children whose parents differ by race. At this point, we do not know whether the current OMB racial classification system will be readily used by these individuals or whether many of them may identify with the race of one parent in some circumstances and that of the other parent in other circumstances. The traditional system of categorizing persons according to membership in a unique race is no longer accurate nor acceptable, but it is far from certain that the approach used in Census 2000 is practical, ideal, or useful (Skerry 2000).

We have yet to determine whether the concept "multiracial" will enter popular discourse. I believe that it will not, and that into the foreseeable future, most people will continue to assume that every American has a "basic" or "essential" race.

The multiple-race option is a dramatic change in the federal statistical system, but there is a telling demographic analogy. From 1870 through 1970 the census asked the birthplaces of respondents' parents. After the restrictive immigration laws of the early twentieth century went into effect, the second-generation population declined, and in 1980, an open-ended question about ancestry supplanted the query on parents' birthplaces. Respondents were encouraged to write in a term or terms to identify their ethnicity, ancestry, or national origin. The Census Bureau coded the first two terms unless the individual had entered a religious identity. At first glance, one might assume that analysts would exploit these new ancestry data to describe patterns of ethnic intermarriage, the nation's ethnic heterogeneity, and the way ancestry or national origin was linked to achievement. Few scholars, however, have analyzed ancestry and multiple-ancestry information from the last three censuses, and as far as I know, these data have not been used by governmental agencies.

Note

1. It is one challenge to create a form that will be administered by an interviewer or computer. It is another to design a questionnaire that will be readily understood by its recipients without benefit of detailed instructions or clear explanation of terms such as "race" or "Hispanic ethnicity." The census questionnaire provokes respondents to cross out terms they do not like, write in new or different terms, or write phrases rather than ticking boxes.

References

Anderson, Margo J. 1988. *The American Census: A Social History.* New Haven, Conn.: Yale University Press.

Cortes, C. E. 1980. "Mexicans." In *The Harvard Encyclopedia of American Ethnic Groups,* edited by Steven Thernstrom. Cambridge, Mass.: Harvard University Press.

Farley, Reynolds. 1999. "Racial Issues: Recent Trends in Residential Patterns and Intermarriage." In *Diversity and Its Discontents: Cultural Conflict and Common*

Ground in Contemporary American Society, edited by Neil J. Smelser and Jeffrey C. Alexander. Princeton, N.J.: Princeton University Press.

Fu, Vincent Kang. 2001. "Racial Intermarriage Pairings." *Demography* 38(2): 147–59.

Gilberston, Greta, Joseph Fitzpatrick, and Lijun Yang. 1996. "Hispanic Intermarriage in New York City: New Evidence from 1991." *International Migration Review* 30(summer): 445–59.

Harris, David. 1994. "The 1990 Census Count of American Indians: What Do the Numbers Really Mean?" *Social Science Quarterly* 75(3): 580–91.

Heer, David. 1974. "The Prevalence of Black-White Intermarriage in the United States: 1960 and 1970." *Journal of Marriage and the Family* 36(2): 246–58.

Hirschman, Charles, Richard Alba, and Reynolds Farley. 2000. "The Meaning and Measurement of Race in the U.S. Census: Glimpses into the Future." *Demography* 37(3): 381–94.

Hwang, Sean-Smong, Rogelio Saenz, and Benigno Aguirre. 1995. "The SES Selectivity of Interracially Married Asians." *International Migration Review* 29(summer): 469–91.

Jones, Nicholas, and Amy Symens Smith. 2001. "Why Can't They Just Choose a Race? Exploring 'Some Other Race' Reporting in Census 2000." Paper presented at the annual meeting of the American Sociological Association. Anaheim, California (August 18).

Kalmijn, Matthijs. 1993. "Trends in Black-White Intermarriage." *Social Forces* 72(1): 19–146.

———. 1998. "Intermarriage and Homogamy: Causes, Patterns, and Trends." *Annual Review of Sociology* 24: 395–421.

Model, Suzanne, and Gene Fisher. 2001. "Black-White Unions: West Indians and African Americans Compared." *Demography* 38(2): 177–85.

Office of Management and Budget (OMB), Executive Office of the President. 1994. "Standard for the Classification of Federal Data on Race and Ethnicity." *Federal Register* 59(June 9): 29831–835.

———. 1997. "Revisions to the Standards for the Classification of Federal Data on Race and Ethnicity." *Federal Register* 62(10): 58782–790.

———. 2000. *Provisional Guidance on the Implementation of the 1997 Standards for Federal Data on Race and Ethnicity.* Washington (December 15). Available at: *www.whitehouse.gov/OMB/fedreg/index.html.*

Petersen, William. 1987. "Politics and the Measurement of Ethnicity." In *The Politics of Numbers*, edited by William Alonso and Paul Starr. New York: Russell Sage Foundation.

Qian, Zhenchao. 1997. "Breaking the Racial Barriers: Variations in Interracial Marriage Between 1980 and 1990." *Demography* 34(3): 263–76.

Rosenfield, Michael J. 2001. "The Salience of Pan-National Hispanic and Asian Identities in U.S. Marriage Markets." *Demography* 38(2): 161–75.

Sandefur, Gary, and Trudy McKinnell. 1986. "American Indian Intermarriage." *Social Science Research* 15(4): 347–71.

Schoen, Robert, and B. Thomas. 1989. "Intergroup Marriage in Hawaii: 1969–1971 and 1979–1981." *Sociological Perspectives* 32: 365–82.

Skerry, Peter. 2000. *Counting on the Census? Race, Group Identity, and the Evasion of Politics.* Washington, D.C.: Brookings Institution.

Skrentny, John David, ed. 1999. *Color Lines: Affirmative Action, Immigration, and Civil Rights Options for America.* Chicago, Ill.: University of Chicago Press.

Smith, Amy Symens, and Nicholas Jones. 2001a. "What About Children? Race Reporting in Interracial Families: New Findings from Census 2000." Paper presented at the annual meeting of the American Sociological Association. Anaheim, Calif. (August 18).

———. 2001b. "Who Is Really Reporting 'Two or More Races'? Exploring the 'Multiple Race' Population in the 1999 American Community Survey." Paper presented at the annual meeting of the Population Association of America. Washington, D.C. (March 29).

Snipp, Matthew C. 1989. *American Indians: First of This Land.* New York: Russell Sage Foundation.

Spencer, John Michael. 1997. *The New Colored People: The Mixed-Race Movement in America.* New York: New York University Press.

U.S. Department of Commerce. U.S. Bureau of the Census. 1973. "Population and Housing Inquiries in the U.S. Decennial Censuses: 1790–1970." Working Paper 39. Washington.

———. 1996. "Findings on Questions on Race and Hispanic Origin Tested in the 1996 National Content Survey." Unpublished paper. Washington (December 5).

———. 1997. *Results of the 1996 Race and Ethnic Targeted Test.* Population Division Working Paper 18. Washington (May). Available at: *www.census/gov/population/www/techpap.html.*

———. 2001. *Overview of Race and Hispanic Origin: 2000.* Census 2000 Brief C2KBR/10. Washington (March).

Williams, Kim. 2000. "Changing Race As We Know It? The Political Location of the Multiracial Movement." Unpublished paper. Taubman Center for State and Local Government, John F. Kennedy School of Government, Harvard University.

2

DOES IT MATTER HOW WE MEASURE? RACIAL CLASSIFICATION AND THE CHARACTERISTICS OF MULTIRACIAL YOUTH

David R. Harris

O N MARCH 12, 2001, the U.S. Census Bureau announced that in the 2000 census, 2.4 percent of Americans had identified with two or more racial groups. This count, the first in census history to enumerate the multiracial U.S. population, has received significant attention from academics, news organizations, and advocacy groups and has been used to support a variety of claims about the increasing diversity of U.S. society, the declining significance of race, and the blurring of lines between racial groups (Martin Kasindorf and Haya El Nasser, "Impact of Census' Race Data Debated," *USA Today,* March 13, 2001, A1; Eric Schmitt, "For 7 Million People in Census, One Race Category Isn't Enough," *New York Times,* March 13, 2001, A1). In a couple of years, individual-level data from Census 2000 will be released, and with it will come numerous articles and books about the multiracial population.

Although interesting findings will no doubt emerge from these studies, what has yet to be adequately appreciated, and will quite likely continue to be ignored, is that the 2000 census count of the multiracial population probably would have been different had an alternative measure of race been used. Although several studies support this hypothesis (Goldstein and Morning 2000; Hahn, Mulinare, and Teutsch 1992; Harris and Sim 2000), research and policy communities have yet to wrestle fully with its implications. Specifically, little is known about the sensitivity of estimates of the characteristics of the multiracial population to the way this population is defined. It may be that different racial classification schemes produce multiracial population estimates of varying sizes but with the same social and demographic characteristics. This would be welcome news for researchers and policy makers, most of whom are more concerned with the characteristics of the multiracial population than with its size. On the other hand, it may be that alternatively defined multiracial populations differ in both size and characteristics. If this turns out to be true, then analyses based on Census 2000, or any other study that uses a single racial classification scheme, will be far from definitive.

Some of the more interesting findings from the 2000 census will relate to the population of multiracial youth. How do racial classification schemes affect the characteristics of multiracial youth? How do multiracial and monoracial youth compare across sociodemographic indicators and racial classification schemes? How do the answers to these questions change when attention shifts from a simple distinction between monoracial and multiracial to distinctions between white–African Americans, white–Native Americans, white–Asian Americans, and their component monoracial groups? In this chapter I use data from the National Longitudinal Study of Adolescent Health (Add Health) to explore these issues and to offer some conclusions about variability in the characteristics of American multiracial populations.

What Do We Know About the Multiracial Population?

Social scientists have long been interested in the conditions of multiracial people in general and of white–African American people in particular. At the dawn of the twentieth century, W. E. B. Du Bois (1996 [1899]) discussed racial intermarriage and color prejudice in *The Philadelphia Negro*. Observing that many blacks with lighter complexions were able to pass into the economic and social worlds of white America, Du Bois concludes that skin color does, indeed, affect the life chances of African Americans. Several decades later, Robert Ezra Park (1928, 1931) and Everett Stonequist (1935, 1937) conducted in-depth studies of the multiracial population, a group Park labeled "marginal men." Both authors concluded that because multiracial people stand between multiple social worlds, they reflect "the discords and harmonies, repulsions and attractions of these worlds" (Stonequist 1937, 8). Although the anxiety resulting from this inner strain leads some to greater creativity, for others "it initiates a process of disorganization which finds expression in statistics of delinquency, crime, suicide and mental instability" (Stonequist 1935, 12).

During the middle decades of the twentieth century, academics made occasional mention of the multiracial population (for example, Myrdal 1996 [1944]; Reed 1969), but for the most part they followed prevailing norms and proceeded as if every person was a member of one and only one race (for example, Gordon 1964; Wilson 1979). Although the multiracial population continues to be absent from most academic studies, the research community has devoted greater attention to this group in recent years, in response to continuing increases in interracial marriage (Qian 1997) and growing acknowledgment of "multiracial" as a legitimate racial identity (OMB 1997; Snipp 1997). Recent studies of multiracial people include work on identity formation (Gibbs and Hines 1992; Jacobs 1992; Twine 1997; Williams 1996), racial classification (Davis 1991; Hahn, Mulinare, and Teutsch 1992; Hirschman, Alba, and Farley 2000; Xie and Goyette 1998), educational achievement (Kao 1999), and self-esteem (Cauce et al. 1992; Field 1996; Mass 1992).

Despite this growing interest in the multiracial population, the research community has produced relatively little information about their sociodemographic characteristics. Studies of interracial marriage represent one indirect source of information about this population. Interracial couples, it is known, tend to have somewhat higher levels of education than racially endogamous couples, and the odds of intermarriage are highest for educationally homogamous couples (Farley 1999; Kalmijn 1993; Qian 1997, 1999). Education effects are stronger for white-Asian couples than for white-black pairs, and they have been increasing faster for the former group than for the latter (Qian 1997). Thus, we might expect multiracial youth to live in better-educated families and to enjoy the socioeconomic status advantages that tend to flow from education. However, the contexts and characteristics of married interracial couples might differ from those of multiracial youth because of differential fertility, nonmarital childbearing, and marital dissolution. A recent study, for example, shows that patterns of interracial partnering differ significantly for marital and cohabiting unions (Harris and Ono 2000). If a substantial share of multiracial youth are born to unmarried partners, then we can expect the characteristics of multiracial youths' households to differ from those of interracially married couples.

In addition to work on interracial marriage, further information about the sociodemographic characteristics of multiracial populations is provided by studies that directly examine these populations. Unfortunately, such studies are few in number. Work by Yu Xie and Kim Goyette (1998), Grace Kao (1999), and William Corrin and Thomas Cook (1999) are among the exceptions. Xie and Goyette use 1990 census data to assess the way children with one Asian and one non-Asian parent are classified. Their descriptive results indicate that this population is disproportionately of preschool age, has highly educated parents, and lives in areas with fairly large Asian populations. Although informative, Xie and Goyette's descriptives are difficult to interpret because no comparable data are presented for youth from either intraracial or non-Asian interracial unions.

Studies by Kao and by Corrin and Cook provide comparative perspectives on multiracial youth. Kao (1999) finds that among a nationally representative sample of eighth-graders, multiracial youth with one Asian parent live in families with average annual incomes of nearly $45,000. Their families are less wealthy than those of monoracial Asian youth but not significantly less affluent than the families of monoracial white youth. The mothers of multiracial Asian youth are less educated than the mothers of monoracial Asian children, and have lower-status jobs than the mothers of monoracial white children. However, the fathers of multiracial Asian children are better educated and have better jobs than the fathers of monoracial whites. Kao also examines the characteristics of multiracial youth with one black parent. In terms of annual family income and parents' education and occupation, multiracial blacks are solidly between monoracial whites and monoracial blacks, although they are somewhat closer to blacks on these indicators. Their families earn an average of $26,483 a year, compared with about $23,000 for monoracial blacks and more than $46,000 for monoracial whites. Although multiracial blacks are advantaged relative to blacks, and multiracial Asians are disadvantaged relative to Asians, there is nevertheless a substantial gap between these two multiracial populations, with multiracial Asians leading on each of the socioeconomic status indicators Kao considers.

Corrin and Cook use a sample of 2,368 suburban Chicago adolescents to compare monoracial white and black youth with two multiracial groups, one that claims partial white ancestry and one that does not. Nonwhite multiracial youth live in families similar to those of monoracial blacks but are significantly less likely than monoracial or multiracial whites to live with both biological parents. In terms of neighborhood poverty, the four groups are significantly different from one another. Monoracial blacks live in neighborhoods with the highest percentage of poor residents (10.4 percent), followed by multiracial blacks (9.1 percent), multiracial whites (7.5 percent), and monoracial whites (5.3 percent). With respect to neighborhood income, education, and occupational status, monoracial whites are significantly more advantaged than monoracial blacks or either of the multiracial groups. This finding of monoracial white exceptionalism also appears on measures of neighborhood racial composition. Corrin and Cook further find that girls are significantly overrepresented in both multiracial populations, a result that they describe as "difficult to explain" (Corrin and Cook 1999, 11).

Although these recent studies add significantly to our knowledge of the multiracial population, our understanding of this group continues to be limited by methodological shortcomings (Root 1992). One problem is that many studies are based on small convenience samples (Field 1996; Funderburg 1994; Gibbs and Hines 1992; Jacobs 1992; Twine 1997; Williams 1996). We learn a great deal about particular groups of multiracial people from this work, and it presents us with interesting hypotheses, but whether any of the observed patterns apply to larger populations is not clear.

Additionally, work on the multiracial population is limited by the tendency to use single, fixed measures of race. One of the most common ways to identify multiracials is by using parents' race (Eschbach 1995; Harrison and Bennett 1995; Tafoya 2000; Twine 1997; Xie and Goyette 1998). This approach assumes that a person is racially mixed if, and only if, he or she has biological parents who identify with different monoracial groups or at least one parent who identifies multiracially. There are three problems with this approach. First, it requires data on the race of both biological parents—information that is usually unavailable for children who do not live with both biological parents. Second, it requires that parents fully report their racial ancestries; previous research indicates widespread selective reporting of race and ethnicity on surveys (Lieberson and Waters 1993; Snipp 1989; Waters 1990). Third, and perhaps most important, this approach assumes that a person's race is simply the sum of his or her parents' racial identities.

A second approach to racial classification appears in the work of Joshua Goldstein and Ann Morning (2000). Acknowledging flaws in parent-based definitions of race, they instead combine self-reported race and ancestry data to define the multiracial population. In their work, people are classified as multiracial if they report an ancestry that is inconsistent with their race. For example, a man would be considered multiracial if he identified racially as black but reported Kenyan and French ancestry. In addition to the problems associated with ancestry simplification that have already been noted, the Goldstein-Morning approach is also limited by its use of proxy reporting of race and ancestry. In the U.S. census, which is the basis for their estimates, one household member provides race and ancestry data for all household members. Although there is no way of telling how households decide who will be their informant, or how (or whether) many informants ask family members how they would like to be identified, it is reasonable to suspect an imperfect correlation between self-identification and proxy identification among those who might be considered multiracial.

Kao offers yet a third approach to identifying the multiracial population. Using the National Education Longitudinal Study (NELS) to assess test scores for multiracial and monoracial youth, she identifies multiracial youth through a combination of reports by children and parents (Kao 1999). Specifically, Kao defines as multiracial anyone whose self-identified race differs from that of his or her interviewed parent. Although resourceful, this strategy nevertheless produces an undercount of multiracial youth because it defines as monoracial any youth whose racial identity differs from that of the noninterviewed biological parent. Kao's approach may also produce biased estimates of the characteristics of the multiracial population if the probability of being identified as multiracial is correlated with these characteristics.

Finally, a growing number of studies use self-identification to define racial populations (Corrin and Cook 1999; Hirschman, Alba, and Farley 2000). Although this is the most straightforward approach, data limitations have long prevented its use. In every U.S. census conducted between 1930 and 1990, data were collected under a "pure race" assumption—a practice that prevented recognition of multiracialism (Lee 1993). However, with the recent Office of Management and Budget decision to allow identification with one or more racial groups in federal data, and the likely adoption of this change by state, local, and private statistical systems, self-identification will soon be the predominant method of identifying the multiracial population (OMB 1997; Snipp 1997).

Although self-identification has many advantages over other methods of racial classification, it is far from ideal. First, selective reporting often affects self-reports of race (Davis 1991; Harris and Sim 2000). This was evident in the collection of the 2000 census, as interest groups launched campaigns to encourage multiracial people to identify with single-race groups (Diana Jean Schemo, "Despite Options on Census, Many to Check 'Black' Only," *New York Times,* February 12, 2000, A1, 9).

Second, most surveys include a single, static measure of race for each respondent, so data users are forced to assume that the race individuals select on any particular survey reflects the way they view themselves, and the way they are viewed by others, in all contexts. There are strong reasons to suspect that this assumption does not apply to many in the multiracial population. In work with Jeremiah Sim (Harris and Sim 2000), I provide empirical support for the hypothesis that multiracial people tend to have fluid racial identities (Root 1996). We demonstrate that 10 percent of youth give inconsistent responses to race questions on separate home and school surveys—in part because one survey is self-administered and the other is a face-to-face interview but also in response to the difference in setting between the two surveys. Further evidence of the fluidity of race appears in work that illustrates discrepancies between the race people select for themselves and the race assigned to them by observers (Hahn, Mulinare, and Teutsch 1992; Harris and Sim 2000; Telles and Lim 1998). The implication of this work is that a single observation of self-identified race is insufficient for identifying the multiracial population; moreover, depending on the outcome of interest (for example, employment discrimination), it is an approach that may yield misleading results.

In critiquing existing methods of identifying the multiracial population, I want to stress two particular problems. First, each approach identifies a subset of the population but offers no estimate of what share of the population is missed. Second, no approach accounts for the fluidity of racial identity. These shortcomings are particularly troublesome because work that uses multiple methods of racial classification shows that different approaches yield significantly different estimates of the size of the multi-racial population (Goldstein and Morning 2000; Harris and Sim 2000; Hirschman, Alba, and Farley 2000). Again, my work with Sim finds that between 3.6 and 11.4 percent of youth can be classified as multiracial, depending on which racial classification scheme is employed (Harris and Sim 2000). The point made in that paper is that all of these estimates are valid because race is a social construction, albeit one with very real consequences. As such, a person's race can vary across contexts, need not be consistent with the expressed racial identities of his or her parents, and may depend on who is asked to identify one's race. Each resulting race provides meaningful information and defines an individual's "true" race from a particular perspective, in a particular context, at a particular point in time. This observation implies that there is not a single multiracial population. Instead, there are numerous multiracial populations that overlap to varying degrees.

Although it is clear that the way race is measured has a significant impact on estimates of the size of the multiracial population, it is less clear what effect measurement decisions have on the characteristics of this population. It is possible that the multiracial populations captured by various racial classification schemes are either sufficiently overlapping, or sufficiently similar, that they have nearly identical sociodemographic characteristics. Alternatively, racial classification schemes might yield quite dissimilar multiracial populations, thereby rendering estimates of sociodemographic characteristics based on any particular classification scheme less definitive than expected. Although there are no studies that examine this issue with representative U.S. data, international evidence suggests that the way race is defined can have a significant impact on a group's reported characteristics. Using data from a 1995 Brazilian survey, Edward Telles and Nelson Lim (1998) define racial populations on the basis of self-identification and interviewer observation. Despite substantial consistency in the classification of individuals under each scheme, they nevertheless find that the regional, educational, and income distributions of whites, browns, and blacks vary depending on whether self-identified or interviewer-identified race is used.

In response to evidence of significant measurement effects on the characteristics of racial populations in Brazil, the dearth of knowledge about similar effects among U.S. multiracial populations, and the attention being given to census data on multiracials, this chapter presents a comparison of the sociodemographic characteristics of U.S. multiracial populations and their component monoracial groups. Race is measured by a question that was asked in both school and home interviews. Thus, my work presents a rare, generalizable response to the question, "Does it matter how race is measured?"

Data

Few data sets contain multiple measures of race for a large U.S. sample. One of those is the National Longitudinal Study of Adolescent Health (Add Health). Add Health is a school-based, longitudinal study of health behaviors for youth in the seventh through twelfth grades. Wave 1 data were collected in 1994 and 1995. Initially, 83,135 in-school interviews were conducted with students from eighty high schools and fifty-two middle schools. In-home interviews were then conducted with 18,924 youth from the school sample.[1] Finally, in-home interviews were conducted with a primary caregiver of each of the youth interviewed at home. In more than 70 percent of cases the interviewed primary caregiver was the youth's biological mother.[2]

For my purposes the key features of Add Health are its large sample size, multiple measures of race, and numerous sociodemographic indicators. The presence of multiple indicators of race distinguishes Add Health from most other surveys. The self-administered school survey asks, "What is your race? If you are of more than one race, you may choose more than one." At home, an interviewer reads the following question: "What is your race? You may give more than one answer." The same five response categories—white, black or African American, Asian or Pacific Islander, American Indian or Native American, and other—are offered for both questions. As in the earlier paper (Harris and Sim 2000), I imposed two restrictions on the Add Health data. First, I excluded all youth who identified as Hispanic on either the school or home surveys. Add Health uses separate race and Hispanic-origin questions, so I was able to examine only the characteristics of non-Hispanic multiracial youth. Second, to facilitate comparisons between the two self-reported measures of race, I restricted the sample to youth who were interviewed both in school and at home.[3]

Methods and Measures

In the analyses that follow, several definitions of multiracial are employed. First, I contrast the sociodemographic characteristics of three distinct populations—those who report being multiracial only at school, those who report being multiracial only at home, and those who report being multiracial in both contexts. I refer to the first two groups as inconsistent identifiers or inconsistent multiracials and the third group as consistent identifiers or consistent multiracials. Next, I compare multiracial and single-race groups. Here, no attempt is made to account for the number of times an individual identifies as multiracial.

The first set of analyses assesses whether context and mode of administration yield significantly different populations of inconsistently identified multiracials as well as how these two groups compare with those who consistently identify as multiracial. The second set of comparisons simulates findings from studies that ask only one race question in one context and assesses the extent to which the comparison of multiracial and component single-race populations depends on the place and manner in which the surveys are administered.

Because they are based on only two measures of race, these analyses admittedly provide only a preliminary assessment of the relation between racial classification schemes and sociodemographic characteristics. However, because they are based on what will most likely be two of the more common ways that multiracial youth will be defined in coming years, the information they provide should prove especially useful for future research.

All analyses are conducted for the full sample of multiracial youth and then repeated for each of the three largest groups—white–Native American, white-black, and white-Asian. Although Add Health has a large sample size, some of my analyses are based on a relatively small number of cases. As a result, for some comparisons only large differences between groups are statistically significant.

Throughout, racial populations are compared on a diverse subset of sociodemographic indicators. First, I consider two individual-level demographic measures—mean age and percentage female. Previous work suggests that sex ratios are closer to parity among monoracial than multiracial populations (Corrin and Cook 1999). Age structure may also differ. I expect that adolescents who identify themselves as multiracial will be found to be younger than their peers for two reasons. First, younger adolescents have had fewer years of exposure to a society that encourages identification with only one racial group (Harris and Sim 2000). Second, interracial unions are more common among younger couples (Farley 1999; Harris and Ono 2000), and so the offspring of these unions should represent a larger share of younger cohorts.

Second, I include a measure of family structure. Living with both biological parents has been shown to affect a child's socioeconomic status, social networks, and success in later life (McLanahan and Sandefur 1994). Few studies examine the family structure of multiracial youth, in part because many of them use the race of coresidential biological parents to classify the child's race. Corrin and Cook (1999), who do examine this issue, find that nonwhite multiracial youth are significantly less likely than their white or part-white peers to live with both biological parents.

Third, I examine several indicators of family socioeconomic status. The income-to-needs ratio is defined as annual family income divided by the poverty line.[4] I consider both mean income-to-needs ratios and the percentage of youth in three ranges of the distribution—less than or equal to one, between one and five, and greater than five. Those with an income-to-needs ratio of less than or equal to one are officially poor. Ratios above five have been used to indicate that families are economically "comfortable" (Farley 1996). Family socioeconomic status is also indicated by the educational attainment of coresidential parents. I use years of schooling of the most educated parent and draw distinctions between those with no more than a high school degree, those who have completed some college, and those who have earned a bachelor's degree.

Finally, I compare groups on a series of sociodemographic variables that describe their context. Two broad aspects of context are region and urbanicity. At a more proximate level, I consider measures of neighborhood racial and economic composition, all of which are based on 1990 census tract data. These include median annual family income, percentage non-Hispanic white, percentage non-Hispanic black, percentage Asian, percentage Hispanic, mean dispersion in racial composition, and percentage poor. The dispersion measure ranges from zero to one. It is at its minimum when all tract residents are members of the same racial group and at its maximum when residents are evenly distributed across the five main race groups— white, black, Asian, Native American, and other. No indicator of the percentage of tract residents who are American Indian is included because the Add Health tract-level data do not distinguish between American Indians and "other" race individuals.

Results

Figure 2.1 presents the distributions of monoracial and multiracial youth for each race measure. Results show significant differences between multiracial self-identification at school (6.6 percent) and at home (3.6 percent). As has been noted previously (Harris and Sim 2000), discrepancies between school and home race are probably attributable to differences in context and mode of administration. The home interview was administered by an interviewer and was often observed by family members. The school interview, by contrast, was self-administered. The heightened sense of confidentiality that accompanied the school interview most likely eased the social pressure on youth to identify with only one racial group.

Table 2.1 reports the sociodemographic characteristics of youth who identify with more than one racial group. Descriptive statistics are in the center of the table, and asterisks to the right indicate whether the differences between groups are statistically significant. Although more than twice as many youth identify themselves as multiracial at school only, as opposed to only in the home interview, these two groups are strikingly similar in their characteristics. The only measure that shows a significant difference is family structure. Forty-seven percent of school-only multiracials live with both biological parents, whereas 59 percent of those who identify as multiracial only at home live with their birth parents. The ab-

FIGURE 2.1   *Racial Composition of Youth Sample, by Race*
             Reported at School and at Home

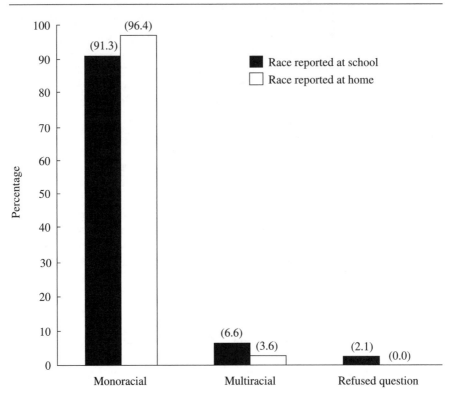

Source: Data from Add Health, Wave 1.
Note: All differences between school and home race are statistically significant (*p* < .05).

sence of further significant differences between these populations suggests that the school and home instruments enumerate multiracial populations that differ significantly in size but have comparable sociodemographic characteristics.

Table 2.1 also compares those who inconsistently identify as multiracial with those who report being multiracial in both interviews. Unlike comparisons between the inconsistently identified groups, these analyses show multiple points of difference. Those who consistently identify as multiracial are significantly more likely than inconsistent identifiers to be female and living apart from at least one of their biological parents. They are also more likely to live in racially diverse neighborhoods in the West that have higher concentrations of Hispanic and nonpoor residents. The geo-

TABLE 2.1   *Descriptive Statistics for Youth Self-Identified As Multiracial in at Least One Context*

Characteristic	Multiracial at School Only	Multiracial Twice	Multiracial at Home Only	At School Only Versus at Home Only	At School Only Versus Twice	At Home Only Versus Twice
Demographics						
Age (mean)	14.91	15.05	15.10			
	(.15)	(.26)	(.21)			
Female	.55	.61	.51			*
Family structure						
Lives with both biological parents	.47	.42	.59	**		***
Family socio-economic status						
Income-to-needs ratio						
≤ 1	.17	.14	.18			
> 1 and ≤ 5	.71	.70	.71			
> 5	.12	.16	.11			
Mean	2.82	3.06	2.82			
	(.15)	(.31)	(.21)			
Parents' highest level of schooling						
High school or less	.38	.33	.34			
Some college	.33	.31	.35			
College degree or higher	.29	.37	.31			
Geographic distribution						
Urban	.24	.29	.20			
Suburban	.60	.57	.60			
Rural	.15	.14	.20			
Region						
West	.19	.33	.16		***	***
Midwest	.31	.27	.33			
South	.34	.28	.35			
Northeast	.15	.11	.16			

TABLE 2.1   *Continued*

Characteristic	Multiracial at School Only	Multiracial Twice	Multiracial at Home Only	At School Only Versus at Home Only	At School Only Versus Twice	At Home Only Versus Twice
Census tract						
Racial composition						
Non-Hispanic white	.74	.74	.76			
Non-Hispanic black	.17	.13	.15			
Asian	.04	.05	.03			
Hispanic	.04	.07	.05	***		
Dispersion in racial composition (mean)	.25 (.02)	.30 (.03)	.27 (.03)	*		
Percentage poor	.14	.13	.15			*
Median annual family income (mean)	33,304.56 (1,033.92)	34,101.90 (1,426.68)	33,183.70 (1,356.51)			
Unweighted *N*— family income variables	469	199	199			
Unweighted *N*— other variables	590	254	243			

Source: Data from Add Health, Wave 1.
Note: For means, standard errors are shown in parentheses.
***$p < .01$, **$p < .05$, *$p < .10$.

graphic and neighborhood differences between these groups are consistent with expectations. In environments that are more encouraging of racial diversity, youth feel encouraged to express a consistent multiracial identity. By contrast, in less progressive and less racially diverse areas outside the West, youth most likely face greater pressure to adopt a single-race identity.

Observed sex-ratio differences between consistently and inconsistently identified multiracials represent an extension of previous findings (Corrin and Cook 1999). They show that although girls are only slightly overrepresented among multiracials in any particular survey, they are significantly more likely than boys to consistently report being multiracial. There are no known biological reasons to suspect that multiracials would be more likely to be girls, so the explanation for this gender imbalance in reporting of multiracial identity must lie in the social lives of adolescent boys and girls. Yet the exact source of this difference is unclear.

It is also not immediately clear why youth who consistently report being multiracial are less likely to live with both biological parents. One would suspect that children who live with biological parents of different races would be the most likely to claim two or more racial ancestries. However, if inconsistent multiracials are more likely to have biological parents who identify with the same single-race group (because, for example, a previous generation included an interracial couple), and marriages between people who identify with different racial groups are both less stable and more likely to produce consistent multiracials, then we would expect the observed results. Alternatively, it may be that adolescents who have less contact with their biological parents, and therefore may have less knowledge about their ancestry, find it easy and desirable to imagine a multiracial identity, especially one that has few immediate consequences (for example, white–American Indian). As these youth would be less likely to live in interracial households, and therefore less likely to be socialized as multiracial—which to many has traditionally meant expressing a monoracial identity (Daniel 1996; Davis 1991)—they would have fewer challenges to their constructed multiracial identity and be more likely to express a consistent multiracial identity. Unfortunately, Add Health data do not allow a test of these hypotheses directly, in part because there is no race data for nonresidential parents. Nevertheless, these hypotheses illustrate both the necessity of treating self-identified race as endogenous and the need for better race data.

The comparisons in table 2.1 capitalize on the multiple reports of self-identified race available in the Add Health data and show significant differences between consistently and inconsistently identified multiracials. Table 2.2 builds on these findings by comparing monoracial and multiracial youth across the two race measures.[5] Responses to the school survey indicate that compared with their monoracial peers, multiracial youth are younger, more likely to be female, less likely to live with both biological parents, and more likely to live in racially diverse and urban areas in the West. The data on home-reported race support similar conclusions about regional and neighborhood differences between monoracial and multiracial youth, though on age, sex, family structure, and urbanicity the gap between monoracial and multiracial youth is somewhat smaller than the data on school-reported race suggest. Observed differences between monoracial and multiracial youth partially reflect patterns of interracial union formation, though as discrepancies between the home-reported and school-reported race measures indicate, differences between these two populations also reflect factors that affect a youth's likelihood of self-identifying as multiracial.

Thus far I have discussed multiracial and monoracial populations and

TABLE 2.2   *Descriptive Statistics for Multiracial and Monoracial Youth, by School-Reported and Home-Reported Race*

Characteristic	School Race		Home Race	
	Monoracial	Multiracial	Monoracial	Multiracial
Demographics				
Age (mean)	15.32***	14.94	15.30	15.07
	(.13)	(.15)	(.13)	(.19)
Female	.50**	.56	.51	.55
Family structure				
Lives with both biological parents	.57***	.46	.57	.51
Family socioeconomic status				
Income-to-needs ratio				
≤ 1	.15	.16	.15	.17
> 1 and ≤ 5	.72	.71	.72	.70
> 5	.13	.13	.13	.13
Mean	3.07	2.88	3.05	2.90
	(.12)	(.15)	(.12)	(.20)
Parents' highest level of schooling				
High school or less	.35	.37	.35	.33
Some college	.31	.32	.31	.33
College degree or higher	.34	.31	.33	.34
Geographic distribution				
Urban	.20	.25	.20	.25
Suburban	.60	.60	.60	.58
Rural	.20**	.15	.20	.17
Region				
West	.12***	.22	.12***	.24
Midwest	.30	.30	.31	.30
South	.43***	.33	.42**	.32
Northeast	.15	.14	.15	.14
Census tract				
Racial composition				
Non-Hispanic white	.79***	.74	.79**	.74
Non-Hispanic black	.14	.16	.14	.15
Asian	.02	.04	.02*	.04
Hispanic	.04***	.05	.04***	.06
Dispersion in racial composition (mean)	.22***	.26	.22***	.29
	(.02)	(.02)	(.02)	(.03)
Percentage poor	.14	.14	.14	.14
Median annual family income (mean)	33,217.58	33,498.51	33,208.60	33,509.66
	(820.24)	(1,013.61)	(812.46)	(1,200.59)

TABLE 2.2   *Continued*

Characteristic	School Race		Home Race	
	Monoracial	Multiracial	Monoracial	Multiracial
Unweighted *N*—family income variables	668	7,939	403	8,372
Unweighted *N*—other variables	844	10,206	504	10,757

Source: Data from Add Health, Wave 1.
Note: For means, standard errors are shown in parentheses.
***$p < .01$, **$p < .05$, *$p < .10$.

made no reference to particular racial groups or combinations of groups, but there are strong reasons to suspect that disaggregating the multiracial population will reveal distinct subgroup patterns. Single-race populations are known to differ from one another on many sociodemographic characteristics (Farley 1996), and the same is probably true of multiracial populations. Although multiracials clearly share some experiences—particularly navigating a society that still has strong biases against identifying with more than one race—they also differ in important ways. Among the four major racial groups, blacks and whites are the furthest apart on most social and economic indicators and have had the longest and most contentious history of interactions (Farley 1996; Massey and Denton 1993). As a result, it is likely that in American society, having a mixed white and black ancestry is very different from having a mixed white and Asian or white and American Indian ancestry. Those with a white–American Indian ancestry are distinct in that many people who claim this identity are believed to be whites who occasionally and symbolically identify as American Indian (Harris and Sim 2000; Snipp 1997). If true, this further suggests that multiracials are a heterogeneous group.

Yet another reason to disaggregate the multiracial population appears in figure 2.2, which shows that there is significant variation in the composition of the school-reported and home-reported multiracial populations. Defining youth by the race they identify with at school yields far more people who identify with three, four, or even five races and fewer who report their race as white–American Indian, white-Asian, or white-black. These response patterns are consistent with the hypothesis that greater confidentiality in the self-administered school interview encourages fewer constraints on self-identified race.

White and Black

Descriptive statistics for inconsistently identified white-black populations are presented in table 2.3. As is true for the aggregate multiracial popula-

FIGURE 2.2   *Racial Composition of Multiracial Youth Sample, by Race Reported at School and at Home*

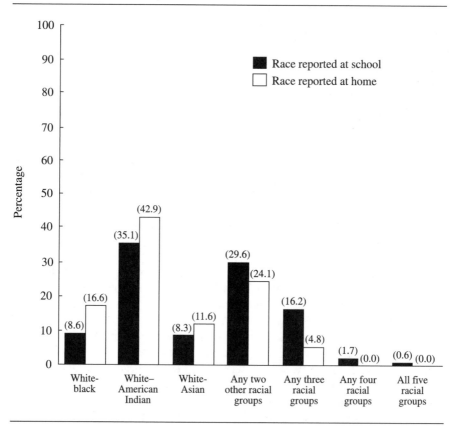

Source: Data from Add Health, Wave 1.
Note: All differences between school and home race are statistically significant ($p < .05$).

tion, there are few differences between these two groups. Those who identify as white-black at home only are somewhat more likely to live in middle-income families and in Hispanic census tracts of the Northeast than are those who select this identity only at school, but no other differences are statistically significant.

Table 2.3 also reports the sociodemographic characteristics of youth who select a white-black identity in both surveys. As was the case for the aggregate multiracial population, the data show numerous differences between consistently and inconsistently identified white-black youth. Those who report being white-black in both contexts are older, more likely to have parents with moderate levels of income and schooling, and more likely to live in racially homogeneous neighborhoods with a high fraction of white residents. The finding that these youth are less likely than inconsistently identified white-black adolescents to live in racially diverse neighborhoods contrasts with results for the full multiracial sample. It suggests that white-black youth who live in predominantly white neighborhoods may be classic examples of Park's "marginal man" (Park 1928). Through constant interaction with whites, some of these youth adopt aspects of "white culture" (Twine 1997), but because of the legacy of the one-drop rule, they are unlikely to be accepted as white. Seeing themselves as culturally different from most blacks, yet not fully white, white-black adolescents in overwhelmingly white neighborhoods may respond by consistently identifying themselves as multiracial. By contrast, white-black youth in neighborhoods with large black populations may find it possible to identify as black, as a statement about both their culture and their race, and so are more apt to inconsistently identify as black and white.

In table 2.4, I compare white-black youth with their white and black peers, beginning with the race reported at school. On the basic demographic characteristics of age and sex, white-black youth are no different from whites or blacks. Similarly, there is only one dimension of socioeconomic status on which white-black youth differed from either whites or blacks. Youth who report being white and black at school live in families with significantly lower income-to-needs ratios than those of the white youth. They are not significantly different from blacks on any of the other measures of family socioeconomic status.

This pattern of similarities between white-black youth and members of their component racial groups stands in stark contrast to comparisons of family structure. White-black youth are less likely than either white or black youth to be living with both biological parents. It is both striking and troubling that only 21 percent of youth who identify as white-black live with both biological parents—striking because it is significantly below the comparable figure for blacks (32 percent), a group known to have a high incidence of single-parent families, and troubling because it suggests that white-black youth face significant obstacles to educational and social achievement (McLanahan and Sandefur 1994).

Although the strong relation between family structure and white-black identity may partially derive from youth who have incomplete information about their ancestry, it is more plausible that social pressure against white-black intermarriage explains why so few of the children of these relationships live with both biological parents. This rare, albeit indirect, evidence about the formation and stability of white-black marital unions is consistent with work showing that white-black couples are significantly more likely than white-white couples to cohabit rather than marry (Harris and Ono

TABLE 2.3   *Descriptive Statistics for Youth Self-Identified As White-Black in at Least One Context*

Characteristic	White-Black at School Only	White-Black Twice	White-Black at Home Only	At School Only Versus at Home Only	At School Only Versus Twice	At Home Only Versus Twice
Demographics						
Age (mean)	14.93	15.62	15.09		*	
	(.42)	(.40)	(.41)			
Female	.59	.58	.44			
Family structure						
Lives with both biological parents	.25	.18	.29			
Family socio-economic status						
Income-to-needs ratio						
≤ 1	.39	.16	.27		*	
> 1 and ≤ 5	.41	.79	.64	*	**	
> 5	.20	.05	.09			
Mean	2.68	2.32	2.49			
	(.90)	(.31)	(.46)			
Parents' highest level of schooling						
High school or less	.45	.20	.40		**	**
Some college	.11	.48	.24		***	**
College degree or higher	.44	.32	.37			
Geographic distribution						
Urban	.42	.30	.40			
Suburban	.57	.53	.55			
Rural	.01	.17	.05			
Region						
West	.14	.17	.15			
Midwest	.45	.32	.35			
South	.30	.37	.24			
Northeast	.11	.14	.26	**		

TABLE 2.3   *Continued*

Characteristic	White-Black at School Only	White-Black Twice	White-Black at Home Only	At School Only Versus at Home Only	At School Only Versus Twice	At Home Only Versus Twice
Census tract						
Racial composition						
Non-Hispanic white	.52	.78	.61		*	**
Non-Hispanic black	.41	.14	.28		*	**
Asian	.04	.03	.04			
Hispanic	.03	.05	.07	**		
Dispersion in racial composition (mean)	.27 (.07)	.29 (.04)	.41 (.06)			*
Percentage poor	.20	.13	.18			
Median annual family income (mean)	33,330.94 (3,998.93)	32,236.13 (1,552.31)	31,416.94 (2,985.27)			
Unweighted *N*— family income variables	28	55	30			
Unweighted *N*— other variables	38	64	38			

Source: Data from Add Health, Wave 1.
Note: For means, standard errors are shown in parentheses.
***p < .01, **p < .05, *p < .10.

2000). The implication of this finding is that although attitudes toward intermarriage have come a long way in the past forty years (Schuman et al. 1997), as a society we still have a long way to go.

With respect to geographic distribution, white-black youth, like their white peers, are somewhat overrepresented in the South and Midwest. This contrasts sharply with regional patterns for blacks, 70 percent of whom live in the South. With respect to urbanicity, white-black youth are more similar to blacks than to whites. Thirty-five percent of white-black youth live in central cities, compared with only 18 percent of whites.

A final basis of comparison in table 2.4 is census-tract characteristics. On this dimension white-black adolescents are solidly between their white and black peers. On average, white-black youth live in tracts that are 68

TABLE 2.4 Descriptive Statistics for White-Black, White, and Black Youth, by School-Reported and Home-Reported Race

Characteristic	School Race			Home Race		
	White	White-Black	Black	White	White-Black	Black
Demographics						
Age (mean)	15.29	15.36	15.50	15.25	15.35	15.46
	(.14)	(.37)	(.22)	(.14)	(.33)	(.23)
Female	.50	.58	.55	.50	.51	.55
Family structure						
Lives with both biological parents	.62***	.21[+]	.32	.62***	.21[+]	.31
Family socioeconomic status						
Income-to-needs ratio						
≤ 1	.11	.24	.35	.11	.19	.36
> 1 and ≤ 5	.75	.65	.59	.75	.74	.59
> 5	.15	.11	.06	.14***	.06	.05
Mean	3.30*	2.45	2.04	3.26***	2.34	2.02
	(.13)	(.45)	(.17)	(.13)	(.30)	(.16)
Parents' highest level of schooling						
High school or less	.33	.29	.47	.33	.26[++]	.47
Some college	.32	.34	.29	.32	.38	.30
College degree or higher	.36	.37	.24	.35	.36[+]	.23

	(1)	(2)	(3)	(4)	(5)	(6)
Geographic distribution						
Urban	.18**	.35	.25	.18**	.36	.26
Surburban	.60	.54	.59	.60	.52	.58
Rural	.22	.11	.16	.22	.12	.16
Region						
West	.10	.16++	.05	.11	.16++	.05
Midwest	.34	.37++	.19	.34	.32	.20
South	.39	.34+++	.70	.38	.34+++	.69
Northeast	.17	.13+	.06	.17	.18++	.06
Census tract						
Racial composition						
Non-Hispanic white	.90***	.68+++	.40	.90****	.70+++	.40
Non-Hispanic black	.06**	.24+++	.55	.06****	.20+++	.55
Asian	.01*	.03+	.01	.01**	.03+++	.01
Hispanic	.03	.04	.03	.03**	.06++	.03
Dispersion in racial composition (mean)	.16***	.28+++	.40	.16****	.34	.40
	(.01)	(.03)	(.03)	(.02)	(.04)	(.03)
Percentage poor	.12*	.15+++	.26	.12**	.15+++	.26
Median annual family income (mean)	34,593.83	32,644.84+++	25,302.22	34,620.04**	31,609.33+++	25,320.08
	(866.34)	(1,863.06)	(1,085.40)	(849.00)	(1,390.52)	(1,094.63)
Unweighted N—family income variables	5,271	83	1,914	5,703	87	2,012
Unweighted N—other variables	6,400	102	2,587	6,923	105	2,727

Source: Data from Add Health, Wave 1.

Note: For means, standard errors are shown in parentheses. For comparisons with blacks, ***p < .01, **p < .05, *p < .10. For comparisons with whites, +++p < .01, ++p < .05, +p < .10.

percent white, 24 percent black, 15 percent poor, and at 28 percent of maximum racial diversity. These tracts are less white, more black, more diverse, and less affluent than whites' tracts but neither as racially diverse nor as poor as blacks' tracts.

When the race question is asked in a face-to-face home interview, as opposed to a self-administered school survey, the responses show few differences from the aforementioned patterns. The most notable differences appear for family socioeconomic status. When youth are classified by their school-reported race, there are no significant racial differences in parents' educational attainment or the income-to-needs ratio. By contrast, those who identify as white-black in the home interview have parents who are significantly better educated than blacks but are significantly less likely than whites to be affluent.

White and American Indian

The white–American Indian population is notable for its extreme fluidity. It is the largest multiracial population among adolescents, but its members are far less likely than white-black or white-Asian youth to express a consistent multiracial identity (Harris and Sim 2000). Despite this fluidity, there are few significant differences between the two groups of inconsistently identifying white–American Indian youth. As indicated in table 2.5, those who identify as white–American Indian at home only are somewhat less affluent and considerably more rural than those who do so only at school. Even more surprising is the pattern of similarities between consistently and inconsistently identifying white–American Indians. Consistent white–American Indians are more likely to be urban and less likely to be suburban than are their inconsistently identifying coethnics, but on all other measures these groups do not significantly differ from one another. The absence of differences between the two groups distinguishes white–American Indian youth from their white-black peers and from the aggregate multiracial population, though the small number of consistently identifying white–American Indian youth may partially explain the paucity of significant differences for this group.

The data presented in table 2.6 allow a comparison of white–American Indian, white, and American Indian youth. Again I begin with school-reported race. Youth who identify as white–American Indian at school are significantly younger than whites and significantly more likely than those who identify as American Indian to be female. Boys and girls represent about equal shares of the white–American Indian population, whereas only 36 percent of those identifying as American Indians are girls. Again, a biological explanation for this discrepancy is difficult to construct, so it is likely that differential socialization is at work. Specifically, the greater like-

TABLE 2.5   *Descriptive Statistics for Youth Self-Identified As*
White–American Indian in at Least One Context

Characteristic	White–American Indian at School Only	White–American Indian Twice	White–American Indian at Home Only	At School Only Versus at Home Only	At School Only Versus Twice	At Home Only Versus Twice
Demographics						
Age (mean)	14.96	14.90	15.06			
	(.19)	(.49)	(.23)			
Female	.50	.56	.49			
Family structure						
Lives with both biological parents	.46	.55	.57			
Family socio-economic status						
Income-to-needs ratio						
≤ 1	.11	.12	.09			
> 1 and ≤ 5	.73	.68	.84	*		
> 5	.15	.20	.07	*		
Mean	3.05	3.51	3.00			
	(.21)	(.75)	(.30)			
Parents' highest level of schooling						
High school or less	.38	.48	.34			
Some college	.36	.31	.47			
College degree or higher	.26	.21	.19			
Geographic distribution						
Urban	.19	.33	.12			*
Suburban	.65	.46	.58		*	
Rural	.15	.22	.30	**		
Region						
West	.17	.23	.18			
Midwest	.35	.35	.39			
South	.37	.34	.33			
Northeast	.10	.08	.10			

(Table continued on p. 86.)

TABLE 2.5   *Continued*

Characteristic	White–American Indian at School Only	White–American Indian Twice	White–American Indian at Home Only	At School Only Versus at Home Only	At School Only Versus Twice	At Home Only Versus Twice
Census tract						
Racial composition						
Non-Hispanic white	.86	.79	.86			
Non-Hispanic black	.07	.14	.08			
Asian	.03	.02	.01			
Hispanic	.04	.04	.04			
Dispersion in racial compo-sition (mean)	.21 (.03)	.23 (.04)	.20 (.03)			
Percentage poor	.12	.14	.14			
Median annual family income (mean)	33,741.08 (1,127.58)	31,345.39 (2,330.20)	33,715.31 (1,582.84)			
Unweighted N— family income variables	140	29	103			
Unweighted N— other variables	171	35	116			

Source: Data from Add Health, Wave 1.
Note: For means, standard errors are shown in parentheses.
***$p < .01$, **$p < .05$, *$p < .10$.

lihood that boys will identify as American Indians may derive from gender-specific stereotypes about American Indians (Deloria 1998). Traditionally, the dominant image of American Indians has been that of the warrior, an image that tends to have greater appeal for boys than for girls. As a result, boys may be more likely to be drawn to an American Indian identity.

On measures of family socioeconomic status, white–American Indians tend to resemble whites. Their families have comparable incomes, and their parents have similar levels of schooling, although whites are somewhat more likely to have at least one parent who has graduated from college. This similarity with whites contrasts sharply with the comparison between white–American Indian and American Indian youth. On nearly all indicators of family socioeconomic status, white–American Indians are more advantaged than American Indians. Their families are less likely to be poor

(12 versus 19 percent), more likely to be affluent (16 versus 4 percent), and more likely to include a college-educated parent (25 versus 11 percent).

Despite the similarities in family socioeconomic status, white and white–American Indian youth differ significantly in family structure. Sixty-two percent of white adolescents live with both of their biological parents, compared with only 48 percent of white–American Indian youth; white–American Indians and American Indians do not significantly differ in family structure. This tendency for white–American Indian youth to live apart from at least one of their biological parents is similar to the pattern observed for white-black adolescents, though in this case the cause is more likely to be identity construction than societal opposition to interracial marriages. Owing to decades of sexual relations between whites and American Indians, there are now few "full-blooded" American Indians (Snipp 1989). The accompanying convergence in physical and cultural attributes between these two populations reduces the opportunity and motivation for opposition to white–American Indian marriages in most of the United States. Moreover, the merging of these two groups has fueled suspicion among many whites that they may have American Indian ancestors, and in recent years increasing numbers of whites have begun to acknowledge these distant, and in some cases fictive, American Indian ancestors. This combination of factors suggests that the reason white–American Indian youth appear unlikely to live with both biological parents is that youth who do not live with both biological parents have less information about their ancestry, and so find it easier to "discover" long-lost American Indian forebears.

Turning to geographic indicators, it is clear from table 2.6 that white–American Indian multiracials are concentrated in suburban areas of the Midwest and the South. They are somewhat less likely than whites to live in rural areas and in the Northeast but more likely to live in the West. There are no significant differences in the geographic distribution of white–American Indian and American Indian youth.

The final set of indicators, those that describe the census tracts where youth live, again show substantial differences between whites and white–American Indian multiracials. Compared with whites, white–American Indian adolescents live in tracts that are less white, more Asian, more Hispanic, and more racially diverse. Despite differences in the racial composition of their tracts, white and white–American Indian youth tend to live in neighborhoods with quite similar economic characteristics. Fewer differences are observed between the neighborhoods of white–American Indians and American Indians. The only two census-tract indicators that show significant differences are percentage white and percentage poor, with American Indians living in tracts with slightly fewer white or nonpoor residents.

When race is classified according to responses to the home interview, the pattern of differences between white–American Indian youth and their

TABLE 2.6 Descriptive Statistics for White–American Indian, White, and American Indian Youth, by School-Reported and Home-Reported Race

	School Race			Home Race		
Characteristic	White	White–American Indian	American Indian	White	White–American Indian	American Indian
Demographics						
Age (mean)	15.29**	14.95	14.75	15.25	15.02	15.03
	(.14)	(.21)	(.22)	(.14)	(.23)	(.33)
Female	.50	.51+++	.36	.50	.51	.49
Family structure						
Lives with both biological parents	.62***	.48	.52	.62	.56++	.41
Family socioeconomic status						
Income-to-needs ratio						
≤ 1	.11	.12+	.28	.11	.10	.32
> 1 and ≤ 5	.75	.73	.68	.75	.80	.67
> 5	.15	.16+++	.04	.14	.10+++	.01
Mean	3.30	3.12+++	2.13	3.26	3.12+++	1.75
	(.13)	(.21)	(.31)	(.13)	(.29)	(.39)
Parents' highest level of schooling						
High school or less	.33	.40	.37	.33	.37	.33
Some college	.32	.35++	.52	.32**	.43	.50
College degree or higher	.36***	.25+++	.11	.35***	.20	.17

Geographic distribution					
Urban	.18	.22	.13	.18	.06
Suburban	.60	.62	.53	.60	.45
Rural	.22*	.16	.34	.22	.49
Region					
West	.10**	.18	.29	.11*	.56
Midwest	.34	.35	.28	.34	.20
South	.39	.37	.36	.38	.17
Northeast	.17***	.10	.07	.17***	.07
Census tract					
Racial composition					
Non-Hispanic white	.90***	.84++	.72	.90*	.64
Non-Hispanic black	.06	.08	.14	.06	.09+
Asian	.01**	.02	.01	.01	.01
Hispanic	.03**	.04	.06	.03	.04++
Dispersion in racial composition	.16***	.22	.34	.16*	.21+
(mean)	(.01)	(.03)	(.09)	(.02)	(.03)
Percentage poor	.12	.13++	.19	.12*	.14++
Median annual family income	34,593.83	33,347.84	28,728.60	34,620.04	33,121.22++
(mean)	(866.34)	(1,108.56)	(2,822.32)	(849.00)	(1,407.44)
Unweighted N—family income variables	5,271	169	101	5,703	132
Unweighted N—other variables	6,400	206	132	6,923	151

Source: Data from Add Health, Wave 1.

Note: For means, standard errors are shown in parentheses. For comparisons with American Indians, ***p < .01, **p < .05, *p < .10. For comparisons with whites, ⁺⁺⁺*p* < .01, ⁺⁺*p* < .05, ⁺*p* < .10.

component single-race groups is quite different from that observed using school-reported race. This is owing to shifts in the white–American Indian and American Indian populations, both of which vary greatly between the two surveys. More than 75 percent of youth who identify as white–American Indian or American Indian at school switch their self-identified race between school and home interviews. This contrasts sharply with whites, blacks, and Asians, among whom there is at least 88 percent agreement between school- and home-reported race, and even with white-black and white-Asian youth, whose agreement between the two race questions is 63 percent and 35 percent, respectively (Harris and Sim 2000).

Given the smaller number of white–American Indian youth in the data on home-reported race, and the less private setting of the home interview, one might expect that adolescents with weaker connections to their American Indian ancestry will be more likely to identify as white, rather than white–American Indian, and that home-reported race will show larger differences between white–American Indians and whites than does school-reported race. However, on most indicators differences between whites and white–American Indians are either comparable with or smaller than those observed in the school-reported race analysis. Exceptions to this trend are parents' education and percentage poor: compared with white–American Indians, whites are more likely to have nonpoor neighbors and at least one parent with a college degree when home-reported race is used.

This pattern of fewer differences between white–American Indians and whites appearing for home-reported race applies unevenly to comparisons between white–American Indians and American Indians. Gaps between the latter two groups are generally smaller for percentage female and parents' educational attainment, but compared with school-reported race results, white–American Indians and American Indians are further apart in family structure, geographic distribution, and the racial and economic composition of their neighborhoods when race is determined by responses to the home interview.

White and Asian

Relatively few differences have been observed between inconsistently identifying white-black and white–American Indian youth. One might therefore conclude that although context of racial self-identification and the mode of administration affect the size of multiracial populations, the race questions asked at home and at school essentially identify similar populations of inconsistent multiracials. However, as table 2.7 illustrates, results for white-Asian youth show that such a conclusion would be mistaken. Compared with those who identify as white-Asian only at school, those who identify as white-Asian only at home are more likely to have moderate-income

TABLE 2.7   *Descriptive Statistics for Youth Self-Identified As White-Asian in at Least One Context*

Characteristic	White-Asian at School Only	White-Asian Twice	White-Asian at Home Only	At School Only Versus at Home Only	At School Only Versus Twice	At Home Only Versus Twice
Demographics						
Age (mean)	14.71	15.01	14.87			
	(.32)	(.47)	(.45)			
Female	.36	.70	.50		***	
Family structure						
Lives with both biological parents	.57	.63	.73			
Family socio-economic status						
Income-to-needs ratio						
≤ 1	.28	.00	.11		**	
> 1 and ≤ 5	.42	.78	.71	*	**	
> 5	.30	.22	.18			
Mean	3.53	3.80	3.64			
	(.73)	(.73)	(.76)			
Parents' highest level of schooling						
High school or less	.23	.22	.36			
Some college	.33	.08	.23		*	
College degree or higher	.45	.69	.41		*	*
Geographic distribution						
Urban	.31	.31	.30			
Suburban	.46	.64	.63			
Rural	.22	.05	.07			
Region						
West	.23	.63	.38		***	
Midwest	.07	.10	.08			
South	.53	.20	.10	***	***	
Northeast	.17	.07	.45	*		***

TABLE 2.7   *Continued*

Characteristic	White-Asian at School Only	White-Asian Twice	White-Asian at Home Only	At School Only Versus at Home Only	At School Only Versus Twice	At Home Only Versus Twice
Census tract						
Racial composition						
Non-Hispanic white	.82	.70	.68			
Non-Hispanic black	.08	.06	.06			
Asian	.04	.15	.18	**	*	
Hispanic	.05	.10	.09		**	
Dispersion in racial composition (mean)	.24 (.07)	.39 (.06)	.36 (.07)		**	
Percentage poor	.13	.09	.07	**	*	
Median annual family income (mean)	33,026.16 (2,454.27)	40,399.94 (3,988.60)	41,214.14 (2,479.52)	**	*	
Unweighted N— family income variables	37	30	28			
Unweighted N— other variables	46	42	39			

Source: Data from Add Health, Wave 1.
Note: For means, standard errors are shown in parentheses.
***$p < .01$, **$p < .05$, *$p < .10$.

families, to live in the Northeast (and less likely to live in the South), and to have Asian or affluent neighbors.

Large differences by racial classification scheme also appear when inconsistent and consistent white-Asian multiracials are compared, yet in a marked departure from observed patterns for other multiracial groups, the data in table 2.7 suggest that comparisons between consistent and inconsistent white-Asians largely depend on which inconsistent population is used. Youth who identify as white-Asian on both surveys are much more likely to be female, less likely to be poor, and more likely to have at least one parent with a college degree, to live in the West, to have Asian and Hispanic neighbors, and to live in an affluent neighborhood than are those who identify as white-Asian only at school. However, there are only two significant differences between consistent white-Asian youth and youth who report being white-Asian at home only: the former group is more likely to have a college-educated parent and less likely to live in the Northeast.

The data presented in table 2.8, which allows comparisons of white-Asians and their component racial groups, suggest several important distinctions among groups by school-reported race. Perhaps because younger adolescents are more likely to identify as multiracial (Harris and Sim 2000), and because intermarriage is more common among younger couples (Farley 1999), mean age for white-Asian youth is .78 years lower than for Asian youth. No significant differences are observed in sex ratios or family structure.

With respect to mean family socioeconomic status, white-Asians appear to be little different from Asians, but they are slightly more advantaged than whites. White-Asian youth are 50 percent more likely than whites to have a parent who has graduated from college. White-Asians and whites also differ in family income—75 percent of white youth, but only 54 percent of white-Asian youth, live in families that have moderate incomes—but the interpretation of the difference is not so straightforward. Rather than indicating a clear economic advantage or disadvantage with whites, the income-to-needs ratio for white-Asians simply has greater variance. Economic heterogeneity among white-Asians is consistent with evidence showing that Asians are a diverse group (Espiritu 1992), a finding that suggests that at least with respect to income, the characteristics of white-Asian multiracials might depend on which Asian ethnic group is involved (Xie and Goyette 1998).

The next set of indicators, those that summarize geographic distribution, display further differences between white-Asians and their component racial groups. Asians are a highly urbanized and western population. White-Asian multiracials are also predominantly an urban and suburban population, but like whites they are more likely than Asians to live in rural areas or in the South. Despite these similarities, the regional distribution of white-Asians also differs from that of whites, with whites being more concentrated in the Midwest and white-Asians in the West.

Finally, table 2.8 displays a familiar pattern for the racial composition of white-Asians' neighborhoods. Adolescents who identify as white and Asian on the school survey live in neighborhoods that are more white than those of Asians but less white than the neighborhoods of white youth. School-reported race data also reveal that white-Asian youth live in tracts that are more Hispanic and more racially diverse than those of whites, though they are less Asian, less Hispanic, and less diverse than Asians' neighborhoods. Poverty rates are nearly identical in the census tracts of the three groups, and the median annual income of their neighbors does not significantly differ.

As the dissimilar patterns for both inconsistently identifying white-

TABLE 2.8 Descriptive Statistics for White-Asian, White, and Asian Youth, by School and Home Race

	School Race			Home Race		
Characteristic	White	White-Asian	Asian	White	White-Asian	Asian
Demographics						
Age (mean)	15.29	14.83++	15.61	15.25	14.94+	15.53
	(.14)	(.29)	(.28)	(.14)	(.34)	(.28)
Female	.50	.49	.47	.50	.59	.47
Family structure						
Lives with both biological parents	.62	.59	.72	.62	.68	.74
Family socioeconomic status						
Income-to-needs ratio						
≤ 1	.11	.19	.15	.11	.06	.16
> 1 and ≤ 5	.75**	.54	.70	.75	.74	.69
>5	.15	.27	.14	.14	.20	.15
Mean	3.30	3.62	3.32	3.26	3.71	3.31
	(.13)	(.51)	(.40)	(.13)	(.53)	(.42)
Parents' highest level of schooling						
High school or less	.33	.23	.30	.33	.30	.34
Some college	.32	.23	.20	.32***	.16	.20
College degree or higher	.36*	.54	.50	.35**	.54	.46

	(1)	(2)	(3)	(4)	(5)	(6)
Geographic distribution						
Urban	.18	.31	.18	.30	.30	.29
Suburban	.60	.53	.60	.69	.63	.69
Rural	.22	.16^{++}	.22**	.02	.06	.02
Region						
West	.10***	.38	.11***	.53	.50	.53
Midwest	.34***	.08	.34***	.15	.09	.15
South	.39	.40^{++}	.38***	.12	.14	.13
Northeast	.17	.13	.17	.20	.27	.19
Census tract						
Racial composition						
Non-Hispanic white	.90**	.77^{+++}	.90***	.55	.69^{+++}	.54
Non-Hispanic black	.06	.07	.06	.09	.06^{+}	.09
Asian	.01	.08^{+++}	.01*	.21	.16	.22
Hispanic	.03***	.07^{+++}	.03***	.16	.10^{++}	.15
Dispersion in racial composition (mean)	.16**	.30^{+++}	.16***	.53	.38^{+++}	.54
	(.01)	(.06)	(.02)	(.05)	(.05)	(.05)
Percentage poor	.12	.11	.12***	.11	.08^{++}	.12
Median annual family income (mean)	34,593.83	35,857.40	34,620.04***	40,560.64	40,834.36	40,125.25
	(866.34)	(2,800.97)	(849.00)	(1,750.27)	(2,428.48)	(1,889.24)
Unweighted N—family income variables	5,271	67	5,703	523	58	527
Unweighted N—other variables	6,400	88	6,923	922	81	930

Source: Data from Add Health, Wave 1.

Note: For means, standard errors are shown in parentheses. For comparisons with Asians, ***$p < .01$, **$p < .05$, *$p < .10$. For comparisons with whites, $^{+++}p < .01$, $^{++}p < .05$, $^{+}p < .10$.

Asian groups suggest, comparisons between whites, white-Asians, and Asians substantially depend on which measure of self-identified race is used. Compared with the findings based on school-reported race, the data based on home-reported race reveal that white-Asians have no geographic distribution differences in comparison with Asians and no significant family income differences in comparison with whites, but significant differences from whites with respect to tract family income, parents' educational attainment, urbanicity, Southern residence, tract percent Asian, and tract poverty rate; and significant differences with Asians in census-tract percentage black and percentage poor. Clearly, what researchers conclude about the sociodemographic characteristics of white-Asian adolescents and how they compare with those of whites and Asians depends on where and how self-identified race is reported.

Conclusions

Youth who identify as multiracial only at home appear to differ little from those who identify as multiracial only at school. White-Asians present the greatest deviation from this pattern, though even for this group there are no significant differences between the two inconsistently identifying populations on basic demographic or family structure indicators and only one significant difference in family socioeconomic status. Quite a different story emerges when consistent and inconsistent multiracials are compared. These groups tend to exhibit quite dissimilar characteristics on many sociodemographic indicators. As a result, racial classification schemes that rely on self-identification but impose more or less stringent conditions for inclusion in multiracial populations (for example, having ever reported being multiracial versus having always reported being multiracial) are likely to support different conclusions about the characteristics of multiracial populations. It is important to note that though this statement applies to a varying degree to each of the multiracial groups examined in this chapter, it is least applicable to white–American Indian multiracials. Only two significant differences are observed between consistent and inconsistent white–American Indian youth, and each is an indicator of urbanicity.

In comparisons between multiracial youth and peers from component single-race groups, I find numerous significant differences. No multiracial population is a replicate of one of its component monoracial groups, despite hypotheses about possible overlaps between whites and white–American Indian multiracials. These comparisons also illustrate the need for care in selecting a racial classification scheme. For each multiracial population, and across many of the sociodemographic indicators, the magnitude and reliability of differences between monoracial and multiracial populations depends on whether school- or home-reported race is used. One reason for this apparent contradiction with earlier findings is that despite the tendency for inconsistently identifying multiracial populations to be similar to one another—and despite the obvious fact that school-reported and home-reported multiracial populations are made up of similar groups of inconsistent identifiers and the same group of consistent identifiers—the share of the multiracial population that consistently identifies as multiracial differs from one context to the other. So, for example, though inconsistent multiracials differ only in family structure (table 2.1), comparisons between monoracials and multiracials significantly differ along the dimensions of percentage female, age, and family structure (table 2.2), because inconsistent identifiers constitute 70 percent of multiracial youth as self-identified at school but only 49 percent of home-reported multiracials. Similar patterns hold for white–American Indian and white-Asian multiracials, but for white-black youth the share of inconsistent identifiers is identical across contexts.

My work reveals that, at least for multiracial populations, how we measure really does matter. By varying the context of self-identified measures of race, it is possible to identify multiracial populations that not only differ from one another but that also compare differentially with their constituent monoracial populations. When combined with previous work (Harris and Sim 2000), this finding suggests that analysts should exercise caution when analyzing Census 2000 race data. New census data provide unique information about people who are identified by household informants as belonging to more than one racial group, but this is just one of several multiracial populations that could have been enumerated; had Census 2000 utilized an alternative racial classification scheme, the data probably would have supported a different set of conclusions about multiracials. Of course, this would be fine if the census captured the most relevant multiracial population. However, which multiracial population is most relevant depends on one's research question. Thus, for example, a researcher who wants to know about employment discrimination would much rather know an individual's race as defined by his or her employer than as identified by household members. What is clear is that the census—and, indeed, all other surveys that use a single measure of race—should be viewed as an opportunity to learn about *a* multiracial population rather than a source for examining *the* multiracial population.

In preparing this chapter, I benefited greatly from discussions with Yu Xie. Jeremiah Sim provided excellent research assistance.

Notes

1. My analyses use weighted data and the survey commands in the statistics software Stata to correct for oversamples in the home sample, clustering in the school sample, and survey nonresponse (Chantala and Tabor 1999).

2. For more information about the design of the Add Health survey, see Bearman, Jones, and Udry 1997.

3. See Harris and Sim 2000 for a further explanation of the rationale and implications of these restrictions. Restricting the sample to youth who were interviewed twice does not significantly affect relative numbers of white-black, white–American Indian, or white-Asian multiracial youth.

4. Smaller samples are used for comparisons involving income-to-needs ratios because there is more missing data for annual income than for other sociodemographic measures.

5. The number of youth identifying as multiracial at home (table 2.2) is not simply the sum of the consistently identifying and home-only multiracial populations (table 2.1), because youth who did not answer the race question at school are dropped from table 2.1 but are included in the counts of race as reported at home in table 2.2. The idea in table 2.1 is to compare race responses given at home and at school, but in table 2.2 it is to simulate findings from studies that have only one race measure. Subsequent tables for white-black, white–American Indian, and white-Asian youth employ similar procedures.

References

Bearman, Peter S., Jo Jones, and J. Richard Udry. 1997. *The National Longitudinal Study of Adolescent Health: Research Design.* Carolina Population Center, University of North Carolina, Chapel Hill. Accessed May 7, 2002 at: *www.cpc.unc. edu/projects/addhealth/design.html.*

Cauce, Ana Mari, Yumi Hiraga, Craig Mason, Tanya Aguilar, Nydia Ordonez, and Nancy Gonzales. 1992. "Between a Rock and a Hard Place: Social Adjustment of Biracial Youth." In *Racially Mixed People in America,* edited by Maria P. P. Root. Newbury Park, Calif.: Sage Publications.

Chantala, Kim, and Joyce Tabor. 1999. *Strategies to Perform a Design-Based Analysis Using the Add Health Data.* Carolina Population Center, University of North Carolina, Chapel Hill. Accessed May 7, 2002 at: *www.cpc.unc.edu/ projects/addhealth/strategies.html.*

Corrin, William J., and Thomas D. Cook. 1999. "Spanning Racial Boundaries: Multiracial Adolescents and Their Families, Peers, Schools, and Neighborhoods." Working Paper 99-20. Evanston, Ill.: Institute for Policy Research, Northwestern University.

Daniel, G. Reginald. 1996. "Black and White Identity in the New Millennium: Unsevering the Ties That Bind." In *The Multiracial Experience: Racial Borders As the New Frontier*, edited by Maria P. P. Root. Thousand Oaks, Calif.: Sage Publications.

Davis, F. James. 1991. *Who Is Black? One Nation's Definition.* University Park: Pennsylvania State University Press.

Deloria, Philip J. 1998. *Playing Indian.* New Haven, Conn.: Yale University Press.

Du Bois, W. E. B. 1996 [1899]. *The Philadelphia Negro*. Philadelphia: University of Pennsylvania Press.

Eschbach, Karl. 1995. "The Enduring and Vanishing American Indian: American Indian Population Growth and Intermarriage in 1990." *Ethnic and Racial Studies* 18(1): 89–108.

Espiritu, Yen Le. 1992. *Asian American Panethnicity: Bridging Institutions and Identities*. Philadelphia: Temple University Press.

Farley, Reynolds. 1996. *The New American Reality*. New York: Russell Sage Foundation.

———. 1999. "Racial Issues: Recent Trends in Residential Patterns and Intermarriage." In *Diversity and Its Discontents: Cultural Conflict and Common Ground in Contemporary American Society*, edited by Neil J. Smelser and Jeffrey C. Alexander. Princeton, N.J.: Princeton University Press.

Field, Lynda D. 1996. "Piecing Together the Puzzle: Self-concept and Group Identity in Biracial Black-White Youth." In *The Multiracial Experience: Racial Borders As the New Frontier*, edited by Maria P. P. Root. Thousand Oaks, Calif.: Sage Publications.

Funderburg, Lise. 1994. *Black, White, Other: Biracial Americans Talk About Race and Identity*. New York: William Morrow.

Gibbs, Jewelle Taylor, and Alice M. Hines. 1992. "Negotiating Ethnic Identity: Issues for Black-White Biracial Adolescents." In *Racially Mixed People in America,* edited by Maria P. P. Root. Newbury Park, Calif.: Sage Publications.

Goldstein, Joshua R., and Ann J. Morning. 2000. "The Multiple Race Population of the United States: Issues and Estimates." *Proceedings of the National Academy of Sciences* 97(11): 6230–35.

Gordon, Milton M. 1964. *Assimilation in American Life*. New York: Oxford University Press.

Hahn, Robert A., Joseph Mulinare, and Steven M. Teutsch. 1992. "Inconsistencies in Coding of Race and Ethnicity Between Birth and Death in U.S. Infants: A New Look at Infant Mortality, 1983 through 1985." *Journal of the American Medical Association* 267(2): 259–63.

Harris, David R., and Hiromi Ono. 2000. "Estimating the Extent of Intimate Contact Between the Races: The Role of Metropolitan Area Factors and Union Type in Mate Selection." Paper presented at the annual meeting of the Population Association of America, Los Angeles (March).

Harris, David R., and Jeremiah Joseph Sim. 2000. "An Empirical Look at the Social Construction of Race: The Case of Multiracial Adolescents." Research Report 00–452. Population Studies Center, University of Michigan.

Harrison, Roderick J., and Claudette Bennett. 1995. "Racial and Ethnic Diversity." In *State of the Union,* vol. 2, edited by Reynolds Farley. New York: Russell Sage Foundation.

Hirschman, Charles, Richard Alba, and Reynolds Farley. 2000. "The Meaning and Measurement of Race in the U.S. Census: Glimpses into the Future." *Demography* 37(3): 381–93.

Jacobs, James H. 1992. "Identity Development in Biracial Children." In *Racially Mixed People in America,* edited by Maria P. P. Root. Newbury Park, Calif.: Sage Publications.

Kalmijn, Matthijs. 1993. "Trends in Black-White Intermarriage." *Social Forces* 72(1): 119–46.

Kao, Grace. 1999. "Racial Identity and Academic Performance: An Examination of Biracial Asian and African Youth." *Journal of Asian American Studies* 2(3): 223–49.

Lee, Sharon M. 1993. "Racial Classification in the U.S. Census: 1890–1990." *Ethnic and Racial Studies* 16(1): 75–94.

Lieberson, Stanley, and Mary C. Waters. 1993. "The Ethnic Responses of Whites: What Causes Their Instability, Simplification, and Inconsistency?" *Social Forces* 72(2): 421–50.

Mass, Amy Iwasaki. 1992. "Interracial Japanese Americans: The Best of Both Worlds or the End of the Japanese American Community?" In *Racially Mixed People in America,* edited by Maria P. P. Root. Newbury Park, Calif.: Sage Publications.

Massey, Douglas S., and Nancy A. Denton. 1993. *American Apartheid: Segregation and the Making of the Underclass.* Cambridge, Mass.: Harvard University Press.

McLanahan, Sara, and Gary Sandefur. 1994. *Growing Up with a Single Parent.* Cambridge, Mass.: Harvard University Press.

Myrdal, Gunnar. 1996 [1944]. *An American Dilemma.* New Brunswick, N.J.: Transaction Press.

Office of Management and Budget (OMB), Executive Office of the President. 1997. *Revision to the Standards for the Classification of Federal Data on Race and Ethnicity.* Washington.

Park, Robert Ezra. 1928. "Human Migration and the Marginal Man." *American Journal of Sociology* 33(8): 881–92.

———. 1931. "Mentality of Racial Hybrids." *American Journal of Sociology* 36(4): 534–51.

Qian, Zhenchao. 1997. "Breaking the Racial Barriers: Variations in Interracial Marriage Between 1980 and 1990." *Demography* 34(2): 263–76.

———. 1999. "Who Intermarries? Education, Nativity, Region, and Interracial Marriage, 1980 and 1990." *Journal of Comparative Family Studies* 30(4): 579–97.

Reed, T. Edward. 1969. "Caucasian Genes in American Negroes." *Science* 165(3895): 762–68.

Root, Maria P. P. 1992. "Back to the Drawing Board: Methodological Issues in Research on Multiracial People." In *Racially Mixed People in America,* edited by Maria P. P. Root. Newbury Park, Calif.: Sage Publications.

———. 1996. "The Multiracial Experience: Racial Borders As a Significant Frontier in Race Relations." In *The Multiracial Experience: Racial Borders As the New Frontier*, edited by Maria P. P. Root. Thousand Oaks, Calif.: Sage Publications.

Schuman, Howard, Charlotte Steeh, Lawrence Bobo, and Maria Krysan. 1997. *Racial Attitudes in America: Trends and Interpretations.* Cambridge, Mass.: Harvard University Press.

Snipp, C. Matthew. 1989. *American Indians: The First of This Land.* New York: Russell Sage Foundation.

———. 1997. "Some Observations About Racial Boundaries and the Experiences of American Indians." *Ethnic and Racial Studies* 20(4): 667–89.

Stonequist, Everett V. 1935. "The Problem of the Marginal Man." *American Journal of Sociology* 41(1): 1–12.

———. 1937. *The Marginal Man: A Study in Personality and Culture Conflict.* New York: Russell and Russell.

Tafoya, Sonya M. 2000. "Check One or More: Mixed Race and Ethnicity in California." *California Counts* 1(2): 1–11.

Telles, Edward E., and Nelson Lim. 1998. "Does It Matter Who Answers the Race Question? Racial Classification and Income Inequality in Brazil." *Demography* 35(4): 465–74.

Twine, France Winddance. 1997. "Brown-Skinned White Girls: Class, Culture, and the Construction of White Identity in Suburban Communities." In *Displacing Whiteness: Essays in Social and Cultural Criticism,* edited by Ruth Frankenberg. Durham, N.C.: Duke University Press.

Waters, Mary C. 1990. *Ethnic Options: Choosing Identities in America.* Berkeley, Calif.: University of California Press.

Williams, Teresa Kay. 1996. "Race As Process: Reassessing the 'What Are You?' Encounters of Biracial Individuals." In *The Multiracial Experience: Racial Borders As the New Frontier*, edited by Maria P. P. Root. Thousand Oaks, Calif.: Sage Publications.

Wilson, William Julius. 1979. *The Declining Significance of Race.* Chicago: University of Chicago Press.

Xie, Yu, and Kim Goyette. 1998. "The Racial Identification of Biracial Children with One Asian Parent: Evidence from the 1990 Census." *Social Forces* 76(2): 547–70.

3

MIXED RACE AND ETHNICITY IN CALIFORNIA

Sonya M. Tafoya

OVER the past thirty years, California has undergone a phenomenal demographic transformation.[1] As recently as 1970, nearly 80 percent of the state's population was classified as white, non-Hispanic (Reyes 2001). By 1999, only 50 percent of the population was estimated to be white, non-Hispanic, whereas 31.6 percent was classified as Hispanic, 12.2 percent as Asian or Pacific Islander, 7.5 percent as black or African American, and fewer than 1 percent as American Indian, Eskimo, or Aleut (U.S. Census Bureau 1999a). California's racial and ethnic diversity derives largely from immigration, yet even without further immigration the growing occurrence of mixed racial and ethnic births will give rise to even greater diversity. California has been on the leading edge of national trends in immigration and intermarriage. Indeed, the California Supreme Court ruling ending legal barriers to intermarriage in California took effect in 1948—nearly two decades before the United States Supreme Court took action, in 1967, to remove all remaining miscegenation laws in the nation (Bancroft Whitney Company 1949). As of 1997, about 25 percent of the state's population was foreign born, compared with 10 percent in the nation as a whole (Schmidley and Alvarado 1998).

Historically, the federal and statewide statistics used to document California's growing diversity have divided the population into discrete monoracial groups. However, new guidelines issued by the Office of Management and Budget (OMB) now allow respondents to check one or more racial categories.[2] Census 2000 marked the first major employment of these new racial and ethnic standards. As a precursor to data that will be available as these standards are more widely employed and reported, this chapter documents the rise in multiracial-multiethnic births in California from 1982 to 1999, addressing the following questions: What is the overall trend in multiracial-multiethnic births in California? What is the relationship between immigration and multiracial-multiethnic births in California? What is the racial-ethnic profile of California's multiracial-multiethnic newborns? How do racial and ethnic group size, maternal age, and maternal education affect the occurrence of multiracial-multiethnic births in California?

Data Source

Data for this chapter are derived from California Vital Statistics Birth Records. The birth records include information for nativity, race, and Hispanic origin of both the mother and the father.[3] The records office employs a two-question format for collecting racial and ethnic information. Although the racial and ethnic data in the birth records distinguish several Asian racial subgroups and several Hispanic ethnic subgroups, in this chapter the data are aggregated into the current OMB one-question format. The racial options are American Indian or Alaska native, Asian, black or African American, Hispanic or Latino (of any race), Native Hawaiian or other Pacific Islander, and white, non-Hispanic.

A multiracial-multiethnic child is defined as one whose father is from one of these six racial or ethnic groups and whose mother is from another. Because data on maternal and paternal race-ethnicity are coded in discrete monoracial and monoethnic categories, it is impossible to determine whether either parent is multiracial or multiethnic; thus, the number of multiracial-multiethnic births reported here may be biased downward. Conversely, because the race or ethnicity of the child in this study is derived data rather than self-identified data, it may overestimate the number of multiracial-multiethnic births. In other words, some infants classified in this chapter as multiracial or multiethnic might be identified by their parents as monoracial or monoethnic (Waters 1990).

Trends and Patterns

Although the state has a racially and ethnically diverse population, and although it abandoned legal barriers to intermarriage relatively early compared with many other states, California has experienced only a moderate increase in multiracial-multiethnic births over the past nineteen years. As a percentage of total births in the state, multiracial-multiethnic births rose from less than 12 percent in 1982 to 15 percent in 1999 (figure 3.1). This change represents a numerical increase in multiracial-multiethnic births from about fifty thousand in 1982 to about seventy thousand in 1999.

The absence of a precipitous increase in the occurrence of multiracial-multiethnic births can be explained by California's status as a large immigrant-receiving state. Numerous studies have shown that compared with the native born, immigrants are less likely to marry a member of a different

FIGURE 3.1   Multiracial-Multiethnic Births As Share of All Births, California, 1982 to 1999

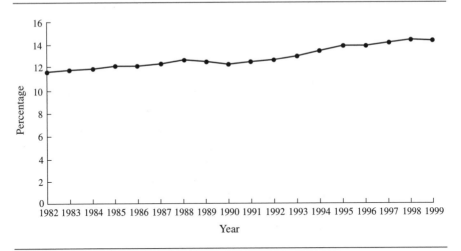

Source: Author's calculations from California Vital Statistics Birth Records.

racial or ethnic group. The literature cites various explanations for this tendency: the foreign born may be already married at the time of immigration, they may be more likely to live in ethnic enclaves, they may be more closely tied to cultures that resist out-marriage, or they may encounter language barriers that discourage out-marriage (Sung 1990; Lee and Fernandez 1998; Gurak 1987). In fact, data on legal immigrants in California for 1996 indicate that 68 percent of new female immigrants and 58 percent of male immigrants were already married when they arrived in California (State of California 1999).

Figure 3.2 charts the trends in multiracial-multiethnic births to California mothers by immigrant status. As the figure illustrates, the rise in multiracial-multiethnic births is a native-born phenomenon. Multiracial-multiethnic births to native-born mothers rose dramatically from 1982 to 1999— from less than 14 percent to more than 21 percent, a 50 percent increase. In contrast, fewer than 8 percent of births to foreign-born mothers were multiracial-multiethnic in 1982; this figure declined slightly in the early 1990s and has remained relatively stable at 7 percent since 1995.

As can be seen in figure 3.3, the share of births to immigrant women has increased by nearly 50 percent since 1982. The sharpest increase in births to foreign-born women began in 1988. The timing of this increase is consistent with the post-IRCA (Immigration Reform and Control Act) immigration of family members of recently amnestied residents (Cornelius

FIGURE 3.2   *Multiracial-Multiethnic Births As Share of All Births, by Mothers' Nativity, California, 1982 to 1999*

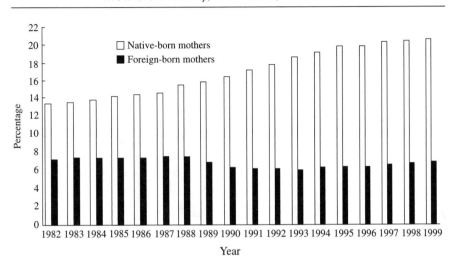

Source: Author's calculations from California Vital Statistics Birth Records.

1989). By 1992 births to foreign-born mothers had stabilized, and in 1999 they accounted for roughly 45 percent of all births to California mothers. The size of the foreign-born population, coupled with the relatively low incidence of multiracial-multiethnic births among this group, has tempered the overall increase in multiracial-multiethnic births in California.

Despite the moderating influence of the foreign-born population, multiracial-multiethnic births in 1999 still constituted a larger share of total births (15 percent) than both monoracial Asian births (9 percent) and monoracial African American births (6 percent). Multiracial-multiethnic births ranked below monoracial-monoethnic Hispanic births (43 percent) and monoracial-monoethnic white, non-Hispanic births (28 percent). The relative size of the multiracial-multiethnic group provides a context for understanding the concerns raised by various civil rights groups.[4]

Figure 3.4 illustrates the relative proportions of California's multiracial-multiethnic births for the largest multiracial-multiethnic groups in 1999. Births to couples in which one partner was white, non-Hispanic and the other was Hispanic, Asian, or African American accounted for roughly 77 percent of all multiracial-multiethnic births in 1999. The majority of these births were to couples in which one partner was white (and non-Hispanic) and the other Hispanic (53 percent). Births to mixed Hispanic-black, Hispanic-Asian, and Asian-black couples accounted for 16 percent

FIGURE 3.3   *Births to Native-Born and Foreign-Born Mothers As Share of All Births, California, 1982 to 1999*

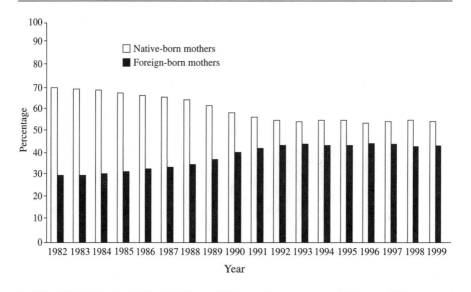

Source: Author's calculations from California Vital Statistics Birth Records.

of multiracial-multiethnic births. The remaining mixed births were to couples in which one partner was American Indian, Alaska native, Native Hawaiian, or other Pacific Islander.

It is unclear how continued immigration will affect the trend in multiracial-multiethnic births in California.[5] The effect will certainly be influenced by immigrant trends in country of origin, immigrant generational effects, residential segregation, and group size. For example, intermarriage rates for Hispanics and Asians increase with immigrant generation. National intermarriage estimates for Hispanics are 0.08, 0.32, and 0.57 for first, second, and third generations, respectively (Edmonston, Lee, and Passel 1994).[6] Consistent with these national data are California data showing that counties with a high percentage of multiracial-multiethnic births tend to be the same as those with a high percentage of native-born, rather than foreign-born, mothers. Residential segregation also plays a role in determining the occurrence of multiracial-multiethnic births. Generally, higher levels of residential segregation are linked to lower levels of multiracial-multiethnic births. For example, Los Angeles not only has a higher share of foreign-born mothers than Sacramento, but it is also, according to indexes

FIGURE 3.4   *Profile of Multiracial-Multiethnic Births, California, 1999*

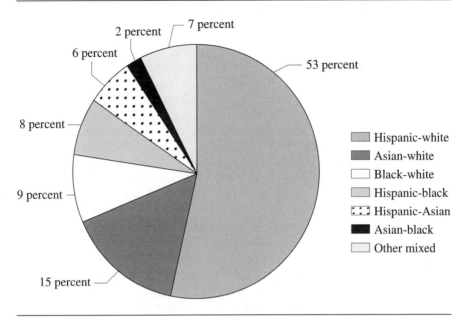

Source: Author's calculations from California Vital Statistics Birth Records.

of segregation, more highly segregated than Sacramento, especially for Hispanics and African Americans (U.S. Census Bureau 1990). Therefore, it is not surprising to find that in 1999 the percentage of multiracial-multi-ethnic births in Sacramento (19 percent) was nearly twice that in Los Angeles (10 percent).

Previous research indicates that members of small populations tend to intermarry because they are less likely to meet potential mates from their own racial or ethnic groups than those from other groups (Blau 1977). Recent estimates indicate that in 1999, 44 percent of the population in Los Angeles County was Hispanic, whereas only 16 percent of Sacramento County's population was Hispanic (U.S. Census Bureau 1999a). In Sacramento County, where Hispanics make up a relatively small share of the population, the proportion of multiracial-multiethnic births to native-born Hispanic mothers was relatively high (45 percent); the proportion of multi-racial-multiethnic births to native-born Hispanics in Los Angeles County, on the other hand, was only 14 percent.

Impact of Maternal Age and Education on Multiracial-Multiethnic Births

In examining the impact of maternal age and education on multiracial-multiethnic births, I focus on the three largest native-born races or ethnic groups in California: white, Hispanic, and African American. Figure 3.5 illustrates the trend in the percentage of multiracial-multiethnic births for each race or ethnic group. In 1982, 22 percent of births to native-born Hispanic mothers were multiracial-multiethnic; the percentage peaked in 1991, at 26 percent, and by 1999 had declined back to 22 percent. For native-born white mothers, 11 percent of births in 1982 were multiracial-multiethnic. The number rose to 19 percent in 1998 and remained at that level in 1999. For native-born African American mothers, 4 percent of 1982 births were multiracial-multiethnic, and by 1999 that figure had more than doubled, to 11 percent. Whereas multiracial-multiethnic births to Hispanic and white mothers appear to be leveling off, multiracial-multiethnic births to African American mothers appear to be continuing on an upward trend.

Although figure 3.5 provides information on the occurrence of multiracial-multiethnic births, it does not account for the effects of relative group size. Even if mate choice were a completely random process, the occurrence of multiracial-multiethnic births by race or ethnic group would differ owing to relative differences in group size among the racial and ethnic groups in California. Thus, to more clearly understand the differences in multiracial-multiethnic birth trends by race or ethnic group, I use odds ratios, which are independent of relative group size. Odds ratios are generally used to measure levels of endogamy—the degree to which members of a given racial or ethnic group marry within their own group. Higher odds ratios indicate a higher degree of in-marriage. In the case of births, the odds ratio employed here for Hispanic mothers is defined as the odds that a Hispanic mother pairs with a Hispanic father, rather than a non-Hispanic father, divided by the odds that a non-Hispanic mother pairs with a Hispanic father, rather than a non-Hispanic father (Kalmijn 1998).[7] High odds ratios indicate a lower degree of multiracial-multiethnic births; low odds ratios indicate a higher degree. The odds ratios presented here are calculated separately for each maternal education and age group. Three maternal age groups are used: younger than twenty-four years of age, twenty-five to twenty-nine years of age, and thirty years of age and older. Two education groups are used: twelve or fewer years of education and thirteen or more years of education.

Figure 3.6 illustrates the odds ratios for native-born African American mothers. In 1989, the first year for which education data is available in this data set, African American mothers, especially those twenty-five years of age and older, showed a low degree of multiracial-multiethnic births (high

FIGURE 3.5   *Multiracial-Multiethnic Births As Share of All Births to Native-Born Mothers, California, 1982 to 1999, by Race or Ethnicity*

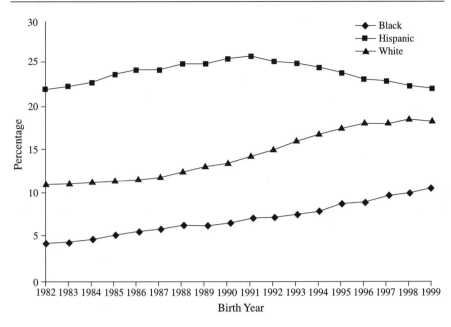

Source: Author's calculations from California Vital Statistics Birth Records.

odds ratios), and compared with mothers' age, mothers' educational attainment was relatively unimportant. A decade later, in 1999, the degree of multiracial-multiethnic births had risen for all age and education groups (odds ratios declined) but had risen fastest for women older than twenty-four years of age. In 1999, education was again relatively unimportant in determining these trends, especially for the older two age groups.

Figures 3.7 and 3.8 illustrate the odds ratios for native-born white and native-born Hispanic mothers. Odds ratios for these groups are far lower than the ratios for African American women, indicating a far higher degree of multiracial-multiethnic births among Hispanic mothers and white mothers. For both of these groups, education and age influence odds ratios. In 1989, women with only a high school education had a lower degree of multiracial-multiethnic births than women with some college education. Over the decade, the odds ratios for white and Hispanic mothers dropped for every age and education group, meaning that the degree of multiracial-multiethnic births for all women was higher for them than for their counterparts

FIGURE 3.6   *Odds Ratios of Monoracial-Monoethnic Birth to Native-Born African American Mothers, California, 1982 to 1999, by Maternal Age and Education*

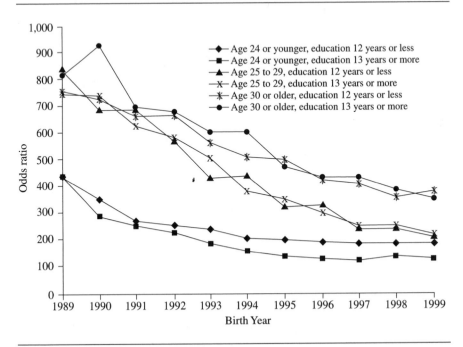

Source: Author's calculations from California Vital Statistics Birth Records.

ten years earlier. By 1999, the odds ratios by age and education group for white and Hispanic mothers ranked in the same order. Women with no more than a high school education had the lowest degree of multiracial-multiethnic births, and within this group, the degree of multiracial-multiethnic births declined with age. The groups with the highest degree of multiracial-multiethnic were the oldest college-educated women, followed by the twenty-five- to twenty-nine-year-old college-educated women and then the youngest college-educated women.

The mid-1990s marked a reversal in the downward trend in odds ratios for the youngest Hispanic and white mothers, meaning that their degree of multiracial-multiethnic births is actually leveling off or declining. Explanations of this trend will require further research. This trend may be due to a selection effect of women who opt to bear children at a relatively young age. Alternatively, it is plausible that the youngest Hispanic age group is made up of more native-born children of Hispanic immigrants, as

FIGURE 3.7   *Odds Ratios of Monoracial-Monoethnic Birth to Native-Born White Mothers, California, 1982 to 1999, by Maternal Age and Education*

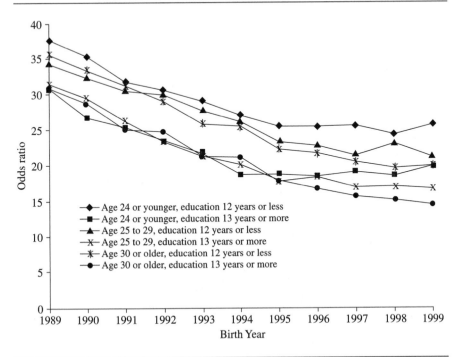

Source: Author's calculations from California Vital Statistics Birth Records.

compared with the older Hispanic age groups, which may comprise more women whose grandparents or great-grandparents were immigrants. Finally, because the geographic distribution of these groups across the state is not uniform, it may be that these ratios are largely driven by births in Los Angeles County, where the population is relatively younger and more likely to be Hispanic than in other parts of the state.

Implications of California's Multiracial-Multiethnic Births

The context for this analysis was the impending release of complete Census 2000 data. At this point, the portions of Census 2000 data that have been released confirm what the Census 2000 Dress Rehearsal data suggested (U.S. Census Bureau 1999b): first, the percentage of people identifying as multiracial was higher in California than in the nation as a whole, and

FIGURE 3.8   *Odds Ratios of Monoracial-Monoethnic Birth to Native-Born Hispanic Mothers, California, 1982 to 1999, by Maternal Age and Education*

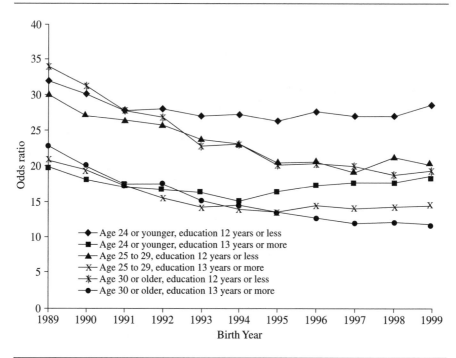

Source: Author's calculations from California Vital Statistics Birth Records.

second, young people are more likely to identify as multiracial than their adult counterparts (U.S. Census Bureau 2000).

A closer look at how Californians identified themselves racially and ethnically in the 2000 census explains why the results presented in this chapter differ from those now available from Census 2000 and why tabulation methods for the Hispanic population are particularly important in California.[8] Clearly, treating Hispanic ethnicity as a race greatly increases estimates by including multiethnic with multiracial data. In the analysis presented here, Hispanic ethnicity was treated as if it were a racial category, yielding a multiracial-multiethnic estimate of 15 percent of total births in 1999. Yet Census 2000, which considers Hispanic ethnicity separately from race, reveals that only 7.3 percent of Californians under the age of eighteen are multiracial.

The appearance of the "some other race" option among the specified racial categories on the 2000 census schedule has particular relevance for California. Many Hispanics identified themselves as multiracial by selecting both "white" and "some other race." In fact, 7.7 percent of California Hispanics under the age of eighteen were reported to be of two or more races, the vast majority of them identified as "white' and "some other race." Extrapolating from these figures, one could calculate a correction factor for the 1999 birth data, converting the multiracial-multiethnic estimate to a strictly multiracial estimate. Assuming that 7.7 percent of all Hispanic births are multiracial, instead of deriving the data from parental responses on the birth records, yields an estimation that 8.9 percent of California births in 1999 were multiracial. Indeed, including only a portion of the multiethnic births closely approximates the Census 2000 results. Although this correction factor serves to bridge the 1999 birth data with Census 2000 data, forthcoming census data will provide a detailed picture of which Californians actually chose to identify as multiracial.

California leads the nation as the state with the largest population of multiracial people, and Hispanics make up a large component of this population. The fact that many Hispanics in California selected the "some other race" category clearly indicates that they do not identify with the specified racial options presented to them in the 2000 census. California birth records illustrate that the potential growth of the multiracial Hispanic population is large. A growing multiracial Hispanic population may be one of the enduring results associated with the change in federal racial classification.

Notes

1. The definitions of race and ethnicity used in this report are derived from current Office of Management and Budget (OMB) standards. "Multiracial" refers to any individual who can claim two or more of the following OMB racial designations: white, black or African American, Asian, Native Hawaiian or other Pacific Islander, Native American or Alaska Native. "Multiethnic" refers to any individual who can claim to be partly of Hispanic or Latino origin and partly not of Hispanic or Latino origin. The terms "multiracial-multiethnic" and "mixed race or ethnicity" refer to any individual who is either multiethnic or multiracial.

2. At this time, the OMB has not included a provision in the standards that would allow multiethnic respondents to select both "Hispanic origin" and "not of Hispanic origin" (OMB 1997). For detailed discussion of tabulation issues, see OMB 1999. To meet redistricting needs, the Census Bureau has decided to provide data with sixty-three categories of race. There are sixty-three potential single- and multiple-race categories consisting of six monoracial categories and fifty-seven categories for biracial and multiracial respondents. There are

two ethnic categories: Hispanic and not Hispanic. Thus the population can now be categorized into 126 unique racial and ethnic combinations.

3. Approximately 1 percent of the data on mother's race and ethnicity is missing. Before 1995 forward, generally less than 4 percent of the data for father's race and ethnicity is missing. From 1995, 4 to 7 percent of these data is missing. Records with missing race and ethnic data are excluded from the analysis. Nationwide, approximately 15 percent of data for father's race and ethnicity in 1997 and 1998 is missing (National Center for Health Statistics 1999).

4. For a detailed discussion of tabulation options, see OMB 1999. For an analysis of the March 2000 OMB guidelines for civil rights monitoring and enforcement, see Goldstein and Morning 2000.

5. Native-born adult children of immigrants out-marry at a higher rate than do their parents. For national-origin population group projections that consider exogamy estimates by generation, see Edmonston, Lee, and Passel 1994.

6. Data based on 1990 census microdata and 1994 birth data from the National Center for Health Statistics; see Smith and Edmonston 1997.

7. Odds ratios are not calculated for fathers because data on father's place of birth are unavailable.

8. A number of factors limit the comparability of these two analyses. These include racial or ethnic self-identification versus research-derived racial or ethnic assignments, and state allocation of virtually all Hispanics to the "white" racial category in the California Vital Statistics Birth Records versus racial self-identification into six different racial categories in the Census Dress Rehearsal data.

References

Bancroft Whitney Company. 1949. *Reports of Cases Determined in the Supreme Court of the State of California, May 25, 1948, to November 1, 1948.* Perez v. Sharp [32 C.2d 711; 198 P.2d 17] Andrea D. Perez et al., Petitioners, v. W. G. Sharp, as County Clerk, etc., Respondent [L.A. No. 20305. In Bank. Oct. 1, 1948.]. Vol. 32. 2d ed. San Francisco: Bancroft Whitney Company.

Blau, Peter M. 1977. *Inequality and Heterogeneity: A Primitive Theory of Social Structure.* New York: Free Press.

Cornelius, Wayne A. 1989. "Impacts of the 1986 U.S. Immigration Law on Emigration from Rural Mexican Sending Communities." *Population and Development Review* 15(4): 689–705.

Edmonston, Barry, Sharon Lee, and Jeffrey Passel. 1994. "U.S. Population Projections for National Origin Groups: Taking into Account Ethnicity and Exogamy." Paper presented at the annual meeting of the American Statistical Association. Toronto, Canada (August 13–18).

Goldstein, Joshua, and Ann Morning. 2000. "Back in the Box: Allocating Multiple-Race Responses Back to Single Races." Paper presented at Jerome Levy Economics Institute conference, Multiraciality: How Will the New Census Data Be Used? Annandale-on-Hudson, N.Y. (September 22–23).

Gurak, Douglas T. 1987. "Family Formation and Marital Selectivity Among Colombian and Dominican Immigrants in New York City." *International Migration Review* 21(2): 275–98.

Kalmijn, Matthijs. 1998. "Intermarriage and Homogamy: Causes, Patterns, Trends." *Annual Review of Sociology* 24:395–421.

Lee, Sharon, and Marilyn Fernandez. 1998. "Trends in Asian American Racial-Ethnic Intermarriage: A Comparison of 1980 and 1990 Census Data." *Sociological Perspectives* 41(2): 323–42.

National Center for Health Statistics. 1999. "Births: Final Data for 1997." *National Vital Statistics Report* 47(18).

Office of Management and Budget (OMB), Executive Office of the President. 1997. "Revisions to the Standards for the Classification of Federal Data on Race and Ethnicity." *Federal Register* 62(210): 58781–790.

———. 1997. "Recommendations from the Interagency Committee for the Review of the Racial and Ethnic Standards to the Office of Management and Budget Concerning Changes to the Standards for the Classification of Federal Data on Race and Ethnicity." *Federal Register* 62(131): 36873–946.

———. 1999. Tabulation Working Group of the Interagency Committee for the Review of Standards for Data on Race and Ethnicity. "Draft Provisional Guidance on the Implementation of the 1997 Standards for the Collection of Federal Data on Race and Ethnicity." *Federal Register* (February 17).

Reyes, Belinda I., ed. 2001. *A Portrait of Race and Ethnicity in California: An Assessment of Social and Economic Well-being.* San Francisco: Public Policy Institute of California.

Schmidley, Diane, and Herman A. Alvarado. 1998. "The Foreign-Born Population in the United States: March 1997 (Update)." *Current Population Reports.* Report P20h507. Washington: U.S. Department of Commerce, U.S. Department of the Census.

Smith, James P., and Barry Edmonston, eds. 1997. *The New Americans: Economic, Demographic, and Fiscal Effects of Immigration.* Washington, D.C.: National Academy Press.

State of California, Department of Finance. 1999. *Legal Immigration to California in Federal Fiscal Year 1996.* Sacramento.

Sung, Betty Lee. 1990. "Chinese American Intermarriage." *Journal of Comparative Family Studies* 29(3): 337–52.

U.S. Department of Commerce. U.S. Bureau of the Census. 1990. *Residential Segregation 1990.* 1990 Census Summary Tape File (STF): 1A. Accessed March 13, 2001 at: *www.census.gov/hhes/www/resseg.html.*

———. 1999a. *Population Estimates for States and Counties by Race and Hispanic Origin.* Washington (July).

———. 1999b. *U.S. Census 2000 Dress Rehearsal.* P.L. 94–171. Redistricting Summary File. Washington (March).

———. 2000. Redistricting Data. P.L. 94–171. *Census 2000 Redistricting Data* (Public Law 94–171). California Summary Files. Washington.

Waters, M. C. 1990. *Ethnic Options: Choosing Identities in America.* Berkeley: University of California Press.

Part II

HOW MUCH WILL IT MATTER?

4

BACK IN THE BOX: THE DILEMMA OF USING MULTIPLE-RACE DATA FOR SINGLE-RACE LAWS

Joshua R. Goldstein and Ann J. Morning

How are multiple-race statistics to be used to enforce laws created in the single-race era? The Office of Management and Budget (OMB) issued revised standards for racial and ethnic statistics, allowing respondents for the first time to mark multiple races on federal forms, including census forms, in 1997. It was not known at the time how multiple-race data would be processed, tabulated, or used. Just weeks before the 2000 census, however, the OMB issued guidelines for the use of multiple-race data: for civil and voting rights purposes, people who marked "white" and a nonwhite race should be counted as members of the nonwhite group (OMB 2000).

The OMB guidelines, known as Bulletin 00-02, are limited in scope to "data on race for use in civil rights monitoring and enforcement" and do not, for example, apply directly to the reporting of the many social, economic, and demographic indicators involving racial statistics. Nor are they meant to preclude the development of alternative allocation methods for preserving the continuity of time-series data collected under the old and new systems (that is, "bridging" methods). Nevertheless, they are the first explicit guidelines covering the use of multiple-race data, and as such they have set a precedent for the systematic reallocation of multiple responses back to single-race categories.[1]

The need for allocation rules results from the disconnection between statistical policy governing the collection of racial data and the laws and precedents for using racial data. The implementation of current civil rights laws calls for single-race categories that unequivocally distinguish between those who are members of minority groups and those who are not. The guidelines provide a way to do this: first, by specifying that any person who marks both "white" and a nonwhite race will be allocated to the nonwhite race; and second, by specifying that allocation of multiple nonwhite responses will depend on the circumstances of the complaint at issue.

The OMB's Bulletin 00-02 has the advantage of being easy to understand and relatively easy to implement. Most important, it does not reduce the overall size of the minority population. As the OMB points out, it also avoids the division of whole people into fractions, a procedure open to criticism because of the history of voting rights under the pre–Civil War constitution, in which slaves were given only three-fifths of the weight of free whites.

However, despite the practical merits of this strategy, the allocation to nonwhite groups may nonetheless prove controversial for both the mixed-race community and the general population. First, the OMB approach reimplements, albeit in a civil rights context, the traditional American "one-drop rule" associated with slavery, segregation, and the history of racial discrimination. In the past, the one-drop rule was used to classify a person with any degree of African ancestry as black and thus to enforce a rigid color line between blacks and whites (Davis 1991). The modern use of a one-drop rule clearly has a different purpose; it is aimed at redressing discrimination rather than enforcing segregation. Despite its intentions, however, the rule is still open to the criticism that it repeats the mistakes of the past, further institutionalizing the divide between the white and nonwhite populations.

A second difficulty in the reallocation plan is that it appears to violate the principle of self-identification. Now that multiracial individuals are finally permitted to "mark one or more" races, many expect to be treated as such without being put back in a single checkbox. Even government reports acknowledge that "congruence with respondent's choice" is an important feature of any tabulation system. As the Tabulation Working Group of the Interagency Committee for the Review of Standards for Data on Race and Ethnicity has noted, "the underlying logic of the tabulation procedures *must reflect to the greatest extent possible the full detail of race reporting*" (OMB 1999, 13; italics added).

A third challenge for the guidance is the risk of making race-based public policies even more controversial than they already are. The system of racial classification may come to be seen as too unwieldy and arbitrary to support civil rights legal decisions. There is probably no escape from this problem. Any assignment of multiple-race people to single races is open to criticism of being ad hoc or arbitrary since there is no way of knowing with which single race mixed-race respondents would most strongly identify, if given the opportunity.

A final challenge that the OMB's reallocation may face is that it errs on the side of extending the coverage of race-based policies, which are already under political attack, to a segment of the population—namely, mixed-race individuals with some white ancestry—who may not have qualified for such protection under past definitions. Some 60 to 80 percent of those likely to mark more than one race choose "white" when asked to mark only a single race (Goldstein and Morning 2000). Yu Xie and Kimberly Goyette's (1997) finding that biracial white-Asian children were nearly equally likely to be reported (presumably by their parents) as white or Asian on the 1990 census may suggest whites' acceptance of biracial white-Asian people to a considerable degree, rather than stigmatization as a minority group. Herbert Gans (1999) and Michael Lind ("The Beige and the Black," *New York Times Magazine*, August 16, 1998, 38–39) further suggest that mixed-race Americans with white ancestry are so well integrated into the white community that in time they too will come to be considered white.

The Guidelines

The federal government's 1997 introduction of the multiple-race format raised the question of how multiple-race statistics would be tabulated and used to monitor and enforce civil rights laws that had previously depended on a single-race classification system. In the past, classification systems had been formalized in response to legislation (Edmonston, Goldstein, and Lott 1996), but now the enforcement and monitoring of laws had to respond to a change in the statistical system. The approach taken by the OMB was to develop a procedure for reallocating mixed-race respondents back into single-race categories.

The OMB (2000, 2) guidelines read in part as follows:

Federal agencies will use the following rules to allocate multiple race responses for use in civil rights monitoring and enforcement.

- Responses in the five single race categories are not allocated.
- Responses that combine one minority race and white are allocated to the minority race.
- Responses that include two or more minority races are allocated as follows:
  - If the enforcement action is in response to a complaint, allocate to the race that the complainant alleges the discrimination was based on.
  - If the enforcement action requires assessing disparate impact or discriminatory patterns, analyze the patterns based on alternative allocations to each of the minority groups.

A precedent for the treatment of multiple identification can be found in the combined treatment of race and Hispanic-origin statistics. The most common joint treatment of race and origin statistics has been in the past to give Hispanic origin priority over race. Five categories emerge from this approach: white, non-Hispanic; black (African American), non-Hispanic; Native American, non-Hispanic; Asian, non-Hispanic; and Hispanic.[2] This system, in which Hispanic origin trumps all other racial categories, is analogous to the allocation rules whereby any "minority" racial identity trumps white identity. Both procedures have a similar aim—namely, to protect those who have historically experienced discrimination.

This decision to allocate in favor of nonwhite populations was greeted with relief by representatives of traditional minority groups, who had been concerned that they might lose numbers because of the shift to the "one or more" format (Steven A. Holmes, "New Policy on Census Says Those Listed As White and Minority Will Be Counted As Minority," *New York Times*, March 11, 2000, A9). On the other hand, it was harshly criticized by some in the multiracial community (for example, Byrd 2000) as a return to the "one-drop rule."

What Is at Stake? The Uses of Racial Statistics in Civil Rights and Voting Rights Act Enforcement

How people are counted—that is, into which racial category they are placed—does not involve the same issues as the question whether people are counted at all. With the census undercount, the area in which a "missed" person lives is credited with one fewer person, and the congressional representation, federal funds, and other benefits that would have gone to that person go elsewhere. If a person is allocated to one race instead of another, however, a state's congressional apportionment is not affected. Similarly, population-based funding will not, in general, be affected by the racial counts. What *is* at stake in racial reallocation are the nominal size of groups, an issue of interest to organizations that claim to represent them; the feelings—and perceived right to self-identification—of mixed-race respondents; enforcement of the Voting Rights Act; and enforcement of civil rights legislation, notably antidiscrimination laws in employment, housing and education.

Although the focus here is on the effect of the allocation rule on the use of racial statistics in redistricting and civil rights, the first two issues should not be taken lightly. The possibility that some, or even many, mixed-race respondents may feel betrayed is a real one. As Susan Graham of Project RACE and James A. Landrith Jr. of the Multiracial Activist have written, "The federal government is going to decide what single race you or your children would pick if you had to pick just one. They not only want people to make a choice of one race, they want to make the choice for us" (Graham and Landrith 2001).

Racial statistics are used for the monitoring and enforcement of both civil rights laws and the Voting Rights Act (Edmonston and Schultze 1995). In civil rights cases, a statistical demonstration of disparate impact is a first step toward proving a discrimination case. Yet statistics are not everything, for, depending on the law, the intent to discriminate must also be shown. In contrast, for the Voting Rights Act, statistical evidence is sufficient for the Department of Justice to find a redistricting plan in violation, even without evidence of discriminatory intent.

Voting Rights

The Voting Rights Act of 1965 (as amended in 1970, 1975, 1982, and 1992) requires that states and political subdivisions demonstrate that their redistricting plans do not reduce the voting strength of minority citizens (Edmonston and Schultze 1995). Plans that split minority voters into multiple districts, for example, can be held to violate the voting rights of minorities by diluting their members' votes. In the 1970s and 1980s, the courts developed numerical standards by which to judge whether minority groups were given a fair chance of electing a candidate from their districts. One such rule was the so-called "65 percent rule," according to which a minority concentration of 65 percent was necessary to ensure representation for minority groups.[3] However, in 1993 the Supreme Court decided in Shaw v. Reno (509 U.S. 630 [1993]) that race could not be "the predominant factor" in the drawing of districts (Persily 2001). The definition of how to determine whether race is "the predominant factor" remains controversial and unresolved.

The effect of this ruling and others is that redistricting plans are subject to competing, and potentially contradictory, criteria. On the one hand, the voting rights statutes forbid the dilution of minority voting power, and statistics on racial composition are employed in judging compliance with those statutes. On the other hand, the Supreme Court's recent rulings appear to forbid the drawing of district lines on the basis of race alone. Thus race must be taken into consideration to assure the protection of voting rights, but not so much that the redistricting plan is likely to be rejected in court.

If numerical thresholds are used, even a slight reallocation of multiracial responses could alter minority counts enough to make a difference in the approval of a redistricting plan. In a hypothetical district in which 60 percent of the voting-age population marked "black" as their only race and in which an additional 10 percent marked "black" as one of their races, the method used for allocating the mixed-race respondents would determine whether or not the district was in compliance with the 65 percent rule. Moreover, the racial reallocation method used would quite likely be hotly contested.

Although, in light of the Supreme Court's ruling in *Shaw*, the 65 percent rule will probably no longer be applied, other numerical criteria may persist. For example, according to the so-called "Gingles criteria" (Persily 2001) a minority group filing a complaint of vote dilution must show that it is large enough that it would be able to form a numerical majority (that is, greater than 50 percent) in a redrawn district.

With numerical thresholds apparently having fallen out of favor with the courts, the allocation of multiple-race responses is likely to be less controversial than in the hypothetical scenario presented here. However, the vast number of voting districts to be redrawn following the 2000 census suggests that even if allocation methods for the multiracial population matter only rarely, at least a few contentious cases may still surface.

Civil Rights

Federal civil rights law prohibits discrimination in employment, housing, and education on the basis of race and color (as well as sex, religion, and national origin). In employment cases, statistical comparisons of a firm's employees with the local labor force are used as the first piece of evidence that an employer may be discriminating against a particular group. Although there is no commonly accepted numerical threshold for determining whether there is evidence of discrimination, statistical tests of significance are typically performed to determine whether the composition of the labor force of a firm and of a local area differ. Statistics are not usually used alone, as they are in the voting rights cases, but rather are just one piece of evidence used in civil rights cases. Thus small, and perhaps even relatively large, changes in population composition may not be sufficient to change the determination of cases.

Nevertheless, the reallocation of racial responses will have consequences for the statistics presented as evidence of discrimination. A hypothetical example illustrates how even the inclusion of equal proportions of mixed-race respondents in the minority shares inside and outside a firm could change evidence of discrimination. Suppose that, according to the old single-race system, 10 percent of a firm's labor force marks "black" as its only race, and that 20 percent of the qualified labor force in the geographic area is similarly "black." In this instance, the firm has hired only half of the black workers it could be expected to employ, signaling a warning sign of possible discrimination. Now suppose that another 30 percent of the workers, both in the firm and in the area, have marked "black" in combination with "white." Under the OMB allocation rules, these workers are defined as black, and thus the firm now has a workforce that is 40 percent black, whereas the workforce in the surrounding community is 50 percent black.

The evidence for discrimination now appears weaker, as the firm can claim that it has hired four-fifths the number of blacks it could be expected to employ.

It is also worth noting that in some cases racial reallocation could have unbalanced effects, adding relatively more or fewer minorities to a firm's labor force than to the area's labor pool. This could happen by chance, or it could happen because of compositional changes in the socioeconomic profile of the minority population as a result of allocation.

The existence of plausible alternative allocation procedures that would be more or less favorable to employers may muddy the waters and make it harder to demonstrate discrimination. Employers and other institutions accused of discrimination may argue that the malleability of racial identification implied by the new system makes statistical arguments less reliable and less convincing.

Unresolved Issues

The current guidelines leave unresolved several potentially contentious issues. One example is how program eligibility will be determined: will a person who marks "white" and a minority race on a form be eligible for the same programs as someone who marks a minority group alone? Such targeted programs include the Small Business Administration's 8-A loans for minority businesses, government contracting programs that reserve a portion of government contracts for minority businesses, and affirmative action programs in hiring. It is hard to imagine that a court case will not arise in which the eligibility of a mixed-race person will be challenged, particularly if it can be shown that that person had in the past identified himself or herself only as white. In the present climate, in which race-targeted programs are under political attack (notably in California), the potential for controversy is great.

A second unresolved issue concerns what will happen in cases in which the method of allocation applied to multiple nonwhite responses (for example, "black" and "Asian") ends up making a substantial difference. As noted earlier, the OMB allocation guidelines allow data users some discretion in this area. Although the amount of such allocation is likely to be small in proportional terms (at least in the short run), it is not at all clear that the current guidelines can withstand application if they actually make a substantive difference in a particular civil rights case.

Finally, the OMB allocation procedure effectively obscures potential differences in the treatment of mixed-race people and single-race people because the two groups are lumped together. Employers or landlords might well discriminate against (or in favor of) people with mixed backgrounds relative to those with single-race backgrounds, but it will not be possible to determine whether such a pattern exists if only allocated racial data is available.

Estimates of Reallocation

At the national level, mixed-race respondents made up 2.4 percent of the population in the 2000 census. This was somewhat larger than had been expected based on census pretests (for example, del Pinal et al. 2001) and somewhat smaller than estimates based on race and ancestry responses in the 1990 census (Goldstein and Morning 2000).

The racial composition of the national population and the effects of reallocation are shown in table 4.1. In the column designated "Maximum Allocation," we show the largest possible size each racial group could assume under the OMB reallocation guidelines. Here each nonwhite group includes all the people who marked that race either alone or in combination with any other race (or races). Each is the count that would be determined for the nonwhite group using both of the reallocation guidelines: allocating white-nonwhite combinations to the "white" category and allocating all combinations of nonwhite races to the nonwhite group in question. In the next column, we present the "Minimum Allocation" that would obtain if only the first guideline were implemented, reclassifying people who marked both "white" and a minority race to the minority category but leaving the allocation of multiple minority races undecided.

Although mixed-race people make up only 2.4 percent of the total population, reallocation can create dramatic increases in the size of single-race populations. For the country as a whole, allocation more than doubles the count of Native Hawaiians and increases the counts of Native Americans by more than half, Asians by nearly one-sixth, and African Americans by about one-twentieth.

The national estimates provide an indication of what will happen "on average." This average, however, hides the great variability in multiple-race reporting in the small local areas in which most civil and voting rights cases are decided. Figure 4.1 illustrates the multiracial population of the United States by county and state. Among the areas with counties with high concentrations of multiple-race responses are Hawaii, Alaska, the Far West, the Southwest, Oklahoma, and the Northeast corridor between Washington, D.C., and Boston.

The multiple-race combinations in these highly multiracial counties are of many types. In Hawaii, the most popular multiple-race responses are white-Asian and white–Native Hawaiian. In Oklahoma, the most popular response is white–Native American. The most common responses in Wash-

TABLE 4.1   *Reallocation of the 2000 Census National Multiple-Race Results (Millions)*

Race	Unallocated Census 2000 Results	Maximum Allocation[a]	Minimum Allocation[b]	Effect of Allocation on Group Size (Percentage)	
				Maximum	Minimum
White	211.5	211.5	211.5	0	0
Black	34.7	36.4	35.4	+ 5	+ 2
American Indian	2.5	4.1	3.6	+ 66	+ 44
Asian	10.2	11.9	11.1	+ 16	+ 8
Native Hawaiian	0.4	0.9	0.5	+ 118	+ 28
Other	15.4	18.5	17.6	+ 21	+ 14
More than one race	6.8				
More than one race, to be allocated			1.8[c]		
Total	281.4	283.3[d]	281.4		

Sources: Jones and Smith 2001; Grieco and Cassidy 2001.

[a]For each nonwhite race, the "maximum allocation" refers to the count of all responses including that race, whether alone or in combination with other races. The single-race "white" category is not affected by the OMB reallocation guidelines.

[b]For each nonwhite race, the "minimum allocation" includes the single-race responses in that category plus the responses that combine that race with "white" in a dual-race combination.

[c]Responses including more than one nonwhite race.

[d]Greater than the national total due to double-counting of responses that combine two or more nonwhite races.

ington state are white-Asian and white–Native American, and in New York, white-other, black-other, and white-black.

The 2000 census data probably represents the lower bound of multiple-race reporting that can be expected in the future. The multiracial population is growing as intermarriage increases. We also expect awareness of the change in question format—that is, the realization that the question actually permits multiple-race responses—to increase with time.

What single race would mixed-race respondents choose if confronted with the choice of reallocating themselves? Although we cannot determine this from the 2000 census, it is possible to use the 1990 census responses to race and ancestry questions to infer multiple responses and the probable single race chosen by mixed-race people.[4] It is clear from figure 4.2 that the "one-drop" aspect of the OMB allocation rule runs counter to the ways many multiracial people would choose to self-identify. Among people of mixed white and American Indian background, the vast majority chose

FIGURE 4.1   Multiple-Race Population As Share of Total Population, 2000, by
              State and County

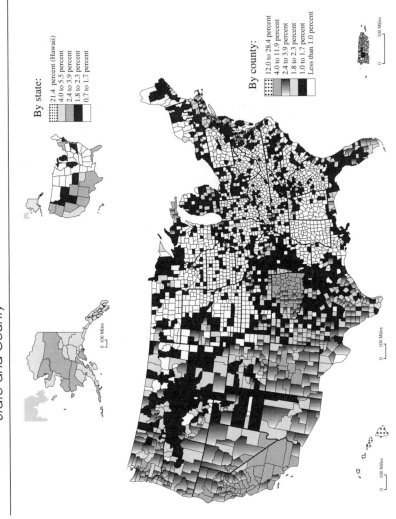

By state:

21.4 percent (Hawaii)
4.0 to 5.5 percent
2.4 to 3.9 percent
1.8 to 2.3 percent
0.7 to 1.7 percent

By county:

12.0 to 28.4 percent
4.0 to 11.9 percent
2.4 to 3.9 percent
1.8 to 2.3 percent
1.0 to 1.7 percent
Less than 1.0 percent

Source: U.S. Bureau of the Census 2000.
Note: The rate of multiple-race reporting for the entire United States was 2.4 percent.

FIGURE 4.2   *Primary Single Race Chosen by Respondents Reporting Multiple-Race Ancestry, 1990*

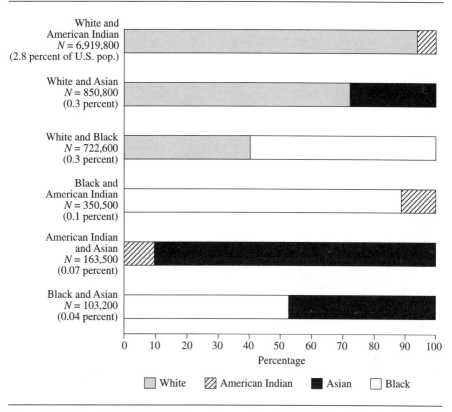

Source: 1-in-100 unweighted 1990 IPUMS sample, as analyzed in Goldstein and Morning 2000.

"white" as their single race. For those with mixed white and Asian background, more than two-thirds identified themselves as "white." Only for blacks does the "one-drop" allocation conform to the majority of responses, but even here nearly 40 percent of white-black respondents would choose "white" as their single race.

Our analysis of the 1990 data may overestimate the white single-race preference of mixed-race respondents in the 2000 census because some of those who reported a combination of white and nonwhite ancestry in 1990—particularly American Indian—appear not to have marked multiple races in the 2000 census. Nevertheless, it is clear that the necessary simplicity of the reallocation rules runs counter to the social complexity of racial identi-

TABLE 4.2   Socioeconomic Characteristics of Adults 1990, by
             Race, by 1990 Census Count and OMB Reallocation

Characteristic	1990 Census Count Estimate	OMB Reallocated Count Estimate
Annual Family Income (dollars)		
White	41,984 (47)	42,281 (48)
Black	28,864 (101)	28,883 (102)
American Indian–Alaska Native	28,739 (343)	32,248 (143)
Asian–Pacific Islander	48,610 (329)	48,231 (324)
Other	29,633 (188)	29,617 (189)
To be determined[a]		37,722 (859)
Educational Level[b]		
White	10.45 (.00)	10.48 (.00)
Black	9.49 (.01)	9.49 (.01)
American Indian–Alaska Native	9.49 (.03)	9.57 (.01)
Asian–Pacific Islander	10.86 (.02)	10.84 (.02)
Other	7.96 (.02)	7.96 (.02)
To be determined[a]		10.55 (.05)

Source: Unweighted 1-in-100 1990 IPUMS sample. See Goldstein and Morning 2000 for additional details of methodology.
Note: Standard errors in parentheses. Sample is limited to adults eighteen years of age and older.
[a]We assign responses including two nonwhite races to the "To be determined" row because the OMB guidelines do not set a single fixed rule for these cases.
[b]Education is coded as follows: 7 = less than eleventh grade; 8 = eleventh grade; 9 = twelfth grade, no diploma; 10 = high school graduate; 11 = some college.

fication. The allocation rules will often be inconsistent with the single-race choices made historically by those of mixed ancestry.

The impact of the new OMB guidance on racial data will be felt not just in terms of the relative sizes of racial groups but also in terms of the characteristics—socioeconomic, demographic, and other—that these newly constructed racial groupings will exhibit. Such statistical profiles may influence the analysis of data for the purpose of detecting discriminatory patterns. In an employment discrimination case, for example, comparisons may focus on the population with a particular level of educational attainment. Statistical profiles may also influence the way researchers understand trends over time in the social status of minorities in the United States, if the "bridging" technique selected resembles the OMB allocation guidelines. We explore how shifts in classification affect racial groups' mean outcomes on two basic socioeconomic characteristics: educational level and family income. Returning to our 1990 census data, we use only the adults eighteen years of age and older in the sample ($N = 1,838,508$) to control somewhat for differing age structures across racial groups. Results for the national population are shown in table 4.2.

At the national level, racial reallocation tends to raise the socioeconomic profile of both the white and American Indian populations. The Asian population is affected slightly, with a small decline in its socioeconomic profile, and the characteristics of the black population remain essentially unchanged. It is important to note, however, that our analysis here does not include the potential effects of reallocating the double-minority population, which we leave instead in the "To be determined" row.

The direction of these effects can best be understood in terms of the population that is being shifted during allocation. The socioeconomic characteristics of those with both American Indian and white ancestry tend to be in between those of the two groups, and thus allocation from the white to the American Indian category raises the socioeconomic levels of both groups. A similar type of selection—but in the reverse direction—slightly lowers the characteristics of the Asian population.

Table 4.3 reports the mean values of our socioeconomic indicators for a selected subset of the multiracial groups in the 1990 census.[5] These indicators can be used to assess whether the allocation guidelines place people in the socioeconomic group they most resemble. This appears to be the case for those with mixed black and white or American Indian and white backgrounds. For example, the average family income of people with mixed black and white backgrounds is $31,000, which is closer to the mean income of single-race blacks ($28,800) than to that of single-race whites ($42,300). On the other hand, for those with both Asian and white backgrounds, allocation to the Asian group actually locates them in a category with people with whom they differ more on average in their socioeconomic characteristics than they would if they were placed in the white group. Such differences suggest that the "one-drop" minority allocation rule is less appropriate for those of mixed Asian and white background than it is for those of mixed black and white and mixed American Indian and white background.

Finally, although the effects of allocation on the socioeconomic characteristics of racial categories tend to be small at the national level, this does not mean they will be uniformly small at all levels of geography. In some localities, there may be cases in which the socioeconomic composition of a racial category could change substantially as a result of allocation decisions.

Concluding Discussion

The Office of Management and Budget's proposed allocation method is easy to understand and to implement. Our message here is not that the OMB made a mistake in its guidelines. Rather, we have tried to point out some of the issues that the allocation method may raise and some of the

TABLE 4.3   Socioeconomic Characteristics of Selected
             Multiple-Race Groups, 1990

Racial Category	Annual Family Income (Dollars)	Education Level[a]
Multiple-race combinations		
White-black	31,000	10.0
White–American Indian	33,300	9.6
White–Asian–Pacific Islander	43,700	10.9
Single-race groups		
White	42,300	10.5
Black	28,800	9.5
American Indian–Alaska Native	27,100	9.3
Asian–Pacific Islander	48,600	10.8

Source: Unweighted 1-in-100 1990 IPUMS sample. See Goldstein and Morning 2000 for additional details of methodology.
Note: The sample is limited to adults eighteen years of age and older.
[a]Education is coded as follows: 7 = less than eleventh grade; 8 = eleventh grade; 9 = twelfth grade, no diploma; 10 = high school graduate; 11 = some college.

difficulties it may encounter. While ease of use is important, success will be judged on many fronts. We have shown that the reallocation procedure does not conform to the single races that respondents could self-identify, nor does it necessarily map individuals to the closest single race in terms of socioeconomic characteristics.

The fundamental challenge of using multiple-race data is that perhaps for the first time, the law and the courts may be playing catch-up to the data rather than the other way around. The use of racial statistics in past decades has been guided by legislation. The separation of Hispanic origin and race into two questions, for example, was a response to legal and administrative requirements (Edmonston, Goldstein, and Lott 1996). This time, however, the change to multiple-race reporting was made to adapt to the changing demography of the United States and to accommodate the mixed-race respondents who had expressed intense dissatisfaction with single-race reporting. Reallocation of mixed-race respondents then becomes a way of bringing the data back into line with preexisting legal requirements.

Any allocation system is controversial because it involves altering the designations that people chose for themselves. What makes such a system even more controversial is that there are many conceivable alternative allocation schemes. Thus not only are responses being changed from what people might have originally intended, but also the changes are being made in an arbitrary, if systematic, manner. Arbitrariness is not a characteristic of the OMB allocation scheme in particular but is rather a feature of any single set of rules.

The "one-drop" aspect of the OMB allocation rule is aimed at preserving the rights and size of minority populations. The effect is to overshoot somewhat, thereby including in minority groups some people who formerly identified themselves as white. Thus there will be some degree of "false positive" allocation of individuals to minority groups, similar to the allocation of people who do not belong to distinct official racial groups to the "multiracial" category that has been tested in the past (McKay 1996).

A potential technical difficulty with the allocation rules is that they can be impossible to implement fully without reporting all sixty-three categories. It is not possible to allocate only from the aggregated categories, which include only the most common dual-race categories and other groups that number more than 1 percent of the total population, because the remaining categories consisting of smaller dual-race combinations also need to be allocated.

Although the scope of the allocation and aggregation rules are explicitly limited to civil rights applications, in the absence of alternative rules they may well end up being applied elsewhere. For example, the original guidelines did not specifically apply to voting rights but have since been extended. We believe a particularly sensitive area will appear in terms of program eligibility, which the guidelines clearly are not meant to cover—in fact, the old racial classification standard (Directive 15) explicitly excluded eligibility—but for which they will nonetheless serve as a precedent.

How large will the effect of allocation be? Our calculations are illustrative and do not include tabulations of small areas, in which most civil and voting rights cases are decided. However, as figure 4.1 illustrates, multiracial people account for as much as a quarter of the total population in some counties.

In terms of the Voting Rights Act, the climate against numerical quotas probably means that numerical thresholds will play a less important role in redistricting litigation and enforcement following the 2000 census than they did following the 1990 census, when the 65 percent rule was fairly firmly in place. Nevertheless, it will take only a few extreme cases in which the allocation rule for deciding how to count multiple-race responses ends up really making a difference for this issue to end up in the courts. This does not mean that the whole system of Voting Rights Act enforcement is in peril, for in most cases the allocation of multiple-race reports will not make a significant difference (Persily 2000). Only one court case in one district is needed, however, to call into question the principles underlying the OMB racial allocation rules.

Civil rights enforcement has traditionally been less subject to strict numerical thresholds. Nonetheless, statistical significance has been used as a standard in the courts, and the method of allocation might end up making a difference here. In particular, we find that the allocation of mixed white-nonwhite people to minority groups can increase some of the socioeconomic characteristics of minority groups. Using 1990 data, we have found that allocation of mixed white-nonwhite individuals to the minority group tends to raise the socioeconomic profiles of the black and American Indian populations but to lower slightly the socioeconomic profile of Asian Americans. This could have consequences for employment discrimination cases, in which comparisons are being made not just by race but also by education level and other characteristics.

For now, the controversy about allocation is likely to center on only a few cases. In the future, as the multiracial population grows, the courts will presumably issue rulings, and lawmakers may modify existing legislation. A possible outcome of the uncertainty and controversy about tabulation may be a weakening of the statistical basis for enforcing existing civil and voting rights laws. In a climate of increasing opposition to racial classification and the use of racial statistics, it is hard to see how multiple-race responses and the problems associated with allocating back to single races will strengthen the case for race-based laws and public policies.

There is some danger that the OMB reallocation rules will automatically become the default method for treating multiple-race responses. As many have noted, official statistical classifications not only are a reflection of the broader society; they also have a tendency to take on a life of their own. As the multiracial population of the United States grows, it would seem unwise for the government to encourage the wholesale reclassification of the mixed-race population toward traditional minority populations. It is not that this particular result is necessarily undesirable but rather that such a decision should be set into motion after sufficient democratic discussion, not as an unintended consequence of a single administrative action. Ideally, the principle of self-identification should give mixed-race people the ability to identify with minority, majority, or multiracial groups. Allocation may be necessary for the enforcement of existing civil rights law, and the OMB guidelines explicitly limit allocation to such enforcement issues. Yet any application of the rules sets a precedent for the legal and statistical treatment of the multiracial population, one that may be difficult to undo in the years ahead.

Notes

1. As of this writing, the Bush administration has not announced whether it plans to revise the OMB guidelines. Since the release of OMB Bulletin 00-02, the Tabulation Working Group (OMB 2000) has issued additional guidance for tabulation, bridging methods, and collection of multiple-race data.

2. In practice, American Indian and Asian responses are not usually specified as "non-Hispanic" because the number of Hispanic responses in these racial cate-

gories is small. The allocation of Hispanic Asians and Hispanic American Indians to the Hispanic category is implicit.

3. The extra margin beyond 50 percent was meant to account for the younger age structure of minority populations and for differences in turnout.

4. It will also eventually be possible to use micro-data from the 2000 census to look at the ancestry ordering in multiple-race responses.

5. We select only multiracial groups with some white ancestry here because their allocation is more clear-cut under the OMB rules than that of other multiracial groups.

References

Byrd, Charles M. 2000. "The Political Realignment: A Jihad Against Race-Consciousness." *Interracial Voice* (September–October). Accessed October 2000 at: *www.webcom/intvoice/jihad.html.*

Davis, F. James. 1991. *Who Is Black? One Nation's Definition.* University Park: Pennsylvania State University Press.

del Pinal, Jorge, Leah M. Taguba, Arthur R. Cresce, and Ann Morning. 2001. "Reporting of Two or More Races in the 1999 American Community Survey." Working Paper 329. Annandale-on-Hudson, N.Y.: Jerome Levy Economics Institute of Bard College (May).

Edmonston, Barry, Joshua R. Goldstein, and Juanita Tamayo Lott, eds. 1996. *Spotlight on Heterogeneity: An Assessment of the Federal Standards for Race and Ethnicity Classification.* Washington, D.C.: National Academy of Sciences.

Edmonston, Barry, and Charles Schultze. 1995. *Modernizing the U.S. Census.* Washington, D.C.: National Academy Press.

Gans, Herbert J. 1999. "The Possibility of a New Racial Hierarchy in the Twenty-first-Century United States." In *The Cultural Territories of Race: Black and White Boundaries,* edited by Michèle Lamont. Chicago and New York: University of Chicago Press and Russell Sage Foundation.

Goldstein, Joshua R., and Ann J. Morning. 2000. "The Multiple-Race Population of the United States: Issues and Estimates." *Proceedings of the National Academy of Sciences* 97(11): 6230–35.

Graham, Susan, and James A. Landrith Jr. 2001. "Blood Pressure." *The Multiracial Activist.* Available at: *www.multiracial.com/news/bloodpressure.html.*

Grieco, Elizabeth M., and Rachel C. Cassidy. 2001. "Overview of Race and Hispanic Origin." Census 2000 Brief CENBR/01-1. Washington: U.S. Bureau of the Census (March).

Jones, Nicholas A., and Amy Symens Smith. 2001. "The Two or More Races Population: 2000." Census 2000 Brief C2KBR/01-6. Washington: U.S. Bureau of the Census (November).

McKay, Ruth B. 1996. "Cognitive Research in Reducing Nonsampling Errors in the Current Population Survey Supplement on Race and Ethnicity." *Statistics Canada Symposium 96*(November): 107–18. Ottawa: Statistics Canada.

Office of Management and Budget (OMB), Executive Office of the President.

1999. Tabulation Working Group of the Interagency Committee for the Review of Standards for Data on Race and Ethnicity. "Draft Provisional Guidance on the Implementation of the 1997 Standards for Federal Data on Race and Ethnicity." February 17.

———. 2000. *Guidance on Aggregation and Allocation of Data on Race for Use in Civil Rights Monitoring and Enforcement.* Bulletin 00-02. Washington (March 9). Accessed March 9, 2000 at: *www.whitehouse.gov/OMB/bulletins/ b00-02.html.*

Persily, Nathaniel. 2000. *The Real Y2K Problem: Census 2000 Data and Redistricting Technology.* New York, N.Y.: Brennan Center for Justice, New York University School of Law.

———. 2001. "Color by Numbers: Race, Redistricting, and the 2000 Census." *Minnesota Law Review* 85: 899–947.

U.S. Department of Commerce. U.S. Bureau of the Census. 2000. *Census 2000 Redistricting Data.* P.L. 94–171 Summary File. Washington.

Xie, Yu, and Kimberly Goyette. 1997. "The Racial Identification of Biracial Children with One Asian Parent: Evidence from the 1990 Census." *Social Forces* 76(2): 547–70.

5

INADEQUACIES OF MULTIPLE-RESPONSE RACE DATA IN THE FEDERAL STATISTICAL SYSTEM

Roderick J. Harrison

Humpty Dumpty was pushed off a wall.
Humpty Dumpty had a great fall.
All the Feds' Guidance and efforts to mend
Couldn't put Humpty together again.

HUMPTY" is, of course, the federal statistical system for classifying race and ethnicity for purposes of measuring and monitoring racial and ethnic differentials in the social, economic, health, education, housing, and other conditions of the population and, where appropriate, for investigating and determining which conditions result from discrimination that violates the civil rights of racial and ethnic minorities. The "push" was the revision of the Office of Management and Budget (OMB) directives for classifying race and ethnicity, mandating that all federal collections allow respondents to report more than one race. How to tabulate those responses for the various purposes for which the federal government collects and analyzes statistics by race and ethnicity is the challenge in putting Humpty together again.

The OMB established a research subcommittee to conduct empirical research that might inform its consideration of the recommended changes, which the OMB eventually adopted. I note for the record that I served with Clyde Tucker as cochair of that subcommittee. I was also a member of the OMB's Tabulation Group until I was removed so that the Census Bureau could "speak with one voice." I thus helped "push" Humpty and subsequently tried to help in mending him. I am no longer affiliated with the Census Bureau, and nothing in this chapter or in remarks that I might contribute to discussions should be misconstrued as reflecting Census Bureau positions or opinions.

The nation's official systems for classifying people by race and ethnicity date to the very establishment of the United States in its Constitution and have been implicit in every U.S. census that has ever been conducted, including the first in 1790. Historians and social scientists have made compelling arguments that statistics on race and racially based constitutional statuses like "slave" and "Indian not subject to taxation" were needed to help sustain systems that enslaved African Americans and expropriated the lands and territories of sovereign American Indian nations and tribes. However, it seems reasonable to argue that since the passage of civil rights legislation in the 1960s, the major use of data on race and ethnicity by the federal government has been to identify and monitor differentials in the conditions of the population by race and ethnicity and to develop or enforce policies designed to reduce or redress those differentials. This notably includes the enforcement of equal access to education, employment, housing, lending, health services, and the like in cases in which discriminatory practices might have denied equal access to all.

In any event, these activities of federal agencies heavily depend on statistical data on race and ethnicity and upon trends evident in these data. To say that the revisions to the classification system have pushed Humpty off the wall is to suggest that they have put the statistical infrastructure required by these efforts in some jeopardy. I argue that the system is, indeed, in serious jeopardy, especially for American Indians and Asians. Alternative tabulation procedures will generate different counts of—and, possibly, different characteristics of—these populations; and the differences are likely to be of sufficient magnitude that federal agencies will need defensible estimates of how these counts and characteristics would have been distributed absent the change in collection and tabulation methods.

This might be especially true in the monitoring and enforcing of civil rights, as parties on both sides of efforts to identify discriminatory patterns will doubtlessly insist—and rightly so—that the determinations depend not on statistical evidence or standards that reflect changes in the way data on race and ethnicity are collected and tabulated but rather on the patterns at issue. Employers, landlords, educational institutions, and health officials in a given locality are likely to object to being held to goals or standards for American Indians, Asians, or African Americans that are 10, 20, or 30 percent higher than they would have been without the methodological revisions. On the other side, those who feel they suffer from inequitable educational, employment, housing, or health conditions are also likely to insist that statistics showing improvements in these conditions not reflect new collection and tabulation methods rather than changes that would have been measured in these conditions absent the revisions.

These issues concern the bridge to the past—a bridge that might have to be constructed and crossed if the nation is to repair the possible damage that methodological revisions may cause to the statistical infrastructure needed to monitor and enforce civil rights and to track and address racial differentials in conditions within the population. A second set of issues concerns the bridge to the future. Some in the OMB process envision a future in which the data on at least some multiple-response combinations will meet the statistical standards of quality required for them to be presented as "official statistics" on these emerging populations. They anticipate that some data on multiple-race combinations will meet these standards, and the interim guidance presents several options for reporting data for these new groups.

The data released thus far in multiple-response and even multiracial categories may be of great interest and value for research on the changing formation of racial identity in the United States; but for the foreseeable future these data will be of dubious validity or meaning for measuring the social, economic, housing, or health characteristics of any nontautologically defined or independently observable population. To present multiple-response data as if it referred to meaningful multiracial populations, federal agencies would have to be willing to argue that the data on the child of one black and one white parent should count toward statistics on an "emergent" black-white population if and only if that child self-identifies as both black and white—not an argument that federal statistical policy should want or try to make. Moreover, it does not logically or necessarily follow that the data collected for the laudable purpose of giving respondents better options for reporting racial identities that might cross traditional categories will represent a meaningful population on which the federal government can validly report statistics.

The Bridge to the Past

In February 1999, the OMB issued a *Draft Provisional Guidance on the Implementation of the 1997 Standards for the Collection of Federal Data on Race and Ethnicity*. The document notes that in instituting the new standards, the OMB identified four areas requiring further research on how to tabulate data under the new standards:

- How should the data be used to evaluate conformance with program objectives in the area of equal employment opportunity and other anti-discrimination programs?
- How should the decennial census data for many small population groups with multiple racial heritages be used to develop sample designs and survey controls for major demographic surveys?
- How do we introduce the use of the new standards in the vital statistics program, which obtains the number of births or deaths from administra-

tive records, but uses intercensal population estimates in determining the rates of births and deaths?

• And more generally, how can we conduct meaningful comparisons of data collected under the previous standards with those that will be collected under the new standards? (OMB 1999, 9–10)

For reasons briefly broached at the beginning of this chapter, statistically defensible answers to all but the second question will almost certainly require, at some point in the process, an ability either to distinguish changes in the measures attributable to the introduction of revised methods for collecting or tabulating the data from changes in the phenomena themselves or to demonstrate that the changes introduced by the revised methods are insignificant enough that their effects on the phenomena measured can be ignored. Some passages in the *Provisional Guidance* suggest that in many important applications, the problems of comparability will be demonstrably negligible. For example, the discussion of redistricting and voting rights applications notes that

it is not expected that provision of the redistricting count data in the new format will lead to significant changes in redistricting practices or decisions. The new data categories will not affect the total population counts used for the apportionment of Congress, or for compliance with one-person, one-vote requirements. . . . Research also has indicated that, at least nationwide, there is unlikely to be a significant difference between the "single count" Black population and the "all-inclusive" Black population." (OMB 1999, 42)

In analyses of several sample surveys that collected multiple-race responses or multiracial category data—including the National Health Interview Surveys (NHIS) from 1993 to 1995, the May 1995 Current Population Survey (CPS) Supplement on Race and Ethnicity, and the Washington State Population Survey, all of which are examined in chapter 19 of this volume—evaluations of allocation schemes for bridging found important differences in the performance of the alternatives on various criteria. Nevertheless, the options examined produced few differences in selected indicators for health (no health insurance, poor or fair health, child of single mother) and employment (unemployment and labor force participation rates), and the largest apparent differences—for the American Indian unemployment rate—were not statistically significant (OMB 1999, 152–53).

As one might expect, however, American Indians and Asians are the groups most sensitive to the choice of allocation method, and are most likely to have high misclassification rates under at least some methods. This is an almost mathematically derivable consequence of relatively high ratios of multiple- to single-race responses in these relatively small U.S. populations, which have had relatively high intermarriage rates over long periods of time. Furthermore, the performance of the methods deteriorates in simulations "as the number of multiple race respondents increases, suggesting that the allocation methods to approximate the old standards may be of decreasing utility over time, especially in some areas of the country" (OMB 1999, 151).

This is perhaps not disturbing to one who expects the need for "bridge" estimates to be sufficiently transitory or finite. The *Provisional Guidance* suggests that "for some period of time, referred to as the bridge period, agencies may display historical data along with two estimates for the present time period. The first, a tabulation of the data collected under the new standard . . . and the second, a 'bridging estimate' or prediction of how the responses would have been collected and coded under the old standard. Once the bridge period is over, the bridge estimates will no longer be needed" (OMB 1999, 151). However, the considerably higher rates of multiple-race reporting that may occur with time are already with us in several localities of the country, especially for American Indians and Asians. In 1999, the American Community Survey (ACS) was conducted in twenty-one sites, most of them counties. The Census Bureau released summary tables from the 1999 sites in July 2000. The matrix for race presents all combinations of multiple responses, making it possible to calculate the population counts one would obtain for four race groups—American Indians and Alaska natives, Asians, blacks or African Americans, and Native Hawaiians and Other Pacific Islanders—at each site, using the allocation method specified in the *Guidance on Aggregation and Allocation of Data on Race for Use in Civil Rights Monitoring and Enforcement* issued in March 2000 (OMB 2000). The ratio of these OMB "civil rights" counts to the single-race counts for these groups were then calculated for each of these populations. The results are shown in table 5.1.

At six of the sites, the American Indian population constituted a share of the site's total population much larger than the 0.9 percent of the nation's population that American Indians represented in recent estimates (U.S. Bureau of the Census 2000). Using the OMB "civil rights" counts, the percentage of American Indians (including Alaska natives) at these six sites ranged from 1.7 percent in Multnomah County, Oregon, to 9.1 percent in Flat Head and Lake Counties, Montana. These sites provide examples of counties in which the American Indian population may well be large enough for local officials, planners, and perhaps even civil rights agencies to have real needs for data on the employment, education, housing, and health conditions of American Indians.

The "civil rights" counts of American Indians at four of these sites ranged from 25 to 45 percent higher than the single-race counts, which constitute the "official" counts of American Indians in the P.L. 94-171 Voting Rights file. The ratios are even larger—approaching two and three

TABLE 5.1   OMB "Civil Rights" Allocation to Single-Race Count and Percentage of Total Population for Selected Racial Groups, American Community Survey, 1999

Site	American Indian and Alaska Native		Asian		Black or African American		Native Hawaiian and Pacific Islander	
	Ratio	Percentage	Ratio	Percentage	Ratio	Percentage	Ratio	Percentage
Flathead and Lake Counties, Montana	1.27	9.1	1.08	0.7	1.32	0.1	1.00	0.08
Yakima County, Washington	1.31	6.1	1.42	1.4	1.34	1.2	1.88	0.10
Pima County, Arizona	1.25	4.0	1.11	1.9	1.07	3.9	2.12	0.10
Tulare County, California	1.45	2.6	1.06	3.8	1.07	2.6	1.10	0.30
Sevier County, Tennessee	1.99	2.0	1.44	0.9	1.64	0.4	—	0.00
Multnomah County, Oregon	1.94	1.7	1.11	5.9	1.06	7.3	1.47	0.54
San Francisco County, California	1.98	0.9	1.02	35.4	1.01	10.4	1.02	0.76
Calvert County, Maryland	2.95	0.9	1.08	1.5	1.01	19.6	0.00	0.06
Douglas County, Nebraska	1.58	0.8	1.06	1.4	1.04	11.9	1.46	0.05
Bronx Borough, New York	1.07	0.8	1.02	3.5	1.01	40.8	1.03	0.04
Jefferson County, Arkansas	2.60	0.7	1.13	0.3	1.01	46.5	0.00	0.01
Hampden County, Massachusetts	2.53	0.7	1.10	2.0	1.06	8.9	1.33	0.11
Black Hawk County, Iowa	3.16	0.5	1.16	0.8	1.10	7.9	1.09	0.18
Lake County, Illinois	1.88	0.5	1.08	3.4	1.03	7.2	3.26	0.02
Fort Bend and Harris Counties, Colorado	1.84	0.4	1.04	6.2	1.02	20.0	1.00	0.02
Broward County, Florida	1.63	0.4	1.11	2.1	1.02	18.6	1.19	0.03
Franklin County, Ohio	2.48	0.4	1.07	2.6	1.03	18.0	1.44	0.03
Star and Zapata Counties, Texas	1.00	0.3	1.00	0.1	—	0.0	—	0.00
Rockland County, New York	3.70	0.3	1.07	6.4	1.05	11.1	1.67	0.09
Madison County, Mississippi	1.33	0.2	1.00	1.0	1.00	46.2	0.00	0.06
Schuykill County, Pennsylvania	—	0.1	1.29	0.4	1.11	0.8	—	0.01

Source: Author's compilation.

Note: "Ratio" is the ratio of the OMB allocation for civil rights purposes to the single-race count. "Percentage" is the group's share of the total population in the site. The OMB "civil rights" allocation reassigns multiple-race respondents into single-race categories, based on a set of formulas laid out in OMB 2000.

times as many American Indians in the "civil rights" count as in the single-race count—for several of the sites at which the percentage of American Indians is about the national average of 1 percent. These sites include Sevier County, Tennessee; Multnomah County, Oregon; San Francisco County, California; and Calvert County, Maryland. Differences this large in the possible estimates of target populations for purposes of assessing equal opportunity in employment, education, or housing certainly raise serious possibilities that affected parties somewhere will question or challenge the fairness—and the statistical appropriateness—of using the numbers generated by the civil rights guidance.

Beyond civil rights issues, this wide a range in tabulation estimates (even wider if the "all inclusive" and single-race counts are compared) portends great challenges in selecting appropriate denominators for health and vital statistics. A denominator that overestimates the counts of American Indians relative to the count that would have been obtained under the previous collection system risks reducing birth and death rates, as well as disease and disease-specific mortality rates, for American Indians.

The ratios for Asians, though far smaller at most 1999 ACS sites, nevertheless provide "civil rights" counts that are at least 10 percent higher than the single-race counts in several sites in which Asians represent at least 2 percent of the population. These include Multnomah County, Oregon; Broward County, Florida; Hampden County, Massachusetts; and Pima County, Arizona. The counts are between 5 and 10 percent higher in Rockland County, New York; Tulare County, California; Lake County, Illinois; and Franklin County, Ohio. The Asian populations of the Rockland (6.4 percent), Multnomah (5.9 percent), Tulare (3.8 percent) and Lake (3.4 percent) County sites were proportionately larger than the Asian population of the United States in 1990 and hence represent relatively large communities for this group. The "civil rights" counts were 40 percent higher in Yakima County, Washington, and Sevier County, Tennessee, two sites with relatively smaller Asian populations (1.4 and 0.9 percent, respectively).

The "civil rights" and single-race counts of African Americans are much closer to each other at almost all of the sites in which African Americans constitute 10 percent or more of the population, falling within 6 percent of each other in all ten sites. However, the ratios grow to between 5 and 10 percent at all of the ACS sites except Lake County, Illinois, with relatively smaller black populations (2.6 to 8.9 percent of total population) and become quite large in Yakima County, Washington (34 percent higher), Sevier County, Tennessee (64 percent higher), and Flathead and Lake Counties, Montana (32 percent higher), where blacks constitute relatively small percentages of the population (1.2, 0.4, and 0.1 percent, respectively).

As might be expected, the ratios of "civil rights" to single-race counts of Native Hawaiians and Other Pacific Islanders are substantial at many sites with relatively high concentrations of this small population, including Multnomah County, Oregon (47 percent higher), Hampden County, Massachusetts (33 percent higher), Yakima County, Washington (88 percent higher), Pima County, Arizona (112 percent higher) and Rockland County, New York (67 percent higher). However, Native Hawaiians and other Pacific Islanders constitute less than 1 percent of the population at all these sites. If this group were combined with the Asian population to reconstitute the former Asian and Pacific Islander category for civil rights and trend applications, however, it would notably increase the ratio of "civil rights" to single-race counts for the combined group.

These comparisons of "civil rights" and single-race counts demonstrate that the multiple responses will create notable differences between these two alternative tabulations for American Indians and for Asians at many of the sites in which these populations represent relatively large percentages of the population by national standards. The two ways of counting the African American population produce much closer results, but at several sites the "civil rights" counts are still 5 to 10 percent higher than the single-race counts.

The actual impact of these differences might be mitigated considerably in some applications. For example, in all populations at the Sacramento Dress Rehearsal site except American Indians, the median age of those who provided multiple responses involving the group was under eighteen years, suggesting that the multiple responses were disproportionately concentrated among children. If this pattern held consistently across the ACS sites, one might find much smaller differences between "civil rights" and single-race counts, except perhaps for American Indians, in equal employment opportunity applications, in measuring educational attainments for the adult population (aged twenty-five years and older), and in efforts to assess the poverty or disability characteristics of the elderly population. On the other hand, the age concentration of multiple-race responses might correspondingly increase the difficulty of assessing racial imbalances in schools, differential performance on academic proficiency tests, and teenage unemployment.

The size of the differences might also be mitigated when multiple-response data are included in the numerators provided by employers, educational institutions, landlords, and others. However, employers will have data using the new classifications only for recent hires, unless they undertake a resurvey of their employees and update their personnel records. Moreover, there is reason to doubt that many who provided multiple responses in the census will do so consistently on other applications: preliminary estimates of consistency between interview and reinterview in the 1998 Dress Rehearsals were only around 50 percent—that is, only half of respondents again reported multiple races.

An adequate assessment of the vulnerability of federal statistical measures of racial differentials to multiple-race responses would require analyses of their effects on a full range of age, education, income and poverty, disability, and employment characteristics. The publicly available data from the 1999 ACS sites do not include cross-classifications of race by such characteristics. The critical information that such analyses might provide federal agencies on how multiple-race responses might affect 2000 census tabulations or denominators that they rely upon at local levels of geography must therefore await the release of either more extensive 1999 ACS tabulations or, preferably, analyses of internal ACS files by Census Bureau staff or specially sworn agents of the OMB tabulation work group.

While awaiting such tabulations and analyses, one might nevertheless urge federal agencies to take even these skimpy comparisons of "civil rights" and single-race counts at the ACS sites as what the already proverbial neologism terms a "wake-up call." The *Washington Post* quotes Census Bureau officials (perhaps erroneously) as being "comfortable" with the relatively small percentages of the populations at ACS sites reporting more than one race (D'Vera Cohn, "Census Race Question Has Limited Impact," July 20, 2000). The effects of multiple-race responses on the utility of race data in virtually all applications depends, however, not on the overall percentage of such responses in the total population but on the ratio of multiple- to single-race responses involving a given group. The problem is whether and how alternative tabulations of multiple responses will affect counts and characteristics for blacks, American Indians, Asians, non-Hispanic whites, and other race groups. The "bridge" section of the OMB's own *Provisional Guidance* does an excellent job of presenting and analyzing these group-specific effects (OMB 1999). Given this fact, assessments by federal agencies that take only the overall percentage into account are, at best, puzzling and scarcely provide a statistically appropriate or sound basis for expecting multiple-race responses to have only marginal or acceptable effects.

The group-specific ratios suggest, instead, that multiple-race responses create sufficiently large differences between "civil rights" and single-race counts of American Indians at most ACS sites, and possibly also of Asians at several sites, to require much more detailed information and analyses of their possible effects on researchers' ability to measure differentials for these groups in statistically defensible ways. The ratios also suggest that although counts of blacks have much narrower ranges under alternative tabulations, they too may fall within vulnerable ranges at specific sites. In civil rights applications, I would urge agencies to consider that the system might be only as strong as its weakest links: the entire system could fall owing to a few challenges in places where "civil rights" and single-race counts or characteristics are sufficiently different for courts to rule against the procedures issued in the civil rights guidance. That these cases might be unusual and atypical of the tabulation differences that arise elsewhere is not likely to save the guidelines, and there are strong reasons they should not: if civil rights guidelines cannot be applied equally everywhere in the country, then the rights of some people will be better protected—or less well protected—than those of others.

Two implications of the weakest-link argument should be made explicit. First, one might be reassured by the relatively small differences between the "civil rights" and single-race counts for blacks at most ACS sites, particularly given the importance of this group to civil rights enforcement. However, the most relevant cases for assessing the viability of the allocation method proposed under the civil rights guidance might well be those in the ACS and in the 2000 census, where the discrepancies are the largest and most consequential. Again, a successful challenge to the guidance might require only a case or two anywhere in the United States, however anomalous, where the allocation performs poorly.

Second, the weakest links will almost certainly lie in the "civil rights" counts for American Indians, and then for Asians, rather than for blacks. It is entirely possible that statistically strong and successful challenges to the guidance could arise in cases involving the "civil rights" counts of American Indians or of Asians in the relatively larger number of localities where counts will differ sharply from single-race counts, and the guidance methods would be struck down for all groups.

Officials from the Justice Department and other civil rights enforcement agencies may be able to provide valid reasons for not being too concerned about this possibility. (See, for example, the next chapter.) Some agencies may have few cases involving the civil rights of American Indians or of Asians that require statistical data, for example, or there may be reason to believe that courts might narrow the application of the guidance to cases in which the determination would not be affected by choice of tabulation method. Indeed, civil rights agencies may well determine not to file or support complaints whose decision might depend on the choice of tabulation method. However, if agencies find that the emergence of alternative counts creates new limits on their ability to pursue enforcement, either through court actions or through their own, then the OMB and the federal agencies should acknowledge the loss as a cost—perhaps unanticipated, perhaps acceptable—of revising the classification standards on race and ethnicity to permit multiple responses.

The problems that multiple responses cause for statistics on American Indians are often discounted by noting that many of these problems long predate the revisions in the standards. It is certainly true that our statistics for this group have been the least reliable in the system, and that growth in this population in recent decades has been more likely attributable to shifting self-identification than to natural increase or immigration. Statistics, such as for mortality rates, that use observer-identified race in the numerator and self-identified race in the denominator, have been especially unreliable for American Indians (Hahn, Mulinare, and Teutsch 1992). However, the tabulation method issued in the civil rights guidance may exacerbate the difficulties in defining and counting American Indians and highlight legitimate and serious problems with the tabulation method that OMB has chosen for civil rights allocations.

Indeed, American Indians are the population for whom the rule to tabulate the minority race is least supported by the data: tabulations of multiple responses of American Indian and white in the NHIS for 1993 to 1995, which used a follow-up question on the race with which respondents primarily identified, have found that 80.9 percent of respondents identified their primary race as white and only 12.4 as American Indian. The remaining 6.7 percent chose neither option. Almost one-half (46.9 percent) of those who reported their race as white and Asian and a quarter (25.2 percent) of those reporting white and black chose white as their primary race; another 18.4 percent of the former and 26.6 percent of the latter chose neither option. Insofar as the NHIS follow-up question on primary racial identification provides an indicator of how respondents would have reported absent the revisions to the collection and tabulation methods, the minority assignment rule correctly assigns only about half of respondents reporting as black and white, 34.6 percent of those reporting as Asian and white, and only 12.4 percent of those who identified as American Indian and white. To this same extent, the "civil rights" allocation inflates the counts of blacks, Asians, and especially American Indians over what might have been expected had the system not been changed.

The foregoing suggests that at the very least it would be prudent for civil rights agencies and the federal statistical system to have a "Plan B" for monitoring and enforcing civil rights in the event of a successful challenge to the "minority" tabulation rule issued in the civil rights guidance. The bridges most likely to produce statistically defensible estimates are those, like the NHIS and CPS data used in the "bridge" section of the *Provisional Guidance*, that can cross-tabulate data from a race question that permits multiple responses or multiracial identities with a question asked under the old standards that instructed respondents to report a single race or with a follow-up question that asks respondents with which of the multiple identities they primarily or most closely identify.

Empirical research on the NHIS and CPS (OMB 1999, 143–54) and of the National Longitudinal Study of Adolescent Health (Harris and Sim 2000) have shown that substantial percentages of those who report as white and one other race are not likely to have reported the minority race in either a follow-up questionnaire or in the past and that these percentages vary considerably with the combined races involved. The "civil rights" allocation nevertheless assigns all such responses to the minority race and therefore consistently overestimates the size of the minority populations that would have emerged absent the changes in collection methods. The census bridge survey, like the studies cited, would provide empirical estimates of the single races that multiple-race respondents provide when given a single-race question or primary identification follow-up, and it therefore can provide demonstrably better approximations of the distributions expected absent the revisions to the questions.

It is crucial for the sample for such a bridge study to provide statistically reliable estimates of the preferred or likely single-race responses for the largest multiple-race combinations at the county level, if at all possible, for counties in which the numbers reporting a combination involving a given group (for example, American Indian and white) exceed a given threshold (for example, 10 or 20 percent) of the single-race count of that population or of an age group within that population (for example, those under the age of eighteen). The issue here is that the preferred or past single-race distributions of multiple-race respondents might differ substantially even across counties within a state. For example, multiple-race respondents in a county that contains an American Indian reservation may be much more likely to report their primary or single-race identity as American Indian than residents of a metropolitan area who report they are American Indian and white or American Indian and black. Examining counties with high numbers and ratios of multiple- to single-race respondents for each major race group should help considerably in developing the sample design. It might also prove useful to identify the major tribes (including "none specified") involved in multiple responses in different counties and states or regions and also to specific Asian nationalities. Both the likelihood of multiple responses and preferred or past single-race responses are likely to vary with these characteristics.

The Bridge to the Future

Collecting "bridge" statistics for counties or county clusters in which the number and ratio of multiple- to single-race responses involving a given minority population were sufficiently large to significantly inflate estimates of that minority population (for example, at the 5 or 10 percent level) would go far toward providing the defensible estimates needed to monitor and enforce civil rights legislation and maintain statistics use for measuring trends in education, health, and social and economic conditions. Such statistics would thus ensure that Humpty could indeed be mended for the central purposes that justify the collection and analysis of federal statistics on race and ethnicity.

A second challenge that multiple responses pose for the integrity and viability of the system of federal statistics on race arises around the presentation and meaning of the data in the multiple-response categories. The implicit assumption underlying the previously cited passage, concluding that "once the bridge period is over, the bridge estimates will no longer be needed," is that each of the thirty-one possible combinations of the OMB minimum reporting categories is an equally valid and "official" race category—or should become one, once it represents a sufficiently large percentage of the responses or observations to meet an agency's standards for the quality and statistical reliability of published data and its confidentiality standards.

Another possible injury to Humpty is neither diagnosed or mentioned in the *Provisional Guidance* but might represent a chronic and progressive ailment. The problem, which can be classified as one of the quality or the very meaning of the data in a multiple-response category, is this: what independently definable and identifiable population does the category represent? What populations, for example, do responses of "white and black" or "white and Asian" represent?

Operationalism provides a simple, tautological answer: the population represented is those individuals who self-identify with these combinations of race groups. This is all well and good, but do the self-identified populations of "white and black" or "white and Asian" people represent groups that federal agencies can define or identify sufficiently well to justify collecting, presenting, and analyzing statistics on them? If the answer is yes, then for which of the many purposes that presently justify federal or state collections of data on race? For monitoring and enforcing civil rights? For measuring racial differentials in education, health, employment, and housing? In any of several applications that one could consider for the sake of discussion, could a federal agency justify a system that counts in the "white and black" or "white and Asian" populations those who self-identify in these groups but excludes from that count or measure people who have one white and one black or Asian parent but identify only a single race?

There are certainly contexts—including surveys or administrative records that ask people to report their race—in which it may be more appropriate to collect data in ways that allow respondents to report their race or races based on their self-identification. Indeed, this is the basis for the revision permitting multiple responses to the race question. However, it does not follow that data collected under this definition can provide viable or meaningful indicators of the conditions that most federal data on race and ethnicity are designed to measure or that the revised collection system can meaningfully address the questions that agencies must address in comparing or analyzing data on these populations.

Consider, for example, the arguments that civil rights agencies would be forced to defend if the federal statistical system bridged toward a future in which statistics on self-identified multiple-race groups were to be used to monitor and enforce civil rights. The agencies would have to affirmatively and explicitly argue, if pressed, that people who self-identify with two or more races should be counted in the data for that combined race group (for example, white and black or white and Asian) but that people who identified with only one race, though they had parents from the component races of the combination (for example, one white and one black or one white and one Asian parent), could not be included in the counts of the combined group for civil rights purposes. In other words, the methodology would then count as members of a white and black or white and Asian population those who self-identified with and reported those race combinations but would exclude those who could be defined as members of these populations based on their parentage or ancestry. Federal agencies then would tell employers, schools, bankers, and landlords that their offers of jobs, admissions, loans, and leases to people who self-identified as "black and white" could be presented as evidence that their practices toward this group is nondiscriminatory, but that their comparable offers to people who had one black and one white parent, and whom they may therefore have assumed belonged to the "black and white" population, could not.

Suppose, for the purposes of this discussion, that the potential discriminator assumes that an applicant belongs to a multiple-race population, basing that assumption on appearance, information drawn from personal essays, organizational memberships or activities, or observations or discourse during visits or interviews (which might involve family members in some school admissions, lending, and housing visits or applications) and not from a race question on the application itself. Indeed, many application processes collect data on the race of the applicant on a separate, voluntary document to permit analyses of the applicant pool without prejudicing initial reviews of the application. The potential discriminator could hypothetically know of several applicants who had parents of different races and might admit, or hire, or lend to them without respect to that mixed parentage. Nevertheless, if most or all of these applicants subsequently reported only a single race to the institution, they could not be counted as evidence that the institution's admissions, hiring, or lending policies toward relevant multiple-race populations were in fact and in practice nondiscriminatory.

A school, employer, landlord, or lender who wished to admit, hire, or lend or rent to multiple-race populations in proportions that civil rights agencies might approve would in fact have to ask applicants to self-identify so that this information could be considered in the decision. Such institutions would then be distinguishing among people whose parentage might define them as multiple race based upon the applicant's inclination to self-identify with multiple races instead of a single race—that is, based upon an applicant's *thoughts and opinions* about racial identification. In the end, trying to monitor and enforce civil rights for multiple-race populations defined solely by the self-identification of respondents would require schools, employers, lenders, and landlords to inquire into and make decisions on the thoughts and opinions of their applicants. It would shift the grounds for believing that a potential discriminator could reasonably have inferred an applicant's membership in a group that he or she has discriminatory tendencies toward from observable characteristics of the applicant (however unreliably correlated to the applicant's self-identification) to thoughts and ideas that he or she could consistently learn about only by explicitly questioning the applicant. Would we really want people's *thinking and choices* concerning racial identity to become the basis for admissions, hiring, lending, and renting decisions? Trying to monitor and enforce civil rights using data only on the self-identified multiple-race population might have just this effect.

Beyond this, it would make sense to treat behavior toward self-identified multiracial people, and not behavior toward the offspring of interracial couples, as relevant only if one also believed that it is the embracing and revelation of a multiracial identity, and not hostility toward miscegenation, that would trigger the discriminatory behavior. Accounts by people who identify as multiracial certainly report anger at their refusal to accept a single-race identity as a prime source of racial conflict and hostility toward them. However, it is just as clear that others, including people in positions of authority (for example, a South Carolina high school principal who barred an interracial student couple from attending a school prom together and, until recently, Bob Jones University), find miscegenation itself problematic or even "sinful." Such officials have been willing to defend these beliefs as explicitly and publicly as officials once did the need for racial segregation.

For both reasons, it is difficult to imagine civil rights agencies arguing that they could monitor and challenge discriminatory, disparate practices against a "white and black" or "white and Asian" population using data only on those who self-identify in those categories. Similar problems also make data exclusively from those who report multiple races of dubious value for measuring the educational, health, housing, or employment conditions of these populations and analyzing how these differ from the conditions for other groups. Once again, the problem is that the illnesses, reading scores, home-ownership rates, and occupations and earnings of persons with parents of two different races would contribute to the statistics for the multiple-race population (for example, white and black, white and American Indian) if the individual reported those multiple races, but not if he or she reported only one race. Thus, for example, a person who has one black and one white parent will be counted in the numerator and denominator of the cancer or coronary rate if that person self-identifies as "white and black" but not if that person self-identifies with only one of those races.

Similarly, people from historically "mixed" populations (for example, Cape Verdeans or Creoles) could count toward the rate if they self-identified with two or more races but not if they reported a single-race group, including "some other race."

Why is this a problem? Cancer rates or reading scores for multiple-race populations defined by parentage (for example, people with one white and one black or one American Indian parent or grandparent) have reasonably straightforward interpretations and can be readily compared with the corresponding statistics for other groups. Such statistics for a multiple-race population defined by parentage or ancestry could indicate whether persons with one black and one white parent (or various combinations of black and white grandparents) have higher or lower cancer rates than those whose parents were both black or both white (or all of whose grandparents were black or white) or whether they are reading at levels above or below their counterparts. More generally, such comparisons could be interpreted as answering questions about whether having possible membership, defined by parentage, in two or more "groups" opens options or generates outcomes different from those for people with parents or ancestors from only one group.

Users might assume that the data from the census and other federal collections will provide statistics that can be similarly interpreted and compared. Indeed, it is possible that the authors of the *Provisional Guidance* have assumed that the data on people who self-identify with two or more races is either equivalent or sufficiently analogous to the parentally defined population of two or more races for the statistics to be meaningfully used and interpreted in the same way. Our uses of racial statistics have implicitly assumed that those who report a single race either have parents of the same race or have lived in communities and faced conditions similar to those of single-race offspring even though their parents were of different races. It might then seem reasonable to assume that a similar assumption can be made that those who reported multiple responses provide reasonable proxies for the population of people with parents of different races.

All available evidence suggests otherwise, however. Only about half of the children in households in which the parents were of different races (itself a poor approximation of the population that may actually have parents of different races given divorces, remarriages, and single-parent households) reported more than one race in the May 1995 CPS Supplement on Race and Ethnicity to the Current Population Survey, the 1996 National Content Survey, and the 1996 Race and Ethic Targeted Test (RAETT).[1] This suggests that the offspring of interracial marriages may be about as likely to report (or to have reported by the actual respondent) a single race as they are to report multiple races.

As a consequence, substantial portions of the populations that one might expect to be represented in the multiple responses to the race question are probably not: they are "multiracial" by parentage but not by self-identification (or the identification of an adult responding to the census or survey). At the same time, others who reported multiple races may have done so on the basis of grandparents or more distant ancestors, and others on their membership in historically mixed populations or based on more general beliefs that their families or all populations are mixed. Questions designed to inquire into these and other reasons for reporting more than one race were included on the reinterview instruments for the National Content Survey and the Race and Ethnic Targeted Test, but to my knowledge this data has never been tabulated and provided to the OMB's Tabulation Working Group. In their reports on the these two surveys, the Census Bureau promised to analyze and release results from the reinterviews in more complete "final" reports. This work was never conducted, and the light that it might have shed on the composition of the population reporting more than one race in these surveys and in the 2000 census will never be cast.

The numbers and characteristics of those who reported specific combinations of more than one race in the 2000 census and subsequent federal surveys are therefore likely to bear complex and at this point unknown relationships to the counts and characteristics of multiple-race populations that might be defined by parentage or ancestry. One cannot assume that the data can be treated or interpreted as a reasonable proxy for the data one might obtain for the multiple-race population defined by parentage without at least gathering evidence that among those with parents of two specific different races, those who reported those multiple races and those who reported a single race did not differ on the characteristics or conditions under consideration. Under such conditions (and ignoring the problems potentially arising from those who reported more than one race on bases other than parentage or ancestry), data on those who did identify with more than one race could be presented and interpreted as an adequate indicator of the characteristics and conditions of those who did not.

In the absence of such evidence and assumptions, it is difficult to define or determine just what population the self-identified multiple-race responses represent beyond the tautological and therefore uninformative population of those who reported more than one race. It is, a fortiori, even more difficult to imagine what cancer rates, reading scores, or poverty rates calculated from these responses would represent and how they could be interpreted and compared with the rates for other race and ethnic groups. Lower coronary rates or higher reading scores for those who reported as black and white than for those who reported as black could not be interpreted as meaning that the offspring of one black and one white parent have lower risks for heart diseases or higher reading proficiency than the offspring of two black parents. The rates and scores for the offspring who identify with two or more races may well differ from the those of offspring who identify with a single race, particularly if the likelihood of choosing multiple- over single-race identification is related to education, income, or neighborhood characteristics that affect risk behaviors for heart disease or access to higher-quality education. Where such differences exist, the data from those who reported as black and white would provide misleading indicators for the population that has one black and one white parent and hence also misleading comparisons with other race groups.

Nowhere in the *Provisional Guidance* does the Office of Statistical Policy acknowledge that the statistics for the self-identified multiple-race populations do not provide good proxies for those that might be obtained from defining these populations by parentage or ancestry; nor does it explicitly define what populations the multiple responses represent. It may not recognize this problem, or it may think that despite the problems, the multiple responses provide informative and useful measures for some as yet undefined (and nontautologically defined) population. If so, the Office of Statistical Policy has a professional obligation to explain just how it thinks those statistics should be appropriately used and compared with statistics for the other groups. It is far from clear how these statistics should be interpreted to be meaningful or useful for the questions that statistics on race have been primarily designed to address. If the Office of Statistical Policy or other federal agencies are going to report such data, they ought to be able to tell users and the public how they think it can be meaningfully used to address the issues that data presented in the same table has typically helped us understand.

The question is neither an idle nor an academic one: prominent advocates of revising the single-race classification standards did so not only to establish their right to report as they identify themselves, but also because they expect the new standards to produce data showing how multiracial populations compare with the single-race groups' characteristics that federal statistics have long permitted researchers to measure. For example, an advocacy group for multiracial causes that decries the "total lack of information about health risks and trends in public health statistics for the multiracial population" notes that "the U.S. Department of Health and Human Services can tell us NOTHING about health risks or trends in public health statistics for multiracial children and adults, although they have studied every other racial and ethnic group" (Project RACE, n.d.).

Should any professional statistician or health official in the Department of Health and Human Services, then, tell Project RACE and the public that they will soon be providing estimates for these and other diseases or health risks for the "black and white" and the "Asian and white" or the "two or more races" populations? Should they tell Project RACE and the public that we can now compare these diseases or health risk with those for "every other racial and ethnic group" in the table? The discussions in the *Provisional Guidance* on when and how to present the data for multiple-response categories, and the vision of "bridge" statistics representing a transition to a future in which reporting in multiple-response categories becomes sufficiently large to report the statistics for more of these "emergent" groups, suggest that the answer would be a naive and resounding yes, representing the federal government's commitment to recognizing the growing diversity to which multiple-response groups contribute.

This chapter has raised doubts that multiple-response data can, or should, be presented as if it represented multiple-race populations defined by parentage or ancestry and has noted that a challenging program of research would have to be undertaken and completed if one hoped ever to determine the relationship between the two. The multiple-response data might represent populations beyond the tautologically defined population that provided multiple responses. If it does, however, the OMB's Office of Statistical Policy and its *Provisional Guidance* have yet to define or even discuss what that population might be. Until then, the effort that the guidance devotes to discussing ways to present data that currently has no well-defined meaning seems illogical and misplaced. At the very least, the OMB and federal agencies should refrain from implying that the multiple-race data that will be collected under the revised standards can provide statistically defensible estimates of the cancer or coronary rates, or the reading scores and poverty or home-ownership rates, for a present or future "white and black" or "white and Asian" race group. The OMB and the agencies should probably refrain from presenting, in the same tabulations with other groups, data for which it cannot define a meaningful—that is, nontautological—referent population. If, for reasons that would have to go beyond statistical policy, the OMB and federal agencies choose to present statistics on the multiple-response population in tabulations for race and ethnic populations, they should also explicitly warn users that the multiple-response statistics should not be compared with those for the other groups. In addition, they should confess to Project RACE and the public that the federal system can provide neither the health, education, employment, housing, and other statistics for multiple-race populations that it has provided for "every other racial and ethnic group" nor professionally responsible and defensible answers to the questions that Project RACE asks.

If the multiple-response data cannot provide reliable statistics on multiple-race or multiracial populations that can be meaningfully and usefully compared with those of other racial populations, then how, beyond providing counts of multiple-race responses, does it really help us better represent and understand the growing racial and ethnic diversity of the nation? The questions raised in this chapter, if valid, suggest that simply allowing people to report more than one race does not provide data that can represent these populations as they would be defined by parentage or ancestry. Nor can it represent any meaningful—that is, nontautologically defined—population in the United States. The decision to revise the standards on race and ethnicity to permit multiple responses to the race question can be defended, and even lauded, on the grounds that it allows respondents to federal data collections to report as they self-identify themselves and thereby substantially reduces the degree to which the federal government imposes upon them definitions of who they are. The problems identified here suggest that multiple-response data on race, as it has been collected in the census and will be in other federal collections by 2003, presently fall far short of helping us understand any nontautologically defined population in the United States. Such data are therefore at best useless and at worst deceptive and misleading for describing or comparing the characteristics and conditions of multiracial or multiple race populations with those of other groups.

If the revision of the standards were intended to actually provide data on the characteristics and conditions of multiple-race populations in the United States comparable with that long collected on other racial and ethnic populations, and if the arguments presented here are valid, one might well wonder why the OMB and the federal agencies have failed so miserably in accomplishing this objective. The likely answer is that the revision was not undertaken because federal agencies or others in the process saw a need for such data or for an ability to compare the characteristics and conditions of multiple-race populations in the United States with those of the racial and ethnic populations on which it has collected and analyzed data in recent decades. Had this been the objective, it is very likely that professionals in the agencies could have pointed out the problems outlined here and suggested that data on multiple-race populations defined by parentage, ancestry, or other criteria, yet to be proposed, would be more useful for such comparisons and analyses than data based solely on self-identification.

Instead, the multiple-response data was collected primarily—and perhaps only—to allow respondents to report their race or races in accordance with the way they identify themselves. There is little or nothing in the July 1997 report and recommendations of the research subcommittee that provided the basis for the OMB's decisions, or in the *Provisional Guidance,* to suggest that the need for or value of data on multiple-race populations comparable with that for other groups was even a serious consideration in the evaluation or decision-making process. Once the decision was made, the only definition for racial and ethnic populations available was that based on their self-identification. The fact that data based on self-identification has been accepted (with perhaps too little critical evaluation) as a proxy for the groups one would have identified by parentage or ancestry under the single-race paradigm perhaps obscured the importance of the tabulations showing that perhaps only half of the children in families with parents (or stepparents) of different races reported multiple races in the surveys examined to inform the decisions.

Defining race and ethnicity based on self-identification has compelling advantages if one believes, as virtually all social and biological scientists do, that these are social constructs—and that there are no "true" white, or black, or "white and black" populations independent of those constructs. If this is true, then the individual respondent may well be the best arbiter of which of several available descriptors are most appropriate or accurate for identifying his or her "true" race and ethnicity. In this sense, defining racial and ethnic populations by self-identification might be deemed scientifically preferable to other bases for defining or measuring these constructs, including parentage.

In the eyes of most philosophers of science, however, nowhere in science, not even in physics or chemistry, are there definitions that can be said to be "objectively" true or correct or preferable to others independent of the theories and paradigms within which they are embedded (Kuhn 1970; Wallace 1971). They are scientifically "true" or preferable only in the very relative sense that, combined with other definitions, assumptions, theories, and methods, they have proved demonstrably more useful than others for guiding and advancing research concerning the phenomena that they are designed to explain. That relativity is underscored by the fact that they are regularly supplanted and superseded by new definitions, in new systems of concepts and assumptions, when they prove more useful or powerful in studying or explaining those phenomena.

The purposes for which federal agencies collect and analyze data on race and ethnicity must be an integral consideration in efforts to select definitions and tabulation strategies that will help meet those research needs and objectives. The purposes for which we have sought to define and measure "race" and "ethnicity" in the post-civil-rights federal statistical system are relatively limited and increasingly debated. They have been to measure differences in a wide range of social, economic, health, justice, and housing conditions among the "race" and "ethnic" groups that we define and construct, and to examine where these differences might represent inequalities and inequities arising from the past, and perhaps continuing discrimination and exclusion of these "groups" from full equality with other "groups" in our society. The historical and possibly ongoing discrimination against these groups has in critical ways been based on and exercised through social constructions of their racial or ethnic group membership defined primarily through their presumably identifiable descent from parents or ancestors who were similarly identified by potential discriminators as members of groups stigmatized as inferior, in various expressed ways, to the groups excluding them from full and equal participation in society. The currently available paradigm has assumed—again, with insufficient critical examination—that self-identified race and ethnicity provide sufficiently good proxies for membership in these populations as defined by potentially discriminating observers and by parentage and ancestry, at least for purposes of analyzing the differences between these groups and, where appropriate, for enacting and enforcing policies designed to reduce or redress inequities that contribute to the differences.

This assumption breaks down when one tries to define multiple-race populations solely on the basis of self-identification, precisely because large portions of the population who can reasonably be defined as multiracial by observers or by parentage and ancestry self-identify with a single race. To develop a new paradigm around self-definition to replace the current paradigm requires far greater attention to the problems and challenges that would have to be resolved than the civil rights guidance currently gives. These serious and difficult problems would have to analyzed, studied, and resolved before one could responsibly talk about bridging to a period in which multiple responses could be treated as representing groups in a manner equivalent or comparable, for the sorts of analyses and tabulations generated by federal agencies, to the data on the race groups collected before the revision of the racial and ethnic classifications. There is little indication that the OMB's Office of Statistical Policy recognizes this. Indeed, in systems in which "policy" often regresses to little more than attempts to justify and defend the behavior and decisions of incumbent policy makers, it may be difficult for the OMB to give serious consideration to the possibility that the data on multiple responses, which it collected for the very good purpose of allowing more people to report the race or races they feel best describe themselves, might not be useful or meaningful for the uses for which federal agencies have and need to collect data on race and ethnicity.

It seems unlikely that serious professionals engaged in health, education, employment, or housing research would publicly argue that statistics that include the offspring of interracial marriages when they self-identify two or more races but exclude people with the same parentage when they do not are comparable to the data collected and provided for other racial and ethnic populations or are useful for the types of tabulations and analyses provided for those populations. If there are grounds for supporting such arguments, they have yet to be advanced. It seems more likely that such arguments might only hold the Office of Statistical Policy and federal statistical agencies open to ridicule among professionals working on these issues.

More is at stake, however, than the professional reputations of the statistical agencies—although one would think that this itself would be more highly valued. The same arguments and positions, advanced in a civil rights context, would almost certainly provide strong ammunition to institutions and a public that is growing increasingly resistant to statistical or numerical "standards" for assessing progress toward equality of opportunity. This chapter has also argued that the OMB's civil rights guidance leaves the entire statistical mechanism for monitoring and enforcing civil rights vulnerable to successful challenge in courts for systematically inflating counts of minorities above what they would have been absent the revision to the standards. The nation certainly should determine, through public discourse, the Congress, and the courts, whether it still wishes to monitor and enforce equal opportunity legislation using the current methods and systems of assessing disparate impact, or should instead make use of alternative approaches and policies that may have become more appropriate. However, the system should not crumble because federal statisticians, in a legitimate and even laudable effort to allow respondents to identify their race as they themselves see it, were insufficiently cognizant of or professionally committed to understanding the full ramifications of their revisions. Unless and until the responsible agencies explicitly and carefully address these potential problems—many of which they might show are nonproblematic or resolvable—they are placing that system in jeopardy.

Note

1. Unpublished tabulations presented in meetings of the Tabulation Working Group of the Interagency Committee for the Review of Racial and Ethnic Standards (Tabulation Working Group 1997).

References

Hahn, Robert, J. Mulinare, and S. Teutsch. 1992. "Inconsistencies in Coding of Race and Ethnicity Between Birth and Death: A New Look at Infant Mortality in the United States, 1983–1985." *Journal of the American Medical Association* 267: 259–63.

Harris, David R., and Jeremiah Joseph Sim. 2000. "An Empirical Look at the Social Construction of Race: The Case of Mixed-Race Adolescents." Research Report 00–452. Ann Arbor, Mich.: Population Studies Center, University of Michigan.

Kuhn, Thomas. 1970. *The Structure of Scientific Revolutions*. Chicago: University of Chicago Press.

Office of Management and Budget (OMB), Executive Office of the President. 1997. Tabulation Working Group of the Interagency Committee for the Review of Racial and Ethnic Standards. Unpublished tabulations.

———. 1999. *Draft Provisional Guidance on the Implementation of the 1997 Standards for the Collection of Federal Data on Race and Ethnicity.* Washington (February 17).

————. 2000. *Guidance on Aggregation and Allocation of Data on Race for Use in Civil Rights Monitoring and Enforcement.* Bulletin 00-02. Washington.

Project Race. N.d. "The Health Status of Multiracial Americans Fact Sheet." Project Race. Accessed May 28, 2002 at: *www.projectrace.com/urgentmedicalconcern.*

U.S. Bureau of the Census. 2000. "Resident Population Estimates of the United States by Sex, Race, and Hispanic Origin: April 1, 1990 to July 1, 1999, with Short-Term Projection to November 1, 2000." U.S. Census Bureau, Washington, D.C.

Wallace, Walter. 1971. *The Logic of Science in Sociology.* Chicago: Aldine.

6

THE LEGAL IMPLICATIONS OF A MULTIRACIAL CENSUS

Nathaniel Persily

BECAUSE it destabilizes established notions and measures of race, the move to a census race question that allows for multiple responses presents novel challenges for social scientists and policy makers. The chief effect of the new format for racial data, however, may be determined as much in the courtroom as in the computer lab. Lawyers and judges, to a large extent, will help decide the societal impact of this new means of expressing racial identity.

Although the short-term legal implications will most likely be minor, the shift in census format from a single response to multiple expressions of racial identity may represent a turning point, as Kenneth Prewitt suggests, in the way Americans conceive of and measure race and also in the way lawyers prove racial discrimination. Racial data, from the census and elsewhere, frequently make their way into litigation whenever a plaintiff seeks to prove that a law, policy, or even private action has had a discriminatory effect on a given racial group. Such discrimination claims may become more challenging to prove as the number of racial categories proliferates and the size of several single-race groups diminishes. The more complicated and debatable the description of a community's racial makeup becomes, the more difficult it may be to use racial data to prove the adverse effects of certain policies on racial groups. Moreover, rules developed to cope with this new complexity—to reaggregate multiracial data back into a single racial format, for example—create their own set of potential legal problems arising from race-based assumptions as to who "really belongs" in which racial category.

The new multiracial format for census data will have some effect on any case in which a legal claim depends on the size of a racial group's population. This chapter discusses three categories of cases. The first type consists of discriminatory impact cases, in which the plaintiff alleges that an employer, the government, or some other defendant has discriminated against him or her on the grounds of race. To prove discrimination the plaintiff compares the racial composition of the advantaged or disadvantaged population to the racial composition of the background population. If the plaintiff can demonstrate a dramatic disparity—for example, if an employer in a heavily African American area hires very few African Americans—the defendant may then bear the sometimes difficult burden of proving that such a disparity arises as a result of something other than discriminatory policies. The second category of cases involves compliance with certain goals or timetables in achieving an appropriate racial composition of the relevant population. In affirmative action and school desegregation cases, for example, courts will often pay attention to racial data to determine whether the relevant governmental unit has successfully integrated its workforce or student population. The final category of cases arises in the context of legislative redistricting under the Voting Rights Act. More than any other area of the law, such litigation makes use of census race data—for example, to force the creation of a legislative district of a certain racial composition. All claims of race-based vote dilution depend on some theory about how the given racial population was packed into one district or split among several, such that the racial minority was unable to elect its candidate of choice.

The different methods of aggregating multiracial data back into a single-race format also present novel legal challenges. Other contributors to this volume have described the Office of Management and Budget's aggregation rules as a new incarnation of the historic "one-drop rule." Judges who will confront the OMB or other aggregation rules in the course of civil rights litigation will need to decide whether the Constitution prevents reaggregation of multiracial census data back into a single-race format. Opponents of the aggregation rules argue that such rules create an unconstitutional presumption that multiracial individuals *really* belong to one of the single race categories.

Although the new format of the census race question poses a series of new legal questions, the number of discrimination claims in the near term that will turn on the new format or how multiracial individuals are counted is relatively small. The overwhelming majority of race discrimination claims are brought by African Americans, who have a low rate of multiracial response on the census, and Hispanics, who are unaffected by the multiracial categorization because they are counted as an ethnicity, not as a race. Moreover, of the universe of race discrimination claims, the ones that turn on racial data are also a small subset, and though some aggregation rules might conceivably raise constitutional questions, not all of them will. The differences between impermissible and permissible modes of reaggregation of the multiracial subset of a racial group will often "come out in the wash" of litigation, so to speak, when other issues submerge reaggregation in importance.

Before discussing these legal problems and scenarios in detail, it should be stated at the start that one needs to tweak the 2000 census data and hypothesize sometimes absurd circumstances in order to highlight the possible problems the new multiracial format could independently cause. Racial statistics are one component of often complicated and drawn-out presentations of evidence in civil rights litigation. Well before the most recent change in racial categorization, the question of which racial statistics should be used often became a subject of vigorous disagreement in court. The new multiracial format for census data adds one more layer of complexity and one more subject for disagreement, but by concentrating on this subject, one should not assume that the use of race statistics was problem-free before the "multiracial question" became relevant.

When Multiraciality "Matters"

The process of racial classification employed by the census does not raise any significant legal issues by itself. As the Office of Management and Budget (OMB) and the Census Bureau remind us at every opportunity, the process of checking off one's race is grounded in a theory of self-identification. The compilation of individual responses at larger and larger levels of aggregation (census blocks, block groups, political subdivisions, and so on) merely represents a collective registration and expression of individual self-identification.[1] Legal issues arise, if ever, when the census race data become evidence used to prove an argument in court or support a finding for a policy.

Because misconceptions about the types of legal claims arising out of the new race data appear to be widely held, let me begin by emphasizing the obvious: no individual has a personal claim arising out of how he or she was categorized by the census. In other words, someone who checks off both "black" and "white" on the census form but is intentionally or erroneously counted as "black" does not suffer a cognizable injury that a court can redress. Although the Constitution requires the taking of a census, it does not give individuals a "right to be counted" or a right to be counted honestly and accurately. The Census Bureau's failure to count an individual accurately does not injure that individual, for the same reason that the National Bureau of Labor Statistics does not injure someone if it counts him or her as unemployed when in reality that person has a job.[2]

However, census data, like all official government statistics, have definite legal consequences based on how the government or individuals use those statistics. As others in this volume have noted in greater detail than is warranted here, the new format has led to the creation of sixty-three possible racial combinations (126 if the Hispanic-origin question is included in the computation). For lawyers, like everyone else who uses the data, the exponential increase in categories creates complexity where previously there was relative simplicity. Lawyers and judges are not immune from the problems identified by social scientists in this volume. Their lives, too, will be made somewhat more difficult by the wholesale change from the data format that preceded it and by new challenges that arise from the need to deal with these additional layers of complexity.

The new multiracial-response format "matters" for the law principally because certain legal claims and arguments depend on the size and characteristics of racial minority groups. Census race data form a benchmark against which subsets of the general population are then compared to see if they "measure up." Only if we know how many African Americas live in a given area, for example, can we advance arguments about how many African Americans we should expect in some other context—a congressional district, a school's student population, or a factory's workforce.

The key impact of the new format on the law derives from its effect on the size of minority group populations as they are expressed in the census. With the opportunity for respondents to express fully their racial identities, did the Asian American share of the population increase or decrease with the recent census? The question implies an agreed-upon definition of who is an Asian American. Is the category limited to the 10.2 million people who checked only "Asian," or does it include the additional 1.7 million people who checked both "Asian" and another race? Depending on one's answer, the count of the Asian population could grow or shrink by 15 percent. Are there 2.5 million American Indians and Alaska natives in the United States or 4.1 million? Whether multiracial respondents are counted as members of that group could shift the number by as much as 65 percent. Admittedly, under either a minimalist or maximalist categorization scheme, Asians and American Indians together account for only 4.5 to 5.7 percent of the national population, but in certain areas of the country each group's numbers represent a greater population share, and their relative numbers (at least with regard to Asians) may be growing.

"Who counts as what?" is not a mere academic question, however. It forms the baseline assumptions about "who deserves and is entitled to what." Civil rights litigation is, in part, about ensuring that members of different racial groups receive equal treatment and are not deprived of opportunities to compete for their equal share. Although a guarantee of equal results is never a constitutional requirement and usually represents a constitutional problem, assessing a group's share of the population is often a much-needed first step in understanding whether unfair or unconstitutional barriers have been placed in its way. As the cases discussed here reveal, identifying the existence or absence of discrimination requires some agreement as to the background racial contours of the general population. The addition of multiracial combinations to the census makes such agreement less likely.

Types of Lawsuits Affected by the New Multiracial Categorization

Any lawsuit that depends on an argument derived from census data about the size and characteristics of a racially defined community will be affected by the new format of the race question. I address three such categories of lawsuits here: disparate impact cases; compliance with goals and timetables, particularly in the area of desegregation and affirmative action; and the unique setting of challenges to legislative districting schemes under the Voting Rights Act. For the first two categories, another word of caution is in order. Although race data are central to the litigation, disparate impact and compliance cases rarely use race data provided by the census. The parties or enforcement agencies usually rely on other sources of data (for example, student records, employee applications, or a special data set developed by an expert witness), or the parties construct the relevant data set themselves. I include a discussion of these categories here for two reasons. First, many of the noncensus data sets used in such lawsuits will also use a multiracial checkoff option similar to that employed on the 2000 census.[3] Second, whichever race-based data set is used for litigation, the multiracial "issue" will become more prevalent in coming years. The problems with categorization may arise largely from the format of the census race question, but they also come from what those questions attempt to capture: that is, the rising number of Americans who identify with more than one race.

Disparate Impact Cases

Most laymen find race discrimination an easy concept to define. At its core, the concept refers to the treatment of individuals differently on account of their race. This relatively simple concept becomes infinitely complex in application, however. The fact that a given policy or decision adversely affects members of a given racial group is generally insufficient, by itself, to prove racial discrimination. After all, random, unintentional behavior or quite legitimate reasons may underlie policies that end up affecting one racial group more than another. The difficulty arises in separating impermissible modes of discrimination from permissible ones. In most cases that difficulty translates into whether the law ought to require discriminatory intent as well as effect. Discrimination claims brought under the Equal Protection Clause require proof of discriminatory intent and impact,[4] whereas a prima facie case of discrimination under various civil rights statutes can sometimes be shown based only on a showing of disparate impact.[5]

Proving discriminatory impact often involves some statistical showing as to how many members of the plaintiff's racial group were affected by a policy and how large a share they constitute of the population. Census data or (more commonly) other statistics describing the racial composition of the population help establish the expectations as to what the racial composition of a work force, housing complex, or some other "treatment" population should be. Thus, if census data reveal a community population that is half Native American but the employer's work force is only 25 percent Native American, the disparity between the work force and the population may give rise to an inference of discrimination. Of course, legitimate non-discriminatory reasons may explain the disparity. But the civil rights statutes sometimes require that the defendant demonstrate what those reasons are and explain why such a discriminatory impact flowed from necessary business policies. To take one real-world example, the Court in Griggs v. Duke Power (401 U.S. 424 [1971]),[6] found illegal discrimination in an intelligence test, which whites passed at a higher rate than African Americans and which, as compared to alternatives, represented a poor indicator of prospective job performance. In finding discriminatory impact, the Court noted the dramatic disparity between the percentage of African Americans in the applicant pool and population, and the percentage that passed the intelligence test.[7] That disparity forced the employer to justify the intelligence test on grounds of business necessity, a burden it could not satisfy.

In addition to claims brought under the civil rights statutes, race statistics often play an important role in discrimination cases brought under the Constitution. Discrimination in jury selection provides a case in point. Although no defendant is constitutionally entitled to a jury with a racial breakdown proportionate to the surrounding community, an unrepresentative jury pool could give rise to an inference of unconstitutional discrimination. If the state cannot rebut that inference by articulating unbiased reasons for the "tainted" jury, a violation of the Equal Protection Clause could be shown. Census race data are frequently used in jury cases to demonstrate the racial composition of the population from which a jury would be selected.[8] In Castaneda v. Partida (430 U.S. 482 [1977]), the Court explained the mode of analysis and the relevance of demographic data:

> In order to show that an equal protection violation has occurred in the context of grand jury selection, the defendant must show that the procedure employed resulted in substantial underrepresentation of his race or of the identifiable group to which he belongs. The first step is to establish that the

group is one that is a recognizable, distinct class, singled out for different treatment under the laws, as written or as applied. . . . Next, the degree of underrepresentation must be proved, by comparing the proportion of the group in the total population to the proportion called to serve as grand jurors, over a significant period of time. . . . Finally, as noted above, a selection procedure that is susceptible of abuse or is not racially neutral supports the presumption of discrimination raised by the statistical showing. . . . Once the defendant has shown substantial underrepresentation of his group, he has made out a prima facie case of discriminatory purpose, and the burden then shifts to the State to rebut that case. (Castaneda v. Partida, 430 U.S. 482, 494–95 [1977], citations omitted)

To make a showing of discriminatory effect or disparate impact, therefore, one must have a baseline against which to judge the benefited or disadvantaged population.

The new multiracial data format could introduce some uncertainty and variation in evaluating the proper benchmark. Before the multiracial checkoff was introduced, statistics were always contested, but usually there existed greater agreement as to which individuals in the background population or applicant pool shared the plaintiff's race, such that they should be counted in the benchmark statistic used to measure the alleged disparity. Two problems now arise. First, the move to the multiple-race checkoff option has drained some single-race categories of many of their "members." Second, courts and parties to the litigation must now decide who should be counted in the benchmark statistic—individuals who just checked off the plaintiff's race or also those who checked off that race plus another one.

To make the point with the worst-case scenario, consider what could happen if a Hawaiian corporation were the defendant in an employment discrimination suit. One of the race categories on the 2000 census form is "Native Hawaiian or Other Pacific Islander." According to the data revealed by the Census Bureau, only 113,539 people in Hawaii, just 9.4 percent of the state's population, checked that category alone. However, 169,128 people, 13.9 percent of the state's population, checked off that category plus another one. Thus, 23.3 percent of the state's population checked "Native Hawaiian or Other Pacific Islander" either alone or in combination with another race. Which percentage, 9.4 or 23.3, should serve as the benchmark for judging the discriminatory effect of a Hawaiian corporation's employment practice? If the workforce is 10 percent "pure" Native Hawaiian and 90 percent white, does a "pure" Native Hawaiian have a claim? Would a "mixed" Native Hawaiian have a claim? What if the workforce were 25 percent mixed Hawaiian but there were no "pure" Hawaiians; would there then be any claim? How a court counts the multiracial population could affect its assessment of the discriminatory impact of the corporation's hiring policies.

There are plenty of problems with the foregoing hypothetical, of course, but the point remains that legal claims often depend on assumptions about the background racial composition of a community.[9] Those assumptions derive from race data provided by the census or some other source. The proliferation of racial categories introduces some uncertainty and complexity into the process of establishing the baseline against which to judge discriminatory impact by producing a new set of arguments over "who counts as what." These complexities are not insurmountable. Aggregation rules such as the ones discussed later in this chapter, as well as others that might be relevant to a given factual context, could go a long way toward reducing the complexity inherent in the litigation. To some extent the new data format may simply lead plaintiffs to tailor their claims to the new data format. Whereas previously an African American plaintiff may have contended that the employer "discriminates against African Americans," now the plaintiff will contend (if it is in his or her interest) that the employer "discriminates against anyone who is at least part African American." A court is still likely to consider such discrimination, if proven, as race-based and against a "protected class" and, therefore, prohibited by the civil rights statutes or the Constitution.

Compliance with Goals of Desegregation and Affirmative Action

Race data can be used not only to support an inference of discrimination but also to set goals and to measure compliance with government measures designed to foster integration. Perhaps the two most contentious arenas of race-based goal setting are school desegregation and affirmative action. In both of these contexts, the question, once again, is whether the jurisdiction, government entity, or private actor "measures up": whether it has created a racial balance in the relevant employee or student pool that does not stray too far from the racial breakdown of the background population.

School desegregation cases come in many forms, as do the types of remedies that courts order to promote integration. Similar to the other cases of unconstitutional discrimination briefly mentioned earlier in this chapter, a court's finding of unconstitutional segregation in violation of the equal protection clause necessarily involves an appeal to racial data to prove that students of different races have been treated differently. Perhaps somewhat unlike the other cases discussed, however, the difference in treatment here manifests itself in separation of the races, which even nonlawyers know is unconstitutional—"separate but equal" no longer being a safe harbor for a state's discriminatory action. To establish the existence of such separation or segregation, a plaintiff must, among other things, identify the racial character or assess the racial imbalance of the relevant schools of the district in question. Race data of the student population, provided by the schools themselves or by the census, become the building blocks for a finding of segregation as well as the critical information used to set goals for integration.

Once the court finds unconstitutional segregation, attention eventually turns to ways to remedy it. Through busing, magnet schools, rezoning, or a host of other possible remedies, jurisdictions acting under court supervision will attempt to move from segregation or "dual-system" status to a "unitary" status in which the vestiges of state-sponsored discrimination and segregation in education have been largely eliminated. A determination as to whether a school system has made the move to unitary status often requires detailed findings about the changing racial composition of school faculties and student bodies. Integration, of course, does not mean every school in a district is 50 percent white and 50 percent black. The precise percentages, which will represent the goal of the integration efforts, will vary based on expectations created from expert testimony as to which students of which race live in which location.

The multiracial format of the data, in theory, could add a complication to oversight of desegregation efforts and measurement of compliance with court-ordered goals. How should the goals of integration be defined when the relevant population has a high multiracial component to it? How should one "count" a black-white student or faculty member? Is a school that is 50 percent white, 25 percent black-white, and 25 percent black more or less integrated than one that is 50 percent white and 50 percent black? Such far-fetched scenarios should not be of concern for some time, because areas in which segregation is a problem generally do not have high multiracial populations. Moreover, one might say that a significant rise in the multiracial population is almost its own metric of integration: what better way to assess the erosion of race-based barriers (de jure or de facto) than through such personal evidence? At the theoretical level, however, this "counting" problem presents novel and difficult issues that might someday require judicial resolution.

Affirmative action presents similar issues involving goal-setting based on current assessments of racial imbalance and subsequent attempts to achieve some sense of proportionality with the background population. For many Americans, the racial checkoff on a university admission application is their earliest significant experience with the racial categories similar to those appearing on the census. The answers to that question are used to assess the racial diversity of the applicant pool and, along with census data, to calculate the benchmark against which the admitted population will be compared for antidiscrimination and affirmative action purposes.[10] Many universities have already adopted the census format of allowing applicants to check off more than one race.[11] Although they have run into opposition at the Supreme Court, affirmative action policies, of course, are not limited to higher education. Racial data, particularly with regard to the identity of owners of certain businesses, are often used for so-called "minority set-aside" programs or programs targeting "disadvantaged business enterprises."[12]

Universities, private firms, and governments at all levels often set goals for admissions, hiring, or contracting based on assessments of the racial diversity of the available pool. The opportunity to check off more than one race, alongside an underlying rise in multiraciality of the population, will force new questions on these entities as to affirmative action goal setting and achievement. As for goals, the question is similar to disparate impact and school desegregation: who in the underlying population or applicant pool should count in the estimate of the desired or target percentage of a racial group in the final group of admittees or employees? Do we treat multiracial individuals as their own category, or do we add them somehow to one of the single-race categories? For if one treats them as their own category, then the number of "target" categories may increase to the point of unmanageability while the single-race categories become more and more depleted. Even the often-used category of "minority" does not remove the questions as to whether the 5.5 million whites (the largest multiracial group) who identified with another race in the 2000 census ought to count as part of "the majority" or as a "minority."

As the goals become uncertain, so will assessments as to whether they were achieved. If affirmative action goals continue to be expressed according to single-race groups, then the question arises whether the hiring of multiracial individuals fulfills such goals. One might also expect that the decision as to whether multiracial individuals "count" for affirmative action purposes might also have an effect on the propensity of at least some individuals to identify with one race as opposed to multiple races on an admissions or employment form. Unlike the checking off of a race question on a census form, there might be real costs or benefits to an individual, depending on whether he or she chooses a single race or multiple races on forms related to employment or education.

With regard to affirmative action, in particular, it should be noted that many of these problems of racial identity seemingly introduced by the multiracial format are not new. Which racial categories "deserve" affirmative action is always a subject of contention. Should Asians (of mixed race or not) or Cubans, for example, receive affirmative action in higher education? Moreover, the "authenticity" of an applicant's racial self-identification sometimes becomes an issue, especially in the context of set-asides for a business owned or operated by a member of a minority group. Questions often arise whether the owner is "really" a minority group member and whether a largely white business that puts forward a single minority member in a leadership position should receive the same affirmative action treatment as a "bona fide" minority business. The most that can be said is that the new multiracial format has made a tricky problem even trickier. Despite the inherent contentiousness of regimes of racial categorization, however, the law has found a way around many problems of similar magnitude in the past. Aggregation rules and other judicial, legislative, and administrative means of coping will emerge to deal with this new layer of complexity.

Voting Rights Act Cases

Litigation arising under the Voting Rights Act of 1965 represents the area of most immediate concern for those grappling with the challenges the 2000 census data present.[13] Census data exist as the building blocks for almost every legislative district in the country—from the smallest town council ward to congressional districts with more than six hundred thousand people. In a context beset by political and interest group power battles, state and local governments have rushed to redraw districts of equal population for the 2002 elections. The stakes could not be higher for this redistricting cycle. The major political parties, which are at near parity in the House of Representatives and in many state legislatures, see the redistricting cycle as an opportunity to define their candidates' electorates and cement their influence for the next ten years. Minority candidates and the interest groups that support them see the redistricting process as the critical juncture in the political process when decisions are made as to which interests will be represented and which will be ignored. These political battles take place on uncertain legal terrain, with statutes and Supreme Court precedents pulling jurisdictions in different directions. The added complexity of the new multiple-race format of the census data presents uncertainty and contentiousness in an already racially charged and unsettled process.

Just as in the legal contexts already discussed, litigation challenging districts alleges that the state's action was motivated by discriminatory intent or caused discriminatory effects (or both).[14] Discriminatory intent plus effect, once again, is required for a constitutional claim, whereas the relevant statute, here the Voting Rights Act of 1965, develops an impact or "results" test. Unlike the affirmative action or employment contexts, voting rights litigation relies almost exclusively on census race data to gauge a redistricting plan's discriminatory impact. Most race-based challenges to redistricting plans allege that a given set of lines "dilutes" the voting strength of a minority population. A plan can cause dilution by spreading the minority population among several districts or packing minorities into one or just a few. Section 2 of the Voting Rights Act prevents any legislative districting scheme anywhere in the country from diluting minority votes. Section 5 of the Voting Rights Act applies only to certain states and jurisdictions and prevents them from enacting redistricting plans that worsen the position of racial minority populations.

Vote Dilution Claims Under Section 2 of the Voting Rights Act

In proving vote dilution under section 2 of the Voting Rights Act, plaintiffs must demonstrate that the voting patterns of racial groups as channeled through a particular districting scheme deprives a racial minority population of an "equal opportunity to elect [its] candidate of choice." The Court has established a three-pronged test for vote dilution in which the plaintiff must show:

- that the minority community is "sufficiently large and geographically compact to constitute a majority in a single member district,"
- that the minority community is "politically cohesive," and
- that the white majority votes "sufficiently as a bloc to enable it . . . usually to defeat the minority's preferred candidate." (Thornburgh v. Gingles, 478 U.S. 30, 50–51 [1986])[15]

The new multiracial format of the census has the potential to affect plaintiffs' abilities to prove each of these "Gingles factors." Once again, I add the caveat that these potential problems are more theoretical than probable in the near term, but they draw our attention to the area of the law in which census race data are most often used.

The first factor, size and compactness of the minority community, assumes that the membership of the minority community in question can be accurately identified. Numerical minorities will always be disadvantaged in a majority-rule electoral system, thus not all racial minorities could possibly (or feasibly) be entitled to their own single-member district. Only minority communities that are "large enough" have the right to a judicial remedy. Therefore, the plaintiff must be able to point to a map overlaid on census race data and be able to say that "members of my racial group live in this area, and we are large enough to constitute a majority in a single-member district."[16] A new question then arises: who should count as a member of the minority community? If the multiracial population is large enough, perhaps the plaintiff might need to count multiracials as members of the minority community in order to prove that the community is sufficiently large. An unrealistic example might help prove the point. Suppose a given neighborhood is one-third African American, one-third white, and one-third biracial (African American–white). Does an African American plaintiff seeking a district that surrounds that neighborhood have a potential claim under section 2? The answer may depend on whether the biracial community is counted as African American. At this stage of the litigation, it is usually in the plaintiff's interest to show that the minority community is as large as possible.

Strangely enough, the same cannot be said for fulfilling the second and third Gingles factors. Here, the size of the minority community is irrelevant; what matters is whether it is politically cohesive and is systematically outvoted by a white bloc-voting majority. Cohesion and bloc voting are demonstrated through statistical methods that suggest the members of the minority community tend to vote alike—that is, the racial minority group tends to rally around and vote for one candidate who is usually defeated because whites vote for his or her opponent. Here, increasing the size of the minority community by counting the multiracial population might actually harm a plaintiff's chances of proving illegal vote dilution. If the multiracial population votes differently from the single-race population (a rare event, to be sure), then treating the two groups together as "one race" would undermine the plaintiff's claims that his or her community is cohesive.

Another unrealistic example might help prove this point. Other authors in this volume have referred to the "Cherokee grandmother" phenomenon, in which a white individual, with some distant relative who is American Indian, checks off both white and American Indian on the census form. Suppose for a moment that a large number of such individuals live in a community alongside a large number of individuals who check off American Indian only. Assume also that the single-race respondents and the "Cherokee grandchildren" tend to vote for different candidates: for example, the American Indians tend to vote Democratic and the "biracial" community tends to vote Republican. If one counts the biracial community as American Indian,[17] it will appear that the American Indian community is not politically cohesive—that is, that they do not support the same candidates. If the community is not cohesive, then one cannot argue that their votes are being diluted by a given set of district lines. Rather, the candidate "preferred" by the American Indian community tends to lose because the community splits its vote.

Although the new multiracial format will have implications for calculating the necessary elements of a vote dilution claim, those implications cut in different directions. On the one hand, a plaintiff may be aided by counting the multiracial population as members of the plaintiff's race, thereby suggesting the largest possible size of the minority community. As the minority community is "enlarged" in this way, however, one runs the risk of "diversifying" the community to the point at which it lacks political cohesion. For those worried about the legal impact of the new race format, these counterbalancing effects ought to be the source of solace, not additional concern. Only politically cohesive minority communities have enforceable voting rights claims. Thus, if the multiracial population is genuinely and systematically different from the single-race population (an improbable occurrence), then the plaintiff has nothing to gain, and perhaps much to lose, from aggregating multiracials with the relevant minority group. However, if it turns out that the multiracial population votes as the single-race population does, then a good argument can be made that the two groups share similar characteristics beyond one box checked on a census form: they constitute a unified political group and also share some racial characteristics.

Retrogression Under Section 5 of the Voting Rights Act   A similar dynamic emerges with regard to litigation under section 5 of the Voting Rights Act, although the standard in section 5 cases is "retrogression" rather than dilution. Section 5 requires certain states and jurisdictions to gain approval from the Department of Justice or a federal district court in Washington, D.C., before they enact their redistricting plans into law. Most of the jurisdictions covered by section 5 have a history of denying or impairing the right to vote of certain racial or "language" minorities.[18] Covered states submit their plans to the Department of Justice for "preclearance" (that is, permission to let them go into effect). The department will deny preclearance if a plan has a "retrogressive" purpose or effect on minority voting power. Retrogression is determined by looking at minority voting power under the previous plan and comparing it with what minority voting power would be under the proposed plan.[19] If the new plan will make minorities "worse off," then the department will deny preclearance. One factor the Department of Justice has considered in its assessment of retrogressions is whether the number of majority-minority districts (that is, districts in which a racial minority, such as African Americans, constitutes a majority of the district) would decrease if the proposed plan were to go into effect.

As in the vote dilution context, retrogression depends on certain assumptions about exactly who "belongs" to the racial minority in question and where they live. If, under a covered jurisdiction's current redistricting plan, for example, African Americans live together in a district, then a new redistricting plan that splits them up among many districts is likely to be considered retrogressive and therefore would be denied preclearance by the Department of Justice. The new question posed then by the multiracial format is whether multiracial respondents will be grouped with single-race respondents for purposes of determining the retrogressive effect of a districting plan. Another absurd example, derived from the American Indian hypothetical presented earlier, might help prove the point. Assume that under the current districting plan in a covered jurisdiction (for example, Arizona) an American Indian community exists as a narrow majority in a single-member district. Suppose further that under the proposed redistricting plan that American Indian community would be split into two districts, but half of it will now be joined with a large biracial "American Indian–white" community (for example, "Cherokee grandchildren"). Is there retrogression? If one counts the biracial population as American Indian, then the number of districts with an American Indian majority has not declined, and preclearance would be warranted. If one counts the biracial community as its own distinct race or as white, however, then perhaps the new redistricting plan does retrogress—that is, it may split up the American Indian community and therefore worsen the position of American Indians by reducing their voting strength. How the multiracial population is counted may affect whether the new district lines retrogress.

Once again we should be cautious in estimating the independent impact of the change in the census data. First, as a result of several Supreme Court decisions in the past decade striking down intentionally created majority-minority districts as unconstitutional, the Department of Justice is much less likely to adhere to rigid numerical thresholds, such as a decrease in the number of districts in which racial minorities constitute more than 50 percent of the population. Thus, the precise size of the single-race community under the current and proposed plans will most likely not be of any determinative significance. Second, in its recent notices on the subject, the Justice Department, while promising to use the OMB's aggregation rules to determine retrogression, has stated that its determinations of retrogression will involve a detailed and multifactor analysis, of which census race data are only a part (U.S. Department of Justice 2001).[20] As in the section 2 context, the Justice Department now promises to analyze polarized voting patterns and other electoral data to evaluate changes in minority voting strength under proposal redistricting plans. Third and most important, the multiracial populations in covered jurisdictions are likely to be so small that they could not conceivably rise to levels of significance required for the Justice Department's retrogression inquiries—almost all of which, like section 2 vote dilution cases, involve examinations of the diminution of African American and Hispanic voting strength. As noted at the beginning of this chapter, African Americans display a low rate of multiracial identification, and Hispanics, counted through a separate "origin" question on the census, are unaffected by the new multiracial format. If any group's voting rights under section 2 or section 5 will be affected during the next ten years by the new race format, it will most likely be American Indians in small covered jurisdictions (for example, a county districting scheme in South Dakota, Arizona, or Alaska) and perhaps Asian Americans in New York City or California. Nevertheless, a remarkable confluence of political and geographic circumstances and a rejection of the OMB's aggregation rules would need to occur before the new racial data present real difficulties for voting rights litigation.

Constitutional and Other Problems Posed by Aggregation Rules

A common feature of these legal claims is the need for some agreed-upon method of counting or categorizing the multiracial population. As others in this volume have noted, an almost infinite number of such aggregation rules could be used. One could simply leave the sixty-three categories as they are, counting each four-race combination, for example, as its own separate "racial group." Another possibility is that one could count a biracial person, for example, as two people of different races or as half a person of each race. If it is decided that reaggregation back into the six single-race categories is desirable, rules of thumb could be developed based on the different probabilities that a given multiracial individual would have checked one or another single-race category. Such probabilities could be developed through survey methods or simply by looking at how members of certain multiracial groups responded to the racial categories on the previous census, when the multiple-response option was not offered. For example, if 80 percent of those who checked Asian American and white in the 2000 census checked only Asian American in the 1990 census, then for each level of geography 80 percent of those who checked that biracial combination would be reallocated to the Asian category and 20 percent to the white category. The OMB has developed its own somewhat controversial aggregation rules, which will apply to civil rights monitoring and enforcement.

The Scope and Meaning of the OMB's Aggregation Rules

Recognizing that its decision to allow for a multiple-race checkoff might spawn confusion in federal agencies that rely on racial data, the OMB developed certain aggregation rules for civil rights monitoring and enforcement. In Bulletin 00-02, the OMB provided the following rules of aggregation:

- Responses in the five single race categories are not allocated.
- Responses that combine one minority race and white are allocated to the minority race.
- Responses that include two or more minority races are allocated as follows:
    - If the enforcement action is in response to a complaint, allocate to the race that the complainant alleges the discrimination was based on.

- If the enforcement action requires assessing disparate impact or discriminatory patterns, analyze the patterns based on alternative allocations to each of the minority groups. (OMB 2000, 61–62)

For all practical purposes, the OMB rules provide that the data should be aggregated in the light most favorable to racial minorities—that is, to increase the size of the nonwhite categories by reallocating to them any who could possibly be counted in those categories. Thus, a person who checks off the white and African American boxes will be reallocated as African American. Some authors in this volume have criticized such a practice as reenacting the "one-drop" rule of the Jim Crow South.

Before assessing the problems with the OMB rules, it is important to understand their scope. As the OMB bulletin itself states, these rules are for "agencies responsible for enforcing civil rights laws, and does not preclude the use of more detailed data if an agency chooses to do so" (OMB 2000, 61). These rules are for government agencies, not for private citizens or federal courts. Thus, to the degree they bind anyone at all, they apply only to the federal government, and only to those parts of the federal government, such as the Department of Justice or the Equal Employment Opportunity Commission, that are responsible for enforcing civil rights laws.[21] Indeed, the Census Bureau itself (not a civil rights enforcement agency) developed different allocation rules when it tried to figure out how to recategorize people for purposes of conducting its method of statistical adjustment (see Persily 2001, 931–33). As Bulletin 00–02 itself also states, nothing in the rules prevents an agency from developing more complicated or sensitive reaggregation rules.

To clarify even further, these rules will become an issue in court only when the federal government is a party to the case. Thus, if a woman sues her employer for racial discrimination on a disparate impact theory, the rules do not bind the court in adjudicating her claim. Moreover, the contending parties could advance alternative theories and procedures for aggregation of multiracial responses, and the courts, on a case-by-case basis, might develop aggregation rules for different legal and demographic contexts. Of course, one would expect the courts to pay some deference to the OMB's rules, but such rules might be highly applicable to one set of facts and highly inapplicable to another.

Moreover, in case the point needs to be reemphasized, no individual has a claim against a federal agency for being reallocated into a category he or she did not check. (I state the point again because so many have suggested otherwise in private conversations.) Individuals cannot be injured by the reallocation process; indeed, they will be unaware that it has happened. The allocation process becomes legally relevant only when it skews the data used as evidence in litigation in a direction favoring either the plaintiff or the defendant.

The Rationale for the OMB Rules and Possible Constitutional Objections

In many respects, one's position on how multiracial respondents should or should not be reallocated depends on whether one believes civil rights actions should be easier or more difficult to pursue. The OMB has taken the position that the new data format ought not to become an additional barrier to proving a civil rights violation. The OMB has decided that, in the unlikely event that a case turns on how the multiracial population is counted, the data should be presented in the light most favorable to the plaintiff in a civil rights action. Recognizing that civil rights cases that depend heavily on racial statistics are often quite difficult to win anyway, the OMB decided not to allow the new data format to become a factor that might tip the scale against the government when it enforces the civil rights statutes.

However well intentioned, the OMB rules may lead to some perverse results and to constitutional challenges. As noted in the discussion of voting rights enforcement, sometimes it is not in the interest of minority plaintiffs to have multiracial respondents reallocated into their single-race category. If systematic differences exist between the multiracial and single-race respondents, then aggregating the two groups might make the group look less cohesive, suggesting that the racial group may be more diverse or "better off" than the plaintiff suggests. Furthermore, by introducing multiracial respondents into a plaintiff's racial group, one runs the (admittedly infinitesimal) risk that a defendant could "make up" for discrimination against the plaintiff by acting favorably toward those of mixed race.

Of greater concern to many observers are potential constitutional problems with the OMB aggregation rules. Some might argue that the rules themselves arise from discriminatory intent and portend discriminatory effects that violate the Equal Protection Clause. Like arguments against affirmative action, the argument against the OMB rules would suggest that the rules seek to advantage minority plaintiffs over white plaintiffs or white defendants; therefore, the rules act as intended to discriminate on the basis of race against some civil rights complainants in favor of others. The Constitution prevents a federal agency from employing the OMB allocation rules, the argument goes, so the civil rights agencies for whom the rules were presented as guidance should develop different allocation rules that treat each race equally or discard allocation rules altogether.

There are several reasons to think a constitutional challenge to the OMB rules either will not happen or will not be successful, at least in the near term. The first is that the OMB rules are subject to challenge only if they actually make a difference. Like other types of discrimination, the rules themselves must have an identifiable discriminatory effect—a person or organization must be injured by the OMB's use of these allocation rules as opposed to some nondiscriminatory ones. As I have tried to emphasize, those injuries will be rare, because few claims will turn on the manner in which multiracial respondents are allocated. More specifically, a plaintiff challenging the OMB rules must show that the choice of the OMB rules over alternative constitutional ones injured the person challenging the rules.

Second, even if the OMB rules were found to be unconstitutional as applied in a given case, the judge, by rejecting them, would probably not strike them down as facially unconstitutional. The judge would simply replace those rules with others that he or she considers more appropriate in the given case. To be sure, that might have the effect of striking down the rules by setting a precedent as to when such rules are inapplicable. The decision, however, as to what allocation rules should be used is ultimately a question of law for the judge, who will interpret the given civil rights statute and arrive at allocation rules that he or she considers as flowing from the statute. There will undoubtedly be some circumstances in which the OMB rules will make absolutely no sense (as in the hypothetical case of vote dilution presented earlier), and a judge will recognize that fact in constructing different rules for a given case.

Finally, it is worth stating that the OMB rules, even in the worst-case scenarios, probably do not violate equal protection; they merely redefine somewhat our notions of what a "protected class" under the civil rights laws may be. As described earlier, plaintiffs will now frame discrimination claims in such a way as to suggest that the defendant discriminates against anyone who is even part African American, for example. Assume for the moment that a defendant actually does discriminate against anyone who is even part African American; is it irrational or unconstitutional, then, to organize the reference group data in such a way as to reflect or prove that fact? Any allocation rule or even refusal to allocate biases the data in favor of or against potential plaintiffs or defendants. The OMB's rule, while certainly inapplicable and maybe unconstitutional in some cases, is not systematically inferior to alternatives, especially given the contexts in which allocation rules will become relevant. So long as some circumstances exist under which the OMB allocation rules could be applied constitutionally, what we can expect is a series of judicial opinions that cabin the OMB rules to appropriate situations. As the multiracial population grows, perhaps even overtaking some of the single-race categories, one would expect judges and the OMB to discard these allocation rules for alternatives that are more sensitive to the demographic dynamics depicted with each census.

Conclusion

The decision to allow respondents to check more than one race on their census forms will have its most significant consequences on the way inherently arbitrary racial categories are understood rather than on the way racial data are used in the courtroom. Nevertheless, there will be some cases in which the new format may have an impact, and over the long term, it is likely that the opportunity for self-identification with more than one race will further erode or make fuzzy the lines separating one racial category from another. Indeed, the "problems" with the multiracial checkoff and resulting sixty-three racial categories highlight difficulties that come with any regime of racial categorization. The choice of categories themselves and assumptions about the groups that belong in them necessarily lead to "unfairness" and misassignment at the individual level. So long as we rely on a process of racial self-identification, though, we run the risk that variation within a given racial category will sometimes exceed variation between them.

In assessing the independent legal consequences of the multiracial checkoff, then, there is cause for both caution and concern. The legal regime has confronted and solved similar problems of racial categorization. For example, in several respects the problems of allocation and creating racial baselines have existed for as long as the census has asked the race question. Consider, for example, the separate question that attempts to capture Hispanic origin. The presence of that question alongside the race question has always led to a multiracial census, of sorts, with which the law coped, in general, by adopting something akin to the OMB allocation rules. When Hispanic origin was relevant—that is, when a plaintiff claimed a defendant had discriminated against him because he was Hispanic or that Hispanic votes were diluted—the court would pay attention to data on Hispanic origin. The court would "reaggregate" those respondents, despite the fact that most who fell into that category also considered themselves black or white and had checked off one of those categories on their census forms. Conversely, for an African American plaintiff alleging racial discrimination, the data were usually retabulated with sole attention to the race question—despite the fact that the relevant category would include recent immigrants from Puerto Rico and the Dominican Republic as well as descendants of American slaves.

A second reason for caution in assessing the independent legal effects of the change in the format of race data is that discrimination claims that will turn on categorization will be few and relatively weak. As emphasized repeatedly throughout this chapter, the overwhelming majority of discrimination claims for all statutes are made on behalf of African Americans and Hispanics. African Americans display a low rate of multiracial response, such that the choice of aggregation rules will not affect them. Data on Hispanics come from a separate question on Hispanic origin, and thus the change in data format leaves their numbers constant. Even for those racial groups with a relatively high rate of multiracial response, such as American Indians and Alaska Natives, Native Hawaiians and other Pacific Islanders, and Asians, a discrimination claim that turns on the way the multiracial population is categorized is probably relatively weak. Most discrimination claims that rely on statistics will not turn on a 10 percent difference in the benchmark population. If a county's population or teacher applicant pool is 33 percent American Indian, for example, but only 30 percent of the teachers employed in the county's public schools are American Indian, one would be hard pressed to find a judge who would suggest that such a disparity gives rise to an inference of discrimination. Numbers that close, in fact, usually suggest that the jurisdiction is doing something right. A plaintiff whose case depends on upping his racial group's numbers to the maximum probably has a pretty weak case in any event.

Finally, rules of aggregation will emerge to deal with this new complexity. We can be sure that the rules developed today will become irrelevant in succeeding censuses, but racial categorization (as the perpetual change even in the census single-race categories suggests) is an inherently evolving process. Indeed, courtrooms will serve as forums in which society arrives at rules for when, if ever, groups should be recategorized as one race or another. The inquiry and result will most likely depend on the circumstances. Different multiracial combinations may require different rules of aggregation, and some combinations may become so large as to warrant their own category.[22] In many respects, the legal rules that are developed will be based more on our underlying beliefs as to how high we think the barriers to bringing civil rights claims should be rather than on some shared agreement as to which type of person belongs in which racial category.

Notes

1. Of course, the method of self-identification and the Census Bureau's procedures for occasionally *assigning* people racial identities have received much deserved criticism; see Skerry 2000, 46–79. For purposes of this chapter, the relevant point is that individuals who fill out census forms are never "injured" by any process that categorizes or miscategorizes them.

2. Although such breaches of official duties may not injure an individual, statistical agencies, like other federal agencies, are forbidden to engage in "arbitrary and capricious" conduct.

3. The OMB guidelines allowing for multiple-race responses do not limit themselves to census data. The 1997 standards apply to all racial information gathered by federal agencies. See OMB 1997.

4. See, generally, Personnel Administrator of Mass. v. Feeney, 442 U.S. 256 (1983) (holding that the equal protection clause is implicated only when a state's legislature selected a course of action at least in part because of, and not merely in spite of, its adverse effects on an identifiable group); and Arlington Heights v. Metropolitan Housing Corporation, 429 U.S. 252 (1977) (reversing a Seventh Circuit decision and finding that while the plaintiff had standing to sue, they had failed to establish racially discriminatory intent or purpose was a motivating factor in the rezoning decision).

5. See Civil Rights Act of 1991, 42 U.S.C.A. § 2000e-2(k) (West Supp. 2000). Disparate impact analysis was an accepted part of Title VII of the Civil Rights Act until 1989 when the Supreme Court, in Ward's Cove Packing Co., Inc. v. Atonio, 490 U.S. 642 (1989), interpreted the Act in such a way as to limit disparate impact claims. The Civil Rights Act of 1991 overruled Ward's Cove and codified disparate impact analysis into the law of employment discrimination. The analysis, which presents a series of shifting burdens between the plaintiff and defendant, begins with the plaintiff's demonstration that a given employment practice has fallen more harshly on plaintiff's racial group. As proof a plaintiff will show that the employer hired members of plaintiff's race at a rate lower than that racial group's percentage in the population or qualified applicant pool. The defendant employer then must show that the practice is "job related for the position in question and consistent with business necessity." If the employer is able to prove business necessity, then the plaintiff must show that an alternative practice would fulfill the necessity but have less of a disparate impact on racial minorities.

6. Griggs v. Duke Power (401 U.S. 424 [1971]). Griggs established the disparate impact test that was limited by Ward's Cove but largely reinstated by the Civil Rights Act of 1991. Griggs also relied somewhat on census race and education data to show disparate impact. (Griggs v. Duke Power, at 430 n.6.)

7. Griggs v. Duke Power, at 430 n.6.

8. See, for example, Batson v. Kentucky, 476 U.S. 79 (1986); Turner v. Fouche, 396 U.S. 346 (1970); Whitus v. Georgia, 385 U.S. 545, 552 (1967); Swain v. Alabama, 380 U.S. 202 (1965).

9. The problems with the hypothetical also reflect the complexity of discrimination suits. First, the relevant benchmark would not be derived from the general population. If the claim is one of discriminatory hiring practices, one must use population statistics limited to those people who applied for the job or, perhaps, those who are of the correct age and education level for the job. Second, it is almost inconceivable that somehow an employer could successfully (let alone intentionally) discriminate just against the mixed-race population. Third, workforce data probably are not compiled with the same sensitivity to multiraciality that the census is. Thus, the 10 percent figure could reflect how many Native Hawaiians are counted by an observer rather than through a process of self-identification along the lines of the census. In other words, employers (at the present time) do not keep data on their work-

force broken down into sixty-three racial categories. However, one might conceive of a future employer, either during litigation or preparing for it, who uses the census multiracial data format. Finally, the "Native Hawaiian or other Pacific Islander" category, even standing alone, falls prey to some of these problems. The category groups together a wide array of diverse groups found on either sides of the Pacific.

10. Sometimes even census race data are used to evaluate an affirmative action program. In the well-known case of Regents of the University of California v. Bakke (438 U.S. 265 [1978]), Justice Powell's opinion announcing the judgment of the Court, as well as the other opinions in the case, used census data to justify their positions. Justice Powell's opinion, for example, made note of the fact that "by 1970, the gap between the proportion of Negroes in medicine and their proportion in the population had widened: The number of Negroes employed in medicine remained frozen at 2.2% . . . while the Negro population had increased to 11.1%. . . . The number of Negro admittees to predominantly white medical schools, moreover, had declined in absolute numbers during the years 1955 to 1964" (438 U.S., at 370). Justice William Brennan's opinion went even further in defending the university's affirmative action program: "True, whites are excluded from participation in the special admissions program, but this fact only operates to reduce the number of whites to be admitted in the regular admissions program in order to permit admission of a reasonable percentage—less than their proportion of the California population [footnote]—of otherwise underrepresented qualified minority applicants [footnote]" (438 U.S., at 374). The footnotes to the quoted section of Brennan's opinion are even more revealing of how racial data work in affirmative action programs and judicial consideration of them: In the first, Brennan notes that "Negroes and Chicanos alone constitute approximately 22% of California's population." The second reads as follows:

> The constitutionality of the special admissions program is buttressed by its restriction to only 16% of the positions in the Medical School, a percentage less than that of the minority population in California. . . . This is consistent with the goal of putting minority applicants in the position they would have been in if not for the evil of racial discrimination. Accordingly, this case does not raise the question whether even a remedial use of race would be unconstitutional if it admitted unqualified minority applicants in preference to qualified applicants or admitted, as a result of preferential consideration, racial minorities in numbers significantly in excess of their proportional representation in the relevant population. Such programs might well be inadequately justified by the legitimate remedial objectives. Our allusion to the proportional percentage of minorities in the population of the State administering the program is not intended to establish either that figure or that population universe as a constitutional benchmark. In this case, even respondent, as we understand him, does not argue that, if the special admissions program is otherwise constitutional, the allotment of 16

places in each entering class for special admittees is unconstitutionally high (438 U.S., at 374, nn. 57 and 58).

11. For example, the University of Pennsylvania, Yale University, the University of Chicago, and Harvard University (which uses the "Common Application," as do approximately two hundred other colleges) now allow applicants to check off more than one race on their college applications. Subtle variations exist between the schools as to the format of the race-ethnicity question and available choices. The applications can be found at *www.upenn.edu/ugao/ forms/Domestic2001.pdf* (February 1, 2002); *www.yale.edu/admit/freshmen/ application/pdf/yale—application.pdf* (February 1, 2002); *www.college. uchicago.edu/College/App-ad/App/freshman0203.pdf* (February 1, 2002); and *admis.fas.harvard.edu/Rollo01/application/49678A11–14.pdf* (February 1, 2002).

12. See, for example, 13 CFR § 124.1008 (describing the Small Business Administration's program for determining "small disadvantaged business" status); 49 CFR § 26.45 (describing the Department of Transportation's program for participation of "disadvantaged business enterprises," which refers to disparity studies and census data).

13. Elsewhere I discuss at greater length the voting rights implications of the new multiracial format; see Persily 2000, 2001. See also Saunders 2001.

14. Unlike the previous contexts, however, race-based intent by itself can, on rare occasions, give rise to a constitutional claim. In a set of controversial decisions beginning with Shaw v. Reno (509 U.S. 630 [1993]), the Court has invalidated districts in which race was the "predominant factor" in their creation.

15. Gingles involved a challenge to a multimember, at-large districting scheme that diluted the votes of African Americans. Dilution was shown there because the use of the multimember form acting alongside racially polarized voting submerged the votes of African Americans and thereby prevented them from electing the candidates of their choice.

16. Although Gingles seems to establish "majority" status as a threshold showing for a vote dilution claim, the Court (in footnote 12 of the Gingles opinion) left open the possibility that a community that did not surmount the "50 percent plus one" threshold might still have a claim under section 2. Although a few lower courts have entertained so-called influence-district claims, no such cases have made their way to the U.S. Supreme Court. In many respects, whether influence-district claims are justiciable under section 2 will determine the importance of the change in the census race format. If rigid numerical or percentage thresholds are unimportant, then how the multiracial community is counted (that is, whether its inclusion would bring the minority community over the 50 percent threshold) might not prevent a plaintiff from getting his or her foot in the courthouse door to argue the rest of a vote dilution claim.

17. Incidentally, this would be the practice under the OMB's aggregation rules.

18. Covered states include Alabama, Alaska, Arizona, Georgia, Louisiana, Mississippi, South Carolina, Texas, and Virginia. States with covered jurisdictions include California, Michigan, New Hampshire, New York, North Carolina, and South Dakota.

19. See Beer v. United States, 425 U.S. 130, 141 (1976). A redistricting plan created with a retrogressive purpose (that is, with an intention to make minorities worse off) can also be denied preclearance by the Justice Department; see Reno v. Bossier Parish School Board, 528 U.S. 320 (2000).

20. The same notice explains that the impact of multiple-race responses on the preclearance process is "expected to be minimal" (66 Fed. Reg at 5414).

21. The Department of Justice is not technically an agency, but as noted in the previous section, it has agreed to use the OMB's aggregation rules, at least with respect to enforcement of the Voting Rights Act.

22. Indeed, OMB Bulletin 00-02 provides that for agencies collecting racial data, any individual multiracial combination that rises above 1 percent will be calculated separately (suggesting such a combination is entitled to its own line on the relevant form). It further specifies that the races on a given form will change based on where such data are collected. As the bulletin's footnote explains, "Based on Census 2000 data, agencies will determine the race combinations that meet the one percent threshold. For example, in Hawaii there may well be combinations of race groups that meet this threshold such as Native Hawaiian or Other Pacific Islander and Asian, or Native Hawaiian or Other Pacific Islander and White, or Native Hawaiian or Other Pacific Islander and Asian and White" (OMB 2000, Appendix B, 3).

References

Office of Management and Budget (OMB), Executive Office of the President. 1997. "Revisions to the Standards for the Classification of Federal Data on Race and Ethnicity." *Federal Register* 62(October 30): 58782–90.

———. 2000. *Guidance on Aggregation and Allocation of Data on Race for Use in Civil Rights Monitoring and Enforcement.* Bulletin 00-02. Washington (March 9). Accessed on February 1, 2002 at: *www.whitehouse.gov/OMB/bulletins/b00-02. html.*

Persily, Nathaniel. 2000. "2000 Census Data: New Format and New Challenges." In *The Real Y2K Problem: Census 2000 Data and Redistricting Technology,* edited by N. Persily. New York: Brennan Center for Justice, New York University School of Law.

———. 2001. "Color by Numbers: Race, Redistricting, and the 2000 Census." *Minnesota Law Review* 85(February): 899–947.

Saunders, Melissa. 2001. "Of Minority Representation, Multiple-Race Responses, and Melting Pots: Redistricting in the New America." *North Carolina Law Review* 79(June): 1367–81.

Skerry, Peter. 2000. *Counting on the Census? Race, Group Identity, and the Evasion of Politics.* Washington, D.C.: Brookings Institution.

U.S. Department of Justice. 2001. "Guidance Concerning Redistricting and Retrogression Under Section 5 of the Voting Rights Act, 42 U.S.C. 1973c." *Federal Register* 66(January 18): 5412, 5414.

Part III

A MULTIRACIAL FUTURE?

7

AMERICAN INDIANS: CLUES TO THE FUTURE OF OTHER RACIAL GROUPS

C. Matthew Snipp

R ACIAL classifications serve as the framework for what is known about the social and cultural diversity of American society. Since 1790, the federal government has kept track of the racial composition of the United States, albeit with a system that has evolved slowly and has been shaped by notions about the substance of racial differences. In 1976, the federal government issued a document, known as Office of Management and Budget (OMB) Directive 15, that sought to impose a standard set of categories to be used by all federal agencies, its grantees, and its contractors for the collection of racial data. Two decades later, the OMB amended this classification. Perhaps the most significant change was the revised instruction that allowed respondents to claim membership in more than one race.

Directive 15, interestingly enough, said little about the criteria by which persons might be assigned to one or another of its specified categories. The 1997 revision implies fairly clearly, though it does not explicitly state, that self-identification is the intended method for eliciting racial ancestry. Perhaps more significantly, it does not explicitly forbid criteria or methods other than self-identification from being used to classify individuals into one or another of its specified categories.

This chapter focuses on American Indians to examine several different criteria that might be used to allocate individuals to these categories and the public policy considerations that are attached to them. American Indians provide a valuable test case for at least two reasons. First, a variety of different criteria are in place for designating persons as American Indians. Furthermore, there is not always a great deal of consistency across these criteria with respect to the populations who are designated as American Indians. Second, the American Indian population includes a large number of persons of mixed ancestry. This heterogeneity leads to a great deal of volatility in the reporting of American Indian race that has been well documented by demographers for nearly twenty years (Passell 1976; Passell and Berman 1986; Snipp 1989; Harris 1994).

This volatility is almost certain to foreshadow a similar experience for other groups with rapidly rising rates of intermarriage and a growing number of mixed-race persons—notably, Asians and Latinos. The instability in the reporting of racial heritage entails a number of thorny legal and political issues, many of which are of deep concern within the American Indian community, and they may soon spread to other communities, as well. Although the experiences of American Indians are unique, nonetheless they offer a glimpse of the future for other racial and ethnic minority groups in American society.

American Indian Taxonomies

In the years since the federal government first tried to identify and classify American Indians, the American Indian population has become larger and more diverse. The federal government and the public policy edifice devoted to American Indian issues has also grown larger and more complex. It should be no surprise that federal efforts to identify and classify American Indians have taken a number of different directions to meet a variety of administrative imperatives. Today, there are at least three different ways of being recognized as an American Indian—blood quantum, tribal membership, and self-identification—each with different nuances for public policy (O'Brien 1989; Wilkins 2002). Each of these approaches carries certain advantages and disadvantages as tools for the implementation of public policy.

Blood Quantum

The concept of blood quantum became popular in the early to mid-nineteenth century in connection with ideas associated with eugenics and scientific racism. "Blood" was a convenient metaphor to describe racial heritage. "Blood quantum" denoted the amount of racial heritage that could be ascribed to an individual. In this era, it was widely believed that ethnicity and cultural practices were mostly the result of inheritance. Thus, blood quantum also indicated the degree to which certain behavioral characteristics might be manifested in individual behavior. The proponents of eugenics, including Lewis Henry Morgan, one of the founding fathers of anthropology, argued that the most efficient means for civilizing American Indians was to encourage them to intermarry with whites (Bieder 1986). The dilution of Indian "blood," he believed, would eventually result in a race of people who would possess few, if any, of the traits regarded as representative of American Indian culture.

As implemented by the federal government, "blood quantum" rules are criteria that define the amount of personal ancestry that must be possessed to be designated as an American Indian. A person with an American Indian full-blood quantum is an individual whose ancestors are exclusively the descendants of the aboriginals who occupied the Western Hemisphere before the arrival of Europeans. A person with one-half blood quantum might have one parent who is a full-blood and another who is not; one-quarter blood quantum denotes a person with one full-blood grandparent, and so forth, in ever smaller increments of ancestry.

One might surmise that the discredited and embarrassing intellectual pedigree behind this approach would have caused it to be cast aside long ago, joining like-minded ideas about racial superiority, Jim Crow, and Social Darwinism. On the contrary, the principle of blood quantum has been used extensively for many years since losing its intellectual credibility. Ironically, many American Indian tribal governments still continue to use this as a standard for tribal membership (Thornton 1996). However, they have not been alone, as the Bureau of Indian Affairs (BIA) and the Indian Health Service also have relied heavily on this criterion for determining eligibility for services.[1]

It should also be said, however, that in recent years federal authorities have made much less use of blood quantum rules than in the past. One reason for this is that blood quantum criteria are problematic in terms of their legality. For example, twenty-six years ago, after careful study, the American Indian Policy Review Commission (AIPRC 1976) concluded that numerous successful legal challenges had rendered blood quantum an unacceptable alternative for determining who should be recognized as an American Indian. Nonetheless, in the mid-1980s the Indian Health Service entertained the idea of reinstituting blood quantum standards for the determination of service eligibility. Despite its many problems, the federal government from time to time seems sorely tempted to revive this practice, and for this reason, it is worth reviewing its merits and liabilities for public policy.

The popularity and long-standing use of blood quantum may be due in part to the veneer it presents as a precise marker for determining ancestral descent. Self-descriptions of fractionated ancestry ("part Italian," "part Polish") are endemic to American culture. However, to say that an individual is three-quarters or one-eighth American Indian indicates, at the very least, the number of persons with an ostensibly undiluted Indian ancestry inhabiting the family tree. Furthermore, for the sake of comparison, it permits individuals to claim in precise language the degree to which they possess more or less Indian ancestry than another—the accuracy of such claims notwithstanding. What separates the fractionated ancestry claims of American Indians from those of other Americans are the legal and fiduciary implications they embody. For the purposes of settling legal claims and establishing entitlements, blood quantum appears to offer a high degree of certainty that is less prone to fraud than other indicators of ancestry. Blood quantum claims for American Indians are established by a paper trail of parentage that yields an exact number of what appears to be a closer or weaker connection to the American Indian population.

However, it is this paper trail and apparent precision that yield the most undesirable results when blood quantum is used as a tool for administration of public services. To establish blood quantum requires an ancestral benchmark—that is, a certified degree of blood quantum to which descent can be traced.[2] Most such benchmarks are followed back to censuses and other official counts conducted in the latter part of the nineteenth century and the early part of the twentieth. In some instances, officials queried respondents about their blood quantum; in other cases, friends and relatives were asked; and in still other cases, a blood quantum degree was simply assigned by an enumerator based on physical and behavioral characteristics. An individual, for example, might be designated a full blood if he or she did not speak English.

By modern standards of survey research, the accuracy of these counts is at best suspect. The Census Bureau, for instance, spends tens of millions of dollars and has access to high levels of technology, as well as roads, rapid transit, and aerial mapping. With all these advantages, there are still segments of the American Indian population it cannot reach or who refuse to disclose accurate information. There is no reason whatsoever to believe that a handful of men on horseback, often working in remote areas, trying to count a fearful or hostile population could have done any better. It seems virtually certain that the documents upon which blood quantum claims are based are flawed. Almost certainly there were individuals who were not counted or whose blood quantum was misjudged. It must be remembered that in this era, anyone disclosing a full-blood identity was acknowledging a powerful stigma when dealing with authorities.

This means that any determination of blood quantum based on these records is itself likely to be flawed. Nonetheless, the BIA and more than a few tribal governments spend enormous amounts of time and money calculating these imperfect estimates of fractionated patrimony. Similarly, individuals displeased with the results of these efforts may also spend enormous amounts of personal resources disputing them. The reason to do so, apart from correcting the historical record, is that one-quarter blood quantum often has been regarded as the minimum amount necessary for one to be recognized as a bona fide Indian (Thornton 1996). Quite simply, by bureaucratic reckoning, a person who has at least a 1/4 degree of Indian blood is an American Indian, and one with a 63/256 degree of blood quantum is not. Yet as a practical matter the only difference between these two individuals is one full-blooded ancestor eight generations removed. Seen from this perspective, the arbitrary nature of this standard is painfully obvious.

In addition to the clerical expense of verifying blood quantum, and the arbitrary quality of this criterion, this standard poses another long-term dilemma for the American Indian population. This dilemma arises because the numbers of American Indians with a "pure" ancestry is almost certainly shrinking, and the numbers of persons with ancestries in addition to American Indian is increasing. In the face of this trend, any criterion based on ancestral descent is virtually certain to disenfranchise from membership many persons who by other standards—linguistically, culturally, socially— would be considered bona fide members of the American Indian community. It is a near certainty that fewer and fewer American Indians will be able to be recognized as such under the blood quantum rules used in the past.

This problem stems from the high rates of intermarriage found among American Indians. In the later decades of the twentieth century, American Indians were more likely to be married to non-Indians than to other Indians (Sandefur and McKinnel 1986; Sandefur and Liebler 1996; Snipp 1989). This is not too surprising, given the long history of intermarriage between American Indians and whites, dating back to Pocahontas and John Rolfe, through the fur trade, and into the nineteenth century, when it most likely was very common. Although there are few sources of data showing intermarriage rates in the nineteenth century or in the early part of the twentieth, the Census Bureau collected information about blood quantum in the 1910 and 1930 counts. Table 7.1 shows the distribution of the American Indian population with respect to those identified as full-blood and mixed-blood in 1910 and 1930. Even nearly a century ago, at least one-third of the American Indian population consisted of multiracial persons. The so-called full-blood population was declining, down 10 percent between 1910 and 1930, made up for by a 7 percent increase in the mixed-race population and a 3 percent gain in the "blood not reported" category.

TABLE 7.1   Distribution of Persons Identified as Full Bloods, Mixed Bloods, and Blood Not Reported, 1910 and 1930

Ancestry	1910	1930
Full blood	150,053	153,933
(Percentage)	(56.5)	(46.3)
Mixed blood	93,423	141,101
(Percentage)	(35.2)	(42.5)
Blood not reported	22,207	37,363
(Percentage)	(8.3)	(11.2)
Total	265,683	332,397
(Percentage)	(100.0)	(100.0)

Source: U.S. Bureau of the Census 1915 (table 12), 1937 (table 12).

FIGURE 7.1   *OTA Population Projections by Blood Quantum*

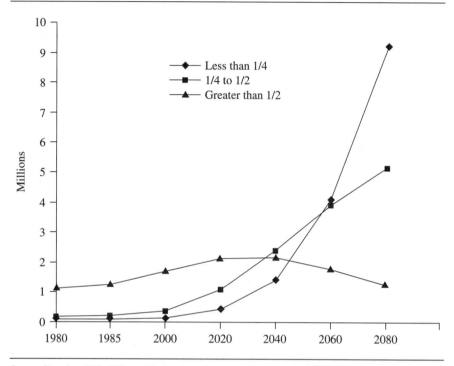

Source: Based on U.S. Office of Technology Assessment 1986 (table 3-9).

It is virtually certain, given high rates of intermarriage, that the full-blood component of the American Indian population has decreased steadily throughout the twentieth century with corresponding growth in the multiracial component. However, this is impossible to substantiate because the Census Bureau did not collect data about blood quantum after 1930, nor has the Bureau of Indian Affairs systematically made this information available. The BIA did conduct one survey of blood quantum in 1950. The results of this survey are noteworthy because they were used by the Office of Technology Assessment (OTA) in 1986 to produce a series of population projections showing changes in the full-blood and mixed-race American Indian populations through the year 2080. It would be a mistake to take the results of long-term population projections too seriously, and the OTA estimates, in particular, have a number of limitations. Nonetheless, the study's findings do have some relevance (see figure 7.1 and 7.2). The proportion of the population that has one-half blood quantum or more is expected to fall dramatically at the same time that the number of persons with less than one-fourth blood quantum is projected to skyrocket. As long as some children marry outside of their community, tribal governments that adhere to

FIGURE 7.2   *OTA Projections of Blood Quantum Composition (Percentage of the Population with Specified Blood Quantums)*

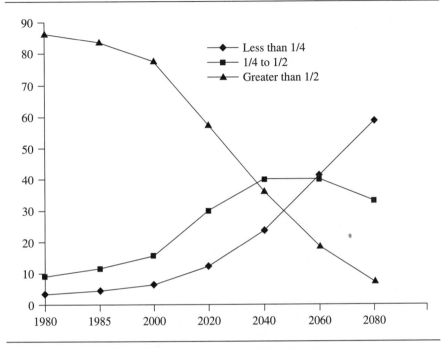

Source: Based on U.S. Office of Technology Assessment 1986 (table 3-9).

this standard run the risk of eventually disinheriting the grandchildren of their people.

Tribal Membership

In 1976, the American Indian Policy Review Commission published its findings about the state of federal Indian policy. One of the more salient issues the commission addressed was the question of who should be recognized as an American Indian. The commission summarized the federal government's position with the following statement:

> Congress can, and has, passed laws to define Indian status for some federal purposes. Although no statute has laid down a general definition of "Indian," Congress has sometimes set standards to define Indian status for special purposes. Older legislation used various degrees of Indian blood for different tribes, but those standards were often arbitrary and conflicted with tribal provisions. Recent congressional legislation, however, has avoided these conflicts and has given recognition to the primary tribal interest in member-

ship by defining "Indian" as a member of an Indian tribe. (AIPRC 1976, 108)

Thus, according to Congress, an American Indian is anyone who belongs to an American Indian tribe. Despite the obvious circularity in this principle, it does one have one special virtue: it recognizes the sovereign rights of tribes to determine their constituencies. However, a closer look at this idea reveals that it actually involves two more or less separate considerations: What constitutes a tribe? And how do individuals qualify for membership within a tribe?

Tribal Recognition   It is far beyond the scope of this discussion to try to disentangle the notion of what constitutes a tribe (see Thornton 1987; Fried 1968). Anthropological theory notwithstanding, it is still important to understand the different kinds of tribes that exist today—especially why some tribes are "recognized" and others are not. For the purposes of public policy there are three categories of tribes in the United States: unrecognized tribes, state recognized tribes, and federally recognized tribes.

In some respects, the situation most complicated to describe involves the standing of those groups who identify themselves as American Indian tribes but who are not recognized as such by any state or federal authority. As the term implies, "unrecognized tribes" are groups of individuals who claim to be American Indians but for one reason or another are not recognized as such by government authorities or, often, by other groups of American Indians. There are many idiosyncratic reasons why this recognition is withheld. However, it is usually on one of two possible accounts. One is that the group in question simply does not conform to what most people would agree constitutes an American Indian tribe by historical or ethnological standards. Suppose a group of individuals who vaguely recall distant Indian ancestors decide to form a collectivity and to call itself the Turtle Bear Tribe. They might gather together once a month to discuss their ancestors (or how to find them), do arts and crafts projects, and share a potluck dinner. One writer has dubbed this "the southeastern syndrome" because it seems to be a common phenomenon in southeastern states (Quinn 1990). Needless to say, the Turtle Bear Tribe would remain unrecognized in perpetuity by the Bureau of Indian Affairs and by most American Indians.

It is easy to see why any claim to tribal identity by the Turtle Bear tribe might be widely regarded as implausible, but in other cases the history is far more complex. For example, there are American Indian groups who were too small, too weak, too peaceful, or too acquiescent ever to have gained the notice of authorities and are thus unrecognized. Another large group includes tribes who lost their recognition during the termination era of federal policy. Historically and ethnologically, all of these groups may have legitimate claims as American Indians. In fact, a number of them have recently been successful in gaining federal recognition. One way this has happened has been through the courts, which in the 1980s restored tribal status to a number of terminated groups in California. Another way has been through congressional legislation, though this has been perhaps least common. More frequently, unrecognized tribes have recourse through a costly and time-consuming process established by the Bureau of Indian Affairs. The BIA recognition process requires extensive documentation showing historical and cultural continuity as a tribe, and only a few tribes have been successful in running this gauntlet. Nonetheless, 237 groups have petitioned or filed papers indicating their intent to petition for recognition. Out of this number, 15 have been denied recognition, and the same number have been approved for recognition, representing the addition of 7,956 "new" Indians to whom the federal government is now obligated.[3] The remainder of applications are still pending within the BIA's Branch of Acknowledgment and Research (Bureau of Indian Affairs 2000).

State-recognized tribes are deemed "official" by their respective state governments but are not recognized as bona fide tribes by the federal government. As such they are not eligible for services from the BIA, nor are they entitled to the sovereign "government-to-government" relationship that exists for federally recognized tribes. The benefits of state recognition vary from state to state but in most instances amount to no more than the benefits that state governments owe to cities, counties, and other forms of local government. Most of these tribes are located in the South in states such as Texas, Louisiana, and Virginia. Some are remnant bands that were overlooked when the federal government was undertaking the removal of American Indians from the Southeast during the early nineteenth century. Others are former federally recognized tribes. For example, federal recognition of the Catawba in South Carolina was terminated in the 1950s. A few, such as the Pamunkey in Virginia, have established reservations, whereas others, such as the Piscataway in Maryland, have no land base. Many, if not most, have petitioned the federal government for recognition.

Federally recognized tribes have what amounts to the highest form of recognition, and this relationship has been written about so extensively that little more need be said. These tribes occupy a highly complicated place in American society and enjoy recognition by virtue of their being sufficiently large or troublesome (sometimes both) that the federal government enacted policies designed to alternately destroy and assimilate them. For these tribes, recognition has been a costly affair, but it is one that is coveted by unrecognized and state-recognized tribes.

Tribal Membership Criteria   The federal government has not in recent years tried to influence the membership criteria that tribes establish. The single exception is that in the past, it has been unwilling to acknowledge persons brought into a tribe through adoption ceremonies. Apart from this exception, each tribe determines the criteria it uses to establish its membership. There is no single or uniform standard that one can state as "the" criterion for tribal membership; hence there are almost as many ways to be an American Indian as there are tribes.

In most cases, proof of descent is a requirement for tribal membership, along with other criteria such as recognition by the community or residence in the community. Some tribes have fairly lax requirements, making it relatively easy to become enrolled in the tribe. Others have exclusive requirements that make it difficult to become an enrolled member. One might expect that tribes with substantial resources, such as casino revenues, would have the most exclusive standards for membership. To some extent, this might be true, but the southwestern pueblos, most of which have relatively few resources, have some of the most stringent criteria.

One way tribal governments can make membership criteria more or less exclusive is by raising or lowering blood quantum requirements—for example, from one-half to one-quarter. Blood quantum is still a widely used criterion by tribal governments. Why so many tribal governments use it is not entirely clear, because it is a fundamentally alien idea imported from Western pseudoscience. Most likely, blood quantum was introduced to tribes during the 1930s and 1940s, when American Indian communities were given the opportunity to establish reservation governments under the Indian Reorganization Act. Tribal constitutions usually stipulated the terms of membership, and during this time, blood quantum was widely used in the administration of Indian affairs.

At the time blood quantum must have seemed a logical basis for establishing tribal membership. In any event, many tribes adopted blood quantum standards, and though a good number have abandoned this standard, it is still a common requirement. Table 7.2 shows the number of tribes using blood quantum membership criterion circa the mid-1980s. No doubt additional tribes have altered their blood quantum requirements since these data were published but the results are still instructive. As the table shows, about two-thirds of all tribal governments maintained some type of blood quantum criterion in the mid-1980s, though in most cases, one-quarter degree or less was the standard requirement.

Tribes vary with respect to the documentation they require to demonstrate blood quantum. One important source of documentation is the Certificate of Degree of Indian Blood (CDIB) issued by the Bureau of Indian Affairs. The CDIB is obtained by furnishing the BIA with documentation about one's ancestors. This documentation permits a link to be created with records such as tribal censuses and enrollments taken in some earlier period of history when blood quantum was recorded. From this information, the

TABLE 7.2   *Blood Quantum Requirements of American Indian Tribes, by Reservation Basis and Size*

	Blood Quantum Requirement		
	More than ¼	¼ or Less	No Minimum Requirement
Number of tribes	21	183	98
Reservation based (percentage)	85.7	83.1	63.9
Median size	1022	1096	1185

Source: Thornton 1996, 107.

BIA issues a document certifying the content of Indian blood possessed by the bearer—that is, a pedigree. It hardly needs mentioning that these documents are as flawed as any other based on blood quantum.

Tribal membership as a standard for circumscribing the Indian population poses a special problem for a small but notable group of persons who might otherwise be entitled to claim American Indian heritage. Adopted persons with little or no information about birth parents are virtually certain to be excluded from identification as American Indian by this standard. This is especially true for children born before the protections offered by the American Indian Child Welfare Act. Before this act went into effect, some unknown but probably large number of children were routinely placed in non-Indian homes with little or no information about their heritage, apart from the fact that they were American Indian. For many of these individuals, it will be impossible for them ever to validate their identity as American Indians to the satisfaction of tribal standards.

Self-Identification

Verifying ancestry and other community connections is a costly exercise. Few organizations are willing to invest the resources required to verify an individual's claim to being an American Indian in the same manner as a tribal government or the BIA might. Few employers, for example, would request and carefully examine documents such as birth certificates to confirm tribal descent. For this reason, self-identification is perhaps the most widely used method of establishing the perimeters of the American Indian population. Apart from cost and convenience, there are also intellectual justifications for relying on self-identification. In his classic essay on ethnicity, Fredrik Barth argues that mutual self-awareness is one of the hallmarks of ethnic group boundaries. Hence, self-identification is an essential element for demarcating ethnic boundaries (Barth 1969).

Ethnic self-identification is perhaps the most common way that American Indians acknowledge their identity. Until recently, the Office of Management and Budget's Directive 15 specifically ordered all federal agencies, its contractors, and grantees to include American Indians and Alaska Natives as groups for whom data should be collected. In practice, this meant that in addition to federal agencies, agencies of state and local governments, educational institutions, and many large and small employers had to provide data about any American Indians with whom they had contact and, hence, the opportunity for clients, students, and employees to self-identify as American Indian or Alaska Native.

Self-identification as a device for eliciting information about ethnic populations has several advantages—and several disadvantages, as well. It is especially attractive to the organizations that must collect and provide ethnic data. It is relatively convenient and inexpensive—certainly less so than any approach that requires verification. Respondents are not required to submit evidence to prove their claim of American Indian identity. It sidesteps the many complexities involved with blood quantum or tribal membership, especially for those persons who belong to unrecognized tribes or who were adopted in childhood. However, these desirable qualities also give rise to some complicated problems.

One especially thorny matter involves the interpretation of reports of American Indian identity. For example, when a respondent indicates that he or she is an American Indian, it is usually not clear whether this person is a member of a federally recognized tribe, a state recognized tribe, or an unrecognized tribe akin to the Turtle Bear tribe. Past and present federal guidelines do not stipulate that respondents should specify the nature of their tribal affiliation. Indeed, the nature of "Indian-ness," and the quality and character of American Indian ethnic identity (and ethnicity in general), is sufficiently nebulous and complex to cast a shadow of ambiguity over the content of racial self-identification. There are quite likely as many different notions about racial identification as there are people to report it. To further complicate matters, a great deal of the data collected about racial characteristics are based on the secondhand reports of individuals, such as teachers, school administrators, friends, neighbors, and family members. Hence, we may know that within a community, there exists a group of individuals who regard themselves (or are regarded by others) as American Indians. This says little, however, about their tribal ties, the degree to which they regard this identity as important, their culture and lifestyle, or anything else that would reveal much about the content of this identity.

The fluidity and instability of self-reported ethnic identity has been frequently commented upon (for example, Waters 1990). However, few other groups in American society have demonstrated more vividly how fluid and changeable self-reports of racial identity can be over time. Because American Indians historically have had high rates of marriage with non-Indians, substantial numbers of multiracial persons have had the "option" of identifying themselves as American Indian or something else. Not surprisingly, census data since 1960 have shown that large numbers of persons have chosen to change their identity to American Indian from some other category of racial heritage—black or white, for instance. Between 1970 and 1980, the American Indian population grew by 73 percent. About a third of this increase derived from births in excess of the number of deaths (Snipp 1989). The remainder was accounted for by what has come to be termed "ethnic switching."

Ethnic switching occurs when an individual identifies with one of his or her multiple ancestries more than another. Data from the 1980 census indicate that large numbers of Americans claim some sort of American Indian or Alaska Native ancestry. In fact, the number of persons who believe they have some amount of American Indian ancestry is much larger than the number of persons who report their racial background as American Indian. Table 7.3 shows the numbers of persons who reported an American Indian ancestry compared with the numbers of persons who reported their race as American Indian in the 1980 and 1990 censuses. Quite clearly, the number of persons who might exercise their option to identify themselves as American Indian is enormous.

The plain fact that so many individuals might plausibly identify themselves as American Indian raises an obvious question about whether they are "real" Indians in any other sense of the term. Questions about the authenticity of American Indian identity are especially problematic for persons with limited contact with a reservation community, limited knowledge about tribal culture, and few visible markers of cultural or phenotypic qualities associated with American Indians. In particular, persons lacking a strong connection with a tribal community may be judged to be ethnic impostors, their identity as American Indians deemed illegitimate, and pejoratively described as "wannabees." Nonetheless, the procedures used by the federal government, most institutions, and private employers do not require verification to establish the credibility of self-reported ethnic identification. Thus, it is impossible to adjudicate claims to American Indian

TABLE 7.3   *American Indian Population by Race and Ancestry, 1980 and 1990 Censuses*

American Indian Definition	1980 Census		1990 Census	
	Number	Percentage	Number	Percentage
By ancestry, total	6,766,000	100	8,798,000	100
By race	1,420,000	21	1,959,000	22
By ancestry, but not race	5,346,000	79	6,839,000	78

Source: Passel 1996, 86.

identity that are patently false or merely trivial from those of the most deeply enmeshed in tribal culture and community life.

Until recently, the policies of the federal government restricted the number of racial and ethnic identities an individual could report to a single category. Changes made in 1997 allow multiracial reporting and may further complicate concerns about ethnic authenticity, creating, in particular, two sources of confusion. One is that given the opportunity to report more than one racial background, persons who in the past may have identified themselves only as black or white may be inclined to add "American Indian" in their responses to the census question on race. This not only will add to the number of persons included in the American Indian population but also will almost certainly alter the American Indian population in significant ways. Quite possibly, it may lead some to conclude that those who report a multiracial heritage including "American Indian" have a weaker claim than others who claim a single American Indian racial heritage.

The second source of confusion arises when persons who formerly identified themselves as American Indians choose to include other racial heritages as well. Unlike the previous scenario, this will not increase the number of American Indians, nor will it significantly alter the population composition. Yet it may add more fuel to the debate about whether the ethnic identities of such persons are as genuine as those who list no identity other than American Indian. It remains to be seen whether these issues emerge as salient concerns to large numbers of individuals, especially to those in policy-making roles. In the event they materialize, they are almost certain to have a corrosive effect on any effort to build a consensus about who may legitimately claim to be an American Indian.

As an endnote to this discussion, it is worth reemphasizing the unparalleled importance of tribal affiliation as a touchstone for American Indian ethnic identification. At the risk of overstating the case, it seems likely that most knowledgeable observers would agree that anyone who does not have an affiliation with a known tribal entity has only the weakest of attachments to the American Indian population. In fact, there is empirical research to support this assertion.

In a study, using data from the 1990 census, comparing the characteristics of American Indians who reported a tribal affiliation with those who did not, Carolyn Liebler (1996) finds several key differences. These findings lead her to conclude that tribal affiliation is the litmus test for the validity of claims to American Indian ethnicity. Liebler concludes the report of her research with this unambiguous summary:

> The absence of a tribal response implies the absence of an American Indian ethnic identity. The principal finding of this paper is that American Indians who do not specify their tribe are usually not people customarily regarded as

American Indians. They have non-Indian ancestries, speak non-Indian, non-English languages, live in cities in non-Indian states and no one else in their household is tribally identified either. Analysts wishing to delineate "real" Indians from others should consider restricting their samples to American Indians who responded to the tribal affiliation item. (Liebler 1996, 30)

Liebler's argument suggests that focusing on tribal affiliation diminishes much of the ambiguity about who can legitimately claim American Indian identity. Her findings also suggest that excluding individuals who cannot disclose a tribal affiliation reduces some of the heterogeneity found within the self-identified American Indian population. These results have important policy implications that are well worth considering.

Lessons for Other Ethnic Minorities

The experiences of American Indians and the efforts to define them offer a number of insights about what the future may hold for other ethnic minority groups in American society. In some instances they presage the future for these groups. In other respects, the uniqueness of American Indians offer a counterpoint that may suggest larger or smaller degrees of complexity with respect to the determination of race, ethnicity, and group membership.

This chapter has focused on blood quantum, tribal or community recognition, and self-identification as devices for establishing racial connections. Before revisiting the ways these standards might be applied to other groups, it is worthwhile to examine how the experiences of American Indians may or may not resemble those of other groups in more general terms.

The most significant difference setting American Indians apart from other ethnic minorities, especially African Americans, is the descent principle that is used to determine group membership. For African Americans, as well as other ethnic minorities, hypodescent—the so-called one-drop rule—has been the historic marker for determining group membership. That is, even a single ancestor ten generations removed is a necessary and sufficient condition for establishing one's claim to being a member of the African American race. The logic behind this rule rests on the assumption that in light of the United States' past history of slavery and Jim Crow segregation, no one would willingly claim to be of African descent. Furthermore, it has been most useful because it has marked a population that was obligated to submit themselves to the service of the dominant white majority. As an inclusive rule, the one-drop rule expanded the number of persons designated for servitude. Thus, by enlarging the pool of subservient lower-caste persons, it diminished their economic value at the same time that it made them more accessible to the white population that needed their labor and desired their social acquiescence.

Historically, hypodescent has seldom been applied for the purpose of determining membership in the American Indian race. In contrast, American Indians have generally been identified by hyperdescent, a principle that stipulates some minimum amount of ancestry as a necessary condition for qualification. Blood quantum rules, for example, have often required that a claimant have a one-fourth degree of American Indian ancestry to receive official recognition as an American Indian. This is equivalent to having one of four grandparents who possesses an ancestry undiluted by any other ethnic affiliation.

Under the rules of hyperdescent, ancestry is a necessary but insufficient condition of establishing one's affiliation as an American Indian. Other characteristics, such as "community recognition" or "cultural retention," may also be required. Predictably, the logic for this rule adheres to the same basic outline as hypodescent. Historically, American Indians have been the possessors of resources—much is owed to them for the expropriation of these resources—most notably, land. In the course of occupying this land, the federal government established a highly complex set of property-related obligations to American Indians that exist in perpetuity. As a result of these obligations, American Indians are eligible for a variety of services ranging from health care to education to land management assistance. Quite plainly, an exclusive rule based on hyperdescent limits the size of the population eligible to receive this assistance, thereby limiting the size of the federal government's financial obligation.

These rules were not the conscious result of a single public debate. Nor were they the result of a single stroke of public policy. Like most social institutions, they evolved slowly over time (Woodward 1974). Nonetheless, they evolved in ways that were dictated by the overarching interests of the dominant white majority. In particular, there were clear incentives for adopting one rule for American Indians and another for African Americans and other ethnic minorities, such as the Chinese in California and Mexicans in Texas. Over time and in hindsight, it is easy to see why these descent rules were applied as they were and to understand the purposes that they served.

Blood Quantum

For the reasons just mentioned, blood quantum has seldom if ever been applied to groups other than American Indians, at least not for most official purposes. There is, however, a historical analogue in a practice used by the federal government in the late nineteenth century. This classification system subdivided the black population into mulattoes, quadroons, and octoroons, corresponding to one-half, one-quarter, and one-eighth degrees of blood quantum, respectively. The purposes served by this classification system are not readily apparent, and, perhaps for this reason, it was relatively short-lived. Moreover, hypodescent rules rendered such distinctions irrelevant: any amount of black is all black. Nonetheless, they also represent a precedent in federal practices that, at least in theory, could be revived if the need arose.

One may reasonably wonder under what sorts of conditions this demonstrably archaic practice might be reinstated. There are at least two scenarios in which fractionated ancestries might once again be used for administrative purposes. One has recently received serious consideration by federal authorities. The other is less likely but still not out of the realm of possibility.

The most recent contemplation by federal authorities of a system of fractionated ancestries reminiscent of the enumeration of blood quantum has taken place in connection with the need to simplify and tabulate the large number of racial categories possible in the 2000 census. The 1997 revision of the federal standards for the collection of racial data allows respondents to identify themselves by marking one or more preselected categories for their racial heritage. In the 2000 census, there were sixty-three unique racial groups and, if overlaid with the distinction of Hispanic and non-Hispanic, 126 separate combinations. For most purposes, and especially for the publication and presentation of these data, 126 distinct categories is simply an unmanageable number. Thus, federal statisticians have been carefully studying ways that these categories might be combined. They have explored a variety of alternatives, including one set of procedures they have aptly dubbed "fractional assignment."

Fractional assignment can be implemented in several ways. The simplest is to divide multiracial respondents evenly across the groups with whom they identify. For instance, a person who lists his or her race as black and white would, for the purpose of estimating population totals, be counted as a 0.5 black person and as a 0.5 white person. Other alternatives have looked at more complicated schemes whereby a person might be counted as one-third or one-fourth of one race and two-thirds or three-fourths of another. Needless to say, the complexity of these schemes using unequal fractions grows exponentially as more races are added for allocation. All of these schemes, of course, beg the question of the actual composition of a respondent's ancestry, about which nothing is known.

The implications of this type of system should be readily apparent. For African Americans who choose to report their multiracial ancestry accurately, most schemes of fractional assignment will result in smaller estimates of the African American population. Whereas hypodescent increased their number, assigning mixed-race African Americans in equal measures across black and white racial categories, for example, will effectively diminish the number of such persons by 50 percent. For purposes of civil rights enforcement, and especially the Voting Rights Act, a reduction in numbers of this magnitude is seriously consequential. Other indicators of social well-being could be seriously affected by this procedure. Residential segregation could be dramatically reduced by this procedure in areas with sizable numbers of multiracial persons who were formerly recognized as African Americans: the numbers of white people would increase, the numbers of black people would decline, and the area would appear more integrated—despite the fact that the composition of the residents remained unchanged.

Although they have seriously considered methods of fractionating ancestry, federal statisticians have not strongly advocated this method of tabulating racial data. Indeed, they point to other problems, not the least of which is that these procedures yield population estimates consisting of fractions of people—a counterintuitive result that is difficult to explain to lay audiences. Thus, it seems unlikely that this methodology will be introduced. However, there is another possible, albeit less likely, circumstance in which blood quantum principles could be invoked: in the event that Congress accedes to demands for reparations to be paid to the descendants of American slaves, fractional assignment would ease the accounting tasks involved.

The proposal that the descendants of African slaves be paid a reparation to recognize the contribution of their labor to the collective wealth of American society has been made from time to time by a variety of African American community advocacy groups, including the Congressional Black Caucus (Feagin 1999). This proposal has never received a great deal of serious consideration in Congress. However, it is not inconceivable that with surpluses in the Treasury, at some point in the future it might be taken more seriously.

Assuming that this idea gains sufficient public support for Congress to take up this issue, and perhaps pass it into law, one of the first questions that must be answered will be the matter of eligibility. Reparations might be paid directly from the Treasury or through some other means, such as an income tax reduction or refund. No matter how it is administered, however, some determination must be made about who is to receive these funds. Otherwise, it is not implausible to expect that millions of Americans will submit a claim for payment. In this scenario, it seems likely that Americans of all races might scour their family trees in search of a black ancestor, real or imagined, that might lead to a claim for a reparation payment. Without question, an open invitation to apply for a payment from the Treasury would evoke some degree of fraud, perhaps widespread fraud. However, there are also some unknown millions of white Americans who might legitimately claim an African American ancestor in their families' distant pasts. The presence of these individuals, combined with the expectation of fraudulent claims, would almost certainly prompt the federal government to institute some sort of eligibility criteria to prevent a wholesale assault on the Treasury.

The most obvious precedent for limiting claims to federal resources can be found in the administration of American Indian affairs—namely, hyperdescent. That is, to decide who might be eligible for reparations for slavery the federal government could establish some minimum level of ancestry traceable to a known slave. For example, the federal government could require proof that any person making a claim for reparation would be required to present proof of ancestry equivalent to having one grandparent who was held in forced servitude before 1865. This would be no different from the standard applied in the past to American Indians, who had to demonstrate the equivalent of having one grandparent with unadulterated American Indian ancestry to receive services from agencies such as the Bureau of Indian Affairs or the Indian Health Service.

At the moment, a scenario involving reparations and a process to establish eligibility seems most unlikely. Beyond the obvious issue of social justice it brings up, this is regrettable for another reason: A program of reparation payments almost certainly would precipitate a genealogical project of breathtaking proportions. At the very least, it would lead to an appreciation of our common ancestries and forever blur the racial fault lines that have marked this nation since its founding.

Community Recognition

Community recognition is one important way that membership in the American Indian population has been established. For American Indians, recognition is a matter of statutory definition for tribes and for individuals. The Bureau of Indian Affairs has criteria for tribal recognition. Tribes, especially those that are federally recognized, have statutes governing who is eligible for membership. This arrangement is peculiar to American Indians, and there is no analogue to it anywhere else in American society.

Community recognition might be implemented for other ethnic minorities in other ways, particularly to serve certain kinds of legal and administrative purposes. The federal government might designate certain community groups or organizations to decide who they consider to be a member of the communities they serve. Thus, for example, local chapters of the Urban League or the National Council of La Raza might issue ethnic identification cards, as many tribes do. This scenario, however, is so implausible, for many reasons, that it borders on the absurd. Assuming even that community-based organizations were willing to take on this daunting task of ethnic certification, they would no doubt face a mountain of legal challenges to their authority.

A more plausible role for community recognition might arise in the courts. Among the many thorny public policy issues surrounding the new OMB procedures allowing multiple response to the question of racial identity is whether multiracial persons are entitled to the same full measure of protection from discrimination as persons who do not claim a multiracial ancestry. On the face of it, this is a simple question. The Office of Management and Budget, in consultation with the Justice Department, issued guidelines in March 1999 clearly suggesting that for the purposes of civil rights enforcement, certain common combinations of multiracial ancestry (for example, American Indian and white) were to be treated as a protected minority. Ironically, the OMB had to resort to a variant of hypodescent to ensure that mixed-race persons were covered by the various civil rights provisions of federal law: for purposes of civil rights enforcement, a person who is black and white is considered black.

As straightforward as the OMB rules may seem, potentially problematic situations might cause the courts to resort to community recognition as a possible device for resolving disputes. Community recognition might resolve many possible disputes, and two examples readily come to mind, one involving an allegation of "ethnic fraud" and another that might stem from a claim of discrimination.

The term "ethnic fraud" was coined by a Detroit reporter who wrote a story in the early 1990s about Michigan college students who were claiming to be American Indians for the purpose of receiving tuition waivers (St. John 1992). As more students learned that they could receive financial assistance simply by self-identifying as American Indian, this program became widely abused. The reporter documented numerous instances in which students with no American Indian ancestry whatsoever had nonetheless claimed to be American Indians solely for the purpose of obtaining tuition assistance, fraudulently claiming an ethnic identity and thereby committing "ethnic fraud."

Although the courts and state electorates have sharply limited affirmative action and grants of race-based financial assistance, considerations of race still play an important role in a variety of settings ranging from college admission to bank loans. For example, Small Business Administration loans for minority-owned businesses require verification that an ethnic minority applicant owns a majority of the company. However, they do not require verification that the minority applicant is indeed a member of an ethnic minority group. Sooner or later, it seems plausible that programs such as this one will become vulnerable to ethnic fraud, and it may be necessary to police them to prevent this practice from becoming widespread. In all likelihood, this type of fraud is already occurring, but as more and more individuals come to understand the malleability of racial boundaries, it is virtually certain to increase.

In cases of racial discrimination, the new OMB standard may eventually result in especially problematic challenges. Consider an employee who identifies himself as African American and white in his personnel file. After being repeatedly passed over for promotion, he may decide to file a complaint of racial discrimination against his supervisor. For the sake of this example, also consider that some small degree of phenotypic ambiguity exists with respect to the employee's racial heritage, a not uncommon occurrence. In this instance, the supervisor may defend herself from the charge of racial discrimination by claiming to be unaware of or uninformed about the employee's ethnic minority ancestry. "This person considers himself to be white and African American. I did not discriminate against him, because I thought he was white." In this dispute, the first matter to be resolved is whether the employee is self-evidently African American—an issue that must be demonstrated even before the allegation of racial discrimination can be heard.

When presented with a case of ethnic fraud or a challenge to a discrimination case, the courts will have to decide whether an individual's claim to being a member of a racial or ethnic minority group is bona fide or false. To date, DNA testing is not sufficiently developed to yield an unambiguous finding with regard to racial heritage, although connections to common male ancestors can be traced. Similarly, birth and death records might be used to establish descent; but records can be notoriously inaccurate with respect to race and may not even exist for distant ancestors. In the absence of indisputable biological evidence, the courts may turn to other means for settling these claims—namely, whether a person is recognized by the community as African American, Latino, or some other ethnic minority.

The application of a community standard is not an unusual test. Perhaps the best-known example of a community standard is with regard to pornography. An image is deemed pornographic if it offends community tastes. Just as there are a multitude of problems in demonstrating community tastes, a host of complex issues would undoubtedly beset any effort to prove or disprove ethnic identity on the basis of community recognition. How does one assemble a preponderance of evidence to prove or disprove such a claim? What evidence is deemed acceptable, and from what sources? What constitutes a "community," and how is recognition established within it? Attorneys are adept at arguing, if not resolving, issues like these, and for that reason community recognition may eventually prove attractive to the judiciary.

Self-Identification

Many of the complexities related to self-identification for American Indians are equally applicable to other racial and ethnic minority groups—to some groups more so than to others. For American Indians, the use of self-identification becomes most problematic with respect to three issues: heterogeneity, authenticity, and response variability. Although perhaps not to the same degree, these same issues are problematic for other ethnic minorities. Like American Indians, growing numbers of multiracial persons will be at the heart of these matters. In the 2000 census, for example, nearly 12.0 million persons identified themselves as Asian; of this number, about 1.7 million reported that their racial heritage also included a non-Asian group (or groups)—in most cases, either black or white.

The problem of heterogeneity in self-identification stems from the fact that it is simply impossible to know exactly what information is being referenced when an individual self-reports a particular ethnic minority ancestry. The Asian population in the United States is a spectacularly diverse group and includes Japanese, Koreans, Cambodians, and East Indians, to name only a few. Some of these groups have been here for generations and include persons who speak uninflected American English and have everyday lives indistinguishable from their non-Asian neighbors. Others include persons who live in immigrant enclaves and speak little or no English and whose everyday lives are steeped in cultural traditions unfamiliar to most Americans. Between these two extremes are millions of persons who lead their lives as Asians but vary enormously with respect to the salience this identity has for their everyday lives and long-term life chances. Add to this group the large and growing numbers who identify with some other ethnic minority heritage, in addition to Asian, and the substantive content of this ethnic category begins to appear very ephemeral indeed.

Given the high levels of heterogeneity in populations like Asian Americans and American Indians, the question of authenticity can be a difficult one to answer. Authenticity speaks to the issue of who is entitled to claim a given ethnic or racial heritage. For most purposes, self-identification permits anyone to claim any racial or ethnic identity they choose. This is true in decennial census, and it is the case in most other applications, as well. Employers and schools, for example, have neither the resources nor the inclination to verify, and if necessary challenge, the identity of an applicant. However, there are those who will argue that this standard is too lax, and that an authentic ethnic identity means more than simply a willingness to report as such. This perspective would argue that, for the reasons described in connection with ethnic fraud, self-identification must be authenticated by some sort of additional information. Proponents of this position would be unlikely to accept some claims to identity because they did not include some minimum number of ethnic trappings. They might argue, for example, that a young man of mixed Asian and white ancestry who is growing up in a predominantly white suburban neighborhood, knows little about his Asian culture, and speaks only English should not be considered as genuinely Asian. Although this young man may have some phenotypically Asian traits, he is Asian in precious few other respects. However, this young man may feel differently about his ethnic status and, perhaps having an affinity for his Asian parent, choose this identity for himself.

Trying to establish a set of criteria that will authenticate beyond dispute claims to ethnicity is virtually certain to be a fool's errand. The impossibility of this exercise notwithstanding, the conflicts, disagreements, disputes, and disquietude caused by assertions of authenticity and lack thereof are unlikely to disappear in the near future. Furthermore, the heightened awareness of these claims, and concern about them, are exacerbated by individuals who alter their racial or ethnic identities at will, on a more or less frequent basis, to suit whatever needs are presently before them. This sort of behavior has been well documented in census data for American Indians, and preliminary evidence indicates that it exists among other groups as well, notably Asians and Latinos (Eschbach and Gómez 1998).

Response variability in racial reporting occurs when individuals decide to switch from one race with which they regularly identify to some other racial identification. This is a particularly acute problem for social scientists, who routinely assume that ascribed characteristics such as age, race, and sex are invariant traits or change in predictable orderly ways. However, response variability has the potential to affect the outcome of research in important ways if its effects are not recognized, especially in studies involving temporal comparisons. It requires a high degree of analytic sophistication to avoid being misled by the artifacts of compositional change.

Methodological problems aside, response variability has another potential downside: this kind of behavior contributes to a growing perception that race is an outmoded idea in American society, one that carries less and less legitimacy. To the extent that race and racial identity come to be perceived as arbitrary, capricious, and largely meaningless ideas, claims of racial injustice will increasingly be undercut. If race is a meaningless concept that depends largely on the whims of personal identity, then claims of racial disadvantage are rendered meaningless. However, this also would mean that one of the fundamental strands of social inequality in American society had finally unraveled, a strand that has existed since the founding of this nation and earlier. Although this might be cause for celebration, it is a fact that should be verified before the party begins.

It is a fact that needs to be established especially because racial discrimination can be, and often is, based wholly on phenotypic traits, regardless of how individuals construct their personal identities. Racial discrimination depends on perceptions of racial heritage and need not be qualified by additional information about how or why a person may claim to be black, white, Latino, or Asian. Indeed, the most malignant forms of racism in American society, physical attacks and verbal abuse, are almost always based on appearances and phenotypic traits. Thus a Chinese man is attacked by auto workers angry about competition from Japanese imports, and Asian Indians are threatened by enraged Americans following the destruction of the World Trade Center in New York City. Quite clearly, racial appearances matter in American society, and until they cease to make a difference in our everyday behavior, race will remain an omnipresent part of American society, no matter how much we acknowledge it to be an arbitrary and socially constructed fiction, purely of our own making.

Concluding Comments

In some respects, the American Indian population represents a truly unique case. No other racial or ethnic minority group has the same legal status as American Indians. This status leads directly to many of the highly complex classification issues discussed in this chapter. However, the experience of American Indians is not so different in one important respect—the matter of how to settle the question of inclusion: who does and does not belong to a particular ethnic group. Although it is easy to see how this has become a contentious matter for American Indians, it could be just as contentious for other groups. In the event that Congress decides to award reparations to the descendants of African slaves in America, questions will no doubt be raised about how to establish ancestral connections to the institution of slavery. The official determination of who is and who is not truly an African American could become an enormously complex question in such circumstances.

Despite their unique history, American Indians also may be an important bellwether for other groups insofar as they have much higher rates and a longer history of interracial marriage than other minorities, though this is a pattern increasingly emulated by other racial and ethnic groups since the 1960s. In the not-too-distant future, rates of interracial marriage among Asians and Latinos could reach the same level as those of American Indians. Even today, about one-third of all Latino children have a non-Latino parent.

High rates of intermarriage and high rates of immigration from Asia and Latin America are almost certain to swell the numbers of interracial persons in future generations. In the face of these growing numbers, the old paradigm for tracking race and ethnicity in American society is going to become ever more obsolete and difficult to handle. For American Indians, the tabulation procedures used to bridge past trends and data to the future amount to pounding a square peg into a round hole, with about the same precision and finesse in result. Based on some of the data presented in this chapter, especially the data for persons identifying themselves as "other" races, the experiences of American Indians presage the future of other racial and ethnic minority groups in America—Asian Americans, Hispanic Americans, and, perhaps to a lesser degree, African Americans.

The stability and invariance of benchmark racial classifications is no longer a realistic assumption. The challenge to social scientists, and anyone else with a serious interest in race and ethnicity, will be to understand the sources of this variability. Absent this knowledge, any effort to comprehend the racial and ethnic composition of American society is likely to be an exercise in futility.

Notes

1. For many years, the Bureau of Indian Affairs required proof that a person was at least one-fourth blood quantum to qualify for services such as scholarship assistance.

2. The Bureau of Indian Affairs routinely issues Certificates of Degree of Indian Blood. The most recent regulations for obtaining these documents were published in the *Federal Register* in 1999.

3. There are a variety of reasons they have been denied recognition. In general, denial of recognition indicates that the petitioning group failed to satisfy the criteria stipulated by the Bureau of Indian Affairs.

References

American Indian Policy Review Commission (AIPRC). 1976. *Final Report.* Volume 1. Washington: U.S. Government Printing Office.

Barth, Fredrik. 1969. Introduction to *Ethnic Groups and Boundaries,* edited by F. Barth. Boston: Little, Brown.

Bieder, Robert E. 1986. *Science Encounters the Indian, 1820–1880: The Early Years of American Ethnology.* Norman: University of Oklahoma Press.

Eschbach, Karl, and Christina Gómez. 1998. "Choosing Hispanic Identity: Ethnic Identity Switching Among Respondents to High School and Beyond." *Social Science Quarterly* 79(1): 74–90.

Feagin, Joe R. 1999. *Racial and Ethnic Relations*, 6th ed. Upper Saddle River, N.J.: Prentice Hall.

Fried, Morton. 1968. "On the Concepts of 'Tribe' and 'Tribal Society.'" In *Essays on the Problem of Tribe,* edited by June Helm. Seattle: University of Washington Press.

Harris, David. 1994. "The 1990 Census Count of American Indians: What Do the Numbers Really Mean?" *Social Science Quarterly* 75: 580–93.

Liebler, Carolyn A. 1996. "American Indian Ethnic Identity: Analysis of Tribal Specification in the 1990 Census." Working Paper 96–20. Madison, Wisc.: Center for Demography and Ecology, University of Wisconsin.

O'Brien, Sharon. 1989. *American Indian Tribal Governments.* Norman: University of Oklahoma Press.

Passel, Jeffrey S. 1976. "Provisional Evaluation of the 1970 Census Count of American Indians." *Demography* 13: 397–409.

————. 1996. "The Growing American Indian Population, 1960–1990: Beyond Demography." In *Changing Numbers, Changing Needs,* edited by Gary D. Sandefur, Ronald R. Rindfuss, and Barney Cohen. Washington, D.C.: National Academy Press.

Passel, Jeffrey S., and Patricia A. Berman. 1986. "Quality of 1980 Census Data for American Indians." *Social Biology* 33: 163–82.

Quinn, William W., Jr. 1990. "The Southeast Syndrome: Notes on Indian Descendant Recruitment Organizations and Their Perceptions of Native American Culture." *American Indian Quarterly* 14: 147–54.

St. John, Paige. 1992. "American Indians Hurt by College Admissions Abuses." *The Detroit News,* April 12: 1A.

Sandefur, Gary D., and Carolyn A. Liebler. 1996. "The Demography of American Indian Families." In *Changing Numbers, Changing Needs,* edited by Gary D. Sandefur, Ronald R. Rindfuss, and Barney Cohen. Washington, D.C.: National Academy Press.

Sandefur, Gary D., and Trudy McKinnel. 1986. "American Indian Intermarriage." *Social Science Research* 15: 347–71.

Snipp, C. Matthew. 1989. *American Indians: The First of This Land.* New York: Russell Sage Foundation.

Thornton, Russell. 1987. *American Indian Holocaust and Survival.* Norman: University of Oklahoma Press.

————. 1996. "Tribal Membership Requirements and the Demography of 'Old' and 'New' Native Americans." In *Changing Numbers, Changing Needs,* edited by Gary D. Sandefur, Ronald R. Rindfuss, and Barney Cohen. Washington, D.C.: National Academy Press.

U.S. Department of Commerce. U.S. Bureau of the Census. 1915. *Indian Population in the United States and Alaska, 1910.* Washington: U.S. Government Printing Office.

————. 1937. *The Indian Population of the United States and Alaska.* Washington: U.S. Government Printing Office.

U.S. Department of Interior. Bureau of Indian Affairs (BIA). 2000. *List of Petitioners.* Washington: Bureau of Indian Affairs, Branch of Acknowledgment and Research.

U.S. Office of Technology Assessment. 1986. *Indian Health Care,* OTA-H-290 (April). Washington: U.S. Government Printing Office.

Waters, Mary. 1990. *Ethnic Options: Choosing Ethnic Identities in America.* Berkeley, Calif.: University of California Press.

Wilkins, David E. 2002. *American Indian Politics and the American Political System.* Lanham, Md.: Rowman and Littlefield.

Woodward, C. Vann. 1974. *The Strange Career of Jim Crow.* New York: Oxford University Press.

8

CENSUS BUREAU LONG-TERM RACIAL PROJECTIONS: INTERPRETING THEIR RESULTS AND SEEKING THEIR RATIONALE

Joel Perlmann

Racial and ethnic projections are connected to the themes of this volume because the projections, like other federal race classifications and tabulations, must find ways to deal with interracial marriages and especially with the offspring of those marriages.[1] Yet today the Census Bureau does not build future intermarriages into the racial and ethnic projection models. Instead, the offspring of today's interracial marriages are assigned the race of the mother, and all future marriages are modeled within single racial categories (or within Hispanic and non-Hispanic ethnicity). The child of two Hispanics will marry another Hispanic; and so too their great-great grandchild will marry another Hispanic.

It is easy to make the assumptions of any model seem simple minded; the real issue is what is gained and what is lost by working with these assumptions. The gains and losses in connection with projections specifically need to be considered; we cannot merely claim that because race counts of the contemporary population are needed, racial projections are useful, too. Nor can we argue that because nonoverlapping racial counts of the contemporary population are important for legal purposes, non-overlapping categories in racial projections are also desirable. Many Americans believe that some form of race tabulation is still a necessity in contemporary society. We may look forward to a day when the situation will be different, when it will still be important to tabulate ages but not to tabulate races; but for today, we need the race counts to monitor progress in redressing the racial oppression of the past (or of the present). Moreover, many believe that race counts are necessary for the present structure of the civil rights laws. The racial counts may involve problems for which there is really no good solution, but those counts are necessary, and the problems do not lead us to conclude that the goals of tabulation are wrong.

However, these two justifications of the race counts for today's population—the need to monitor progress toward racial equality and the need to have accurate count for purposes of civil rights enforcement—do not apply to the racial projections. Consequently, we need to ask whether the federal government has any justification for projecting the racial composition of the population. One might ask first if there is legislative or executive directive mandating racial projections; such a directive might not amount to a reasoned justification for the projections, but the existence of a legislative or executive directive would at least explain why the Census Bureau produces and publishes the projections. Yet to the best of my knowledge, there is no law or executive order that directs bureau officials to issue these reports.

Where, then, do the projections come from, and why does the bureau produce them? My impression is that the reports on racial projections are an outgrowth of the need to project the size and age structure of the population. In the middle third of the twentieth century, as government planners asked for population estimates—both estimates for points in time between decennial censuses and estimates for points in time in the future—the Current Population Survey (CPS) estimates and projections came into being. In those years it made sense, for almost any purpose, to build up total population figures from figures of the white and black populations considered separately: fertility, mortality, age, and sex structure were all different for blacks and whites. Moreover, blacks were not merely a numerically important segment of the national population; they were a huge proportion in the South. Ignoring the white-black demographic differences would create avoidable errors in national figures, and ignoring those white-black differences would spell disaster for figures that were specific to the southern region. Moreover, white-black intermarriage rates were extremely low—indeed, white-black intermarriage was still illegal in much of the nation during the entire middle third of this century. Consequently, working with closed population estimates was a simplifying assumption for a projection model, an assumption that involved relatively little distortion.

Whether at that time American Indians and Asians were counted with blacks, with whites, or in a separate grouping was a much smaller concern numerically than it would become after 1970. Over the past three decades, the size of the Asian and Hispanic populations rose as the data about them became regularly available, and it seemed a reasonable step to treat Asians and Hispanics explicitly in the model, as well. In addition, of course, ethnic interest groups may have urged the decision to model the population growth of Asian and Hispanic populations explicitly; but there was also good reason to do so from the point of view of the demographers. Immigrants were rapidly coming to dominate the Asian and Hispanic groups numerically, and new immigrant populations differed from native-born Americans in age structure, fertility, and mortality. What is more, new immigrants tended to marry their own. Thus, projecting the figures for Asians and Hispanics separately could refine total population projections—especially if the most useful projections were those concerned with the next decade or two, during which period the dominance of the immigrant generation within Asian and Hispanic America was quite certain. Finally, projecting figures for black, white, Asian, and Hispanic Americans (rather than simply white and nonwhite) also more or less paralleled the 1977 OMB categories, and that must have seemed an advantage, as well.

I suspect, therefore, that the projections, especially the initial black and white projections, were not at first undertaken as an end in themselves; rather, they were undertaken principally because they were useful for a larger purpose—namely, the refinement of total population projections. A fateful decision followed: since the projections were available by race, why not release them by race, too? Indeed, how could the Census Bureau's procedures claim to be open to scrutiny and review if a critical feature of the modeling (calculations on multiple closed populations) were not published? Finally, I suspect that all these developments resulted from the decisions of demographic experts at the middle levels of the bureau's officialdom; they were not major policy decisions over which presidents, commerce secretaries, or even Census Bureau directors huddled.

However, during the 1980s, and certainly by 1989, the racial projections themselves highlighted a novel finding, a finding interesting in itself to racially conscious America: namely, that the country would become much less white in the future. The projections had not been created to explore that issue, although the result could hardly have been ignored. Even a 1989 projection report, which generated more press attention than any other racial projection up to that time, treated the finding as interesting but secondary to the bigger news that the American population would peak and then decline numerically in the twenty-first century (U.S. Bureau of the Census 1989). The "big break" for the fame of racial projections came, if I understand correctly, during the following year, when *Time* ran its piece about "the browning of America."

The *Time* piece was issued at about the same time that the 1990 census forms were mailed out. Nowhere does the piece mention the Census Bureau's racial projections, and it presents its projections as "*Time* estimates." Still, it is hard to believe that one stimulus was not the bureau's projections of the 1980s, especially that of 1989. The article is striking because it stresses the cultural conflicts that could be expected to intensify as a result of a sharp increase in new immigrant populations of Asians and Hispanics in the context of American race relations of the 1980s and 1990s—language issues, multiculturalism in education, race discrimination and outspoken opposition to it, affirmative action, and so on. At the same time, the numerical point stressed in the article is about the long-run racial projections (over six decades) that will create a nonwhite majority. By juxtaposing the issues and racial divisions of 1990 with long-term population trends and by failing even to mention intermarriage, the article leaves the clear impression that calculations about future race counts mean that race divisions and race issues as Americans knew them in 1990 would grow by 2050 in something like the proportions that the count of minority race and ethnic groups would grow:

> Someday soon . . . White Americans will become a minority group. . . . By 2056 . . . the "average" U.S. resident, as defined by Census statistics, will trace his or her descent to Africa, Asia, the Hispanic world, the Pacific Islands, Arabia—almost anywhere but white Europe. . . . A truly multiracial society will undoubtedly prove much harder to govern. . . . Racial and ethnic conflict remains an ugly fact of American life everywhere. . . . As the numbers of minorities increase, their demands for a share of the national bounty are bound to intensify. ("Beyond the Melting Pot: The Browning of America," *Time*, April 9, 1990: 28–30)

By contrast, it is worth noting in passing, the *Time* story on Tiger Woods and multiraciality seven years later stressed a future of multiraciality and the opaque nature of the future meaning of race (again using the term "browning of America" but making no explicit reference to the magazine's earlier piece): "An explosion of interracial, interethnic and interreligious marriages will swell the ranks of children whose mere existence makes a mockery of age-old racial categories and attitudes. . . . [Many Americans haven't] got a clue about what to call the growing ranks of people like Woods who inconveniently refused to be pigeonholed into one of the neat, over-simplified racial classifications used by government agencies—and let's face it, most people" ("I'm Just Who I Am," *Time,* May 6, 1997: 33).

In any case, if this reconstruction of the development of racial and ethnic projections is not too far off the mark, one conclusion that can be drawn from it is that an important justification for the projections is not in their explicit treatment of race and ethnicity at all but in their use for refining projections of the total American population. In any case, we should still ask about the gains and losses that the racial projections entail for the understanding of their specific subject, race. In particular, what are the effects of ignoring racial intermarriage? I do not spend long on the latter question, because I think most of the key points are now well known (Hirschman 1996; Perlmann 1997; Smith and Edmonston 1997; Hout and Goldstein 1991); but what I hope may be new here, and of some use in making the issues more concrete, is a comparison of projection methods, on the one hand, and a historical study, on the other.

Specifically, I present some findings from a study (based on census data) of Italian immigrants and their descendants over four generations. This is not a study of the census ancestry question, however. My goal was to find the actual origins of recent ancestors, not to explore the reporting of which origins the respondent "identifies with." I was interested in the origins that the genealogist would report rather than those that the social psychologist, interested in subjective thought patterns, would report; I was interested in patterns of descent, not patterns of consent.[2]

The method used is explained briefly in the note to table 8.1, and the full study is also available (Perlmann 2000). The method is surely imperfect, but it does have the great advantage of describing descent across three generations, descent as the genealogist would ask about it, rather than relying on identity, as the ancestry question does.

Italians were the largest immigrant group of the early twentieth century. The great majority started out in low-skilled jobs; they surely were not characterized by especially rapid upward mobility, rapid cultural assimilation, or high rates of intermarriage. If anything, the Italian experience would be a kind of acid test for intermarriage patterns of past European immigrant groups. Italian immigrants would have been considered white in 1910, but only in a limited sense; perhaps, as the cultural historians tell us, it makes sense to think of the Italian immigrants as an "in-between people" (Roediger 1991; Orsi 1992; Barrett and Roediger 1997; Higham 1992 [1955]).[3]

The immigrant generation rarely intermarried, and so their children, the second generation, were mostly of unmixed origins, with two Italian immigrant parents. However, these second-generation Italian Americans often intermarried. This much is well known; the implication for the third generation, presented in table 8.1, needs to be appreciated. Among those third-generation children (who were twelve to sixteen years of age in the 1960 Census)—that is, children who had at least one Italian immigrant grandparent—only 38 percent were the descendants only of Italians. In the fourth generation, no more than 11 percent of the children who had an Italian immigrant great-grandparent were the descendants only of Italians.

Table 8.2 focuses on the time involved in this transition across generations. An Italian immigrant who arrived in 1907 (the midpoint of the great wave of Italian immigration that occurred between 1900 and 1914) could well have had a grandchild entering American schools in 1953—some forty-six years later; and that grandchild was a good deal more likely to be of mixed than of single origins.

The experience of Italians can be compared with that of immigrants in our own time. Second-generation Asians and Hispanics of today are out-marrying at rates that are roughly comparable to the rates at which the Italian second generation out-married earlier in this century (Perlmann

219

TABLE 8.1   *Single and Mixed Ethnic Origins Among Italian Immigrants and Their Descendants (Percentage)*

Characteristic	First Generation	Second Generation	Third Generation[a]	Fourth Generation[b]
Origins				
Single (Italian only)	100	90	38[c]	11
Mixed (Italian and other)	0	10	62	89
Intermarriage among single-origin	5	40	67	n.a.

Source: Data from Perlmann 2000.

Note: Figures for intermarriage rates and for second-generation origins are approximate, based on parents of third- and fourth-generation sample members.

[a]The sample of third-generation members is selected using the birthplace and parental birthplace questions in the 1960 census (IPUMS data set); the sample includes native-born children twelve to sixteen years of age who were living with at least one parent who, in turn, was native-born of at least one Italian-born parent.

[b]The sample of fourth-generation members is selected using the birthplace, parental birthplace, and ancestry questions in the October 1979 CPS; the sample includes children living with at least one parent who, in turn, was native-born and of native parentage and claimed Italian ancestry. These parents would be members of third or later generations; however, since nearly all Italian immigrants arrived after 1880 (and, in fact, most arrived after 1900), the third- or later-generation Italians of 1979 are nearly all third-generation Italians, and their children, the sample members, are nearly all fourth-generation descendants of at least one Italian immigrant.

[c]The percentage declines to 25 if this row is restricted to people of unmixed generational standing (four Italian immigrant grandparents and two native-born parents). Note that the percentages for the third generation (38) involve a range (32 to 42 percent) because some estimation is involved; see Perlmann 2000 for details. Here the approximate midpoint of the range is used. Also, the shift from third to fourth generation in Italian-only origin—38 percent to 11 percent—is slightly exaggerated by changes in method required by the datasets; using comparable methods, the shift would be 33 percent to 11 percent. See Perlmann 2000, 18.

1997; Alba 1995). A Hispanic or Asian immigrant who arrived in 1980 might well have a grandchild in first grade by 2026—not so very distant a horizon. Similarly, we could also turn the question around and ask about the children in the year 2050, for that is a year that much of the discussion of racial forecasting highlights. Imagine a third-generation Asian or Hispanic first-grader starting school in 2050; according to the time frame established for Italian immigrant and later generations, this child's immigrant grandparent will not arrive from Asia or Latin America until 2004. The passage of time to the fourth generation does take us into more distant projection times, of course, adding three more decades, but even that time frame is within the outer years of recent projection periods (seventy-five years).

The grandchild or great-grandchild of these Asian or Hispanic immigrants is considerably more likely to be of mixed origin than of only Asian or only Hispanic origin. Although the Census Bureau projects that the

TABLE 8.2   *Time from First to Fourth Generation: Examples*

		Asian or Hispanic	
Generation and Event	Italian	Example 1	Example 2
Immigrant arrives at age twenty	1907	1980	2004
Second-generation member born	1917	1990	2014
Third-generation member born	1947	2020	2044
Third-generation member enters first grade	1953	2026	2050
Fourth-generation member born	1977	2050	2074
Fourth-generation member enters first grade	1983	2056	2080

Source: Author's compilation.

great-grandchild will be of single origin only, our example suggests that *eight times as many* of the great grandchildren will be of mixed origin as of single origin.

The example of Italian descent can also highlight the difference in the membership numbers generated when we define populations in terms of whether or not they intermarry (that is, marry outside of their racial or ethnic group). Table 8.3 presents the data. As noted in table 8.1, no more than thirty-eight of every one hundred grandchildren of Italian immigrants were of Italian-only origin, and at least sixty-two of every hundred were of mixed origin—that is, at least one of their parents was at least part not Italian. Assume that these third-generation children were born to one hundred different couples. Sixty-two of these couples were of mixed origin, with at least one of the parents having some non-Italian origins, and so sixty-two of the third-generation children are of mixed origin. Given the projection's assumption that no future intermarriage will occur, these mixed couples (of the second generation) cannot exit; instead, the sixty-two Italian members of these couples are assumed to have married other Italians, (for simplicity, assume these sixty-two marry each other) and the sixty-two non-Italian members to have married non-Italians (again, assume they marry each other). We still end up with sixty-two couples, but only half of them, thirty-one couples, are going to be counted as Italians in the projections. Instead of thirty-eight single-origin individuals and sixty-two mixed-origin individuals, then, the Census Bureau would project sixty-nine single-origin Italian individuals (the thirty-eight original single-origin and the thirty-one just discussed) and no mixed-origin individuals. Thus, by ignoring inter-marriage, the projection is for more third-generation people of Italian-only descent than we would project if we took into account intermarriage—sixty-nine as opposed to thirty-eight.

On the other hand, the projection foresees notably fewer individuals with some Italian descent (single or mixed)—sixty-nine as opposed to one hundred. Also noteworthy are the implications for the question "In what

TABLE 8.3   *Origins of Third Generation of Italian Immigrants,
Under Various Methods of Defining Who Is "Italian
American" (Percentage)*

Origin	Descent[a]	Projection (Assumes No Intermarriage)	Self-Identification[b]	Projected Identification Under OMB Guidance Procedure[c]
Single	38	69	$38 \times x$	
Mixed	62	0	$62 \times y$	
Total	100	69[d]	$38x + 62y$ total	$38x + 62y$ total

Source: Perlmann 2000.

Note: The examples assume no differences in fertility across Italian-only, Italian-mixed and non-Italian couples in the preceding generation.

[a]The example is based on the midpoint of the range in table 8.1.

[b]x and y are the proportions in each group that self-identify as Italians (for example, on the census ancestry question).

[c]The breakdown of mixed versus single origin is ignored; both are counted if they identify as Italian. Note that this column refers to a hypothetical example only: the OMB guidance does not deal with Italians, nor does it deal only with later-generation members.

[d]Based on adjusting the sixty-two children from mixed-origin couples. For every sixty-two such mixed couples, the projection assumes the Italian members marry only other Italians—producing thirty-one single-origin couples (62/2). The total number of Italians projected is thus $38 + 31 = 69$. The sixty-two non-Italians marry other non-Italians (producing thirty-one non-Italian couples whose offspring would appear among non-Italians).

year will the population of the United States be x percent Italian?" When asked of the bureau's projections, such a question must be understood as referring to those with *only* Italian origins, because the projection cannot answer the question for a group with mixed origins (they fall outside the assumptions of the projection). By recognizing only single-origin Italians, and thereby also reducing the total number of those descended from an Italian immigrant (the contrast between the projected sixty-nine with single origins and the original group of one hundred with single or mixed origins), the projection finds fewer descendants of Italians. Consequently, such a projection will report the year at which Italian descendants reach x percent of the population to be later in time than if the mixed-origin individuals were included. This is the dynamic operating when the Census Bureau announces that the population of the United States will reach 50 percent nonwhite in a certain year, if individuals of mixed origins—notably white and nonwhite—could be included in the projection. The year in which 50 percent of the population will report some nonwhite origins would be earlier than the census now reports, but many of the individuals with nonwhite origins would also report white origins. Specific figures for such a revised projection appear in chapter 9 of this volume. (See table 9.8; one row captures descent and another specifies total population, allowing calculation of the proportion of Americans projected to have some nonwhite ancestors in a given census year.)

The example of Italian descent is also useful for highlighting the difference between the origins that the genealogist might highlight and those based on subjective self-identity. We can make assumptions about what proportion of individuals will identify themselves as Italian among those who are of Italian-only descent and among those who are of mixed Italian and other descent—here called the (unknown) proportions x and y respectively. Thus the identity question adds another level of uncertainty; and if self-identification of later-generation Hispanics and Asians will be as fluid as identification of Italian ancestry on the censuses of our own time, the uncertainty level may be pretty high.

Finally, this exercise with Americans of Italian descent also illuminates the OMB directive on tabulating race and ethnicity for civil rights law. If Italian descendants entering school in 2026 were at issue (for example, in terms of school desegregation), the OMB guidance would be counting all of those of mixed Italian and non-Italian origin as well as all of those of single origin in the protected group (OMB 2000). If Asians and Hispanics or American Indians were at issue, the implications could be similar, the group would comprise mainly those who were also non-Asian, non-Hispanic, or non–American Indian.

Before closing I add three important caveats. First, I have stressed the distortion created in thinking of the third and later generations of today's immigrants. That emphasis is justified because the message sent by the projections is in fact about what will happen to the descendants of today's racially divided Americans. On the other hand, the third- and later-generation descendants of Asians and Hispanics will not constitute a majority among Asians and Hispanics for a very long time (assuming that Asian and Hispanic immigration continues at levels not unlike those of today). Projections deal with the whole ethnic group, not just with the members of its third and later generations; for that reason it is perhaps best to say that immigrants and second-generation members will be mostly of single origin, and most of the group with Asian and Hispanic origins will be immigrants or members of the second generation, but most of the third- and later-generation descendants of Asian and Hispanic immigrants will have origins in other groups, too.

The second caveat, which follows in part from the first, concerns the use of the Italian example for highlighting the OMB guidance. Even in the unlikely event that the OMB guidance were still in effect in the year 2050, the majority of Asian and Hispanic people covered by it probably will be first- and second-generation members and therefore mostly of single origins. It is only the majority of that subset of Asians and Hispanics in the third and later generations of the group that will be heavily of mixed origins.

The third caveat concerns the connection between immigration and race. The dynamics I have described here pertain to Asian and Hispanic groups, peoples the OMB defines as races but whose experience in contemporary America is shaped by the dynamics of immigration—and particularly by the dynamics of generation. But what of African Americans? We cannot assume that the future rate of black intermarriage will remain at its current low level (a point taken up in the introduction to this volume), and models with alternative assumptions need to be created. However, we certainly want to be careful not to assume that the degree of mixed origins in 2050 will be as great for blacks as it is expected to be for Asians and Hispanics.

In closing this review, I want to ask explicitly whether the Census Bureau should be reporting racial and ethnic projections. I suspect that discarding them today would be hard for political reasons—because of the great interest they have attracted. Moreover, as I stress earlier in this chapter, the racial projections help us project more precise figures for the total population than we otherwise could. Still, it is one thing to use the modeling assumption and another to report all the findings as though they are significant end products. Perhaps it would be possible to stop publishing the detailed tabulations of racial projections (or at any rate projections that extend beyond ten or twenty years), even if the numbers would be available to researchers who want to download raw data. The text of the report could explain the reasons for the changes and include a careful statement about the year in which a majority of the population would be nonwhite in the sense of having some nonwhite ancestors. If no change to accommodate intermarriage and generational standing is contemplated in the Census Bureau's projections, some modification of the published reports in this direction seems critical to avoid popular misunderstandings.

Perhaps intermarriage and generational status can be incorporated into the projections. Doing so, of course would require resources. Still, even then, the question of whether these racial projections are more than an intermediate step needs to be considered. First, why are we bothering to publish the figures as ends in themselves? Second, if they are to be published, what additional effort can be taken to clarify their meaning? The bureau generally devotes effort and funds to ensure public understanding of its work; if it continues to produce race projections (not, I have stressed, necessarily the wisest course), it will need to devote attention and resources to ensure public understanding in this seemingly narrow and technical domain. I suspect the public thinks about the projections mostly in terms of descent and mostly in terms of unmixed descent—essentially treating the marriage projections in table 8.3 as though they were the reality. Given what the Census Bureau has published about projections to date, why would the public think otherwise?

Notes

1. More precisely, in this context, the projections must be refined to deal with the individuals whose recent ancestors had been classified in more than one OMB-defined racial group.

2. This distinction is similar to that between descent and consent, except that typically the interest in using descent and consent is to show how respondents select and chose among the elements of their descent (or create altogether new elements) to forge their ethnic identity, whereas I stress that descent pure and simple is also crucial. On consent and descent, see, for example, Barth 1969, Dominguez 1986, and Sollors 1986.

3. For our purposes, the Italian immigrant experience probably differs most from that of contemporary Hispanics and Asians not in terms of racial isolation but in the duration of the period of mass immigration: whereas some Italians arrived throughout the half-century between 1880 and 1930, the majority arrived in a decade and a half, between 1900 and 1914. The Asian and Hispanic immigrations of today have already taken a different course in that high levels of immigration have continued for a longer period, and the "middle-series" projection assumes consistent future immigration. Italian immigration, of course, also differed from that of contemporary Asians in that the latter includes relatively high proportions of highly educated immigrants or others who enter the American class structure well above the level that was typical for Italians. However, this difference would not lead me to predict a slower process of assimilation and intermarriage for the former. Finally, it should be clear throughout that in discussing the discrimination faced by Asians and Hispanic immigrants I am discussing only today's immigrant Asians and Hispanics, not those who experienced much higher levels of discrimination in earlier centuries and in much of this century.

References

Alba, Richard. 1995. "Assimilation's Quiet Tide." *Public Interest* 119(spring): 1–18.

Barrett, David, and David Roediger. 1997. "In-Between Peoples: Race, Nationality, and the New Immigrant Working Class." *Journal of American Ethnic History* (spring): 3–44.

Barth, Fredrik. 1969. *Ethnic Groups and Boundaries: The Social Organization of Culture Difference.* Boston: Little, Brown.

Dominguez, Virginia R. 1986. *White by Definition: Social Classification in Creole Louisiana.* New Brunswick, N.J.: Rutgers University Press.

Higham, John. 1992 [1955]. *Strangers in the Land: Patterns of American Nativism, 1860–1925*. New Brunswick, N.J.: Rutgers University Press.

Hirschman, Charles. 1996. "Race and Ethnic Population Projections: A Critical Evaluation of Their Content and Meaning." Unpublished manuscript.

Hout, Michael, and Joshua Goldstein. 1991. "How 4.5 Million Irish Immigrants Became 40 Million Irish Americans: Demographic and Subjective Aspects of the Ethnic Composition of White Americans." *American Sociological Review* 59(1): 64–82.

Office of Management and Budget (OMB), Executive Office of the President. 2000. *Guidance on Aggregation and Allocation of Data on Race for Use in Civil Rights Monitoring and Enforcement.* Bulletin 00–02. Washington (March 9).

Orsi, David. 1992. "The Religious Boundaries of an In-Between People: Street Feste and the Problem of the Dark-Skinned 'Other' in Italian Harlem, 1920–1990."*American Quarterly* 44 (September): 313–47.

Perlmann, Joel. 1997. *Reflecting the Changing Face of America*. Public Policy Brief 35. Annandale-on-Hudson, N.Y.: Jerome Levy Economics Institute (October).

———. 2000. "Demographic Outcomes of Ethnic Intermarriage in American History: Italian Americans Through Four Generations." Working Paper 312. Annandale-on-Hudson, N.Y.: Levy Economics Institute.

Roediger, David. 1991. *The Wages of Whiteness: Race and the Making of the American Working Class*. London: Verso.

Smith, James P., and Barry Edmonston, eds. 1997. *The New Americans: Economic, Demographic, and Fiscal Effects of Immigration.* Washington, D.C.: National Academy Press.

Sollors, Werner. 1986. *Beyond Ethnicity: Consent and Descent in American Culture*. New York: Oxford University Press.

U.S. Department of Commerce. U.S. Bureau of the Census. 1989. *Population Projections of the United States, by Age, Sex, and Race, 1988 to 2080.* Current Population Reports, series no. 1018. Washington.

9

RECENT TRENDS IN INTERMARRIAGE AND IMMIGRATION AND THEIR EFFECTS ON THE FUTURE RACIAL COMPOSITION OF THE U.S. POPULATION

Barry Edmonston, Sharon M. Lee, and Jeffrey S. Passel

THROUGHOUT U.S. history, immigration has been a major force in shaping population growth and ethnic composition. As the countries of origin of immigrants shifted, so did the ethnic composition of the nation's population. The role of immigration was and remains closely linked to a second major force in U.S. society: beliefs and attitudes about race. The passage of the Chinese Exclusion Act of 1882, the creation of the "barred zone" (the Asia-Pacific triangle) in 1917, and the implementation of national origins quotas in immigration laws in the 1920s exemplify the influence of racial attitudes on immigration policies. When immigrants from southern, eastern, and central Europe dominated immigrant flows at the turn of the twentieth century, nativist reactions and exaggerated fears of racial suicide were widespread (Dinnerstein and Reimers 1988; Higham 1972).

Given the powerful effects of immigration and racial ideology in shaping U.S. society, it is not surprising that efforts to describe and track the population have always used race as a critical variable. The first census of 1790 classified the population into slaves and free persons. Because no whites were slaves, this was a de facto counting of the population by race (Anderson 1988). Race was used in subsequent censuses to track the growth and relative sizes of different racial populations. Population projections by race have also been routinely performed by official agencies, including the U.S. Census Bureau, which released its first set of population projections by race in 1947 (Whelpton 1947).

The nation is once again experiencing a substantial shift in the national origins of immigrants. Over the past forty years, Europe has ceased to be the primary source of immigrants to the United States. More than 80 percent of today's immigrants come from Asia and Latin America, compared with less than 35 percent in the 1950s. Recent immigration has fueled the rapid growth of the Asian and Hispanic populations and brought about a new phase of racial and ethnic transformation in the United States. A population once dominated by people of European and African descent is becoming more diverse. The effects of continued immigration from Asia and Latin America on the future racial and ethnic composition of the U.S. population is a key concern for government officials, educators, researchers, and others involved in responding to these changes. There are also broad social and political ramifications as the diversity of the population increases.

Recent projections by the Census Bureau depict further dramatic shifts in the racial and ethnic composition of the population. In our previous work, we developed a population projection approach that characterizes the U.S. population by race, Hispanic-origin, and immigrant generation (Edmonston and Passel 1992, 1994). Our use of immigrant generation in population projections is a novel approach. It allows the model to make different assumptions and to provide separate results for the foreign born (the first generation), children of the foreign born (the second generation), and subsequent descendants (the third and higher generations). Our new projection results underscore the impact of immigration on both short- and long-term population growth.

A second important aspect of recent demographic trends is increased racial intermarriage. Conventional population projections assume no intermarriage. The assumption of complete endogamy implies that all children inherit the racial and ethnic identities of their parents. In our projection model, we take into account the effects of racial-ethnic intermarriage and, along with it, the likelihood that children are born with multiple racial-ethnic backgrounds. We follow current federal standards on racial and ethnic classification. Official races are white, black, Asian, American Indian or Alaska Native, and Native Hawaiian or other Pacific Islander. Ethnicity refers to Hispanic origin. When we speak of race-ethnicity, then, we mean race and Hispanic origin. Racial-ethnic intermarriage refers to marriages between members of different races and marriages between Hispanics and non-Hispanics. The inclusion of the effects of intermarriage on the future racial-ethnic composition of the U.S. population is another novel feature of our approach. By explicitly considering the effects of intermarriage, we highlight the blurring of racial-ethnic group boundaries and the error of assuming endogamous populations classified into mutually exclusive racial-ethnic categories.

The problems surrounding classification and measurement of race have been noted in earlier work (Edmonston et al. 1994; Lee 1993). The process of racial and ethnic identity has also been shown to be fluid and influenced by situational and other factors (Eschbach 1995; Passel 1997; Root 1996; Snipp 1997; Waters 1990). The significance of intermarriage lies in the growth of the population of people with multiple racial-ethnic backgrounds on demographic trends (Goldstein 1999; Perlmann 1997; Sandefur 1986). We view the process of racial identification by such individuals and their subsequent marital and fertility behavior as critical to understanding future population trends. The growth of the population with multiple origins creates a momentum toward further mixing of the population as multiple-origin people tend to be less tied to a particular origin, be it race, Hispanic origin, language, or religion (Finnas 1988; Labov and Jacobs 1998). Unlike previous censuses, the 2000 census permitted individuals to mark more than one race. This shift in the method of reporting racial data underlines the importance of considering intermarriage and its consequences on population projections by race and ethnicity.

In this chapter we present new findings from our population projection model, using recent data on immigration, emigration, fertility, mortality, and intermarriage. The limits of population projections, employing current knowledge about fertility, mortality, and migration to estimate future trends, are well known (Hirschman 1994; Preston 1993; Romaniuc 1990; Tabah 1993). All three components are subject to unknown amounts of change, and long-term projections are particularly risky and tenuous. Despite the well-known shortcomings of population projections, they fulfill the important task of providing clues to the future. The specific parameters of population projections may prove to be incorrect, but the general pattern of projected trends may be close to actual demographic changes.

Population Projection Approach

The population projections reported in this chapter are obtained with a modified cohort-component method. The conventional cohort-component model assumes a population that is affected by births, deaths, and in- and out-migration. For a national population, the migration streams are international migration flows. The model used here introduces two new features in population projections. First, it explicitly considers the role of generation by describing the population in terms of first-generation immigrants, the second-generation sons and daughters of immigrants, and members of the third and higher generations. Second, it does not assume that all members of the population group, considered here as racial or ethnic groups, will have descendants who inherit and retain membership in the group. The projection models vary group membership by assuming intermarriage and subsequent multiple racial-ethnic membership.[1]

Overall Population Model

The initial population is characterized by age, sex, and ethnicity, as in a standard population projection. The model makes separate demographic assumptions for each of five race-ethnic groups: American Indians, Asians and Pacific Islanders, blacks, Hispanics, and whites.[2] The base population, starting in 2000, is moved forward in five-year intervals, with successive application of the demographic dynamics. Births are added, deaths are subtracted, and net migration is added, depending on levels of immigration and emigration in each group.

The projection model provides population estimates, by age and sex, for each of the five groups for the period 2000 to 2100. Different assumptions are made for changes over time in fertility and mortality rates and for the level and age composition of immigrants and emigrants. The fertility, mortality, and migration assumptions for the projection period are described in a later section.

The conventional population projection model is modified to distinguish generations: the foreign born (the first generation), the native-born sons and daughters of foreign-born parents (the second generation), and the native-born offspring of native-born parents (the third and higher generations). For a generational population projection, assumptions need to be made for each of the three generations. For mortality, each generation by age and sex experiences mortality that may differ by generation. Deaths in a generation reduce the numbers of that generation. For fertility, births to a generation produce an addition to the next generation. Births to foreign-born immigrants (the first generation) are members of the second generation and add to the second-generation zero-to-four-years age group in the next interval of the population projection. For international migration, assumptions need to be made about the generational composition of migrants. Immigrants to a population are principally foreign born. Emigrants from the United States are usually members of the first generation: they are people who immigrated to the United States and then later decided to return to their country of birth.

The Dynamics of Intermarriage and Racial-Ethnic Origin

Population projections of immigrant groups, characterized by race and ethnicity, also need to consider the persistence of such membership. Members of a racial or ethnic group who always marry and reproduce within the group would have perfect endogamy and maintain single race-ethnicity membership. Marriage to persons of other racial and ethnic groups (that is, intermarriage) and reproduction of a new generation would produce offspring of multiple racial-ethnic origins. It is important therefore to include

an estimate of intermarriage in the population projection to obtain an estimate of the single-race-or-ethnicity versus multiple-race-or-ethnicity populations of subsequent generations.

It should be noted that the 2000 census categorizes the U.S. population into the following official races: American Indian and Alaska Native,
Asian, black or African American, Native Hawaiian and other Pacific Islander, white, and "some other race." Hispanic status is explicitly defined
for purposes of identifying a Hispanic population. Hispanics can be of any
race. In practice, more than 90 percent of the Hispanic population reports
itself as either white or "other" (reports of "other" race include individuals
who do not check a specific, listed race but write in such responses as
"Mexican").

The official current classification system is based on an arbitrary separation of race and ethnicity, defining Asians, blacks, American Indians,
Hawaiians, and whites as "races," not ethnic groups. There have been
many previous and current discussions of the logical and statistical problems with federal racial classification standards (Edmonston et al. 1994;
Lee 1993; Hirschman 1994; Lieberson 1993). We recognize that official
classifications of race and ethnicity are problematic. However, for purposes
of population projections for racial-ethnic groups, we employ the standard
categories. Indeed, our efforts to incorporate the effects of intermarriage in
population projections support the viewpoint that such classifications dis-
tort demographic and social reality.

The main implication of the current official classification system is
that population projections for the Hispanic population overlap with the
overall projections for the main-race groups. Because of the overlap of
Hispanics with the race groups in current population counts produced by
the Census Bureau, census data do not present mutually exclusive racial-
ethnic groups. We calculate a base population in which the white, black,
Asian, and American Indian and Alaska Native population do not include a
Hispanic component. This approach avoids a double counting of Hispanic
persons. We offer projection results for five racial-ethnic groups: American
Indian, Asian, black, Hispanic, and white.

In the population projections, we define intermarriage as the union
between persons of different racial-ethnic origins, and we take into account
the racial origins for their offspring. Standard population projection models
of racial and ethnic groups make one crucial and highly questionable assumption: they assume perfect endogamy for the group for the projection
period. Standard models assume that all members of a given group marry
members of the same group and produce children of a single racial or
ethnic origin. This is a false assumption for many groups, and such projections potentially present a misleading picture of future population composition.

A growing literature on racial and ethnic intermarriage reveals increasing levels of intermarriage. High rates of intermarriage across racial lines are particularly significant for population projections by racial groups because they contribute to the increased blurring of racial boundaries. Intermarriage between Asian and non-Asian Americans varies from 21 percent overall to more than 40 percent among native-born Asian Americans (Lee and Fernandez 1998; Liang and Ito 1999). Hispanic intermarriage rates are also high and increasing (Qian 1999). About one-third of married Hispanics has a non-Hispanic partner. The traditionally low racial intermarriage rate for blacks has tripled in recent years, from 2 percent in 1980 to 6 percent in 1990 (Heaton and Albrecht 1996). Matthijs Kalmijn (1993) has examined marriage license data and reports substantial increases in the black intermarriage rate during the 1980s, particularly among men and residents of nonsouthern states. The case of Asian Americans is particularly instructive because Asians are considered a racial group whereas most Hispanics report their race as white or "other." Moreover, persons with partial Asian origins appear to have greater flexibility in their racial identity (Xie and Goyette 1997)—that is, they do not tend to report their race as single-race Asian—unlike what seems to be the case for persons of black-white origins.

Previous research has described important factors associated with intermarriage (Kalmijn 1998). Foreign birth is negatively related to intermarriage, perhaps because of lower acculturation and fewer opportunities to meet potential partners outside the racial-ethnic community (Lee and Fernandez 1998). In addition, many immigrants arrive as married adults (Hwang and Saenz 1990). Thus prior research suggests that, all other factors being equal, the native born will have higher levels of intermarriage. Intermarriage also varies by sex for some racial groups (Heaton and Albrecht 1996). Intermarriage differentials by sex are affected by the age-sex structure within a racial-ethnic community, the conditions of intergroup contact, differences in the socialization of males and females, and differential access to marital opportunities and rewards by gender. It is therefore not easy to explain observed sex differentials in intermarriage, even when they are consistent over time. For example, black males have higher rates of intermarriage than black females, whereas among Hispanics and Asians, both sexes are equally likely to intermarry, with a slightly higher intermarriage rate among females. Intermarriage is also more likely among the younger age groups and among persons with higher levels of schooling (Heaton and Albrecht 1996; Qian 1999).

A review of recent research on race and ethnic marriage patterns leads to three conclusions about intermarriage and its demographic effects. First, considerable intermarriage occurs for many U.S. racial and ethnic groups, leading to growing numbers of people with crosscutting racial and His-panic-origin backgrounds. Second, intermarriage varies significantly by generation. Levels of intermarriage are certain to increase as the native-born generations of Asian and Hispanic Americans expand. Finally, other covariates of intermarriage, such as younger age, higher education, and native birth, suggest that intermarriage rates will continue to increase in the future.

Births of Single and Multiple Racial and Ethnic Origins

The population projection model incorporates intermarriage by including assumptions about the proportion of births that have the same race or eth-nicity as the mother. Intermarriage is assumed to vary by immigrant gener-ation, and different intermarriage levels are assumed for different genera-tions for each race or ethnicity group. Births to women with a partner of a different race or ethnic origin are considered to have multiple racial-ethnic origins and are then tabulated separately in the projection model.

We consider two types of births: single-origin births are births to par-ents who are both of the same racial-ethnic identification, and multiple-origin births are those to parents of different racial-ethnic identifications. The distinction between single- and multiple-origin births has no pejorative implications. We make no assumptions that single-ancestry births are racially or ethnically "pure." Indeed, available evidence indicates that all commonly recognized racial and ethnic groups are of mixed descent in the evolutionary history of human populations. "Single origin," in the context of this chapter, means only that both parents report themselves (in a popu-lation census or survey) as sharing a common racial-ethnic origin.

There are challenges to modeling intermarriage as single- or multiple-origin births. Our population modeling involves an intermarriage coeffi-cient that determines the proportion of births that are of single origin. We assume that all other births to the group of women are multiple-origin births. Moreover, we assume that births to multiple-origin women are also multiple-origin births.

We make no assertions about the ethnic identification of multiple-origin persons. The meanings of racial and ethnic labels have changed in the past and will undoubtedly change in the future (Lee 1993). Such changes are further facilitated by the extensive use of self-reporting in col-lecting racial and ethnic data. Theoretically, one can consider two outcomes of racial and ethnic identification for persons of multiple origins. These are avoidance and affiliation. In the simplest case of persons who are of multi-ple origins, "P" and "Q," avoidance of one origin, let us say "P," would mean that only people of single-origin "P" would report "P" origin. On the other hand, if all persons of mixed "P" and "Q" origins affiliate with "P," then the reported number of people with "P" origin will include those of single "P" origin as well as those who report a multiple "P-Q" ancestry.

For our population projections, we do not know, without making some assumptions about the ethnic self-identification of multiple-origin persons, what the future size of a given ethnic group will be. We limit ourselves, therefore, to reporting the numbers of persons of multiple origins. We do not attempt to interpret how these persons might choose to identify themselves in future censuses and surveys. Many researchers have shown that the process of racial and ethnic identification is dynamic, situational, and subject to influence by numerous factors (Snipp 1997; Stephan and Stephan 1989; Waters 1990, 1998).

Uses of Population Projections

Demographers use population projections for several purposes: as predictions or forecasts, for prospective analysis, and as simulations. Population projections as predictions may be undertaken as a statistical exercise (either as a function of statistical regularities or as a probabilistic function) or on the basis of a "law" of population change (such as a logistic growth curve). Yet human population growth, especially for racial groups in the United States, is neither purely probabilistic nor deterministic. Efforts to predict future population growth using a statistical apparatus are probably fruitless and certainly misleading.

The purpose of population projections as prospective analysis is to examine the implications of a plausible and credible set of demographic assumptions. Plausible parameters should reflect the likely variety of future values for such key demographic input values as fertility, mortality, and immigration. Credible parameters should depend on state-of-the-art research about current demographic levels and reasonable forecasts for the demographic input values. By nature of the emphasis on analytical credibility, prospective analysis projections are directed at the immediate future. Current demographic research, it seems to us, provides plausible and credible parameters for intermediate-term projections for, say, fifteen to twenty-five years for the U.S. national population and, for a lesser period of time, for state populations. Population projections cannot, at this time, be regarded as based on credible parameters for plausible longer-term forecasts. Nor can projections of U.S. racial groups be regarded as plausible, given the state-of-the-art research on intermarriage and racial identity.

The population projections reported here are produced from a simulation perspective. The simulations are designed to generate results on the racial-ethnic distribution of the U.S. population implied in an assumed time path of fertility, mortality, international migration, and intermarriage. We select demographic parameters consistent with current observed levels for a narrow heuristic purpose—to examine the demographic consequences that flow from the assumed conditions. Given the consistency of our assumptions with current demographic conditions, however, the projections may have a prospective character for the next five to ten years. We do not argue that these projections are based on plausible demographic parameters for the next century. Although we provide projections from the present to 2100, our results are neither a prediction nor prospective analysis for long-term racial-ethnic population change. Rather, they indicate the variation and uncertainty in outlooks based on alternative assumptions.

Data

The base population includes five races or ethnic groups, and separate assumptions for demographic processes are made for each group. The discussion that follows addresses the assumptions made for the projection period 2000 to 2100.

Base Population

The base populations were defined for April 1, 2000, the official date for the 2000 U.S. Census of Population. Because data required for this analysis from the 2000 census are not yet available, the age-sex distribution for each race-ethnic group was taken from a thirteen-month extrapolation of the March 1999 Current Population Survey (CPS).[3] The CPS includes self-reported race or ethnic origin (American Indian, Asian and Pacific Islander, black, Hispanic, and white) for respondents as well as questions about nativity and parental nativity. We rely on the nativity questions to define three generations.

For this work, we used 1990 census data to estimate the proportion of persons in major ethnic groups who report a race or ethnicity (as self-reported in the census "ancestry" question) that differs from their self-reported race-ethnic identity on the 1990 census. Overall, about 5 percent of the U.S. population in 1990 reported a race or ethnic origin that differs from their primary racial or ethnic affiliation. In 2000, we estimate that 8 percent of the U.S. population has multiple racial origins, based on our previous work (Edmonston and Passel 1999).[4] Table 9.1 shows the single- and multiple-origin estimates for population groups in 2000.

Fertility Assumptions

The fertility assumptions in this chapter assume changes that stem from two sources. First, we assume that there are differences in fertility by generation and that overall fertility will be affected as the generational compo-

TABLE 9.1   Single- and Multiple-Origin Base Population, by Race or
             Ethnic Group, 2000 (Millions)

Population Group	Single Origin	Race (Census Base)	Multiple Origins	Total	Multiple Origins As Share of Total (Percentage)
American Indian	1.4	2.1	7.6	9.0	84.4
Asian and Pacific Islander	9.5	10.6	1.8	11.3	15.9
Black	31.5	34.8	2.9	34.4	8.4
Hispanic	29.7	33.4	7.2	36.9	19.5
White	184.7	197.9	17.9	202.6	8.8
All groups	256.8	278.8	22.0	278.0	7.9

Source: Authors' calculations based on 1990 Census PUMS data.
Note: "Single-origin" is the estimated number of persons reporting themselves as having a single racial origin. "Race (Census Base)" is the estimated number of persons reporting their primary racial identification in 2000 as one of the main race-ethnicity groups, assuming that the racial question was asked using the format of the 1990 census. "Multiple-origin" is the estimated number of persons reporting themselves as having multiple racial origins. "Total" equals the single-origin plus the multiple-origin population. The race (or Census Base) numbers lie between the single and total estimates and indicate the proportion of multiple-origin persons who have a primary racial identification with the population group, based on analysis of 1990 census PUMS data.

sition of the racial-ethnic group changes. Second, we assume that long-term fertility rates for third-generation groups move toward replacement level of 2.1 children per woman in 2150. The second assumption is made in recent U.S. Census Bureau projections (Hollmann et al. 2000).

To estimate fertility levels by generation for racial-ethnic groups, we relied on the June 1994 CPS supplement, which asked women several fer-

TABLE 9.2   Fertility Assumptions: Projected Total Fertility Rates for
             Racial and Ethnic-Group Populations, 2000 and 2100,
             by Generation (Percentage)

Population Group	2000				2100			
	Overall	1st	2d	3d and Later	Overall	1st	2d	3d and Later
American Indian	2.41	2.41	2.41	2.41	2.16	2.16	2.16	2.16
Asian and Pacific Islander	2.44	2.60	2.27	1.80	2.19	2.44	2.07	2.08
Black	2.11	2.53	2.30	2.08	2.17	2.53	2.30	2.08
Hispanic	2.90	3.51	2.91	2.04	2.67	3.51	2.91	2.09
White	1.84	1.86	1.85	1.84	2.09	2.09	2.08	2.07

Source: Authors' calculations.

tility questions, including how many children they have ever borne and whether they had a child within the past year. Using the CPS nativity data, we tabulated the population by generation for each race or ethnic-origin group.[5] We adjust the generational fertility rates in 2100 to match, as closely as possible, the long-term fertility trends assumed in the Census Bureau's projections. Specifically, we assume the total fertility rates shown in table 9.2.

Mortality Assumptions

We rely on mortality projections of the Census Bureau (Hollmann et al. 2000) for our assumptions about survival rates by age, sex, and race-ethnicity. The Census Bureau's survival rates are based on a set of target life tables for 2150 and interpolations of life tables for the period between 2000 and 2100. The target life tables are based on projected life expectancies using the approach taken by Ronald Lee and Shripad Tuljapurkar (1998), which is an updated application of Lee and Lawrence Carter's (1992) model. We assume that mortality across generations does not vary. Specifically, we assume the life expectancy levels at birth shown in table 9.3.

TABLE 9.3   *Mortality Assumptions: Projected Life Expectancy at Birth, 2000 Baseline and 2100 Ultimate Year, by Population Group (Years)*

	2000			2100		
Population Group	First	Second	Third and Later	First	Second	Third and Later
Males						
American Indian	72.9	72.9	72.9	88.5	88.5	88.5
Asian and Pacific Islander	80.9	80.9	80.9	89.4	89.4	89.4
Black	68.4	68.4	68.4	86.9	86.9	86.9
Hispanic	77.2	77.2	77.2	88.6	88.6	88.6
White	74.7	74.7	74.7	87.6	87.6	87.6
All groups	74.1	74.1	74.1	88.0	88.0	88.0
Females						
American Indian	82.0	82.0	82.0	93.6	93.6	93.6
Asian and Pacific Islander	86.5	86.5	86.5	93.4	93.4	93.4
Black	75.1	75.1	75.1	91.5	91.5	91.5
Hispanic	83.7	83.7	83.7	92.9	92.9	92.9
White	80.1	80.1	80.1	91.8	91.8	91.8
All groups	79.8	79.8	79.8	92.3	92.3	92.3

Source: Authors' calculations.

International Migration Assumptions

Our population projection model includes three types of international migration assumptions: the immigration of the foreign born, the emigration of the foreign born, and the international migration of the native born. Our immigration assumptions are similar to those made in the Census Bureau's population projections (Hollmann et al., 2000).[6]

Regarding immigration of the foreign born, we assume that there is a modest increase in immigration from about 1.2 million per year in 2000 to about 1.3 million in 2002, a decline to about 1.0 million in 2010, followed by a gradual increase to about 1.1 million in 2020. These fluctuations are, in turn, the likely result of trends in immigration from Mexico (based on IRCA [Immigration Reform and Control Act of 1986]-related family reunifications), refugee movements, and gradual increases in immigration from Asia, Africa, and the Middle East. After 2020, we assume a gradual

TABLE 9.4   *Foreign-Born International Migration Assumptions: Projected Annual Immigration and Emigration, 2000 to 2100, by Population Group (Thousands)*

	Net Immigration		Components	
Time Period	Number	Percentage	Immigration	Emigration
2000 to 2005				
American Indian	45	0.9	48	3
Asian and Pacific Islander	1,168	23.1	1,599	431
Black	685	13.5	740	55
Hispanic	2,228	44.0	2,588	360
White	932	18.4	1,525	593
Total	5,058	100.0	6,500	1,442
2045 to 2050				
American Indian	40	0.7	43	3
Asian and Pacific Islander	2,135	35.6	2,609	474
Black	1,110	18.5	1,177	67
Hispanic	1,419	23.6	1,767	348
White	1,297	21.6	1,906	609
Total	6,001	100.0	7,502	1,501
2095 to 2100				
American Indian	39	0.7	42	3
Asian and Pacific Islander	2,595	43.3	3,089	494
Black	1,286	21.5	1,358	72
Hispanic	1,035	17.3	1,378	343
White	1,032	17.2	1,635	603
Total	5,987	100.0	7,502	1,525

Source: Authors' calculations.

rise in immigration to about 1.45 million per year in 2050. We assume that immigration will then remain constant at about 1.45 million per year.[7] Table 9.4 displays the assumptions made for overall immigration by race and ethnic-origin group for the years 2000 to 2005, 2045 to 2050, and 2095 to 2100 (showing immigration figures for five-year periods).

Emigration is modeled in these projections as age-specific rates of emigration applied to the foreign-born population for each race-ethnicity group.[8] Table 9.4 presents information on the implied emigration levels for the three projection periods.

International migration of the native born includes four components: native-born emigration, net movement from Puerto Rico, Armed Forces inductions less discharges overseas, and net returns of government officials and overseas Armed Forces dependents.[9] We assume the net international migration flows of the native born for each race-ethnicity group as shown in table 9.5. We assume that these numbers remain constant for the 2000 to 2100 projection period.

Intermarriage Assumptions

American Indians have high rates of intermarriage. Based on 1979 survey data, Richard Alba and Reid Golden (1986) report that 79 percent of American Indians were married to someone who was not reported as American Indian. Using information from the National Center for Health Statistics (NCHS) on the racial identification of parents for birth data, we estimate an exogamy level for American Indians of .27 in 1980 and .42 in 1988. We assume an intermarriage rate of .40 for American Indians for our population projections.

Asian Americans have moderate levels of intermarriage. Available research reports similar intermarriage rates for this population for the past fifteen years. Alba and Golden (1986) estimate an out-marriage rate of 23

TABLE 9.5   *Native-Born International Migration Assumptions: Projected Five-Year Net Immigration, 2000 to 2100, by Population Group (Thousands)*

Population Group	Total	Male	Female
American Indian	−2	−1	−1
Asian and Pacific Islander	−2	−1	−1
Black	−24	−12	−12
Hispanic	40	17	23
White	−162	−86	−76
Total	−150	−83	−67

Source: Authors' calculations.

percent using 1979 CPS data. Sharon Lee and Keiko Yamanaka's (1990) examination of public-use microdata sample (PUMS) data from the 1980 census also report a racial intermarriage rate of 23 percent. Data from the NCHS reveal an intermarriage rate of 24 percent for 1980 and 21 percent for 1988. However, racial intermarriage among Asian Americans had declined to about 12 percent based on 1990 census PUMS data (Lee and Fernandez 1998). The intermarriage data for 1979 to 1980 are fairly stable, but the intermarriage rate appears to have declined during the 1980s, perhaps reflecting the large immigration from Asia during the decade. Based on these reports, we estimate an overall intermarriage coefficient of 20 percent for the Asian population for our projections.

Information on the black population indicates low levels of intermarriage. The long-term historical record shows an intermarriage rate of at most 1 percent between 1900 and 1960. More recent studies confirm the generally lower level of intermarriage among blacks, with an estimated 7 percent using 1979 CPS data (Alba and Golden 1986) and an estimated 2 percent using 1980 census PUMS data (Lee and Yamanaka 1990). Intermarriage among blacks is apparently increasing, however (Kalmijn 1993). There were 65,000 black-white married couples reported in 1970; this number increased to 231,000 in 1991 (Kalish 1992). Data from the NCHS suggest 1 percent intermarriage in 1980 and 3 percent in 1988. Data from the 1990 census indicate that 7 percent of married blacks have nonblack partners (U.S. Census Bureau 1998a). We assume a black intermarriage coefficient of 10 percent for our projections.

The Hispanic population has moderate levels of intermarriage. Using 1980 census PUMS data, we have estimated in earlier work that 13 percent of all married Hispanic persons were married to a non-Hispanic (Lee and Edmonston 1992). Earlier data for New York State reported by Douglas Gurak and Joseph Fitzpatrick (1982) suggest that about 20 percent of Hispanic immigrants were married to non-Hispanics and that the out-marriage rate rose to 40 percent for second-generation Hispanics. Sharon Lee and Marilyn Fernandez (1998) report an intermarriage rate of about 20 percent among Hispanics based on 1990 census PUMS data. Jorge del Pinal and Audrey Singer (1997) report an overall intermarriage rate of 18 percent, using March 1996 CPS data. We assume an overall intermarriage coefficient of 30 percent for the Hispanic population in our projections.

The white population shows very low intermarriage rates, which is expected, given the large relative size of this population and the well-known effect of group size on out-marriage. Only 1 percent of all married whites in 1980 reported being married to a person of a different ethnic background (Lee and Edmonston 1992). Intermarriage rates, using NCHS data, are 1 percent for 1980 and 2 percent for 1988. Data from the 1990 census PUMS show an intermarriage rate of almost 3 percent (Lee and

Fernandez 1998; U.S. Census Bureau 1998b). To maintain consistency for our projections, we assume an intermarriage coefficient of 8 percent for the white group.[10]

We currently lack consistent estimates of intermarriage for major race-ethnicity groups by immigrant generation. To derive the estimates shown in table 9.6, we rely on the studies cited earlier for the intermarriage of overall population groups and then estimate intermarriage coefficients by generation. For Asians and Hispanics, we assume that the native-born population provides an estimate of intermarriage for the third and higher generations, then interpolate intermarriage for the second generation as the average of the intermarriage rates for the first and third generations. For blacks, we assume moderately low levels of intermarriage for the foreign born, consistent with the overall rate. For whites, we assume no generational change because there is no obvious reason why foreign-born whites would be less likely to out-marry than the native born. Finally, we validated our intermarriage estimates by calculating the distribution for births for a matrix of race of mother and race of father, comparing it with the similar 1990 matrix of births published by the NCHS for 1990 data. The estimated exogamy rates approximate the current maternal-paternal race distribution for U.S. birth data. Table 9.6 shows intermarriage estimates, by generation, for the five race and ethnicity groups in our population projections.

We make five important assumptions for the modeling of intermarriage in our population projections. First, we assume that intermarriage varies by race and ethnicity group and by generation. We assume, however, that intermarriage rates are constant by age and that the rates do not vary over time. Second, we assume for some of our estimates that intermarriage rates (the proportion of women of a specific race or ethnicity group who marry someone of a different group) are reasonable indicators of all interracial and interethnic unions. This assumption would hold if all race and ethnicity groups show similar levels of intergroup nonmarital sexual rela-

TABLE 9.6   *Intermarriage Assumptions: Projected Marriages to Other Groups, 2000 to 2100, by Population Group and Generation (Percentage)*

| Population Group | Overall Total (2000) | Generation | | |
		First	Second	Third and Higher
American Indian	40	20	30	50
Asian and Pacific Islander	20	13	34	54
Black	10	14	12	10
Hispanic	30	8	32	57
White	8	10	9	8

Source: Authors' calculations.

tions. Third, we assume that intermarriage and fertility are independent. This assumption means that women who marry (or are in sexual unions with) men of a different race or ethnicity will have the same fertility as couples of the same race or ethnicity. Fourth, we assume that multiple-origin births produce only future multiple-origin generations, regardless of the race or ethnicity of the partners. Finally, we assume that male out-marriage rates are the same as female out-marriage rates.

Many of these assumptions do not accurately represent current and probable future intermarriage trends. Further refinements to the way inter-marriage is modeled are necessary in future work, as we incorporate new data and research on intermarriage and births in our projections.[11]

Results

Even without immigration and with the maintenance of currently low fertil-ity levels, the U.S. population would continue to grow over the next forty years (Smith and Edmonston 1997, 95). The current momentum of popula-tion growth—the result of a younger age distribution—provides a cushion of about 50 million more people in the next decades, even if immigration were to cease immediately. A population projection with no immigration would, however, produce a U.S. population peaking at about 310 million and then slowly declining.

Our first set of projections assume a primary racial identification for each person in 2000 and do not assume intermarriage. The purpose of these projections is to establish a baseline for comparisons with projections that assume intermarriage. With net immigration continuing at current rates, the 2000 total U.S. population of 279 million will top 400 million by 2050 and reach 554 million in 2100, almost doubling from present levels (see table 9.7). Thus, the levels of international migration assumed in these projec-tions produces population increases over the next hundred years.

Growth of Race-Ethnicity Groups

If immigration were zero, then the future ethnic composition would be determined solely by fertility and mortality differentials in the present pop-ulation. This implies that, even with no immigration, the ethnic composi-tion would not remain static. The immigrant component plays the central role in determining the future size of the U.S. population by ethnic groups. There are two ways in which immigration affects ethnic population trends. First, the level of immigration matters. The number of immigrants has a direct effect on population growth, with each new immigrant adding one new person to an ethnic group. Second, the immigrant's age and fertility affects the population by adding descendants. A young immigrant with

TABLE 9.7   *Projected U.S. Population, 2000, 2025, 2050, 2075, and 2100, by Population Group*

Population Group	2000	2025	2050	2075	2100
Projected population (millions)					
American Indian	2.1	3.1	4.0	4.8	5.6
Asian and Pacific Islander	10.6	21.5	37.6	56.2	77.2
Black	34.8	46.6	59.0	71.9	86.6
Hispanic	33.4	63.3	97.9	133.6	169.3
White	197.9	209.4	209.1	210.2	215.0
All groups	278.8	343.9	407.6	476.7	553.7
Projected share of total population (percentage)					
American Indian	0.8	0.9	1.0	1.0	1.0
Asian and Pacific Islander	3.8	6.3	9.2	11.8	13.9
Black	12.5	13.6	14.5	15.1	15.6
Hispanic	12.0	18.4	24.0	28.0	30.6
White	71.0	60.9	51.3	44.1	38.8
Projected increase in prior twenty-five years (percentage)					
American Indian	—	47.6	29.0	20.0	16.7
Asian and Pacific Islander	—	102.8	74.9	49.5	37.4
Black	—	33.9	26.6	21.9	20.4
Hispanic	—	89.5	54.7	36.5	26.7
White	—	5.8	−0.1	0.5	2.3
All groups		23.4	18.5	17.0	16.2

Source: Authors' compilation.

high fertility will add the most descendants, while an old immigrant or one with low fertility will add few. Hence, the future growth of ethnic groups is the product of several interacting factors.

In 2000, the U.S. population was 71 percent white, 12 percent black, 12 percent Hispanic, 4 percent Asian, and about 1 percent American Indian. Future trends in immigration and differential fertility and mortality levels will lead to major changes in these proportions.

The white population is expected to increase its numbers from 198 million in 2000 to 211 million in 2030, decreasing to 209 million in 2060, and then increasing to 215 million in 2100. Nevertheless, because other race and ethnicity groups are growing more rapidly, the white population as a share of the total population will steadily decline from 71 percent in 2000, dropping below 50 percent between 2050 and 2060 and reaching 39 percent in 2100.

Over the next century, the black population will increase substantially from 35 million in 2000 to 87 million in 2100 (again assuming the immigration levels and fertility and mortality trends in these projections). Their proportion of the total population will increase modestly from 12 percent in 2000 to 16 percent in 2100.

Two groups are likely to experience substantial growth during the next century: Asians, including Pacific Islanders, and Hispanics. Under the conditions of this projection, the Asian population will grow at rates exceeding 1 percent for the next century, increasing from 11 million in 2000 to 77 million in 2100. These gains would increase the Asian population's share of the population from 4 percent in 1990 to 14 percent in 2100.

Hispanics are assumed to have a larger share of immigration in the early part of the projection period, and their numbers will grow substantially over the next century. The Hispanic population is likely to increase from 33 million in 2000 to 98 million in 2050 and to 169 million in 2100, rising from 12 percent of the total population in 2000 to 31 percent in 2100. The Hispanic population will have passed blacks to become the largest ethnic minority group in the nation by about 2005, according to our projections.

Intermarriage and Changes in the Single- and Multiple-Origin Population

The results cited in the foregoing material start with an initial 2000 population by racial or ethnic origin based on self-reported primary racial identity. These results also assume that there is no intermarriage and, hence, that all descendants are of the same racial or ethnic origin as their parents. To examine projected populations under conditions of intermarriage, we make two changes from the initial results. First, we assume that the 2000 population includes persons of single and multiple racial and ethnic origins. Second, we conduct a series of population projections to establish possible future boundaries for each race and ethnicity population group under conditions of intermarriage. This requires several different population projections, including the single race and ethnicity population with intermarriage, to establish the size of future single-origin populations; the sum of the single- and multiple-origin populations, to identify the size of the future population for each race or ethnicity group; and the baseline or census population with no intermarriage, to provide a comparison with the conventional population projections cited earlier. We refer to the first as the single-origin race-ethnicity population projection, the second as the overall population projection, and the third as the baseline population projection. The difference between the overall and the single projection yields the multiple-origin population. Table 9.8 reports population projections for each of these race and ethnic origin groups, for American Indians, Asians and Pacific Islanders, blacks, Hispanics, and whites.

The single-origin population includes only persons who have single racial or ethnic origins: they represent the population who reported only one race or ethnic origin in the 1990 census and their descendants who marry within the same race or ethnicity group. The multiple-origins population includes persons who reported multiple race-ethnicity origins in the 1990 census, their descendants, and the offspring of racial-ethnic intermarriages in the future. The overall population is the sum of the single- and multiple-origin groups. Multiple-origin persons have two or more racial-ethnic backgrounds and, hence, are counted in two or more population groups. The number of single-origin persons in the total population equals the sum for each of the five population groups. The number of multiple-origin persons in the total population, however, is not the sum of multiple-origin persons in each of the five groups because there is some double counting.

Table 9.8 also shows the share of multiple-origin persons in the overall population for the total population and for each racial-ethnic population group. The ratios of baseline to total U.S. population are also given for each population group.

More than 84 percent of the overall American Indian population was of multiple origin in 2000, with 2.1 million self-reporting American Indian as their primary race identity. The single-origin population is projected to increase slightly from 1.4 million in 2000 to 1.5 million in 2010, to remain steady at 1.5 million until about 2050, and then to decline thereafter. The multiple-origin population is expected to grow steadily from 7.6 million in 2000 to 15 million in 2100, increasing the share of multiple-origin persons to 95 percent in 2100.

According to our projections, the single-origin Asian population will grow rapidly from 2000 to 2100, and there will be substantial gains in the multiple-origin population, as well. Our results indicate a single-origin population of 56 million and a multiple-origin population of 42 million by 2100. If all multiple-origin persons choose to report themselves primarily as Asian, then the enumerated Asian population could be as large as 98 million in 2100, or 21 million greater than the baseline population projection that assumes no intermarriage. At the other extreme, if no multiple-origin persons choose to report themselves primarily as Asian, then the enumerated Asian population will consist only of single-origin persons, or 56 million in 2100—that is, 21 million fewer than the baseline population projection.

There are increases in the multiple-origin black population from 2000 to 2100, under the assumptions made in this population projection. By 2100, there is a single-origin black population of 66 million and a multiple-origin population of 39 million. The reported black population could vary between 66 and 105 million in 2100, depending upon the self-identification of multiple-origin black persons.

TABLE 9.8   Projected U. S. Population, by Population Group and Single or Multiple Origin, 2000 to 2100

Population Group	2000	2010	2020	2030	2040	2050	2060	2070	2080	2090	2100
Total population											
Single origin (millions)	256.8	277.5	297.1	313.5	325.7	335.0	343.4	349.6	354.7	359.8	364.6
Multiple origin (millions)	22.0	27.6	34.4	44.0	56.8	72.6	91.3	113.0	137.1	162.5	189.1
Overall (millions)	278.8	305.1	331.5	357.5	382.5	407.6	434.7	462.6	491.8	522.3	553.7
Baseline (millions)	278.8	305.1	331.5	357.5	382.5	407.6	434.7	462.6	491.8	522.3	553.7
Ratio of multiple origin to total population (percentage)	7.9	9.0	10.4	12.3	14.8	17.8	21.0	24.4	27.9	31.1	34.2
Ratio of baseline to total population (percentage)	100.0	100.0	100.0	100.0	100.0	100.0	100.0	100.0	100.0	100.0	100.0
Ratio of nonwhite to total population (percentage)	25.9 to 33.8	29.3 to 38.3	31.9 to 42.3	34.2 to 46.5	36.2 to 51.0	37.4 to 55.2	37.9 to 58.9	37.9 to 62.3	37.4 to 65.3	36.8 to 67.9	36.0 to 70.2
American Indian											
Single origin (millions)	1.4	1.5	1.5	1.5	1.5	1.5	1.4	1.2	1.1	0.9	0.8
Multiple origin (millions)	7.6	8.1	8.7	9.4	10.2	10.8	11.8	12.8	13.6	14.6	15.4
Overall (millions)	9.0	9.6	10.2	10.9	11.7	12.3	13.2	14.0	14.7	15.5	16.2
Baseline (millions)	2.1	2.5	2.9	3.3	3.7	4.0	4.4	4.7	5.0	5.3	5.6
Ratio of multiple origin to total population (percentage)	84.4	84.4	85.3	86.2	87.2	87.8	89.4	91.4	92.5	94.2	95.1
Ratio of baseline to total population (percentage)	0.8	0.8	0.9	0.9	1.0	1.0	1.0	1.0	1.0	1.0	1.0
Asian and Pacific Islander											
Single origin (millions)	9.5	13.2	16.9	21.3	26.4	31.4	36.4	41.4	46.3	51.1	55.8
Multiple origin (millions)	1.8	2.8	3.8	5.8	8.4	12.0	16.2	21.4	27.8	34.6	42.4
Overall (millions)	11.3	16.0	20.7	27.1	34.8	43.4	52.6	62.8	74.1	85.7	98.2
Baseline (millions)	10.6	14.8	19.0	24.4	30.8	37.6	44.7	52.3	60.4	68.6	77.2
Ratio of multiple origin to total population (percentage)	15.9	17.5	18.4	21.4	24.1	27.6	30.8	34.1	37.5	40.4	43.2

Ratio of baseline to total population (percentage)	3.8	4.9	5.7	6.8	8.1	9.2	10.3	11.3	12.3	13.1	13.9
African American											
Single origin (millions)	31.5	35.6	39.6	43.5	47.1	50.3	53.5	56.5	59.4	62.6	65.8
Multiple origin (millions)	2.9	4.1	6.8	8.6	11.4	14.8	18.6	23.0	28.0	33.2	39.0
Overall (millions)	34.4	39.7	46.4	52.1	58.5	65.1	72.1	79.5	87.4	95.8	104.8
Baseline (millions)	34.8	39.5	44.3	49.1	54.1	59.0	64.1	69.3	74.7	80.5	86.6
Ratio of multiple origin to total population (percentage)	8.4	10.3	14.7	16.5	19.5	22.7	25.8	28.9	32.0	34.7	37.2
Ratio of baseline to total population (percentage)	12.5	12.9	13.4	13.7	14.1	14.5	14.7	15.0	15.2	15.4	15.6
Hispanic											
Single origin (millions)	29.7	39.0	47.9	56.1	63.4	69.1	73.3	76.0	77.3	77.7	77.2
Multiple origin (millions)	7.2	11.8	18.2	27.8	40.8	57.4	77.6	101.0	127.2	155.2	184.0
Overall (millions)	36.9	50.8	66.1	83.9	104.2	126.5	150.9	177.0	204.5	232.9	261.2
Baseline (millions)	33.4	45.0	57.1	70.1	83.9	97.9	112.2	126.6	141.0	155.4	169.3
Ratio of multiple origin to total population (percentage)	19.5	23.2	27.5	33.1	39.2	45.4	51.4	57.1	62.2	66.6	70.4
Ratio of baseline to total population (percentage)	12.0	14.7	17.2	19.6	21.9	24.0	25.8	27.4	28.7	29.8	30.6
White											
Single origin (millions)	184.7	188.2	191.2	191.1	187.3	182.7	178.8	174.5	170.6	167.5	165.0
Multiple origin (millions)	17.9	21.7	24.3	29.3	35.7	43.1	51.3	60.7	70.5	80.3	90.3
Overall (millions)	202.6	209.9	215.5	220.4	223.0	225.8	230.1	235.2	241.1	247.8	255.3
Baseline (millions)	197.9	203.3	208.2	210.6	210.0	209.1	209.3	209.7	210.7	212.5	215.0
Ratio of multiple origin to total population (percentage)	8.8	10.3	11.3	13.3	16.0	19.1	22.3	25.8	29.2	32.4	35.4
Radio of baseline of total population (percentage)	71.0	66.6	62.8	58.9	54.9	51.3	48.1	45.3	42.8	40.7	38.8

Source: Authors' compilation.

With sizable immigration and moderate levels of intermarriage, our projections suggest rapid growth in the single- and multiple-origin Hispanic population. These results suggest a single-origin Hispanic population of 77 million and a multiple-origin population of 184 million by 2100. The future Hispanic population has a wide range, possibly between 77 and 261 million, depending upon future intermarriage rates and the self-identification of the multiple-origin Hispanic population.

Although the proportion of multiple-origin persons in the white population in 2000 was modest, there will be a substantial increase in the numbers of multiple-origin white persons between 2000 and 2100. The projections indicate a decrease of single-origin persons from 185 million in 2000 to 165 million in 2100 and a gain of multiple-origin persons from 18 million in 2000 to 90 million in 2100. Depending upon intermarriage rates and the primary self-identification of multiple-origin persons, the white population could vary between 165 and 255 million in 2100.

The first panel of table 9.8 shows the overall effect of intermarriage on the total U.S. population. As a result of the effects of intermarriage for the major race and ethnicity groups, the multiple-origin population is expected to grow from 22 million in 2000 to 189 million in 2100, an increase from 8 percent of the total population in 2000 to 34 percent in 2100.

We can also examine the influence of intermarriage from the perspective of the nonwhite minority population. The 2000 minority population, shown as a percentage of the total population in the top panel of table 9.8, varied between 72 and 94 million, or 26 to 34 percent, depending upon the self-reporting of the multiple-origin nonwhite population. By 2100, an increasing component of the U.S. population will have multiple racial and ethnic origins, with at least one minority ancestor. If only single-origin minority persons were reported as members of minority groups, the population would be 200 million, or 36 percent of the total population, in 2100. With a multiple-origin nonwhite population of 189 million, or 34 percent of the total population in 2100, however, the minority population could be reported as large as 389 million, or 70 of the total population. There are great variations in the projected future minority population, therefore, depending on the self-reporting of the multiple-origin minority persons.

Discussion and Conclusions

The U.S. population is becoming more racially and ethnically diverse. Racial and ethnic intermarriage is becoming more common, and growing numbers of people have multiple racial-ethnic origins. Each of these three trends challenges conventional methods of population projections. This chapter modifies conventional population projections by including an exploration of the effects of intermarriage and immigration on future population trends for major race and ethnicity groups. Such modified population projections make it apparent that it is necessary to be fairly bold in the assumptions. Mortality projections can rely on long-term trends in death rates, with a reasonably sound basis for anticipating future trends in mortality rates by age and sex. Although existing research by demographers on fertility do not offer definitive evidence for long-term trends, fertility has been fairly constant for the past decade, and the range for future fertility levels can be reasonably assumed to be in the area of replacement-level fertility. Demographic science offers little guidance, however, for the future path of U.S. international migration. Legal immigration is restricted in the short run by U.S. immigration policies. Illegal immigration, however, is not subject to current laws and is only moderately influenced by present U.S. policies. In the long term, immigration laws may change, and immigration levels may be quite different from current anticipations. Finally, there is great uncertainty about the future course of racial and ethnic intermarriage. Shifts in intermarriage rates, as implemented in this chapter's projection model, would have noticeable effects on the estimates for the single- and multiple-origin populations.

Our work suggests three main findings. First, regardless of the assumptions made about intermarriage, there will be a substantial increase in the Hispanic and Asian and Pacific Islander populations. The Hispanic and Asian populations, fueled by immigration, will be the fastest-growing ethnic groups in the United States in the future.

Second, the growing rate of intermarriages among American Indians, Asians, blacks, Hispanics, and whites (although most intermarriages involve whites with other groups) ensures that there will be a rapid growth in the number of persons with multiple racial and ethnic origins. In the future, the population of the United States will not be made up of distinct groups, each with an associated culture, language, or unique race-ethnicity identification. Because of the number of intermarriages, there will be more people with multiple racial-ethnic parental and grandparental ties and more children with multiple racial-ethnic origins.

This chapter does not directly address the issue of the self-reporting of persons of multiple racial-ethnic origins. Our results, however, call attention to the fact that the official size of the future multiple-origins groups depends heavily on the racial self-reporting of multiple-origin persons. It is unlikely that the extremes presented in our results—varying from a lower bound of single-origin persons to an upper limit of all single- and multiple-origin persons—will be the range for observed self-reporting in the future. Some multiple-origin persons may choose a single primary race or ethnicity, whereas others will choose to report all their racial and ethnic origins.

Third, implicit in these projections is that the use of conventional population projections for race and ethnic groups needs to be questioned. The increasingly multiple racial and ethnic origins of the U.S. population, stemming from continued immigration and intermarriage, will substantially increase the multiple-origin population in coming decades. This increase comes on top of the present multiple-origin population, by some indications presently about 8 percent of the current population. Population projections suggest that there will probably be about a 2 to 3 percentage point increase in the multiple-origin population each decade for the next century. By 2100, based on the assumptions in these projections, the American Indian population will be 95 percent multiple origin, the Asian population 43 percent, the black population 37 percent, the Hispanic population 70 percent, and the white population 35 percent. Such trends suggest that great caution is needed in interpreting the number of persons who may be reported in the next century for each of the major race and ethnicity groups.

The growth of the multiple-origin population has several implications. The process of racial and ethnic identification will become more complex and dynamic as racial group boundaries shift, with the possibility for rapid redefinitions of groups. New, specific group identifications may develop for individuals with multiple racial and ethnic backgrounds, as happened with the Metis in Canada, Anglo-Indians in South Asia, Eurasians in colonial Southeast Asia, and mestizos in Mexico. There may be an expansion of the use of multiple identifications for multiple-origin persons. The increase in the proportion of multiple-origin persons is expected to change the ways in which the identification of race and ethnicity, including its definition and measurement in official statistics, are used.

Increases in the future multiple-origin population challenges directly the interpretations placed on population projections for major racial and ethnic groups. Once the criticism is accepted that not everyone has a unique, exclusive racial or ethnic identity, what are the appropriate demographic interpretations for projections? What interpretation, for example, should be given to a projection of the Asian (including Pacific Islander) population, when the 2100 population might vary plus or minus 25 percent around the baseline population (that assumes no intermarriage), depending upon the self-identification of Asian persons with multiple origins? What cautions should be exercised in projecting the Hispanic population in 2100 when 184 million Hispanics, representing 33 percent of the total U.S. population, are likely to have multiple racial and ethnic origins?

In this situation, interpreting population projections might take various approaches. First, demographers could discard population projections for major race and ethnicity groups altogether, admitting that we lack adequate information about intermarriage and racial and ethnic self-identification. However, if population projections are considered important and necessary tools for understanding racial and ethnic population trends, a second option would be to limit such projections to a shorter period—say, ten to twenty years. This would allow the use of racial-ethnic data from a recent population census and also would increase the plausibility of assumptions.

A third approach, suggested by Leon Tabah (1993), the eminent French demographer and past chief of the U.N. Population Division, would be to restrict ethnic projections to major immigrant groups. In the United States, we could produce population projections for Asian, Middle Eastern, Latin American, Caribbean, and African immigrants and project the future population for the immigrants and their children. Such projections would recognize that there are significant and unknown possibilities for intermarriage and ethnic self-reporting and that useful projections might be best limited to immigrants and their children.

Finally, a fourth option is to note explicitly the assumptions made about intermarriage and their effects on the projected population. In order to make point estimates from such projections, it would be necessary to make specific assumptions about the future self-identification of multiple-origin persons. Such a task is obviously challenging, given what is known about the process of racial and ethnic identification. Although we did not attempt to make such estimates and include them in this chapter because of lack of data, we show that it is possible to estimate ranges in the projected population size for racial-ethnic groups after considering the effects of intermarriage. This approach yields population numbers that are plausible for the near term and illustrative for the longer term.

Notes

1. A more detailed exposition of the projection model can be found in Edmonston and Passel 1992, 1994; and Edmonston, Lee, and Passel 1994.

2. Although in 2000 census data Native Hawaiian and other Pacific Islander is a separate race from Asian, we use a combined Asian and Pacific Islander group in this chapter because 2000 census race data are not yet available. We rely on census and federal statistics from the 1990s for information on the combined Asian and Pacific Islander population (referred to as "Asian" in this chapter).

3. Aggregate data for the U.S. population by race and Hispanic origin have been released since we first wrote this chapter. The 2000 census public-use microdata sample (PUMS) files with information on age, sex, race or ethnicity, and nativity, however, are needed for our projection models, and these have not yet been released.

4. This estimate is based on demographic analysis of 1990 census PUMS data and a projection of trends to 2000. It is likely to differ from self-reported multiracial data in the 2000 census because of the effects of various factors that influence the self-reporting of race. Our 1990 estimates are based on

multiracial data self-reported in the 1990 census's ancestry and race-and eth-nic-origin questions. Further work is needed, once 2000 census PUMS data are released, to study changes in multiple race-ethnicity reporting between 1990 and 2000 and to establish a 2000 baseline population using 2000 census data.

5. We tabulated the number of births from vital statistics and race or ethnic origin from the CPS, along with the adjustment factors needed to scale CPS data to the known levels of births by race of mother. From these adjusted data, we calculated age-specific birth rates for each race or ethnic-origin group for the first, second, and third-plus generations for 1994. We scaled the generational fertility rates for each race or ethnic group to match the fertility assumptions made for 2000 in the Census Bureau's projections: a total fertil-ity rate of 2.4 for American Indians, 2.4 for Asians and Pacific Islanders, 2.1 for blacks, 2.9 for Hispanics, and 1.8 for whites. There seems to be little consensus among demographers about the long-run fertility levels for the United States. We assume, as does the Census Bureau for its long-term popu-lation projections (Hollmann et al. 2000), that total fertility rates move to-ward replacement-level fertility, 2.1 children, for native-born women for all race and Hispanic-origin groups.

6. Hollmann, Mulder, and Kallan (2000) provides the reasoning for the immi-gration assumptions. In an earlier paper (Edmonston and Passel 1999), we make a range of assumptions for immigration levels to illustrate the effects of the volume and racial composition of immigration on the growth of racial groups in the United States.

7. Our projections assume that more rapid population growth will occur in the next fifty years in South Asia, Africa, and the Middle East than in Mexico and other countries of the Western Hemisphere. We assume that there will be a shift in the national origins of immigrants between 2000 and 2050, reduc-ing the number of Hispanic-origin immigrants and increasing Asian, black, and white immigration.

8. We adapt emigration rates from ones developed by the Census Bureau (Holl-mann et al. 2000), assuming variations by age and sex for each race-ethnicity group. We assume that the foreign-born emigration rates, by age and sex, are constant from 2000 to 2100. Overall emigration levels, however, will fluctu-ate with changes in the size of the foreign-born population.

9. The overall international migration figures for the native-born population are generally negative, suggesting a net emigration of about thirty thousand a year. The migration figures are negative for blacks and whites, positive for Hispanics, and negligible for American Indians and Asians and Pacific Is-landers.

10. Data from the NCHS, however, report a sizable number of births to white women with partners of unknown race. If all the fathers of births with un-known race of father were presumed to be other than white, then the inter-marriage coefficient for 1988 could be as high as 10 percent. We stress the

variation in intermarriage rates because the intermarriage coefficient for non-Hispanic whites would have to be about 8 percent if the estimated intermarriage coefficients for the other race and ethnicity groups are reasonable.

11. In our population projections we select only one value for the intermarriage rate for each racial group by immigrant generation, based on current empirical analysis. If future research provides analysis on plausible trends in intermarriage rates, and reasonable bounds for variation, it would be worthwhile to replicate our projections, making a range of assumptions for intermarriage rates.

References

Alba, Richard D., and Reid M. Golden. 1986. "Patterns of Ethnic Marriage in the United States." *Social Forces* 65: 202–23.

Anderson, Margo. 1988. *The American Census: A Social History.* New Haven, Conn.: Yale University Press.

del Pinal, Jorge, and Audrey Singer. 1997. "Generations of Diversity: Latinos in the United States." *Population Bulletin* 52(3). Washington, D.C.: Population Reference Bureau.

Dinnerstein, Leonard, and David Reimers. 1988. *Ethnic Americans.* New York: Harper and Row.

Edmonston, Barry, and Jeffrey S. Passel. 1992. "Immigration and Immigrant Generations in Population Projections." *International Journal of Forecasting* 8: 459–76.

———. 1994. "The Future Immigrant Population of the United States." In *Immigration and Ethnicity: The Integration of America's Newest Arrivals,* edited by B. Edmonston and J. S. Passel. Washington, D.C.: The Urban Institute Press.

———. 1999. "How Immigration and Intermarriage Affect the Racial and Ethnic Composition of the U.S. Population." In *Immigration and Opportunity*, edited by Frank Bean and Stephanie Bell-Rose. New York: Russell Sage Foundation.

Edmonston, Barry, Joshua Goldstein, and Juanita Tamayo Lott, eds. 1996. *Spotlight on Heterogeneity: The Federal Standards for Racial and Ethnic Classification.* Washington, D.C.: National Research Council.

Edmonston, Barry, Sharon M. Lee, and Jeffrey S. Passel. 1994. "Ethnicity, Ancestry, and Exogamy in U.S. Population Projections." Paper presented at the annual meetings of the Population Association of America, Miami.

Eschbach, Karl. 1995. "The Enduring and Vanishing American Indian: American Indian Population Growth and Intermarriage in 1990." *Ethnic and Racial Studies* 18(1): 89–108.

Finnas, Fjalar. 1988. "The Demographic Effect of Mixed Marriages." *European Journal of Population* 4(2): 145–56.

Goldstein, Joshua. 1999. "Kinship Ties that Cross Racial Lines: The Exception or the Rule?" *Demography* 36(3): 399–407.

Gurak, Douglas T., and Joseph P. Fitzpatrick. 1982. "Intermarriage Among Hispanic Ethnic Groups in New York City." *American Journal of Sociology* 87: 921–34.

Heaton, Tim B., and Stan L. Albrecht. 1996. "The Changing Pattern of Interracial Marriage." *Social Biology* 43(3–4): 203–17.

Higham, John. 1972. *Strangers in the Land.* New York: Atheneum.

Hirschman, Charles. 1994. "Race and Ethnic Projections: A Critical Evaluation of their Content and Meaning." Paper presented at SUNY-Albany Conference on "American Diversity: A Demographic Challenge for the 21st Century."

Hollmann, Frederick, Tammany J. Mulder, and Jeffrey E. Kallan. 2000. "Methodology and Assumptions for the Population Projections of the United States: 1999 to 2100." Population Division Working Paper No. 38. Washington: U.S. Census Bureau, January 13.

Hwang, Sean-Shong, and Rogelio Saenz. 1990. "The Problem Posed by Immigrants Married Abroad on Intermarriage Research: The Case of Asian Americans." *International Migration Review* 24(fall): 563–76.

Kalish, Susan. 1992 "Interracial Baby Boomlet in Progress?" *Population Today* 20(December): 1–2, 9.

Kalmijn, Matthijs. 1993. "Trends in Black/White Intermarriage." *Social Forces* 72: 119–46.

———. 1998. "Intermarriage and Homogamy: Causes, Patterns, Trends." *Annual Review of Sociology* 24: 395–421.

Labov, Teresa, and Jerry Jacobs. 1998. "Preserving Multiple Ancestry: Intermarriage and Mixed Births in Hawaii." *Journal of Comparative Family Studies* 29(3): 481–502.

Lee, Ronald, and Lawrence Carter. 1992. "Modeling and Forecasting U.S. Mortality," *Journal of the American Statistical Association* 87(419): 659–75.

Lee, Ronald, and Shripad Tuljapurkar. 1998. "Population Forecasting for Fiscal Planning: Issues and Innovations." Unpublished manuscript.

Lee, Sharon M. 1993. "Racial Classifications in the U.S. Census, 1890 to 1990." *Ethnic and Racial Studies* 16(1): 75–94.

Lee, Sharon M., and Barry Edmonston. 1992. "Ethnic Endogamy Among Asian Americans: An Analysis of Demographic Effects." Unpublished manuscript.

Lee, Sharon M., and Marilyn Fernandez. 1998. "Trends in Asian American Racial/ Ethnic Intermarriage: A Comparison of 1980 and 1990 Census Data." *Sociological Perspectives* 41(2): 323–42.

Lee, Sharon M., and Keiko Yamanaka. 1990. "Patterns of Asian American Intermarriage and Marital Assimilation." *Journal of Comparative Family Studies* 21: 287–305.

Liang, Zai, and Naomi Ito. 1999. "Intermarriage of Asian Americans in the New York City Region: Contemporary Patterns and Future Prospects." *International Migration Review* 33(4): 876–900.

Lieberson, Stanley. 1993. "The Enumeration of Ethnic and Racial Groups in the Census: Some Devilish Principles." In *Challenges of Measuring an Ethnic World: Science, Politics, and Reality.* Statistics Canada and U.S. Census Bureau. Washington: U.S. Government Printing Office.

Passel, Jeffrey S. 1997. "The Growing American Indian Population, 1960–1990: Beyond Demography." *Population Research and Policy Review* 16(1–2): 11–31.

Perlmann, Joel. 1997. "Multiracials, Intermarriage, Ethnicity." *Society* 34(6): 20–23.

Preston, Samuel H. 1993. "Demographic Change in the United States, 1970–2050." In *Forecasting the Health of Elderly Populations*, edited by Kenneth G. Manton, Burton H. Singer, and Richard M. Suzman. New York: Springer-Verlag.

Qian, Zhenchao. 1999. "Who Intermarries? Education, Nativity, Region, and Interracial Marriage, 1980 to 1990." *Journal of Comparative Family Studies* 30(4): 579–97.

Romaniuc, Anatole. 1990. "Population Projection as Prediction, Simulation, and Prospective Analysis." *Population Bulletin of the United Nations* 29: 16–31.

Root, Maria P. P. 1996. "The Multiracial Experience: Racial Borders as a Significant Frontier in Race Relations." In *The Multiracial Experience: Racial Borders as the New Frontier*, edited by Maria P. P. Root. Thousand Oaks, Calif.: Sage Publications.

Sandefur, Gary. 1986. "American Indian Intermarriage." *Social Science Research* 15: 347–71.

Smith, James P., and Barry Edmonston, eds. 1997. *The New Americans: Economic, Demographic, and Fiscal Effects of Immigration.* Washington, D.C.: National Academy Press.

Snipp, Matthew. 1997. "Some Observations about Racial Boundaries and the Experiences of American Indians." *Ethnic and Racial Studies* 20(4): 667–89.

Stephan, Cookie W., and William G. Stephan. 1989. "After Intermarriage: Ethnic Identity among Mixed-Heritage Japanese Americans and Hispanics." *Journal of Marriage and the Family* 51(2): 507–19.

Tabah, Leon. 1993. "Remarks on Population Projections." Presentation at the Meeting of the International Union for the Scientific Study of Population, Montreal (August 27).

U.S. Bureau of the Census. 1986. "Projections of the Hispanic Population: 1983 to 2080." *Population Estimates and Projections.* Series P-25, no. 995. Washington: U.S. Government Printing Office.

———. 1998a. "Projections of the Population of the United States by Age, Sex, and Race: 1988 to 2080." *Population Estimates and Projections.* Series P-25, no. 1018. Washington: U.S. Government Printing Office.

———. 1998b. "Race of Couples: 1990." Accessed June 2002 at: *www.census.gov/population/socdemo/race/interreactab2.txt.*

———. 1999. "Interracial Married Couples: 1960 to Present." Accessed June 2002 at: *www.census.gov/population/socdemo/ms-la/tabms-3.txt.*

Waters, Mary. 1990. *Ethnic Options: Choosing Identities in America.* Berkeley: University of California Press.

———. 1998. "Multiple Ethnic Identity Choices." In *Beyond Pluralism: The Conception of Groups and Group Identities in America,* edited by Wendy Katkin, Ned Landsman, and Andrea Tyree. Urbana: University of Illinois Press.

Whelpton, Pascal K. 1947. "Forecasts of the Population of the United States, 1945–1975." Washington: U.S. Bureau of the Census.

Xie, Yu, and Kimberly Goyette. 1997. "The Racial Identification of Biracial Children with One Asian Parent: Evidence from the 1990 Census." *Social Forces* 76(2): 547–70.

Part IV

THE POLITICS OF
RACE NUMBERS

10

HISTORY, HISTORICITY, AND THE CENSUS COUNT BY RACE

Matthew Frye Jacobson

Although few use the words "moral" or "morality" in their discussion of census taking, the urgency and the tone of much of the recent debate suggest that many in fact do see questions of morality attaching to this matter of counting by race. Allow me to underscore some of the major themes that unite the essays of this collection and to articulate some of the problems they raise as moral problems.

The first major theme running through these essays is the long history of the state's practice of counting by race: the 2000 census is only the most recent chapter in a very long story, and, as many of these essays urge us to recognize, the story has largely been an ugly one. It is a history rooted in questions of slavery and governance, of conquest, of white supremacy and various white supremacist anxieties, and the census count carries with it still a legacy or a residue of that long, ugly history. The project of counting by race has been only partially redeemed—and only recently, in the past forty years or so—as census data have been redeployed in formulating various protections and instruments of redress for aggrieved racial groups.

Although the first moral imperative might seem to be to eradicate race from the statistical portraiture developed by the state, several essayists have reminded us that, in the post-civil-rights era, any assault on the race concept is also an assault on the vital protections that are the legacies of the civil rights struggle. So there seems an equal imperative to defend these protections and, ironically, to defend "race" and the racialized data upon which those protections rely. This is the fundamental dilemma that resides at the core of census taking as a state practice.

The second major theme, intersecting with this, is not just the long history of race counting and its political uses but the historicity of any given moment within that chronological sweep: racial perceptions and conceptions change over time and hence so, too, do our statistical portraits.

Races come and go. Yesterday's "Celt" is among today's "Caucasians" (though "Celts" were never named and enumerated by the Census Bureau as they were by other government agencies). Yesterday's "Negro" might become today's "quadroon," who in turn might yet become tomorrow's "black-white multiracial." These categories are constantly shifting; and the supreme irony is that, of all practices, census taking would seem to be the one that rests most squarely upon the notion that races are stable, fixed, clearly defined, indisputable—in other words, real; and yet no better evidence exists of the contingency of race itself than the history of the census and its ever changing nomenclature and categorical schemes.

There is a moral imperative to hold fast to this insight and not to shy away from it. The "constructed" nature of race has become a commonplace in the academic disciplines; and in recent years the idea has even occasionally crossed over into the pages of *Time* and *Newsweek*. As an organizing principle of American political life, however—in public debate or in discussion among those interested in coalition building—the idea is rather quickly set aside. The implicit argument seems to be that, though it is easy to talk about race as a social construction or a public fiction, it is a construction that has, in fact, translated into social realities that are dangerous to ignore—if that is even possible. A prominent black scholar once remarked, "I notice that my recent work deconstructing race hasn't made it any easier to catch a cab in New York." We have to keep this in mind; and, certainly, turning our insights on the constructedness of race into something that is politically usable is a difficult thing to do. Nonetheless, if we truly believe that race is a public fiction, then we ought not simply to shelve this truth. So, for example, we might take note of and really examine the paradoxical reifying power of the "multiracial" category for the notion of essentially fixed races that happen to "mix" from time to time. The notion of a stable whiteness and a stable blackness that in some instances come together in multiracial hybridity seems to tip its hat to the complexity and the historical messiness of race; but it quietly effaces the long history of race mixing that is in fact the norm. In the 1930s, George Schuyler slyly, and I think quite brilliantly, dedicated his novel, *Black No More*, "to all Caucasians in the great republic who can trace their ancestry back ten generations and confidently assert that there are no Black leaves, twigs, or branches on their family trees" (Schuyler 1989 [1931]). This history—a centuries-long history on all sides of the color lines—is utterly effaced by the "multiracial" category, which posits "mixture" as only an occasional phenomenon in a setting otherwise characterized by racial purity. At stake is how to define and understand not only the "we" who are being counted but also the "we" who are doing the counting.

We might also take closer account of what is afoot when a significant percentage of the population refuses to be interpolated racially on the government's terms and demands a change in the ways that race is conceived. There seems to be a moral imperative not only to grapple with the practical, legal, or political complexities of these new categorizations and their consequences, but also to try to understand the historical or sociological moment that gives rise to new categories and contests. There might be something in that understanding that is politically useful, even if we are still unsure of how to mobilize and develop political strategies on the basis of the race-as-construct model.

This brings us to the third major theme running through these papers, the participation of the state in the process of racial formation. Science, historically, has been the most potent actor in the drama of making race; indeed, science, historically, is what makes "race" what it is. We can have stratification, we can have conceptions of "difference," we can have a politicized notion of "we" and "they," but until science arrives on the scene— the natural and biological sciences of two centuries ago, then the emergent social sciences of one century ago—until we have that kind of authority and epistemology, that particular regime of knowledge, "race" is not yet "race."

Historically, the state has been second only to science in this business of making race and races. At one end of the process, the state is adopting certain racial conceptions or regimes of understanding at the expense of others; and at the other end it is verifying, and so reifying, those conceptions. It is doing this in different ways and for different reasons at different moments, but the state is quite a powerful force when it comes to thinking about what "race" in the abstract is or who "races," specifically, are. We can count Anglo-Saxons, we can count Celts, we can count Malays or Mongolians or Montenegrins—we can count anybody we want to, but only if it occurs to us to do so. If we do count these peoples and name them as racial types, and if we do it with the power of the state behind us, then we are also in the business of creating these peoples and these types and of policing the perceptual or conceptual boundaries that separate them.

The census holds a special place in state practices, not only because the data it generates are used in so many politically significant ways but also because the census itself leaves such a huge imprint on the popular conception of the nation—upon what might be called the ethnological imagination. The anxious pieces that periodically appeared in *Time* or *Newsweek* in response to the racialized census projections of the early 1990s give some sense of the power the census wields over our conceptions of who we are as a nation. At the very least, I think, there is a moral imperative to recognize and grapple with this authenticating power of the state in the matter of racial formation; and perhaps there is a moral imperative to deploy that power only with a certain sense of responsibility and awe.

This is my main reservation about Nathan Glazer's intriguing proposal (chapter 15) to reduce the racial scheme of the census to the simpler, and in some ways quite sensible, two-tiered taxonomy of "black" and "not black." I would argue that the black-white binary in American popular thought is inherently full of trouble and that the state should not promote that sort of simplified view. In this respect, perhaps we are better off as a polity if we think of race as consisting of this impossible maze of 163 categories than in simpler binary terms. American liberalism has too long and rather too conveniently viewed the African American experience as an unfortunate anomaly in an otherwise inclusive and grand democratic tradition. Although the black-white divide has indeed been the most salient and explosive of the racial distinctions in this country over time, still if the United States is viewed through the lens of Asian American history, for instance, a very different but equally important view of how race operates in our political culture emerges. We ought not to lose sight of this, and yet the census, with its authenticating powers, actually has the capacity to *make* us lose sight of it.

I do not pretend to have answers to the moral questions that I raise. We will be well served, however—as practitioners, as professionals, and as citizens—if we keep these questions before us as moral questions.

Reference

Schuyler, George. 1989 [1931]. *Black No More, Being an Account of the Strange and Wonderful Workings of Science in the Land of the Free, A.D. 1933–1940.* Boston: Northeastern University Press.

11

WHAT RACE ARE YOU?

Werner Sollors

There is only one pure race—and this is the *human* race. We all belong to it—and this is the most and the least that can be said of any of us with accuracy. For the rest, it is mere talk, mere labelling, merely a manner of speaking, merely a sociological, not a biological, thing. I myself merely talk when I speak of the blending of the bloods of the white, black, red, and brown races giving rise to a new race, to a new unique blood, when I liken the combination of these strains to the combination of hydrogen and oxygen producing water. For the blood of all the races is *human* blood. There are no differences between the blood of a Caucasian and the blood of a Negro as there are between hydrogen and oxygen. In the mixing and blending of so-called races there are mixtures and blending of the same stuff.

—Jean Toomer, "The Americans"

I N THE five hundred years of its existence, the word "race" has probably done more harm than good. Derived from the Italian "razza," the Spanish and Castilian "raza," and the Portuguese "raça," the word became widespread in the fifteenth and sixteenth centuries. An English example from 1570, referring to the "race & stocke of Abraham," supports the theory that the obscure ultimate roots of "race" may lie in the word "generation" (Oxford English Dictionary). Verena Stolcke has shown that the word "race" could mean "the succession of generations (*de raza en raza*) as well as all the members of a given generation" (Stolcke 1994, 272–86). In addition to the word's relation of "generation," in fifteenth-century Spain "race" connoted "quality" and "nobility of blood" (an aristocratic sense) as well as "taint" and "contamination" (a meaning opposite to that of "nobility"). "Race" in its negative sense appeared in the doctrine of purity of blood (limpieza de sangre), "understood as the quality of having no admixture of the races of Moors, Jews, heretics, or *penitenciados* (those condemned by the Inquisition)" (Sollors 1999, 92–93 and 446–47).

With such a legacy it is not surprising that "race" can evoke both the generational pride of "nobility" and the "taint" of those descended from socially ostracized groups and their descendants. "Race" was used to expel from Spain people "tainted" by Jewish and Moorish blood—hence "race" in the "physical" and "visible" modern American sense, we might think. Yet the list of people to whom the doctrine of purity of blood was applied included descendants of heretics and of penitenciados. Thus at its terrible inception, the concept of race was hardly based on the perception of visible, phenotypic differences but on a religiously and politically, hence culturally, defined distinction that was successfully legislated, however, to be considered hereditary, innate, and immutable.

Against the particular past of the U.S. census and race, which includes fractional counting (of slaves) and noncounting (of Indians), counting to see racial peril (of the Chinese), and the use of counts for deportation purposes (of Japanese Americans)—a past in which mixed-race categories were introduced to find evidence for the mulatto-sterility hypothesis ("mulatto" being thought etymologically derived from "mules") on which rested biological racism and its presumption that races were like species and that intermarriage was therefore "unnatural" and had to be prohibited by the state—the unraveling of "race" might not be the worst thing that could happen in census history (Sollors 1999, 61–63, 127–28), though I am sensitive to the question of which tools shall be needed to keep enforcing antidiscrimination law in the future. Still, the combination of state power, census, and race has wreaked too much havoc and has produced too many Kafkaesque absurdities to be too naively or carelessly adopted, even for well-intentioned policies.

Discussions of such matters often refer to the "one-drop rule"—which was, in fact, probably the exception rather than the rule in U.S. racial fractional bookkeeping in the past. Classifications more typically followed a murkier model resembling that of the European aristocracy (in which the general rule that partial lower-caste descent trumps and "contaminates" nobility), and could easily lead to wars of succession in which the finer applications of the general rule were determined. The big difference was, of course, that American white blood took the place of European blue blood. Hence Josiah Clark Nott referred to whites as "nature's noblemen" (quoted in Sollors 1999, 130).[1] This general rule hardly meant that anyone with any nonwhite ancestry (with the "taint" of that "one drop") was therefore excluded from white nobility. George S. Schuyler (1940) pointed out sarcastically in "Who Is 'Negro'? Who Is 'White'?" that in Nebraska, North Dakota, Maryland, Louisiana, Missouri, Mississippi, or South Carolina a person with less than one-eighth "Negro blood" was not legally a "Negro" and could marry a "white" person and receive the sanction of law and society; but that marriage would be null and void in Arizona, Montana,

Virginia, Georgia, Alabama, Oklahoma, Arkansas, and Texas (Schuyler 1940, 53–56; see also Sollors 1999 and W.A.S. 1927).[2]

These definitions changed over time and were not always easy to apply to particular legal cases (Kennedy 2000, 140–62).[3] Is this murkiness also what characterizes the method applied by the new census tabulations and what would indeed seem to be "taking back what they had been giving"?

We may, in fact, still be operating on a set of assumptions that go back to the very core of racism. When the Virginia judge Leon M. Bazile ruled against the Lovings, he stated that "Almighty God created the races white, black, yellow, malay and red, and he placed them on separate continents. And but for the interference with his arrangement there would be no cause for such marriages. The fact that he separated the races shows that he did not intend for the races to mix." This statement was overruled in Loving v. Virginia (87 S. Ct. 1967 [1817]), in which the Supreme Court also invoked the Japanese American detention cases involving Gordon Hirabayashi and Fred Toyosaburo Korematsu and repudiated "distinctions between citizens solely because of their ancestry" as "odious to a free people whose institutions are founded upon the doctrine of equality" (quoted in Sollors 2000, 7, 33).

Whether in the name of "Almighty God" or of "social and political construction" (usually not declared as such by the government), we seem to be bent on continuing to make these odious distinctions that were invented, and given the name we still use, at the time of the Spanish Inquisition. In this scheme of things, the mixed-race category is not a mere footnote. As George Hutchinson (2000) has argued, the mixed-race category is the "scapegoat" whose sacrifice signifies the origin of racist discourse and also sustains it. It seems particularly troubling that the 2000 census tabulations seem to be making the old familiar sacrifice once again.

The U.S. census quite obviously prefers "pure" races to mixed and multiple affiliations. Joel Perlmann (2000) has pointed out the strangely illogical forms of population predictions in the branch of the Census Bureau that does projections. Its famous projection that became widely known as "the browning of America," for example, was based on the "bizarre assumption that there will be no further intermixing of peoples across racial lines. Specifically, they assume that a child born to an interracial couple today will take the race of the mother and that, starting tomorrow, neither that child nor any other American child will marry across lines" (Perlmann 2000, 524–25). Will such types of taxpayer-supported and state-agency-authorized prophecies—the underlying assumptions of which are not even openly declared—get further fuel from the new tabulation rules?

The question of racial and mixed-race self-description stems not just from a wish to have ever smaller (and statistically annoying) identities recognized and coddled but rather from a principled confrontation with the legacy of racism in the United States. It is a legacy that confuses skin color with culture. David A. Hollinger, who has famously referred to the Office of Management and Budget principle as an "ethnoracial pentagon," offers the following proposal for a two-tier census question:

> The Census might . . . ask two questions, one about color giving free play to the politics of distribution and one about culture giving free play to the politics of recognition. "Do you have the physical characteristics that render you at risk of discrimination at the hands of white people, and if so, do those characteristics make you black, red, yellow, or brown?" This question speaks exactly to the justified concerns of opponents of the mixed-race category. Many mixed-descent individuals, moreover, could easily answer yes without violating their cultural identity. The latter could be elicited by another question, "Do you consider yourself to be a member of any of the following ethnoracially defined cultural groups?" This second question might be asked in relation to a list of ethnoracial categories that would include various specific mixtures, and should include the opportunity to write in something not included in the list. (Hollinger 1999, 116–27)

Let me amend this proposal ever so slightly. The first question could, and really should, carry an explanation. I propose something like the following:

> The Attorney General has determined that the United States government has discriminated against people on the basis of what were once believed to be black, red, yellow, and brown "races." Though there is no scientific basis for this belief, it is important to collect information about the following five categories in order to protect citizens' rights and to enforce antidiscrimination legislation today. These data are used only for these specific purposes and do not reflect the belief of the U.S. government or the Census Bureau that such "races" actually exist. Which of the following "races" might have once been used to describe you?

The second question could ask for the respondent's ethnic origins and have an added phrase about the continuous emergence of cultural groupings—perhaps something like this:

> In many citizens' lives, cultural groups, be they old or new, play an important part. Which, if any, ethnic, cultural, or religious group do you feel the strongest sense of belonging to?

To the fact finders of the nation such questions may seem too complicated for actual use and a mere nuisance that makes their mission difficult. But will it be better to go on pretending that the census practice of data collection was just fine? Will future historians have any reason to look at "our" racial categories in Census 2000 more generously than present-day historians view the Three-Fifths Compromise in the eighteenth-century fractional counting of slaves?

Notes

1. It was Nott who also thought, on the basis of the 1840 U.S. census data, that mulattoes were disappearing.

2. "Some of the statutes prohibit marriages between white persons and persons of African descent (Georgia, Oklahoma, Texas), or between white persons and persons of negro blood to the third generation (Alabama, Maryland, North Carolina, Tennessee), or between white persons and persons of more than one-fourth (Oregon, West Virginia), or one-eighth (Florida, Indiana, Mississippi, Nebraska, North Dakota), or one-sixteenth (Virginia) negro blood; other statutes in more general terms prohibit marriages between white persons and Negroes or mulattoes (Arkansas, Colorado, Delaware, Idaho, Kentucky, Louisiana, Missouri, Montana, Nevada, South Carolina, South Dakota, Utah, Wyoming)" (W.A.S. 1927).

3. Randall Kennedy stresses that the "one-drop rule has by no means exercised easy or uncontested dominance" and even "where the one-drop rule has governed there remained problems of proof" (Kennedy 2000, 147).

References

Hollinger, David A. 1999. "Authority, Solidarity, and the Political Economy of Identity: The Case of the United States." *Diacritics* 29(4): 116–27.

Hutchinson, George. 2000. "Jean Toomer and American Racial Discourse." In *Interracialism: Black-White Intermarriage in American History, Literature, and Law,* edited by Werner Sollors. New York: Oxford University Press.

Kennedy, Randall. 2000. "The Enforcement of Anti-Miscegenation Laws." In *Interracialism: Black-White Intermarriage in American History, Literature, and Law,* edited by Werner Sollors. New York: Oxford University Press.

Oxford English Dictionary. Available at: *www.oed.com.*

Perlmann, Joel. 2000. "Reflecting the Changing Face of America: Multiracials, Racial Classification, and American Intermarriage." In *Interracialism: Black-White Intermarriage in American History, Literature, and Law,* edited by Werner Sollors. New York: Oxford University Press.

Schuyler, George S. 1940. "Who Is Negro? Who Is White?" *Common Ground* 1(autumn): 53–56.

Sollors, Werner 1999. *Neither Black nor White yet Both: Thematic Explorations of Interracial Literature.* Cambridge, Mass.: Harvard University Press.

———, ed. 2000. *Interracialism: Black-White Intermarriage in American History, Literature, and Law.* New York: Oxford University Press.

Stolcke, Verena. 1994. "Invaded Women: Gender, Race, and Class in the Formation of Colonial Society." In *Women, "Race," and Writing in the Early Modern Period,* edited by Margo Hendricks and Patricia Parker. London: Routledge.

W.A.S. 1927. "Intermarriage with Negroes—A Survey of State Statutes." *Yale Law Journal* 36(April): 858–66.

12

COUNTING BY RACE:
THE ANTEBELLUM LEGACY

Margo J. Anderson

AMERICANS made "counting by race" a state practice during the revolutionary and antebellum eras. Revolutionary leaders invented the practice of counting the slave and free populations to allocate tax obligations at the federal level. They expanded the practice to allocate political representation among the states in the federal Constitution. After 1820, Congress elaborated on the practice as it tried unsuccessfully to forestall the political crisis over slavery and civil war. The particular character of race classifications and the meanings attached to them must be understood as emerging from these conflicts among states and the failure of the founding generations of Americans to abolish slavery and integrate the African American population into the polity on equal terms with whites.

Proposal for National Population Counting: Tax Policy

Between 1763 and 1790, representatives of the thirteen colonies formed Committees of Correspondence, then a Continental Congress, then a Confederation of United States under the Articles of Confederation, and then a Union of the people of the United States. One issue they faced was the development of a national system of taxation. Until the 1780s the revolutionary government was supported by funds requisitioned from the individual states, based upon land assessments. Supplying the Treasury with funds was a chronic problem, and by 1783 Congress debated alternative assessment mechanisms based upon population. As they did so, they confronted the problem of who precisely was to be counted in such an assessment system and, in particular, whether slaves were equivalent to free persons for the purposes of tax assessment. Northerners were in favor of a full assessment of slaves for tax purposes; Southerners proposed various ratios of slaves to free persons for tax assessment (Madison 1900, 434–35, 439–41). On March 28, Congress debated a variety of ratios. They discussed the implications of valuing a slave as equivalent to one-fourth, one-third, one-half, three-fifths, two-thirds, three-fourths, or one free person. Several days later, the members returned to the issue and approved a motion to change the assessment system from one based upon land to one based upon population, with a state's slave population counted at a ratio of three-fifths of its free population. The politics of the debate turned on the North's efforts to lower its exposure to taxation by including slaves at the highest ratio and the South's effort to reduce the impact of the slave population on its tax exposure. Northerners defended the value of slaves for the purposes of the fiscal stability of the national state; Southerners played it down. Eventually the two sides settled upon a compromise without further confronting the legitimacy of a slave labor system as a whole.

The new system was not ratified by the states and thus was not implemented, but it would have a profound impact on the formation of the national government created in the federal Constitution of 1787. The framers retrieved the principle in the new structure for political decision making and changed its meaning considerably (see Rakove 1979; Sigler 1966; Ohline 1971; Einhorn 2000).

Constitution Making: Extending the Logic of Population Counting

The framers grounded the authority of the state in the sovereignty of the "people" (Anderson 1988; Wood 1969, 1992; Bailyn 1967; Morgan 1988). "We the people of the United States . . . do ordain and establish this Constitution for the United States of America." The framers used the notion of a population count and the three-fifths rule to allocate the seats among the states in the House of Representatives, the votes for each state in the Electoral College, and the apportionment of "direct taxes." Article 1, section 2, paragraph 3, reads:

> Representatives and direct taxes shall be apportioned among the several States which may be included within this Union, according to their respective Numbers, which shall be determined by adding the whole number of free persons, including those bound to service for a term of years, and excluding Indians not taxed, three-fifths of all other persons. The actual enumeration shall be made within three years after the first meeting of the Congress of the United States, and within every subsequent term of ten years, in such manner as they shall by law direct.

The language of this paragraph is similar to that proposed for taxation, but its political implications were quite different. In the Constitutional Convention, it was Northerners who objected to allocating political power to states on the basis of a population of slaves who had no political rights and raised the larger questions of the need of the federal government to end race-based slavery. Southerners defended the inclusion of slaves in the formula for representation. As in 1783, compromise governed the final decision, since the three-fifths rule also applied to tax requisitions upon the states.

Counting the population is a deceptively simple idea, which on further examination is much more complex. Who actually are "the people"? How, practically, does one go about counting them? Slaves were both "people" and a "species of property" expressly excluded from the possibility of political action. If sovereignty derives from the people, what about other "people" who exercise no political power and had no political authority: women, children, criminals, aliens, the poor? Practically speaking, "voting"—that is, official participation in electing a representative—was exercised by about 10 percent of the total population in the United States of the late eighteenth century. The framers debated these issues but did not resolve them. They settled on a census that counted practically the entire population. The enumeration would count everyone except "Indians not taxed" and would distinguish the slave population from the free population so the slave population could be "discounted" to 60 percent of the free for the apportionment of House seats and direct taxes (Lewis 1995; Zagarri 1987).

Implementing the New System: Separating Whites from Others

The question of the administration of the population count was left to the First Congress to resolve. The legislation enacted in early 1790 mandated a minimal administrative operation (Anderson 1988, 1994; Anderson and Fienberg 1999; Fliss 2000). Congress asked six brief questions of each household: the name of the household head, the number of free white males sixteen years of age and older and under the age of sixteen; the number of free white females, "other free persons," and slaves. The language of the statute itself reflects some interesting slippage with this form: the "marshals of the several districts . . . are hereby authorized and required to cause the number of inhabitants within their respective districts to be taken; omitting in such enumeration Indians not taxed, and distinguishing free persons, including those bound to service for a term of years, from all others" (Wright and Hunt 1900, 925).

This language responded directly to the Constitutional mandate. The statute expanded on the mandate for the count, requiring the marshals to gather information "distinguishing also the sexes and colours of free persons, and the free males of sixteen years and upwards from those under that age" (Wright and Hunt 1900, 925). The age and sex distinctions were justified as a means of measuring potential militia strength. Although the form in which such language became operational would seem to imply a distinction of the "free colored" by sex and age, the actual form used specified only "free white males" were to be distinguished by age.

The conceptual slippage here is revealing. Congress spent considerable time weighing the technical issues and clarifying the statutory language involved in conducting the population count. For example, in debate they clarified that women household heads were required to respond to the marshal. They did not see the need to clarify the nature of data required of the "other free persons." The classification was designed to distinguish "white males" from others, and once accomplished, ambiguities might remain in residual categories. Categories in a classification are not necessarily equivalent. The goal of this first race classification was to identify whites by age and sex.

The chief function of the census at the time was congressional apportionment (Fliss 2000; Balinski and Young 1982; Anderson and Fienberg 2001). What really struck the observers of the day were the demographic results of the count and the implications of those results for the political life of the nation. By the 1810s, Americans recognized that the population was growing rapidly (from 3.9 million in 1790 to 7.2 million in 1810, or 30 to 35 percent a decade nationally). The populations of the states were growing at different rates. The House of Representatives expanded from a temporary constitutional apportionment of 65 members in 1789 to 186 members after the 1810 count. The western state of Kentucky, admitted to the Union in 1792 with two representatives, had ten after the 1810 apportionment, an allocation larger than that of nine of the original thirteen states. American politicians came to recognize that differential population growth could affect their political fortunes.

The First Political Controversy over Counting by Race

The Three-Fifths Compromise had been a troublesome pill for the North to swallow during the ratification of the Constitution and was justified on the grounds that the Northern states retained a majority of seats in the House despite the inclusion of slaves in the apportionment ratio. The conceptual problem remained, however, and after Thomas Jefferson won the presidency in 1800, Federalist critics of the ratio charged that "slave representation" had elected Jefferson. Critics claimed that "500,000 slaves (at least their masters for them) chose 15 Electors of President!" (*Columbian Centinel*, quoted in Simpson 1941, 321–22). Jefferson and Aaron Burr "[rode] into the TEMPLE OF LIBERTY, upon the *shoulders of slaves*" (Simpson

1941, 324). In later years, as New England saw its influence in the nation's politics decline, the rhetoric escalated. "Are the rotten boroughs of England more infamous than our negro boroughs?" wrote the *Hartford Courant* in 1804 (Simpson 1941, 324). Federalists proposed a constitutional amendment to change the ratio and, even more dramatically, by the War of 1812, secession from the Union.

The rhetoric reflected the impact of the relentless shift in political power resulting from the decennial reapportionment process. New England would not be the last area of the country to cry that the rules of the game were rigged against them when they saw their relative political power decline because of population growth in other areas. Nor were their complaints over "slave representation" a call for the abolition of slavery and the inclusion of the freed population on the basis of equality with the free. A reading of Sereno Edwards Dwight's analysis of "slave representation," one of the more elaborate pamphlets on the issue, makes this clear. Dwight, writing as "Boreas," devoted twenty-three pages of close quantitative analysis to the census population data and election results of "Whites" and "Blacks" in "The North" and "The Slave Country" in the first three censuses (Dwight 1812). He extrapolated trends to the 1830s to alert his readers to the dangers ahead. "Awake! O Spirit of the North," he wrote; the Republic was in danger. Dwight could not conceive of a black population with political rights. His proposals found voice in the Hartford Convention of 1814 (Drake and Nelson 1999, 90). The convention proposed that the apportionment clause of the Constitution be changed to read, "Representatives and direct taxes shall be apportioned among the several States which may be included within this Union, according to their respective numbers of free persons, including those bound to service for a term of years, and excluding Indians not taxed, and all other persons."

The language would have repealed the Three-Fifths Compromise by requiring that the apportionment of Congress be based upon the free population only. The interesting question is whether the amendment would have had the overtly racist impact that the rhetoric of its supporters implied. On the one hand, in the context of the debates of the time, including Dwight's rhetoric, it clearly excluded "Indians not taxed" and "other persons" from the political community. On the other hand, it theoretically required simply that people be "free" and members of the political community (that is, "taxed") to be included. It thus offered an apportionment incentive for states to abolish slavery and guarantee that Indians who renounced tribal allegiance would be included in the polity. In the context of the time, the proposal represents the contingency of questions concerning the future of the institution of slavery and questions of race. The slave trade had officially ended only six years earlier. Northern states were still in the process of gradual emancipation, and Southerners had yet to mount a formal defense of the Three-Fifths Compromise and the institution of slavery. That would change within five years as Congress debated the admission of Missouri to the Union in 1819 (Fehrenbacher 1995; Moore 1953).

The Missouri Debates and the Black Population

The rhetoric and argument over the Three-Fifths Compromise did not garner serious national support to change the apportionment clause in the Constitution. They did, however, make Americans acutely conscious of the relation between the political power of the South and the demographics of slavery. In early 1819, the issue was revived again in new form as James Talmadge proposed an amendment to the Missouri statehood bill that would have banned the introduction of slaves to the state and mandated gradual emancipation at the age of twenty-five of children born to slaves. The amendment "provided . . . That the further introduction of slavery or involuntary servitude be prohibited, except for the punishment of crimes, whereof the party shall be duly convicted; and that all children of slaves, born within the said state, after the admission thereof into the Union, shall be free, but may be held to service until the age of twenty-five years" (*House Journal,* 15th Congress, 2d sess., February 16, 1819, 272).

Talmadge and supporters of the amendment made plain their opposition to the extension of slavery into the new states of the West and to "slave representation" in principle. They were willing to concede the Three-Fifths Compromise to the original states that had fought to free the country from the British; but they were unwilling to extend the principle to new states and sought to "protect 'the rights of freemen against further abridgement by the virtual representation of slaves'" (quoted in Simpson 1941, 336). The amendment passed the House but was struck from the bill in the Senate. The two houses deadlocked on further action, and Congress adjourned in March 1819.

The Talmadge amendment set in motion two years of impassioned rhetoric about the constitutional authority of Congress, the future of slavery in the West, and the likelihood of ultimate conflict between Northern and Southern states over slavery. Thomas Jefferson called the Missouri debates "a fire bell in the night," and they are generally seen as the beginning of the sectional conflict that led to the Civil War. The debates also represented the first time that Southerners responded to the attack on "slave representation" and defended slavery as an institution and the three-fifths ratio broadly. The attack on the ratio and its defense hardened conceptions on race, slavery, and representation on both sides of the issue and forced to the fore the contradictions inherent in the original constitutional language (Simpson 1941; Moore 1953; Fehrenbacher 1995).

The implications of the Three-Fifths Compromise and the apportionment of representation on the basis of the slave population came in for elaborate argument and rhetorical debate. Supporters of the Talmadge amendment argued that Congress should extend the principle banning slavery that governed the Northwest Ordinance. Missouri would be a "new sovereignty," and "slavery ought to be extinguished in the limits of every sovereignty, if it can be effected without dangerous consequences" (*Annals of Congress,* 16th Congress, 1st sess., 1133–44). In response to claims that "slaves are as happy as the lower class of white people," Representative Joseph Hemphill responded that "it must be in consequence of the degradation to which they are reduced; their faculties are not allowed that expansion which nature intended; they are kept in darkness, and are unacquainted with their true situation" (*Annals,* 1133–34).

Hemphill continued by making the political argument:

Independent of any considerations of humanity, many of a political character exist. The balance of power between the original States will be disturbed; as, according to the mode prescribed by the Constitution, the owner of one hundred slaves has as much influence in the representation as sixty-one freemen; and as direct taxation is but seldom resorted to, it is by no means an equivalent. This may often give a minority of the freemen a control over the politics of the country. This unquestionably is a hard bargain, but it is one that has not been made with the inhabitants of Missouri. (*Annals,* 1133–34)

Supporters of banning slavery in Missouri also saw that the principle of expanding slavery westward would come up when statehood was debated for future states or when future territories were acquired. Congress had eyed additional territory in the Caribbean and Spanish Florida. Representative John W. Taylor of New York asked rhetorically, "Are the millions of slaves inhabiting these countries, too, to be incorporated into the Union and represented in Congress? Are the freemen of the old States to become the slaves of the representatives of foreign slaves?" (*Annals,* 966). Members of Congress were quite willing to consider as primary the impact of congressional decision making on white Americans. "Preference ought to be given to a white population over a black population, as it regards the strength and prosperity of the nation. Slaves have no ambition; they can never become expert as soldiers, sailors, or artificers; in time of war, the country would be weakened by them. . . . In time of peace, slavery has a pernicious tendency on the industry of white people" (*Annals,* 1134).

The Southern defense of the three-fifths rule and the institution of slavery more generally underscored weaknesses in the argument presented by supporters of the Talmadge amendment, even when they did not defend slavery explicitly. Exploiting the racism inherent in many of the Talmadge amendment arguments, Southern members of Congress conjured up the implications of emancipation and asked about the situation of free blacks in the states that had already emancipated the slaves. "There is no place for the free blacks in the United States—no place where they are not degraded. If there was such a place, the society for colonizing them would not have been formed; their benevolent design never known. A country wanting inhabitants, and a society formed to colonize a part of them, prove there is no place for them." Senator Nathaniel Macon of North Carolina pointed to the convulsions in Haiti. "And are you willing to have black members of Congress? But if the scenes of St. Domingo should be reacted [sic], would not the tomahawk and scalping knife be mercy?" (*Annals*, 227–28).

Southerners also challenged the claim that slaves should not be represented because they had no political rights:

> In what way, I would ask, is the just principle of representation violated, by taking three-fifths of the slaves in the calculation? The answer is given, because slaves have no political rights. And what political rights have the female and the minor? And how many free persons of full age are excluded from the exercise of the elective franchise in the different states? Yet all are taken into the enumeration as the basis of representation. (*Annals*, 356–57)

If Northerners found the three-fifths rule and slavery wrong, Southerners were perfectly willing to drive home the logic of emancipation: "Emancipate them and they stay where they are; and two-fifths of their number will be added to the representation, though they are not permitted to enlist in our army" (*Annals*, 229).

The resolution to the controversy over slavery and the admission of Missouri to statehood is well known. Ultimately, Northerners and Southerners in Congress compromised once again, admitting Missouri as a slave state, Maine as a free state, and setting a line at 36°30' latitude to determine territory in which new states could be created with slavery. The rhetoric on both sides was agonized and stilted: Northerners emphasized the illegitimacy of slavery as an institution and the threat it posed to freemen and the Republic, while saying little about the future of the slave population once freed. Southerners by and large continued to deplore the institution but claimed it could not so easily be reformed. The escalating rhetoric on both sides overshadowed the issue Talmadge had originally posed—one that, in hindsight, clearly needed to be addressed—namely, how to determine a way to end race-based slavery and provide for the emancipation and economic, political, and social integration of the enslaved population and their descendants into American life as freemen. Moreover, despite all the discussion about the three-fifths rule and the future population movements, the Missouri debates seemed to have little effect on the census procedures.

But not quite. At the same time that Congress debated statehood for Missouri, it also debated the 1820 census legislation. On the surface, there was little connection between the two issues, as Congress considered other issues of census innovation, particularly the addition of questions on occupation and on naturalization of the foreign born. The brief record of debate does suggest a connection, however, one that looms larger in hindsight than it did at the time. In the 1800 and 1810 censuses, Congress had expanded the age cohorts for the white population to five and mandated that the marshals distinguish white females in the same age cohorts identified for white males. In 1820, Congress mandated distinctions by age and sex cohorts for the slave and free black population and, more significantly, called for the same cohorts for both groups—cohorts that were slightly less detailed than those used for the white population. The data permitted the identification of the slave and free black population in two age cohorts, those under the age of twenty-six and those twenty-six and older, thereby permitting a count of the population affected by emancipation proposals such as Talmadge's. In addition, they firmly conceptualized the population dynamics of the free black population in comparison with the slave population rather than in comparison with the free white population. Now the African American population as well as the white population was to be the subject of analysis in census data (see Hodgson 1995; Rodriguez 2000).[1]

Sectional Conflict and Counting by Race

The Missouri debates and the new questions on the age structure of the slave and free black population represent a turning point in the conceptualization of issues of population counting. Within ten years of the Missouri Compromise, a permanent abolitionist movement emerged in the United States. After 1830, abolitionists lobbied the public and the political system to deal with the future of slavery. Immediatists such as William Lloyd Garrison labeled the Constitution a proslavery document and called for immediate emancipation of the slave population. Gradualists proposed that slavery in the territories be restricted and pressed for colonization schemes, but they were much reluctant to interfere with slavery in the Southern states in which it existed.

As the political differences between the North and the South grew, the demographic changes in the two sections exacerbated the conflict. Table 12.1 and figure 12.1 trace the relative strength of the slave states in the House and Senate and as a proportion of the population from 1790 to 1870. The slave states represented a declining proportion of the population and an even smaller proportion of the seats in the House because of the 40 percent discounting of the slave population in the apportionment calculations. Hence, the South struggled to maintain parity in the Senate as its proportion of the U.S. population dwindled. Each decennial census reminded the country of these issues because Congress had to be reapportioned, new

FIGURE 12.1   *Slave State Strength, 1790 to 1870*

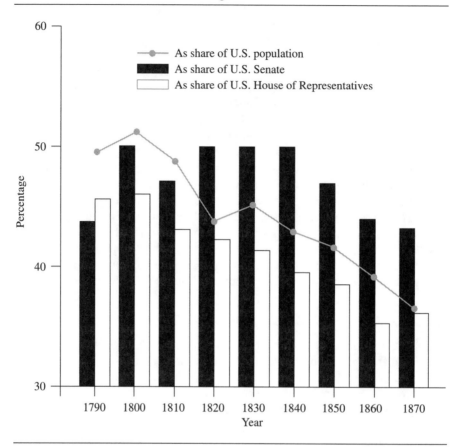

Source: Author's configuration.

TABLE 12.1   *Slave State Power, 1790 to 1870 (Percentage)*

Year	Share of U.S. Population	Share of House Apportionment	Share of Senate
1790	49.5	45.7	43.8
1800	51.2	46.1	50.0
1810	48.8	43.1	47.1
1820	43.8	42.3	50.0
1830	45.2	41.3	50.0
1840	42.9	39.5	50.0
1850	41.7	38.5	46.9
1860	39.3	35.3	44.1
1870	36.5	36.1	43.2

Source: Proportion of House and Senate apportionments from Martis and Elmes 1993. Other figures calculated from U.S. Historical Census Data Browser, available at: *fisher.lib.virginia.edu/census*.

states admitted to the Union, and the precarious balancing act crafted in the Missouri debates maintained.

The South sought to maintain ideological dominance over the question of the future place of the black population in American society and deployed census data to do so. By 1840, Congress had expanded the census to include questions on disability, asking, in particular, for the number of "insane and idiots" "at public charge" and "at private charge" by color as well as the number of blind and deaf and dumb. The 1840 results seemed to show dramatically higher rates of insanity for free blacks in the North as compared with rates for the predominantly slave black population in the South. Northerners claimed the census data had to be wrong. Southerners claimed the results proved that slavery was the appropriate civil status for the African American population. The historical consensus is that the data were flawed, though they were never officially corrected (Cohen 1982). The controversy led directly to efforts to reform the census in 1850 and to an even more complex debate about the place of the African American population in American society.

The 1850 Census: Racial Prognostication and Counting Mulattoes

In March 1849, Congress created a Census Board to reform the procedures. The new procedures were indeed revolutionary. The board recommended an individual-level schedule and an enlarged census office in Washington and proposed that a wide variety of scientific projects be added to the census (Anderson 1988). For questions of counting by race, the most important innovation was the proposal to scrap the household schedule used from 1790 to 1840 and substitute an individual-level schedule.

The shift to the individual level required a new conceptual framework for the census. The board argued that it was harder to count cohorts of people within households than to list individuals and their characteristics. Households contained particular numbers of slaves and free colored and white persons, males and females, children, youth, and so on. The lesson of the 1840 fiasco was that one could no longer expand the detail of the cohorts for households without introducing error in the census. The new individual-level census made it possible to return to a relatively small number of questions for each individual while expanding the scope of the census considerably.

The individual-level census required officials to rethink the categories of inquiry. Some changes were straightforward. One simply asked for the age and sex of each person, for example, or whether the person had married or attended school within the year, was illiterate, was blind or deaf, or had some other disability. Color or race, nativity, occupation, and the value of real estate could have varied responses, however, and the census takers had to think through and explain what kind of answers they sought. It is in the context of the new schedule that the concept of "color" was defined in the census for individuals.

The "color" categories in the censuses from 1790 to 1840 were designed to identify slaves, assumed to be "colored," and free persons, who could be "white" or "colored." All Americans were characterized by color and by whether they were free or slave. The mortality schedule of the 1850 census reflects these distinctions. Separate columns identified the color and the civil status of the person who had died. This was not the proposal for the main population schedule, however, for which the officials proposed separate schedules for free persons and slaves. The new free schedule proposed three "color" categories: white, black, and mulatto. The slave schedule proposed two: black and mulatto.

The reason for two schedules is obvious. Most of the new questions anticipated for the free population did not apply to the slave. Slaves did not own property, go to school, or marry, so it would have been inappropriate to ask them these questions. Interestingly, though, the original plan for the slave schedule asked a different and highly controversial set of questions, including the number of children ever born and "the degree of removal from pure white and black races."

These questions, suggested by Josiah Nott of Mobile, were designed to provide data on a raging scientific controversy, which also had major political implications for the sectional conflict over slavery. Nott and Louis Agassiz denied the unity of the human race and proposed that blacks and whites were literally not of the same species; hence, in their view, the offspring of interracial unions were inferior biologically to the "pure" black or white parents. The political implications of the theory were dramatic. First, if true, the theory implied that whites and blacks could never successfully intermarry or "amalgamate." Second, the theory implied that the existing mixed-race population in the United States, particularly the mulatto communities of cities like Charleston and New Orleans, did not represent the upwardly mobile but should be seen instead as biologically inferior to both white and black, destined to "follow the fate of the Indians" (Nobles 2000; Horsman 1987). The question on the slave schedule relating to children ever born was designed to test the theory. To do so required that slaves be differentiated by "color"—namely, as "mulatto" or "black"—so a new race classification was needed. The final schedule approved by Congress deleted some questions but left the changes in the color categories. The debates on the floor of the Senate provide a window through which to view the implicit meanings in the color categories.

The key debate took place on April 9, 1850. The Senate took up the slave schedule in the midst of the better-known debate on the future of slavery and another sectional compromise, the Compromise of 1850. Interestingly, the main opposition to the form came from slave-state senators, despite Nott's impeccable proslavery credentials. These men challenged the propriety of recording the names of slaves and asking questions on their place of birth, number of children born, and "degree of removal from pure white and black races." Supporters of the planned questions tried to placate the opposition by noting that they "were adopted in compliance with the wishes of southern gentlemen" (*Congressional Globe,* 31st Congress, 1st sess., 1850, 674). As Joseph Underwood of Kentucky put it, the new forms represented "a number of philosophical inquiries . . . as well as the mere basis of representation. . . . And the tables have been constructed, as gentlemen will perceive, in reference to age, in reference to degrees of the blood, in reference to the number of children, and other tables developing the subject of comparative longevity. Now if the information can be obtained, every Senator will see at once the deductions which may be made from it" (*Congressional Globe,* 674).

Opponents of the new questions were not satisfied. They saw dangerous implications in the questions and somewhat disingenuously argued that the information would be too hard to collect. Senators suggested, for example, that a slave woman would not be able to remember how many children she had born: "The woman herself, in nine out of ten cases," claimed William King of Alabama, "when she has had ten or fifteen children, does not know how many she has actually had. [A laugh.]" To this William Seward of New York rose to articulate new possibilities for the questions and to challenge King:

> I hope the motion to strike out [the questions] will not prevail. It appears to me that the information sought to be obtained by this clause is essential, and that it will be found to be so. It is interesting to us all, as a question of political science, to know the actual conditions of every class of population in this country; and certainly it concerns the public, as well as the Government to know the actual *relative* condition of the different classes of population. As I understand the proposition of the committee, they desire to procure information in regard to the comparative longevity of the white and black races in their various conditions. If this information be obtained, it will be useful with reference to that purpose. They desire to ascertain the number of children that each woman has borne, the number that are living, and the number that are dead, with reference to the question of comparative longevity. It is very desirable that we ascertain whatever affects the social and physical condition of the masses of society.
>
> But there is another point. There is no woman, with great deference to the Senator from Alabama, who can have forgotten the number of children that she had borne. If it be true, as it is said, that there are women who do not know whether their children be living or dead, and even how many they have borne, I should like to ascertain the number of such that there are of all

races. And I desire this information because we have all cherished a hope that the condition of African servitude in this country was a stage of transition from a state of barbarism to a state of improvement hereafter. I wish to know how rapid that progress is. I believe it cannot be possible that there are any women, even in Africa, who have forgotten the number of children they have borne. If there be any in America who have forgotten that fact, so important and interesting to themselves, I wish to know it, for the purpose of ascertaining the operation of our social system, and the success of that system as leading to the improvement of the African race. I wish to know also what is the extent of the education or of instruction that prevails, so as to ascertain whether they are advancing toward that better condition which constitutes the only excuse, as I understand, that we have for holding them in servitude. (*Congressional Globe*, 675)

King's suspicions were confirmed by Seward's remarks. King responded angrily to Seward and was ruled out of order by the vice president. Debate continued, with supporters and opponents of the questions making plain their uses. King acknowledged that the questions "would enable us to determine whether the really black race or the intermediate colors are the longest lived and the most prolific." "I have no doubt," he continued, "the fact would be established that the black race are longer lived and increase faster." But the question was "impracticable," he concluded, and "not at all beneficial if it were practicable." William Dayton of New Jersey noted that he was "informed . . . That the black has, in the South, an admitted greater value than the mulatto; that he consumes more, and can do more; that the power of endurance of plantation labor diminishes in proportion to the admixture of white blood; that the mulatto has, in a word, neither the better properties of the white man nor the negro" and was "in a certain degree . . . a *hybrid*." Arthur Butler of South Carolina disagreed, claiming that "the mulatto exceeds the black both in intelligence and pride."

Finally, David Yulee of Florida pointed out a fatal flaw: "It is very well known to every gentleman that the population of the mixed colors is mostly belonging to the free classes," but, he noted, the question on children ever born was not on the free schedule. Underwood acknowledged the problem, debate closed, and the Senate voted to delete the item. Once this question was removed, the Senate deleted the related question on the "degree of removal from pure blood," rejected further changes, approved the schedule, and went on to the consider the remaining schedules (*Congressional Globe*, 676–77). The slave and free schedules as finally approved retained a color classification of white, black, and mulatto without further specification.

Within a month, Congress completed action on the 1850 census bill, and on June 1, 1850, the census began. In the debates in both the Senate and the House, Congress ranged widely over the theories and themes surrounding the crisis of slavery. They also had embarked on a dramatic expansion of the decennial census as an instrument to measure and monitor the demography, economy, and politics of American society. But they had not found a new formula for using the census and the measurement of population as an instrument to manage or end slavery and plan for a transition for the African American population as free Americans.

Each section faced a deeply ironic dilemma embedded in these debates about the census and the trajectory of the African American population. For Northern politicians, it was the obvious vitality of the system of slavery. As is well known, the American slave population grew sufficiently to permit rapid expansion of the Southern plantation economy after the end of the slave trade. Antislavery hopes that the labor system would collapse from its own internal demographic contradictions proved wrong. Each census showed the slave population growing at a good clip, not quite as rapidly as the free population but nevertheless very rapidly by world standards. In 1790, the slave population of 698,000 accounted for about 18 percent of the U.S. population. In 1856, 3.9 million slaves accounted for 13 percent of the American population. Southerners used this demographic growth as evidence of the benign character of the institution. For antislavery advocates, such vigorous population growth complicated schemes for colonization, gradual emancipation, or the integration of millions of freed slaves into the larger society, because the issue loomed larger—literally—each decade. As the taunts of Southerners reminded Northerners, few Northern whites advocated "amalgamation" of the races, intermarriage, or political equality with whites. As noted in the debates over the three-fifths rule and "slave representation," most Northern politicians stumbled when confronted with the consequences of abolition. "White" society was not a "colorblind" society.

If Northerners had trouble interpreting and accepting the demographic dynamism of the slave population, Southerners faced similar conceptual problems when confronted with the free black population. Antislavery advocates pointed out that free black communities were visible evidence that the African American population lived apart from the slave economy, particularly in cities. The free black population represented about 2 percent of the national population. Free blacks faced discrimination in voting and participation in the larger national society but also represented a clear alternative to slavery as the locus of African American intellectual life and culture and as a haven for runaway slaves. The free black community also provided visible evidence of the "amalgamation" of previous generations of white and black Americans, in that the "colors" of free blacks ranged widely (Williamson 1980; Berlin 1974). The 1850 census reported a mulatto population of 406,000, or 1.8 percent of the total U.S. population;

about 40 percent of mulattoes were free. Hence the ironic character of the debate on the Senate floor as the radical antislavery advocate William Seward endorsed the proposals of the racist theorist Josiah Nott for new inquiries on race mixture and the future demography of the slave population.

Conclusions

During the antebellum period, the three-fifths rule required that slave and free be counted separately in the census. Census counting by color or race always went further, however. There were three distinct phases. In the first period, for the censuses of 1790 to 1810, Congress sought to identify the characteristics of the white population, treating the free colored and the slave as simply residuals. From 1820 to 1840, Congress continued the use of a color category to identify characteristics of the white population. As the question of the future of slavery began to loom, however, Congress added a second level of analysis to permit a comparison of the demographic trajectory of the slave and free colored by age, sex, and disability. The year 1850 marked the third phase, as Congress added a category for mixed race, mulatto, to gauge the extent of amalgamation between whites and blacks.

The Civil War cut short any further possibilities of deliberate intellectual analysis of the complex demography of the slave and free populations. Northerners and Southerners fought out the issue of slavery on the battlefield, not in the pages of *DeBow's Review*. The compromises among the states broke down in 1860, as Abraham Lincoln was elected president and the census results signaled further relative losses for the South in Congress and the Electoral College. No more tinkering with formulas for taxation, representation, or statehood would serve to push the issue into the future. Secession seemed the only solution for the South. Yet, after the war, as Southerners had long noted, abolition strengthened somewhat the position of the returning Southern states in the national government as the freed population was counted at full strength for House apportionment and votes in the Electoral College (see table 12.1). That fact presented an immediate political problem for Northern Republicans, and the wartime amendments reflect that reality.

Counting by race continued to saturate the postbellum reconstruction of the political order. National political debate about the humanitarian obligations the nation owed to the freed population were filtered through the more immediate political realities faced by the national decision makers, who had, first of all, to make sure they were around in the next session of Congress or after the next presidential election. For Northern Republicans, that required black votes (Anderson 1988; Gillette 1965; Du Bois 1961 [1903]; Kousser 1974). Section 2 of the Fourteenth Amendment reduced a state's representation in the House and the Electoral College if the state denied the vote to adult male citizens. The Fifteenth Amendment mandated that "the right to vote . . . shall not be abridged . . . on account of race, color, or previous condition of servitude." These measures affirmed that African Americans were citizens and a permanent constituent element of the American population. They provided the mandate for continued congressional attention to the racial demography of the nation. They also provided the potential, as in the antebellum era, for cynical interpretation and manipulation of census data for partisan political ends and for further coalitions of very strange bedfellows in discussions of the racial trajectory of the American population.

Note

1. The other big change of the period was the beginning of democratization of voting at the state level. From the 1780s to the late 1810s, the deferential society of earlier times both persisted and came under political attack (Wood 1992). Ironically, in the first years of the Republic, the conceptual slippage between counts of people for apportionment and counts of votes determining elections was less obvious than it later became because the "voting population" was so small, restricted to adult propertied white males. It was hard for Northern politicians to complain that Southern politicians received undue representation from the "slave" population when Northern politicians also represented an overwhelmingly nonvoting population. Once states began to expand the franchise to poor white men and to debate voter requirements, however, the obvious contradictions between a representative democracy and the enslavement of a huge segment of the population became harder to justify. In fact, the contradiction led directly to the intensification to racism in both regions, because other justifications for disfranchisement—for example, wealth and residency—were being demolished.

References

Anderson, Margo. 1988. *The American Census: A Social History.* New Haven, Conn.: Yale University Press.

———. 1994. "Only White Men Have Class: Reflections on Early Nineteenth-Century Occupational Classification Systems." *Work and Occupations* 21(February): 5–32.

Anderson, Margo, and Stephen E. Fienberg. 1999. "The History of the First American Census and the Constitutional Language on Censustaking: Report of a Workshop." Report to the Donner Foundation (July). Available at: *lib.stat.cmu. edu/~fienberg/DonnerReports.*

———. 2001. *Who Counts? The Politics of Census Taking in Contemporary America.* Revised edition. New York: Russell Sage Foundation.

Annals of the Congress of the United States, 1789–1824. 42 vols. Washington, 1834–1856.

Bailyn, Bernard. 1967. *The Origin of American Politics.* New York: Vintage Books.

Balinski, Michel, and H. Peyton Young. 1982. *Fair Representation: Meeting the Ideal of One Man, One Vote.* New Haven, Conn.: Yale University Press.

Berlin, Ira. 1974. *Slaves Without Masters: The Free Negro in the Antebellum South.* New York: Pantheon Books.

Cohen, Patricia Cline. 1982. *A Calculating People: The Spread of Numeracy in Early America.* Chicago, Ill.: University of Chicago Press.

Congressional Globe. 46 vols. Washington, 1834–1873.

Drake, Frederick D., and Lynn R. Nelson. 1999. *States' Rights and American Federalism: A Documentary History.* Westport, Conn.: Greenwood Press.

Du Bois, W. E. Burghardt. 1961 [1903]. *The Souls of Black Folks.* Greenwich, Conn.: Fawcett Publications.

Dwight, Sereno Edwards [Boreas]. 1812. *Slave Representation.* New Haven.

Einhorn, Robin L. 2000. "Slavery and the Politics of Taxation in the Early United States." *Studies in American Political Development* 14(2): 156–83.

Fehrenbacher, Don. 1995. *Sectional Crisis and Southern Constitutionalism.* Baton Rouge, La.: Louisiana State University Press.

Fliss, William. 2000. "An Administrative and Political History of the Early Federal Census, 1790–1810." Master's thesis, University of Wisconsin, Milwaukee.

Gillette, William. 1965. *The Right to Vote.* Baltimore, Md.: Johns Hopkins University Press.

Hodgson, Dennis. 1995. "Images of Race and Responses to Malthus: The Study of Population in Antebellum America." Paper presented at the Annual Meeting of the American Sociological Association, Washington, D.C. (August 21).

Horsman, Reginald. 1987. *Dr. Nott of Mobile: Southerner, Physician, and Racial Theorist.* New Orleans, La.: Louisiana State University Press.

Kousser, Morgan. 1974. *The Shaping of Southern Politics: Suffrage Restriction and the Establishment of the One-Party South, 1880–1910.* New Haven, Conn.: Yale University Press.

Lewis, Jan. 1995. "'Of Every Age, Sex, and Condition': The Representation of Women in the Constitution." *Journal of the Early Republic* 15(fall): 359–87.

Madison, James. 1900. *The Writings of James Madison,* edited by Gaillard Hunt. Vol. 1. New York: G. P. Putnam's Sons.

Martis, Kenneth, and Gregory Elmes. 1993. *The Historical Atlas of State Power in Congress, 1790–1990.* Washington: Congressional Quarterly Inc.

Moore, Glover. 1953. *The Missouri Controversy, 1819–1821.* Lexington: University of Kentucky Press.

Morgan, Edmund. 1988. *Inventing the People: The Rise of Popular Sovereignty in England and America.* New York: W. W. Norton.

Nobles, Melissa. 2000. *Shades of Citizenship: Race and the Census in Modern Politics.* Stanford, Calif.: Stanford University Press.

Ohline, Howard. 1971. "Republicanism and Slavery: Origins of the Three-Fifths Clause in the United States Constitution." *William and Mary Quarterly* 28(October): 563–84.

Rakove, Jack. 1979. *The Beginnings of National Politics: An Interpretive History of the Continental Congress.* New York: A. A. Knopf.

Rodriguez, Clara. 2000. *Changing Race: Latinos, the Census, and the History of Ethnicity in the United States.* New York, N.Y.: New York University Press.

Sigler, Jay. 1966. "The Rise and Fall of the Three-Fifths Clause." *MidAmerica* 48(October): 271–77.

Simpson, Albert. 1941. "The Political Significance of Slave Representation, 1787–1821." *Journal of Southern History* 7(August): 315–42.

U.S. Congress. *House Journal.* 15th Congress, 2d sess., February 16, 1819.

Williamson, Joel. 1980. *New People: Miscegenation and Mulattoes in the United States.* New York, N.Y.: Free Press.

Wood, Gordon. 1969. *The Creation of the American Republic, 1776–1787.* Chapel Hill, N.C.: University of North Carolina Press.

———. 1992. *The Radicalism of the American Revolution.* New York: A. A. Knopf.

Wright, Carroll, and William C. Hunt. 1900. *History and Growth of the U.S. Census.* Washington: U.S. Government Printing Office.

Zagarri, Rosemarie. 1987. *The Politics of Size: Representation in the United States, 1776–1850.* Ithaca, N.Y.: Cornell University Press.

13

THE ORIGINS OF OFFICIAL MINORITY DESIGNATION

Hugh Davis Graham

THE FINAL decade of the twentieth century was marked by intense controversy in the United States over the role of race and ethnicity in government policy. The U.S. Supreme Court sharply narrowed the scope of race-conscious affirmative action in government contracting and electoral redistricting. In California, voters passed initiatives curbing state services to illegal immigrants and barring minority preferences in employment, contracts, and higher education admissions. Also in California, Asian and Latino entrepreneurs, many of them immigrants, surpassed African Americans in winning minority business enterprise contracts. Nationwide, the controversy over including a new multiracial category in the 2000 census raised questions about the origins and purpose of the federal government's one-race-only rule. The debate over which minority groups deserved affirmative action preferences, and why, raised questions about how, why, and when various groups were included or excluded as official minorities in the first place (Graham 2002). But there were few answers.

Books on the civil rights revolution, published by the thousands, either never asked such questions or threw no light on the answers (Eagles 2000). Scrutiny of the hearings and debates surrounding the nation's revolution in civil rights policy since the 1950s produced abundant discussion of the brutal legacy of slavery and caste. Proponents of affirmative action cited this history as a unique burden that justified race-conscious remedies for African Americans. The record showed almost no discussion, however, of why other groups in America were included as protected-class minorities (for example, Chinese, Argentineans, Pakistanis, Cubans, Spaniards, Portuguese) or excluded (Jews, Italians, Jehovah's Witnesses, Mormons, Palestinians, Iranians).

The answers to the why, when, and how questions could not be found in the public record of elected officials in shaping civil rights policy. Instead, the answers had to be teased out of reports and archival documents left by rather obscure government bureaucrats, men (rarely women) largely unknown to the public and not answerable to voters for their decisions. The documents they wrote date from the 1940s through the mid-1960s. Ironically, their work was largely completed before the federal government, during the Nixon presidency, developed affirmative action programs with controversial, race-conscious remedies. The story these documents reveal about the way official minorities were designated is one shaped not only by the country's history of past discrimination but also by the vagaries of chance, historical accident, logical contradiction, and inadvertence. Above all, none of the career civil servants and appointed officials who shaped the outcomes had any awareness that they were sorting out winners and losers in a process that, by the end of the century, would grant preference in jobs, government contracts, and university admissions to government-designated official minorities, including approximately 26 million immigrants from Latin America and Asia who came to the United States after 1965.

The process began in 1941, when President Franklin Roosevelt by executive order established the Fair Employment Practices Committee (FEPC), a small, temporary agency created under wartime emergency powers. The FEPC's charge was to police discrimination on account of race, color, creed (meaning religion), or national origin. The FEPC expired at the end of the war, with few successes. The momentum of liberal nondiscrimination, however, continued at the state level under the leadership of New York. In 1945, New York passed the State Law Against Discrimination, enforced by the State Commission Against Discrimination, New York's version of the FEPC. The law banned discrimination in private as well as government employment on account of race, religion, and national origin. By the end of the 1940s, race and national origin were tightly linked in the rapidly expanding law of antidiscrimination. By 1960, almost all urban industrial states in the North and West had established antidiscrimination commissions similar to New York's with cease-and-desist enforcement powers (Burstein 1998).

Similarly, although FEPC bills presented to Congress from 1946 to 1964 could not overcome Senate filibusters by southern Democrats protecting segregation and conservative Republicans objecting to government control of business, Presidents Harry Truman, Dwight Eisenhower, and John Kennedy all signed executive orders creating FEPC-like, White House–level committees to police discrimination by government contractors (Graham 1990). When President Lyndon Johnson signed into law the Civil Rights Act of 1964, which established the Equal Employment Opportunity Commission (EEOC) and provided a statutory basis for the president's executive order programs in contract compliance, he joined Congress in affirming the ruling principle of nondiscrimination. It rested on liberalism's command not to discriminate on account of race, color, religion, or national origin (in Title VII, on employment discrimination, the Civil Rights Act additionally prohibited employment discrimination on account of sex). In all this statutory and executive order language, there was no mention of particular groups—not even of "Negroes," the prime group behind the civil rights revolution. In the liberal doctrine of equal individual rights, the goal was to ensure that all Americans enjoyed the full exercise of the same rights. The way to achieve that goal, in classic liberalism's negative command, was to stop doing harm (Graham 1994).

How, then, did particular groups get singled out under the nondiscrimination law? The record shows two paths leading to specific group identification. One was primarily political, the other administrative. The political path, more visible but less determinative in this process than the administrative path, involved the national investigations and reports of advisory bodies. The most important of these were the President's Committee on Civil Rights, appointed by President Truman in 1946, and the U.S. Commission on Civil Rights, established by the Civil Rights Act of 1957. Truman's committee, like all civil rights inquiries and reports in the postwar era, emphasized discrimination against black Americans. The Truman committee's 1947 report, *To Secure These Rights*, also described discrimination against other groups, however. The report noted the wartime evacuation and internment of Japanese Americans, citizenship limitations on Chinese and Japanese, voting restrictions on American Indians, and school segregation and jury duty restrictions on Mexican Americans. The Truman Committee briefly mentioned incidents of past bias against whites—against Jews, in particular, and against Italians during World War II. But *To Secure These Rights* marked a shift away from the concerns over religious discrimination that had characterized New York's pioneering campaign—for example, against Jewish quotas at Ivy League colleges and bias against Catholic immigrants—toward an emphasis on color. "Groups whose color makes them more easily identified are set apart from the 'dominant majority' much more than are the Caucasian minorities," the report notes (President's Committee on Civil Rights 1947, x).

The hearings and reports of the Civil Rights Commission, beginning in the late 1950s, continued this shift. The commission concentrated in the early years on African Americans and segregation in the South, then shifted after 1965 to emphasize nationwide discrimination against blacks and Hispanics. Advisory panels such as the Truman committee and the Civil Rights Commission served important political needs in the national campaign against discrimination. They identified victim groups in order to convince the nation of the pervasiveness of discrimination and the need for reform. Discrimination "on account of" race and national origin were abstract sins; segregating black Americans, denying them the vote, and murdering civil rights workers were palpable offenses that stirred the emotions and fueled reform.

Nonetheless, the advisory bodies had no regulatory or enforcement authority, and their efforts in the decade following the Brown v. Board of Education decision concentrated increasingly on the civil rights of African Americans. More important to the story about the origins of official minorities, the role of the government's one-race-only rule, and the expansion of protected classes—to include, by the end of the century, 26 million immigrants—were the decisions of obscure government officials providing staff support in the fledgling civil rights compliance bureaucracy. Needing information about employment patterns to support the work of the president's contract compliance committees in the 1950s and 1960s, they designed forms for government contractors to fill out showing the distribution of their employees by race, ethnicity, and sex (but not by religion, an attribute of individuals that was barred to government inquiry by the First Amendment).

Because the concept of group rights was alien to the civil rights bureaucracy until the end of the 1960s, the career civil servants designing survey forms for the contract compliance committees had no notion that their rather amateurish efforts would have such far-reaching consequences. The sociologist John Skrentny, in his book *The Minority Rights Revolution* (2002), calls attention, for example, to the decisions of David Mann, the director of surveys for Eisenhower's contract compliance committee and later for Kennedy's committee as well. In 1956, Eisenhower's committee asked government contractors to count their "Negro," "other minority," and "total" employees. For contractors with large numbers of "other minority" employees, the survey questionnaire added that "the contractor may be able to furnish employment statistics for such groups," including "Spanish-Americans, Orientals, Indians, Jews, Puerto Ricans, etc." Contractors were not provided with definitions to guide their count of such groups. Because employment records presumably did not list the religious affiliation of employees, it was unclear how a contractor's visual inspection might identify Jewish workers or how employers should define Spanish Americans or distinguish between Spanish Americans and Puerto Ricans. Presumably, employers were given wide latitude by the form's permissive invitation—contractors "*may*" be able to furnish further information—and by the enigmatic "etc."[1]

This was a clumsy beginning. The only minority group that contractors were required to identify in the 1956 form was "Negroes." Once minority groups started getting named on the government's civil rights compliance forms, however, the ethnic organizations kicked into play. The League of United Latin American Citizens (LULAC), the GI Forum, and the Mexican-American Political Action Committee argued that Hispanics had also suffered discrimination and deserved equal billing with blacks on the government's new form. The Hispanic organizations recruited support from Mexican American members of Congress—Representatives Henry Gonzales (Texas), Joseph Montoya (New Mexico), and Edward Roybal (California), all Democrats. By 1962, when President Kennedy's contract compliance committee revised the early survey questionnaire into Standard Form 40, "Spanish-Americans" were included with "Negroes" as obligatory reporting categories. A similar campaign led by the Japanese American Citizens League and supported by two Asian American legislators from Hawaii, Republican Hiram L. Fong in the Senate and Democrat Daniel K. Inouye in the House, persuaded Mann to add "Orientals" as a required category on the standard form. Mann also added American Indians, even though Indian groups had not lobbied. Jews, on the other hand, were dropped from the form. Some black groups had objected to their inclusion, and Jewish organizations did not contest the matter (Orlans 1986, 3–7).

Thus by 1965, when the newly established EEOC used the contract compliance committee's Standard Form 40 as the basis for construction of its own form, the EEO-1, the government had already produced a de facto list of official minorities that employers were required to count and report. Workers were assigned to five ethnic categories: Negro, Spanish American, Oriental, American Indian, and white. Because the Civil Rights Act, which created the EEOC and provided, for the first time, a statutory basis for the president's executive order programs in contract compliance, prohibited discrimination on account of race and national origin, none of the five groups could legally be discriminated against in 1965, including whites. However, whites, alone among the five groups, were not considered a minority.

Thus when the ghetto riots of 1965 to 1968 prompted federal agency officials and judges to speed up black job recruitment by devising race-conscious affirmative action programs such as the Philadelphia Plan, the government already had at hand a list of four official minorities. Although individual ethnic organizations lobbied federal officials for more attention, there is no record of civil rights leaders addressing the issue of which groups to include on the EEO-1 form, no hearings or record of discussion by the president's contract compliance committees or by the EEOC, and no record of minority rights or women's organizations during that period asking for race-conscious or gender-specific remedies. Instead, as Skrentny has pointed out, the initiative in both the earlier minority-counting projects and, later, in developing race-conscious affirmative action programs came from appointed federal officials and served their political needs (Skrentny 1996).

The exploding racial crisis triggered by the Watts, California, riot of 1965 provided alarmed and harried government officials in the new civil rights enforcement agencies with an opportunity to increase their authority and effectiveness by shifting from nondiscrimination to underutilization as an enforcement model. Federal requirements for affirmative action in civil rights enforcement, first stipulated (but without explanation) in President Kennedy's 1961 executive order on contract compliance and repeated in President Johnson's order of 1965, were grounded in classic liberalism's colorblind doctrine of nondiscrimination. But they invited unspecified outreach efforts, such as targeted recruiting and job training, toward previously excluded groups. These efforts produced dramatic jumps in black employment in the prosperous 1960s, especially in the desegregating South. "Soft" affirmative action under Kennedy and Johnson, however, brought little change to the restless inner cities outside the South. When the ghettos exploded in the urban riots of 1965 to 1968, the new civil rights enforcement agencies turned toward "hard" or race-conscious affirmative action, replacing nondiscrimination with underutilization.

The EEOC, stripped by the legislative compromises of 1964 of the authority to order employers to stop discriminating and attacked as timid and ineffective by impatient civil rights organizations, turned eagerly to underutilization analysis as a way to appease its complaining clients. By 1968, the EEOC had largely dropped discussion of nondiscrimination in favor of underutilization. A group-based concept, underutilization implied a norm of proportional representation, and it occurred when employers hired and promoted fewer workers in a stipulated category than were available in the labor pool. Instead of identifying specific acts of discrimination and proving that they were intentional—a slow, uncertain process even for state fair-employment commissions that could punish offending employers, which the EEOC could not—underutilization analysis allowed the EEOC to infer discrimination from employment statistics supplied by employers on the EEO-1 form. By 1970, the EEOC had developed a "disparate impact" theory of discrimination that disregarded intent and inferred discrimination from statistical underutilization of minorities in the workforce. In 1971, the U.S. Supreme Court upheld this approach in Griggs v. Duke Power Company (401 U.S. 424 [1971]), deferring to the EEOC's expertise in employment policy.

Compliance officials at the Labor Department followed the same path. When the department's Office of Federal Contract Compliance (OFCC) instituted the Philadelphia Plan in 1969, its chief political goal was to speed job redistribution to African Americans in the riot-torn inner cities. Bureaucratically, however, the OFCC drew on the EEO-1 form's current list of official minorities—"Negro, Oriental, American Indian, and Spanish Surnamed Americans"—to establish the Labor Department's own form of underutilization analysis. The OFCC held hearings to document discrimination against black workers in Philadelphia's construction trades. However, there is no record of hearings or discussion about identifying other minorities, beyond black workers, for statistical reporting purposes. In 1970, the Labor Department issued Order 4, extending the Philadelphia Plan from the construction industry in Philadelphia to all federal contractors throughout the United States.

During these tumultuous years of urban riots and violence commissions, a third federal agency, the Small Business Administration (SBA), used the new bureaucratic concept of official minorities to reshape its programs. Established in 1953 under the Commerce Department to help small businesses recover from natural disasters such as floods and hurricanes, the SBA broadened its program scope in the 1960s to include helping economically and socially disadvantaged small businesses succeed. This was consistent with the Great Society's War on Poverty and equal economic opportunity programs. In 1968 the SBA, responding to appeals from the Kerner riot commission for special outreach programs to build economic opportunity in the inner cities, established the 8(a) program. Deriving its title from section 8 of a 1958 law that authorized the SBA to contract with other federal agencies and to subcontract the work to small firms, the 8(a) program channeled procurement contracts to small businesses owned by "economically or culturally disadvantaged individuals." The SBA thus in effect acted as an agent for 8(a)-certified companies, searching out available contracts and persuading other agencies to set aside procurement work for these companies. Aimed at the black ghettos, the SBA's 8(a) program nonetheless did not define what it meant by economic or, especially, cultural disadvantage. Owing to this vague foundation, the 8(a) program developed slowly, its focus unclear. Black and Hispanic organizations criticized the program as cumbersome and ineffective, charges not new to the SBA, which since its inception had been criticized in General Accounting Office reports and newspaper accounts as inefficient (GAO 1993).

In response, the SBA reached out to the new and growing civil rights constituencies to bolster its support in Congress. In 1973, the SBA published new regulations for the 8(a) program in the *Federal Register*. Henceforth, the status of cultural disadvantage would be *presumed* for all program applicants identifying themselves as black, Hispanic, Asian American, or American Indian. The key to eligibility for the 8(a) program's federally subsidized grants, loans, and above all its coveted procurement contracts was cultural disadvantage. This status was conferred automatically on official minorities, who were deemed "presumptively eligible" under the SBA's 1973 regulation.[2] Section 8(a) was a minority business enterprise (MBE) program. Presumptive eligibility in MBE programs automatically conferred on designated minorities a status of economic as well as cultural disadvantage. Nonminority applicants, however, were obliged to prove that they were both economically and culturally disadvantaged. This meant that white Americans alone had to demonstrate, through "clear and convincing evidence," that they had suffered "chronic or ethnic prejudice or cultural bias." Because the 8(a) bureaucracy, like counterpart bureaucracies at the EEOC and the OFCC, was unsympathetic to nonminority claims, participation by whites in the 8(a) program never reached even 1 percent of participating firms (La Noue and Sullivan 1998).[3]

Thus by 1973, when the leading federal agencies in civil rights enforcement had consolidated their shift from nondiscrimination to an underutilization model of affirmative action, they already had at hand a list of four minority groups on whose behalf the new model would be applied. What were the most significant attributes and consequences of this process, which evolved unevenly in fits and starts over three decades? First, it was not an open process of public policy making. The democratic model of policy making features elected officials who hold public hearings, debate the goals of policy, argue the strengths and weaknesses of alternative means, cast their votes on the record, and are held accountable by voters. Instead, the government's minority sorting quest was a closed process of bureaucratic policy making. It was largely devoid not only of public testimony but even of public awareness that policy was being made.

Second, the closed, in-house nature of the government's deliberations narrowed the goals of policy from meeting broad public needs to meeting the more immediate political needs of the agency. Closed deliberations facilitated sheltered bargaining between agency officials, constituent groups, and members of Congress, bargaining that is neither unusual nor inherently improper but that often marks the "iron triangle" deal making associated with the client model of politics, whereby clients "capture" agencies that regulate their industry or sponsor their benefit programs (Wilson 1989, 75–89; Graham 1999). The government's rather clumsy, trial-and-error search for useful survey categories before 1965 seems innocent enough. When nondiscrimination and equal individual rights were the agreed anchors of policy, getting one's ethnic group added to a questionnaire promised little in benefits beyond elevated visibility and prestige. But the subsequent shift, during the Nixon administration, to "hard" or race-conscious affirmative action and adverse impact claims, however, radically changed the stakes of policy.

It is not surprising that the agencies shaping the new definition of official minorities in America—the EEOC, the OFCC, the Office of Civil Rights in the Department of Health, Education and Welfare, the 8(a) program bureaucracy in the SBA—became largely captured bureaucracies whose policies rewarded the protected classes recognized by the official minority designations. For these agencies, hard affirmative action was a risky creative act that paid rich dividends by serving multiple agency goals. It radically enlarged the policy repertoire of the agencies. It allowed them to appease volatile, radicalizing constituencies, quieting criticism by directing a robust new stream of benefits to reward racial and ethnic clientele groups. Best of all, by requiring private firms and other government agencies to pay the cost of the new benefits to minority constituencies (jobs, promotions, government contracts), it freed the civil rights bureaucracy from the necessity of persuading Congress to provide appropriations to pay for the benefits.

Third, the agencies provided no rationale to justify their racial and ethnic categories. Dealing with inherited notions of race that were being abandoned in science and social science, government officials drew up questionnaires that reflected assumptions they took for granted. No explanations were provided. What was a race? Did Spanish Americans constitute a race? Should the list of minorities suffering discrimination in America include Jews, Catholics, Mormons, Jehovah's Witnesses? Were Portuguese Americans Spanish Americans? Were persons from the Middle East or North Africa white? How should the government categorize persons of racially or ethnically mixed ancestry? Not having to answer questions like these in public made it easier for government officials to adjust their lists pragmatically, winnowing the official minorities down by 1965 to a core of four. By that year the new EEO-1 form, by isolating four minority groups that corresponded to the racial color-coding of American popular culture—black, yellow, red, and brown—reified a cluster of assumptions about American society that agency officials, shielded from public debate by their closed process, simply took for granted. This was a fourth important attribute of the long process that identified official minorities: it reified taken-for-granted assumptions that hindsight reveals to have been problematic. One implicit assumption was that membership in a minority group carried a presumption of disadvantage in American society. Other attributes of minority individuals that might reflect socioeconomic success, such as income, wealth, and educational achievement, were disregarded. Minority status, in effect, trumped socioeconomic class. A second implicit assumption was that all minority groups were equal in their disadvantage. Although the paradigmatic disadvantaged minority group was indisputably, in 1950s parlance, the American Negro, there was no implication that civil rights remedies could differ for blacks, Hispanics, Asians, or American Indians (Skrentny 2002, chapter 4). Third, the government listing of enumerated minority groups, which erased the lines separating official minorities from one another, drew a bright line separating official minorities from all other Americans. By 1965, when the EEO-1 form asked employers to use visual identification rather than employee records or queries to assign workers to EEOC categories, the white ethnics and religious groups had all been excluded.

Finally, the government officials making these decisions had from the beginning privileged the rights claims of African Americans. Black claims came first; all other minority groups played a distant tag-along. This taken-for-granted assumption was almost universally shared by postwar liberal reformers. When speaking of the civil rights movement, one meant the black civil rights movement. Presidents Kennedy and Johnson, when pressing the civil rights bills of the mid-1960s, rallied Americans exclusively to the justice claims of African Americans. The early EEOC, in its race-centered commitment to mission, resented the demands by feminist groups for aggressive enforcement of gender equality, even though a third of EEOC complaints charged sex discrimination. Historically, the assumption of African American primacy seemed self-evident. Politically, it provided the moral power behind the breakthrough legislation of 1964 to 1965. Subsequently, it also provided the rationale for adopting race-conscious remedies under affirmative action, speeding government-subsidized jobs to the residents of riot-torn inner city areas. Yet paradoxically, it gave African Americans no legal advantage over other official minorities. The political tradition of black primacy coexisted uneasily with the legal tradition that all official minorities were equally disadvantaged and were entitled to the same remedies in civil rights enforcement.

The tradition of closed federal agency decision making concerning official minorities continued through the 1970s and into the 1980s. As controversy over affirmative action and mass immigration increased, however, especially during periods of economic downturn, it became more difficult for agencies to avoid public debate. When the Office of Management and Budget (OMB) in 1977 codified in Directive 15 the federal government's official categories for classifying Americans, it capped a complex chain of interagency deliberations that had continued the tradition of closed decision making (OMB 1977). The five categories specified in OMB Directive 15 codified the five-color taxonomy found in the EEO-1 form in 1965, categories that, in turn, corresponded to American popular culture's cartoonlike depiction of Americans as being either black, white, yellow, red, or brown. David Hollinger calls this schema "the ethno-racial pentagon" (Hollinger 1995).

In the 1980s, as large-scale immigration strengthened multicultural political currents, the ethnoracial pentagon came under attack. Polls showed that four out of five whites, women as well as men, opposed minority preferences that excluded them because of their race. As large-scale immigration and increased intermarriage strengthened multiracial constituencies, demand grew for a multiracial option in the 1990 census. This led the OMB in 1988 to consider providing such an option. Rights-based racial and ethnic organizations, such as the National Association for the Advancement of Colored People (NAACP) and La Raza Unida, fearing that competing multiracial options would weaken their numbers and solidarity, counter-attacked and defeated the effort. The surging mixed-race population in immigrant-rich America, however, increased pressure against the government's ethnoracial pentagon. Following hearings by the House Census Committee in 1993, the OMB reopened the question in 1994. Multiracial organizations, using new Internet-based lobbying techniques, hammered federal agencies and Congress for refusing to recognize their unique and proud identities (Payne 1998, 161–73). In 1997, the OMB, responding to this pressure, approved an option for Americans to select more than one racial identity in the 2000 census (OMB 1997). By this time, deliberations by the OMB and other government agencies had grown more open, and the network of players in the debate had significantly expanded.

Against this background, in March 2000—a presidential election year— the OMB directed the Census Bureau to classify as a minority all individuals who claimed both white and minority ancestry on the 2000 census forms (OMB 2000). The directive read, in part, "Mixed-race people who mark both White and a non-White race will be counted as the latter for purposes of civil rights monitoring and enforcement" (quoted in Steven A. Holmes, "New Policy on Census Says Those Listed as White and Minority Will Be Counted as Minority," *New York Times*, March 11, 2000, A9). Under heavy lobbying by both African American and Hispanic groups, the Clinton administration acceded in its final year, effectively reaffirming the one-drop rule, a relic of the slave codes and Jim Crow laws of the nineteenth century. In so doing the administration also reverted to the federal government's tradition of closed decision making and color-coded citizenship. It is doubtful, however, that in the twenty-first century, in which the shape of America's demographic future finds representation in Tiger Woods, this tradition can be maintained.

Notes

1. Skrentny's discussion of Mann's construction of survey forms for the president's contract compliance committee is based on an unpublished manuscript by Harold Orlans (1986). Orlans's paper, prepared as part of a Commission on Civil Rights study of affirmative action in higher education in 1986 that was not completed, was generously provided to the author by John Skrentny.

2. The SBA's 1973 regulation named five groups as presumed culturally disadvantaged: "blacks, American Indians, Spanish-Americans, Asian-Americans, and Puerto Ricans." The curious distinction between Spanish Americans and Puerto Ricans testifies to the imprecision and general sloppiness that characterized the closed bureaucratic processes that produced official minority designations to govern affirmative action policy during its formative years.

3. In fiscal 1994, for example, of the 5,628 firms participating in the 8(a) program, only twenty-six of the owners were not in the presumptively eligible groups (nine women, nine disabled, and eighteen white men).

References

Burstein, Paul. 1998. *Discrimination, Jobs, and Politics.* Chicago: University of Chicago Press.

Eagles, Charles W. 2000. "Toward New Histories of the Civil Rights Era." *Journal of Southern History* 66(4): 815–48.

Graham, Hugh Davis. 1990. *The Civil Rights Era.* New York: Oxford University Press.

———. 1994. "Race, History, and Policy: African-Americans and Civil Rights Since 1964." *Journal of Policy History* 6(1): 12–39.

———. 1999. "Since 1964: The Paradox of American Civil Rights Regulation." In *Taking Stock,* edited by Morton Keller and R. Shep Melnick. Washington: Woodrow Wilson Center Press and Cambridge University Press.

———. 2002. *Collision Course: The Strange Convergence of Affirmative Action and Immigration Policy in America.* New York: Oxford University Press.

Hollinger, David. A. 1995. *Postethnic America.* New York: Basic Books.

La Noue, George R., and John C. Sullivan. 1998. "Deconstructing the Affirmative Action Categories." *American Behavioral Scientist* 41(2): 913–26.

Office of Management and Budget (OMB), Executive Office of the President. 1977. "Directive 15: Race and Ethnic Standards for Federal Statistics and Administrative Reporting." May 12.

———. 1997. "Revisions to the Standards for the Classification of Federal Data on Race and Ethnicity." *Federal Register* 62(October 30): 58782–90.

———. 2000. *Guidance on Aggregation and Allocation of Data on Race for Use in Civil Rights Monitoring and Enforcement.* Bulletin 00–02. Washington (March 9).

Orlans, Harold. 1986. "The Origins of Protected Groups." Unpublished paper. Washington: U.S. Commission on Civil Rights.

Payne, Richard J. 1998. *Getting Beyond Race.* Boulder, Colo.: Westview Press.

President's Committee on Civil Rights. 1947. *To Secure These Rights.* Washington: U.S. Government Printing Office.

Skrentny, John David. 1996. *The Ironies of Affirmative Action.* Chicago: University of Chicago Press.

———. 2002. *The Minority Rights Revolution.* Cambridge, Mass.: Harvard University Press.

U.S. General Accounting Office (GAO). 1993. *Small Business: Problems Continue with SBA's Minority Business Development Program.* Washington (September 17).

Wilson, James Q. 1989. *Bureaucracy.* New York: Basic Books.

14

LESSONS FROM BRAZIL: THE IDEATIONAL AND POLITICAL DIMENSIONS OF MULTIRACIALITY

Melissa Nobles

A MERICANS have long perceived Brazil as a multiracial society. Positive assessments have flowed from this perception, the most important being that Brazil is a relatively, if not absolutely, harmonious society. By "harmonious" it is meant that social, political, and economic life is not now, nor has it been, rigidly marked by racial lines. These views of Brazil have been created and advanced, in important ways, by the methods of the Brazilian Institute of Geography and Statistics (IBGE) and its official interpretations of color data. Up through the mid-twentieth century, Brazilian census texts happily reported the "whitening" of the population. Since the 1960s, categorization methods have themselves been questioned and contested by statisticians within the IBGE and by organized groups within civil society. The idea of Brazil as a "racial democracy" has been the dominant lens through which census color data have been interpreted, although as this chapter observes, this interpretation is an embattled one.

If Brazil has enjoyed a reputation as a racial democracy, the United States has borne the stigma of a racial tyranny. American politics and economy have been deeply divided along racial lines. Whereas Brazilians are presumed to be "racially mixed," Americans are presumed to be forever racially distinct, as individuals and as members of groups. American methods of census categorization have not merely reflected these presumptions, they have helped to create and further them. Yet for all of the ways in which Brazilian and American histories and their methods of counting by color or race differ, they share a fundamental similarity: the idea of race has been a central organizing principle of political, economic, and social life in both countries. Moreover, their census bureaus have been active incubators, repositories, and disseminators of racial thought and not mere reporters of racial data.

Indeed, it is this very centrality that explains why the census bureaus in both countries have been recently subjected to intense public scrutiny of their methods and of the underlying rationales for counting by color or race. Even more significant, this scrutiny has led each census bureau to consider employing the methods of the other. While the Office of Management and Budget (OMB) debated the introduction of a separate "multiracial" category in the 1990s, Brazil's IBGE weighed the possibility of eliminating the "pardo" category, which has historically connoted "mixture."[1] In both cases, what were and remain at stake are the very meanings of color and race and the ideational and political purposes that color and race serve or can be made to serve. Here in the United States we are as much concerned about the politics that our purportedly "new" multiracialism will engender as about ascertaining the most "accurate" data. Brazil provides an example of a highly developed discursive and political history of multiracialism, from which I think we may profitably learn.

In the United States, those concerned about civil rights have worried about the impact of multiple-race responses on the implementation, efficacy, and very coherence of race-conscious legislation. With these concerns in mind, the experience of Brazil is instructive because it shows that neither multiracial ideas nor multiracial data mean that discrimination does not exist or cannot be proved. "Multiracial" data, just like "monoracial" data, must be interpreted. The color categories in Brazilian censuses are not free floating; ideas undergird them. Thus, the same multiracial data that were effectively used, for most of the twentieth century, to paint a portrait of a racially harmonious and nondiscriminatory Brazilian society are now being used to paint a portrait of a racially stratified society. Whether U.S. civil rights enforcement will be positively or negatively impacted by multiracial data depends, in significant measure, not only on the mere existence of multiracial data but also on the interpretations of those data and their political significance.

The Idea of Race and Multiracialism in Latin America

As is well known, racial and color identifications in Latin America are flexible, although never arbitrarily assigned or assumed. Indeed, Latin Americans have complex ways of determining an individual's proper "color" designation (Harris 1970; Wade 1993). This identity calculus, which is based principally on physical appearance, also includes assessments of class standing, educational training, place of origin, and the relationship of each person to the others. It is the very complexity and multiplicity of such identifications that at once discloses the pervasiveness of racial thinking and its mooted, but powerful, presence in political and economic life and history.

Political, economic, and social life in Latin America have not been rigidly organized around the idea of race as they have been in the United States, South Africa, Australia, colonial Africa, and Asia, for example. This does not mean that racial ideas have been unimportant. To the contrary, Latin American elites have always been deeply concerned with the "racial" stocks of their populations and have always considered the European antecedents of their peoples and cultures to be the most important and valuable. Race has been a central preoccupation precisely because Latin Americans have thought of themselves in racial terms on two levels. First, Latin American societies are presumed to be the products of persons of different races. Discrete races are presumed to exist. Second, extensive "racial mixture" has resulted in the formation of new "national" races (Brazilian, Cuban, and the like); according to certain thinkers, these new "races" will become white, or whiter, over time. The Mexican philosopher José Vasconcelos has famously celebrated the idea of racial mixture in his formulation of the "raza cósmica" (cosmic race). Mexicans, he claims, are a new, mixed race, made up of both Spanish and indigenous peoples. As scholars have observed, this cosmic race idea gave indigenous Mexicans a place within the new national identity while simultaneously relegating all things Indian to a backward and romantic past (Knight 1990).

In Brazil, the idea of racial mixture has also been the cornerstone of national identity. It is given its fullest expression in the writings of the Brazilian anthropologist Gilberto Freyre: Brazilians are forever becoming a new race, derived from the fusion of the three original races of Europeans, Africans, and Indians (Freyre 1986 [1946]). The Brazilian census apparatus has been an important agent in upholding and sustaining this idea, both in the ways that it measures (it counts by color, not by race) and in its interpretations of census data. The idea of racial mixture has not just served as mere demographic description or a particular cultural artifact; it has also served as both description and explanation of Brazilian social and political relations. The idea of racial mixture has been inextricably linked to the image of Brazil as a "racial democracy." On this view, Brazil is a racial democracy because racial identification has neither enhanced nor diminished social or political life. The meanings of and experiences engendered by "racial democracy" are bound up in the idea of multiracial identity itself.

In short, the principal difference between Latin American countries and the United States is that in Latin America, color has referred to physical appearance, not merely to racial origins. Color and race are conceptually distinguished but related: color refers to appearance, race refers to origins (Nogueira 1985). However, racial origins are not disconnected from color, because color is itself derived from the mixture of races—in the Brazilian case, the mixture of European, African, and Indian. By contrast, in the United States, color and race are often used interchangeably. Historically, there has been no meaningful conceptual distinction between color and race. For example, when black "racial" identification seems incongruous with "color" (for example, a "light-skinned black"), known African origins have served as the arbiter (commonly referred to as "the one-drop rule"). In Brazil, color trumps race; in the United States, race trumps color. Although these distinctions are hardly unambiguous, they go a long way in explaining how race is conceived and matters differently in Latin America and in the United States.

Racial Discrimination and Inequality in a Racial Democracy?

Desperate poverty and large inequalities are enduring features of Latin American economies and societies (Garfar 1998). Because income inequalities are so deeply and complexly rooted in basic issues of land ownership and of the political organization and regulation of economic life in Latin America, it is small wonder that poverty exists and persists. How, then, to address inequalities and reduce poverty is a fundamentally political and ideological question.

The question of how to reduce poverty is even more hotly contested when it is claimed or appears to be especially disadvantageous to a particular group within society. That is, though virtually all countries of the world are plagued by unacceptably high levels of inequality and poverty, this burden is deemed all the more unacceptable if it appears to be inequitably and unequally borne by a particular group. Racial and ethnic distinctions have been widely used to determine how public and private goods are distributed. Latin American elites, however, as well as many foreign observers, have declared Latin American countries exempt from this particular concern precisely because of their racially mixed populations. Thus, though there is no gainsaying the existence of poverty and inequality in Latin America, political and intellectual elites have largely dismissed the racial and color dimensions of that poverty and inequality as nonexistent.

This view of color's purportedly inconsequential character has not gone unchallenged. The challengers face formidable odds, however, mostly because ideologies all along the political spectrum have historically embraced this view, for different reasons. According to the Brazilian right and center, there is no systematic color or racial prejudice and discrimination. Racial discrimination, which is nearly always equated with U.S. "Jim Crow" segregation or South African apartheid, has not historically existed in Brazil precisely because of extensive racial mixture. As they see it, there are no pure races from which either racial antagonisms emerge or to which racial activists can appeal. Brazilians are simply Brazilians, with their many colors. Prejudicial incidences are isolated occurrences, not the products of systemic mechanisms. The words of a Brazilian ambassador are illustrative. In a written response to two 1993 *Washington Post* articles about the size of Latin America's black population and that population's impoverished condition, the ambassador wrote that "a far greater degree of intermarriage between races and the presence of intermediate categories make it inappropriate and irrelevant to transplant to these societies measurement criteria in narrow terms of 'black' and 'white' which have been developed in the context of civil rights in the United States" (Rubens Ricupero, "Racial Harmony in Brazil," *Washington Post*, August 30, 1993).

For the Brazilian left, the principal dividing line is that of class. Color lines may weakly divide Brazil's working rural and urban poor, but these divisions in no way override class. More deeply, color inequalities are derived from and reducible to more fundamental class inequalities. Brazil's "colored" people do not suffer or bear more of the burden of poverty. Far too many Brazilians, regardless of color, are poor, and class struggle is, therefore, the most appropriate political strategy. In sum, according to both right and left views of Brazilian politics and economy, color is of no causal significance. That is, the colors of individuals play no singular, determinative role in the distribution of goods, however poorly distributed such goods may be.

Although these interpretations of the significance—or, more precisely, the insignificance—of color remain influential, they have not gone unchallenged, and they retain their influence with increasing difficulty. Not surprisingly, census data have been crucially important in undermining the image of a nondiscriminatory, racially democratic Brazil precisely because they have been used for so long to uphold the image. The history of Brazilian census taking clearly reveals the connection between the idea of racial democracy, claims of nondiscrimination, and census methods.

Counting by Color

Compared with the American experience, census taking in Brazil seems relatively simple, if erratic. The color question has appeared inconsistently on Brazilian censuses from the first modern census taken in 1872 to the 2000 census. The two nineteenth-century censuses, 1872 and 1890, asked a color question. Of the twentieth-century censuses, those taken in 1940, 1950, 1960, 1980, and 1991 all asked color questions, although the 1960 color data were never fully released. The list that follows gives the response alternatives of these censuses:

- 1872: branco (white), preto (black), pardo (mixed), caboclo (mestizo Indian)
- 1890: branco, preto, mestiço (mixed white and black), caboclo

- 1940: branco, preto, amarelo (yellow)
- 1950: branco, preto, pardo, amarelo
- 1960: branco, preto, amarelo, pardo, Índio (Indian)
- 1980: branco, preto, pardo, amarelo
- 1991: branco, preto, pardo, amarelo, indígena (indigenous). (IBGE, various years)

No censuses were taken in 1910 and 1930, and those of 1900, 1920, and 1970 censuses did not have a color question.

Categorization itself has been more consistent, with the three color categories of white (branco), brown or mixed (pardo), and black (preto) used in nearly every census. The history of color categorization can be divided into three periods. From 1872 to 1910, categorization largely reflected elite and popular conceptions of Brazil's racial composition. From 1920 to 1950, census texts actively promoted and happily reported the whitening of Brazil's population. From 1960 to the present, categorization methods have themselves been questioned and contested by statisticians within the census bureau and by organized groups within civil society. Table 14.1 gives the raw population figures and each color category's share of the total population from the censuses conducted from 1940 to 1991.

Brazilian censuses have included a color question for the same basic reason that American censuses have included a race question. Brazilian elites viewed race as a natural component of human identity and as an independent factor in human affairs. Brazilian censuses have not counted by race, as such, but by color. The thinking is as follows: Brazilians are racially mixed, making the counting by race exceedingly imprecise. However, the census question and categories have themselves organized the fluid boundaries of the very racial mixture presumed to exist. Brazil's intelligentsia, political elite, and census officials have emphasized racial mixture with the same vigilance that their American counterparts have emphasized racial purity. Brazilian social scientists have largely accepted the scientific validity of races and their inequality, though not with the same intensity as have Americans and Europeans. As in America, the elites of Brazil have been obsessed with racial mixture, but they have concluded that Brazilians were becoming a whiter race, not a racially degraded and disadvantaged one.

Censuses from 1872 to 1919

Nineteenth-century Brazilian censuses were not involved in slavery debates, nor did they directly advance racial thought, unlike nineteenth-century American censuses. Although the 1872 census was conducted one year

TABLE 14.1   *Color Composition of Brazilian Population, by Federal Census Decennial Census Count, 1940 to 1991 (Thousands)*

Color	1940	1950	1960	1980	1991
White	26,172 (63.5)	32,028 (61.7)	42,838 (61.0)	64,540 (54.2)	75,704 (52.0)
Brown	8,744 (21.2)	13,786 (26.5)	20,706 (29.5)	46,233 (38.8)	62,316 (42.0)
Black	6,036 (14.6)	5,692 (11.0)	6,117 (8.7)	7,047 (5.9)	7,335 (5.0)
Yellow	242 (0.6)	329 (0.6)	483 (0.7)	673 (0.7)	630 (0.4)
Indigenous[a]	—	—	—	—	294 (0.3)
Missing	42 (0.1)	108 (0.2)	47 (0.1)	517 (0.4)	534 (0.3)
Total	41,236	51,944	70,191	119,011	146,813

Source: IBGE 1950, 1956, 1983, 1998.
Note: Each group's share of the total population in each census year is given as a percentage, in parentheses. No color question was asked on the 1970 census form.
[a]No data available for indigenous category until 1991, when it was first used on the census.

after the passage of major abolitionist legislation, neither census inquiries nor census data were marshaled for slavery debates. Although Brazilian intellectual and political elites were preoccupied with the perceived calamity of racial mixture, unlike their American counterparts they did not use the census to examine the problem. The categories on both the 1872 and the 1890 Brazilian censuses were nearly identical: white (branco), black (preto), brown or mixed (pardo), and caboclo (mestizo Indian). The 1890 added to these four the category of "mestiço" (mixture).

Paradoxically, the census was one of the few late-nineteenth-century undertakings that was not preoccupied with or used to discern the national disaster that Brazilian elites were convinced would accompany racial mixture. As the Brazilian historian Lilia Moritz Schwarcz has richly documented, museums, historical societies, law schools, medical schools, and scientists all fixed on racial mixture because they saw it as the key to understanding Brazil and its national possibilities (Schwarcz 1999). The silence of the census quite likely derived from the modest institutionalization of the statistical institute and the underdevelopment of statistical methods. The creation of the General Directory of Statistics (DGE) accompanied the abolition of slavery in 1888 and the establishment of the Old

Republic in 1890. Historians consider all three of the censuses conducted by the DGE (1890, 1900, and 1920) unreliable (Goyer and Domschke 1983). Brazil's modern federal census bureau, the Brazilian Institute of Geography and Statistics (IBGE), was established in 1938.

Censuses from 1920 to 1950

In the twentieth century the role of the census changed dramatically, as did the Brazilian establishment's ideas about racial mixture. In a sharp reversal, intellectuals posited that the disastrous consequences of racial mixture would be averted because Brazilians would become whiter over time. Racial mixture was not degenerative but fortifying for whites and cleansing for nonwhites (Skidmore 1993 [1974]). Whitening would also be achieved through European immigration.

It is hard to overemphasize the centrality of census data to twentieth-century claims of a racially mixed Brazilian people and the political and social arguments that have flowed from such claims. In the first half of the century, census texts happily reported that Brazilians were becoming whiter. The 1920 census included an extended discussion of the whitening of Brazil's population. In a section of the census entitled "Evolution of the Race" (which was later published separately as a book), the social theorist Oliveira Vianna explained that the "aryanization" of the Brazilian people was under way (Vianna 1956 [1923]). Within mestiço (meaning racially mixed) groups, the quantum of barbaric bloods was decreasing and the quantum of white blood increasing, refining the Brazilian race with each generation. Given the pervasiveness of the elites' belief in whitening, it is not surprising that this belief found its way into census texts. However, the text is surprising because the 1920 census itself did not include a color question. Predictions of whitening were not based on data collected contemporaneously, however unreliable and ambiguous such data certainly would have been. Vianna most likely wrote the whitening text to assure elites that Brazil's future as a white country was certain, thereby making the continued recruitment of European workers unnecessary. By 1920, industrialists and politicians were becoming exasperated with the militancy of immigrant workers (Maram 1977).

The 1940 census was the first twentieth-century census to ask a color question. Census enumerators were instructed to check either white, black, or yellow. If the respondent did not fit into one of these three categories, the enumerator was to place a horizontal line on the census schedule. These blank lines were later tabulated under the pardo category. Indigenous persons were reported as pardo as well. The IBGE excluded explicit reference to "pardo" from the enumeration in response to the rise of European fascism. According to IBGE documents, the category's exclusion would assure Brazilians that census data would not be used for discriminatory purposes (IBGE 1950). It is important to note also that the meaning of "pardo" was then and remains ambiguous. Portuguese language dictionaries define it as both gray and brown. Its connotations are equally ambiguous because Brazilians infrequently use it in common parlance. Its most significant use is as a census term. Although "preto" (black) was not the subject of controversy at the time, it has also been a peculiar term for the IBGE to use. Brazilians usually use it in the third person, not the first person, as the census requires. Even more illuminating, Brazilians use it most commonly to describe objects, not human beings. Black activists raised the issue of terminology most forcefully as the IBGE prepared for the 1991 and 2000 censuses.

The 1940 census also celebrated whitening. The author and esteemed educator Fernando de Azevedo wrote the census text, which was also published separately as a book and (this time) translated into English. Azevedo concluded the chapter entitled "Land and Race" (race, like land, was assigned a natural and fundamental status) with the prediction that "if we admit that Negroes and Indians are continuing to disappear, both in the successive dilutions of white blood and in the constant progress of biological and social selection," Brazil would soon be white (Azevedo 1950, 41).

The pardo category was added to the 1950 census schedule, making the four choices white, black, brown or mixed, and yellow. Self-identification replaced enumerator determination in 1950, as well. Self-identification meant that enumerators were bound to record the respondents' actual answers rather their own subjective assessments.

Censuses from 1960 to 2000

From the 1950s onward, census texts spoke little about whitening. The profound shifts in scientific racial thought following World War II largely account for this change. Census texts spoke less aggressively and frequently of both whitening and of the regenerative and redemptive powers of mixture. Instead, racial mixture was reported in a matter-of-fact way and was not equated automatically with whitening. However, Brazilians in general still believed in distinct races, if not in their inherent superiority or inferiority, and in the benefits of racial mixture. Moreover, the Brazilian establishment has used color data to promote the image of Brazil as a racial democracy. On this view, Brazilian citizenship has been neither enhanced, diminished, nor stratified because of race. Presumed racial differences are not a way of distinguishing among Brazilians because they are a racially mixed people. Brazilians are simply Brazilians, with their different colors. The census, in counting by color (and not race), has thus been instrumental in the discourse of racial democracy. The IBGE has been reluctant either to cross-tabulate color categories with socioeconomic variables or to release color data in a timely fashion. Until the early 1980s, the lack of such socioeconomic data made it impossible to test the claim that color was economically and socially inconsequential in Brazil. It also stymied the advocacy efforts of scholars, policy makers, and activists for remedial and positive public policies.

The National Census Commission, appointed by the military government, removed the color question from the 1970 census, against the recommendations of two experts whom the military itself had solicited. In the late 1970s, scholars and black activists lobbied to have the question restored. It appeared again on the 1980 census, although the IBGE's president remained opposed and called the question unconstitutional. Since Brazil's redemocratization in the mid-1980s (after twenty-one years of military rule), activists and scholars have aggressively challenged the discourse of racial democracy. They have also necessarily challenged census methods and terminology. Their efforts have prompted reexamination within the IBGE. In the early 1980s, for example, a group of statisticians and analysts within the IBGE's Department of Social Studies and Indicators (DIESO) decided to unite pardo and preto data under the term "negro" (black) in socioeconomic analyses and tables. The new inclusive term was deemed more appropriate than the older terms because the two groups had similar socioeconomic profiles and because it was the preferred term of black activists and certain academics (Oliveira, Porcaro, and Araújo 1985).

Activists and academics again raised the issue of terminology through a grassroots campaign around the 1991 census. The campaign, titled "Don't Let Your Color Pass in White: Respond with Good Sense," urged Brazilians to check the darkest appropriate color category on their census schedules. The campaign publicly raised two fundamental issues. First, it confronted the IBGE by asking why the terms "color," "preto," and "pardo" were used rather than "race" and "negro." Second, it challenged the preferences of most Brazilians to choose lighter colors, especially their decision not to self-select black (preto) on census schedules.

The 1991 color question was like past questions, with one important exception: the terms "raça" (race) and "indígena" (indigenous) were added. The question was rephrased to ask "What is your color or race?" and "indigenous" was added to the list of colors. (Since 1940, indigenous persons had been classified as pardo.) These two new terms were linked: race applied only to the indigenous population, and thus the new terminology implied that indigenous persons belong to one race and Brazilians, with their many colors, to another. The IBGE's decision to include "indigenous" was reportedly made after consultations with anthropologists and representatives of the Federal Indian Affairs Bureau. Campaign organizers speculated, however, that it was included at the request of the World Bank, which wanted demographic information for its initiatives on the protection of indigenous territories.

In the midst of preparations for the 2000 census, there was growing public and scholarly debate about the IBGE's methods and terminology. In these debates the IBGE has had to explain and often defend its past and current methods. The sources of pressure on the IBGE vary; they include demographers, black activists, academics, and politicians. With the unraveling of racial democracy, the question of who Brazilians "really" are racially has reemerged powerfully. There is clear reason for this connection. The image of a racially democratic and nondiscriminatory society has hinged on the idea of racial mixture. In fact, a causal link was drawn that was often presented tautologically: Brazilians are racially mixed, and therefore there can be no discrimination; there can be no racial discrimination because Brazilians are racially mixed. The acceptance of the existence of discrimination—an existence substantiated by census data—has lead unavoidably to the abandonment of the racial democracy idea and to a rethinking of the terms and methods used by the census bureau. The discourses of whitening and of racial democracy have resided in census methods and texts as much as they have existed (or not) in the real world. As Brazilians now consider whether their society is made up of distinct racial groups rather than one racially mixed people, the census has been enlisted in advancing a new racial discourse.

As for the 2000 census itself, it began on August 1, with the same terms and methods of the 1991 census. The color question took the form of "Your color or race is . . . ," and the available options were "branco" (white), "preto" (black), "pardo" (brown or mixed), "amarelo" (yellow), "indígeno" (Indian). Unlike U.S. census schedules, the color question has not appeared on the Brazilian census in the basic (short) schedule, only on the long form. Given the incomplete records of IBGE methods currently available to scholars, it is unknown when the long form was introduced. Nor is it known whether the color question was included on the census schedule before the introduction of the long form. For the 2000 census, the long form was used in one of every five households. Enumeration is conducted through door-to-door visits by census enumerators.

Discrimination Revealed: What Do the Data Say?

As mentioned, for most of the twentieth century, the IBGE had not cross-tabulated color categories with socioeconomic indicators; it was not until the 1976 household survey that color data were pegged to health, education, and housing. Furthermore, before the color question was reintroduced to the 1980 census, researchers using census data were forced to use data from the 1950 census. (The 1960 census asked a color question, but these color data were belatedly and not fully released. The color question was removed from the 1970 census.) Since 1980, there has been a veritable boom in scholarly and policy literatures on color inequalities and discrimination. The availability of these data has made the claim of color's inconsequential nature increasingly difficult to sustain.

Using data from the 1976 household survey, the sociologist Carlos Hasenbalg has found that along measures of educational attainment, labor force participation, and wages, "nonwhites" were disadvantaged in comparison with whites. Hasenbalg uses the term "nonwhite" to include "pretos" and "pardos" because, in his words, "although the mulatto group occupies an intermediate position . . . , its position is always closer to the black than to the white group" (Hasenbalg 1985, 28). In terms of educational attainment, Hasenbalg finds that 46 percent of nonwhites had no more than one year of instruction, compared with 26.7 percent of whites. At the other end of the educational ladder, 11 percent of whites had nine years or more of education, compared with only 3.5 percent of nonwhites. One result of low educational attainment is limited employment opportunities. Not surprisingly, nonwhites were largely employed in low-skill and low-wage sectors of the economy: agriculture, construction, and personal services (for example, domestic maids, day laborers). Nearly 68 percent of nonwhites were employed in these sectors, compared with 52 percent of whites. Finally, Hasenbalg finds that 53.6 percent of nonwhites earned only the monthly minimum wage (in 1976, approximately sixty-five American dollars), compared with 23.2 percent of whites. At the other end, 16.4 percent of whites earned more than five times the minimum wage, compared with just 4.2 percent of nonwhites.

The picture that emerged from the 1976 survey of households was not the one Brazil's racial democracy narrative had predicted. Brazil was not a society in which color did not significantly influence life's chances. Instead, Brazil was revealed to be a society in which, though the majority of Brazilians, both white and nonwhite, suffered, the privileged minority was most certainly white. It is important to note, as Hasenbalg does, that nonwhites disproportionately live in the underdeveloped, northeastern region of the country, whereas whites for the most part live in the industrial Southeast. These regional patterns are enduring legacies both of Brazilian slavery and postabolition immigration policies. During slavery, large plantations were located in the Northeast. After slavery's abolition, the planters of the southeastern state of São Paulo actively recruited Italian immigrants to work on their coffee plantations rather than employ Brazil's former slaves.

Using 1980 census data, the sociologist Peggy Lovell and the demographer Charles Wood have found that racial disparities persist (Lovell and Wood 1998).[2] Controlling for parents' education, household income, and place of residence, they find that white children were consistently more likely to be enrolled in school. Although educational attainment has increased for all Brazilians since the 1960s, nonwhites still trail behind whites. Their findings also appear to support those of Hasenbalg. Comparing wages across two decades (from 1960 to 1980), Lovell and Wood find that differentials persist between whites and nonwhites despite the structural changes that have increased opportunities and wages for all. By 1980, 18 percent of the wage gap between nonwhite and white women was attributable to labor market discrimination, and 32 percent of the wage gap between nonwhite and white men could be so attributed—that is, similarly qualified nonwhites were paid less than their white counterparts.

The availability of census and other survey data has proved a powerful weapon in recent and current battles to pass legislation outlawing racial discrimination and to advocate the introduction of affirmative action policies. Activists and some academics have argued that employers are discriminating against nonwhites in hiring and promotion in ways that require legislative action. This action, they argue, should be both punitive and affirmative. On the punitive side, laws should be in place whereby nonwhites who think they have been discriminated against at work can sue their employers. On the positive side, employers and public institutions should be encouraged to develop affirmative action policies to address past and enduring disadvantage. As these activists see it, the analyses of census data have laid low the claim of nondiscrimination and racial democracy.

At the same time, the same census data have been used to undercut some of these political gains. Although black activists and academics have been successful in unraveling the claims of nondiscrimination and racial democracy, they have been far less successful in reconfiguring and hardening the boundaries of color identities themselves. Black activists and many academics claim that grouping "blacks" and "browns" under an umbrella term "black" or "nonwhite" more accurately reflects the character of stratification in Brazil. One of the first venues in which they have sought to push for such a change has been the census schedule itself—namely, with the removal of the "pardo" category. Opponents of this view have argued against both the removal of the category and the public policies that such a removal might facilitate. In 1998, Simon Schwartzman, the president of the IBGE, argued in the *Jornal do Brasil*, a national daily newspaper, that color categorization in Brazilian society is richly complex, defying easy (let alone precise) measurement (Simon Schwartzman, "Cor discriminação e identidade social," *Jornal do Brasil*, May 5, 1998). Although he acknowledges the evident importance of color identification in the distribution of public goods and in the texture of social life, he also casts doubt on the ability of the census to measure the material significance of color, even imperfectly. Defending the IBGE's methods, he simultaneously discounts any alternative significance that might be imputed to color data. By claiming that all color statistics show is that color identification is complex, Schwartzman renders suspect those positive public policies that might be based upon them.

Thus the debate between activists and academics, on the one side, and IBGE officials, on the other, is now about the meanings and purposes of color enumeration. (This debate continues, although the 2000 census was conducted using the same color terms as the 1991 census.) Activists and academics argue that color enumeration should serve broad social and political purposes. To accurately measure Brazilian economic and social stratification, the census should use color terms that reflect the nature of that stratification. In their view, "white and nonwhite" or "white and black" most accurately reflects this stratification. The multiplicity of color terms that Brazilians use to describe themselves and others do not much matter in understanding the distribution of public and private goods. Although "white and nonwhite" or "white and black" may obscure the richness of Brazil's color lexicon, they help to illuminate the structure of inequality. Officials from the IBGE argue that census terms must in some way reflect the complexity of Brazilian color terminology if they are to have any legitimacy at all. Use of the categories "white" and "nonwhite" or "black" distorts Brazil's national identity, both by oversimplifying color categorization and by recasting Brazil, in terms of its racial politics, as some pale version of the United States.

The Lessons

What, then, are the lessons to be drawn from Brazil's experience? The first, if obvious, lesson is that the idea of multiracialism *differently* complicates our understandings of race and politics, but it neither diminishes nor eliminates the salience of race as an idea. This is true precisely because the idea of multiracialism is itself based upon notions of discrete races. The salience of race and, by extension, of color is not diminished because it continues to play an important role in the distribution of political power, economic wealth, and social standing. As socioeconomic analyses of Brazil continue to show, the way a person looks has some connection to the way a person lives and dies. The nature of that connection is a complicated one, however, in which color emerges as a significant, if not determinative, variable. The same is certainly true of the United States. At the same time, the now open acknowledgment and celebration of "multiracialism" in the United States portends the redrawing of group boundaries in largely uncertain ways. In the present context, neither the law, nor science, nor social mores stand in the way. How Americans choose to identify will certainly change, in the absence of restraints. However, the role of the census in engendering such change should not be overstated. As the histories of racial and color categorization in American and Brazilian censuses show, such categorization is embedded within and derived from larger institutional practices, political arrangements, and ideas. As important as censuses are—if mostly because they are overlooked—racial politics do not alone hinge on the existence or absence of a census category.

Nonetheless, it is clear that census categorization and data are often complexly intertwined with social knowledge and political processes. Brazil's narrative of mulitracialism, racial democracy, and nondiscrimination has been upheld and transmitted by the census. The census has not merely measured "whitening" and then "multiracialism"; it has helped to create these ideas through its methods. These ideas, in turn, have profoundly shaped political action. Pointing to census data, the Brazilian right has long argued that Brazilians are becoming "whiter" and are, in any case, "racially mixed," thereby making racial discrimination impossible. The Brazilian left, pointing to that same data, has argued that poverty has no color.

What happens, then, when the data change or are reinterpreted? Most obviously, views about society are challenged and political behavior changes. In Brazil, the introduction of socioeconomic analyses that empirically prove color to be materially and socially consequential has engendered new political strategies among the Brazilian right and left. The right still holds to a defense of Brazil's uniqueness, even if that uniqueness no longer resides in the much vaunted idea of racial democracy. They are generally opposed to the introduction of affirmative action policies for two reasons. First, they argue, such policies would be impossible to implement because of the difficulty in isolating a protected "color" class, given the multiplicity of color terms. Second, affirmative action policies have developed in countries, such as the United States, South Africa, and Malaysia, with histories very different from that of Brazil. Brazilian problems, they argue, require Brazilian solutions.

The Brazilian left, at the urging of black activists, has become far more attentive to combating color discrimination in the workplace and has supported, rhetorically at least, the implementation of affirmative action policies. The São Paulo–based Center for the Study of Labor Relations and Inequality, established in the late 1980s, has sensitized trade unionists to color discrimination and has counseled schoolteachers on how to counteract racial stereotypes; and one of Brazil's leading labor confederations, the Central Union of Workers (CUT), established the National Commission of Blacks in the early 1990s (Reichmann 1999, 16). The views of the Brazilian public also appear to be changing, if in contradictory ways. In a public survey published in June 1995, 89 percent of the five thousand Brazilians polled agreed that racism against blacks exists, although only ten stated that they themselves had behaved in prejudicial ways. Even more interesting and puzzling, 64 percent of pretos and 84 percent of pardos stated that they themselves had never felt discriminated against. According to this survey, Brazil is a racially prejudicial society without either conscious perpetrators or conscious victims (Turra and Venturi 1995).

American observers of Brazilian politics have argued that Brazil's idea of multiracialism serves as a cautionary tale about the purported efficacy of a colorblind doctrine in the remedy of racial discrimination. The second lesson from Brazil, then, is that the idea of multiracialism need not either imply or endorse an idea of colorblindness. Indeed, Brazilian multiracialism and American colorblindness are two distinct ideas, which ironically talk past each other on the very issue of discrimination and its remedy. While American colorblind jurisprudence recognizes the existence of racial discrimination in society, it maintains that race should not be considered in its remedy. On the other hand, Brazilian multiracialism freely recognizes color but denies the existence of discrimination based upon color. Brazilians think of themselves as a multiracial people, and such multiracialism has purportedly lead to a racially harmonious and nondiscriminatory society. Color is inconsequential, particularly in negative ways, and thus does not require remedy.

Advocates for and against colorblindness in the United States, then, cannot look to Brazil for guidance precisely because prevailing (albeit embattled) versions of multiracialism there deny the very possibility of discrimination. In the United States, there is no such widespread denial of discrimination's existence, although there is deep contention over the proper methods of remedy.

Finally, new interpretations of census color data have dramatically altered the tenor and direction of political discourse in Brazil. The same will eventually come to pass in the United States because multiracial census data will require interpretation. Census Bureau officials, politicians, scholars, group leadership, and individual citizens will undoubtedly offer competing interpretations about what these data say about American political, social, and economic life. Brazil, in the early decades of the twentieth century, was heralded as a racial democracy; by century's end it was being compared, albeit hyperbolically, with apartheid South Africa. Both of these assessments were derived from census data. As Brazil moves into the twenty-first century, the census will undoubtedly assist in the telling of Brazil's new story. At present, it appears that this story will focus on Brazil's "racial diversity" rather than the "multiracialism" of old. It is also likely that this new story will obscure certain dimensions of Brazilian society and economy even as it illuminates others. What is seen depends largely on the political and social purposes that such data are intended to advance and to retard.

Notes

1. In the end, the IBGE kept the "pardo" category.
2. Color data from the 1991 census were not released to the public until 1998.

References

Azevedo, Fernando de. 1950. *Brazilian Culture: An Introduction to the Study of Culture in Brazil.* Translated by William Rex Crawford. New York: Macmillan.

Freyre, Gilberto. 1986 [1946]. *The Masters and the Slaves: A Study in the Development of Brazilian Civilization.* Berkeley, Calif.: University of California Press.

Garfar, John. 1998. "Growth, Inequality, and Poverty in Selected Caribbean and Latin American Countries, with Emphasis on Guyana." *Journal of Latin American Studies* 30(3): 591–617.

Goyer, Doreen S., and Elaine Domschke. 1983. *The Handbook of National Population Censuses: Latin America and the Caribbean, North America, and Oceania.* Westport, Conn.: Greenwood Press.

Harris, Marvin. 1970. "Referential Ambiguity in the Calculus of Brazilian Racial Identity." *Southwestern Journal of Anthropology* 26: 1–14.

Hasenbalg, Carlos. 1985. "Race and Socioeconomic Inequalities in Brazil." In *Race, Class, and Power in Brazil,* edited by Pierre-Michel Fontaine. Los Angeles: Center for Afro-American Studies, University of California, Los Angeles.

Instituto Brasileiro de Geográfia e Estatística (IBGE). 1950. *Estudos de estatística teórica e aplicada, estatística demográfica.* Rio de Janeiro: Fundação IBGE.

———. 1950. Censo demográfico 1940. Vol. 2. Rio de Janiero: IBGE.

———. 1956. Censo demográfico 1950. Vol. 1. Rio de Janiero: IBGE.

———. Undated. Censo demográfico 1960. Vol. 1. Rio de Janiero: IBGE.

———. 1983. Censo demográfico 1980. Vol. 1. Rio de Janiero: IBGE.

———. 1998. "População Residente Por Con ou Raça, Segundo As Grandes Regiões, 1980–1991." Rio de Janiero: IBGE, Diretoria de Pesquisas, Departamento de População e Indicadores Sociais.

Knight, Alan. 1990. "Racism, Revolution, and *Indigenismo*: Mexico, 1910–1940." In *The Idea of Race in Latin America, 1870–1940,* edited by Richard Graham. Austin: University of Texas Press.

Lovell, Peggy A., and Charles H. Wood. 1998. "Skin Color, Racial Identity, and Life Chances in Brazil." *Latin American Perspectives* 25(3): 90–109.

Maram, Sheldon. 1977. "Labor and the Left in Brazil, 1890–1921: A Movement Aborted." *Hispanic American Historical Review* 57(2): 254–72.

Nogueira, Oracy. 1985. *Tanto preto quanto branco: Estudos de relaçoes raciais.* São Paulo, Brazil: T. A. Queiroz.

Oliveira, Lúcia Elena Garcia de, Rosa Maria Porcaro, and Tereza Cristina N. Araújo. 1985. *O lugar do negro na força de trabalho.* Rio de Janeiro, Brazil: Instituto Brasileiro de Geográfia e Estatística.

Reichmann, Rebecca. 1999. Introduction to *Race in Contemporary Brazil: From*

Indifference to Inequality, edited by R. Reichmann. University Park: Pennsylvania State University Press.

Schwarcz, Lilia Moritz. 1999. *The Spectacle of the Races: Scientists, Institutions, and the Race Question in Brazil.* New York: Hill and Wang.

Skidmore, Thomas. 1993 [1974]. *Black into White: Race and Nationality in Brazilian Thought.* Durham, N.C.: Duke University Press.

Turra, Cleusa, and Gustavo Venturi. 1995. *Racismo cordial: A mais completa análise sobre preconceito de côr no Brasil.* São Paulo, Brazil: Ática.

Vianna, Oliveira. 1956 [1923]. *Evolução do povo brasileiro.* 4th ed. Rio de Janeiro, Brazil: José Olympio.

Wade, Peter. 1993. *Blackness and Race Mixture: The Dynamics of Racial Identity in Colombia.* Baltimore: Johns Hopkins University Press.

15

REFLECTIONS ON RACE, HISPANICITY, AND ANCESTRY IN THE U.S. CENSUS

Nathan Glazer

A FEW years ago, when I was asked to comment on the controversy over how best to handle the demand of so-called multiracial advocacy groups for a "multiracial" category in the census, I made a brash and wildly unrealistic proposal.[1] Before describing my proposal, however, I should explain what concerned me about the existing questions on race, Hispanicity, and ancestry in the census. These questions had evolved by the 1980 and 1990 censuses in a way that was to my mind false to American racial and ethnic reality and incapable of getting coherent responses, to the degree that that is possible and that is normally expected in a census.

The census short form is the piece of official government paper that is probably seen by more Americans than any other, surpassing in the extent of its distribution the income tax forms. It is a message to the American people, and like any message it educates them to some reality: This is what the government needs, this what it wants, this is what it thinks is important. The census tells the American people that the government thinks the most important thing about them is to get them classified by race and ethnicity—ethnicity, that is, only if it qualifies as something called "Hispanic"; otherwise, the government is not interested. The census asks Americans first for the kinds of information that almost any form does, whether for a credit card or a driver's license—name, sex, age, family status—but then it turns out the main thing the government is interested in is their "race," described in the greatest detail, down to distinctions between Samoan and Guamanian and, if the respondent is Hispanic, between Argentinean, Colombian, Dominican, Nicaraguan, and even Spanish.

The government, in this message sent to all of us, apparently considers these matters more important than how educated we are, or whether we are citizens, or whether we are foreign born, or whether we voted in the last election. Scholars and researchers who follow the matter closely know why these questions are there, so prominently, so fully detailed. Do the American people in general know? If they do not—and it is hardly likely they are fully briefed on the legislation and regulations and politics and the pressures that have made the census form, with respect to race and Hispanicity, what it is today—what are they to conclude?

The census is supposed to give us a portrait of America. Is this what America looks like? Is the matter of race so important that it deserves this prominence and degree of detail?

A further problem is evident: that these questions are trying to impose on identities in flux—not all, of course, but many—a categorization scheme that will inevitably confuse many people. It is a scheme in which many cannot place themselves, and one that requires all sorts of manipulations by the census professionals to put the results into a form in which it can be presented to Congress, the press, and the American people. There is bound to be a substantial degree of error in these final figures, which are never rounded to indicate their uncertainty nor presented with any indication of their degree of error—in contrast with public opinion polls. Yet asking about race and ethnicity has many similarities to public opinion polls about attitudes, compared with questions about age, or amount of schooling, or a number of other topics on which respondents are pretty clear.

Finally, there is simply the irrationality of the categories. Why does Hispanicity include people from Argentina and Spain but not those from Brazil or Portugal? Are there really all those races in Asia, where each country seems to consist of a single and different race, compared with simply "white" for all of Europe and the Middle East? Why, indeed, do people of Spanish origin rate special treatment, as against people from Italy, Poland, or Greece?

All this is familiar. And so I made my proposal. I confess that underlying my proposal was an ideological or political position—just as ideological and political positions underlie the present census arrangements. My position was that it is necessary and desirable to recognize and encourage the ongoing assimilation of the many strands that make the American people into a common culture. It is, I realize, a delicate task to draw a line between "recognize"—which is what the census should do—and "encourage," which it should not see as part of its task. Any form of recognition or nonrecognition is also, however, a form of encouragement or dissuasion. One encourages what one recognizes and dissuades what one does not. My proposal also responded to my interest as a social scientist in recording the progress of this change, which has been continuous in American history, affecting all groups in different degree but tragically leaving aside, for most of our history, one major group.

So then, my brash and unrealistic proposal: I proposed reducing the mishmash of race, Hispanicity, and ancestry to basically two questions. One question would determine whether a person considered himself or herself black or African American. That would remain the only race for which the census requested information. A second question or group of questions would ask in which country the respondent was born and in which country his or her parents were born and could be extended to ask where that person's grandparents were born. These questions on the country of birth of parents and grandparents would be filled in by respondents rather than presented in a multiple-choice format with predetermined options.

Why the interest in only one race? The census has counted blacks, slave and free, since the first enumeration of 1790. History alone and the virtues of continuity would make a claim that that determination be continued. There are, of course, far more potent reasons. This is the group that has suffered from prejudice, discrimination, and a lower-caste status since the origins of the Republic. In law, all this is now overcome and does not exist, but African Americans, we know, despite their presence in large numbers from our origins as a group of British colonies on the Atlantic shore, are less integrated in American society than any other large group. They are more segregated residentially. The rate of intermarriage with others outside the group, even if rapidly increasing, is still the lowest for any large group. They have a clear sense of their identity. One can depend on a high degree of reliability in the answers they give to the race question, as census research has shown.

The second question or group of questions replaces the "ancestry" question because of the rapid rate of assimilation of all groups except blacks or African Americans. The limitation of these questions to the parental generation, and possibly the grandparental, is first a response to the reality that by the third generation and certainly by the fourth, the mix of ethnicities is extensive; second, it serves as an indication that the census and the government are not interested in group characteristics in the third generation and beyond.[2] With intermarriage rates in new nonblack immigrant groups of 30 percent or thereabouts, we assume that by the third generation assimilation has progressed to the point at which identity is mixed and fluctuating and its ethnic character has become largely symbolic. We leave the question of what that identity consists of to the excellent sociologists, such as Richard Alba and Mary Waters, who have studied the nature of ethnic identification in these later generations. The census thereby gets out of the business of trying to affix an ancestry to each American.

If one thinks that each of the peoples of Asia forms a distinct race, this question will be able to encompass all the immigrants from that country and their children. There are not many yet in the third generation. By the time there is a substantial third generation of the post-1960s wave of immigrants, many will be of mixed ancestry, and the question of their identity will be left to them. Intermarriage statistics suggest the same for Hispanics, the great majority of whom are now immigrants and the children of immigrants. The only distinct group for which the census will try to get statistics on all those identified with it is the black or African American, for historical reasons we all know but also because black or African American identity does not fade after a few generations in this country but maintains itself in a varying but full form generation after generation.

I realize that problems remain regarding American Indians, Alaska Natives, Hawaiians, and part-Hawaiians. All these groups have a legal status, and there are means for determining who does and does not belong to each of these groups. I can see the virtue of specific questions beyond those I have suggested for Hawaii and Alaska, but I do not think 280 million Americans have to be troubled to determine the numbers of these very small groups.

Questions on birthplace and parental birthplace as posed today, as against the same questions during the last great wave of immigration, have one virtue: during that earlier wave, immigrants came from Europe, where many ethnic groups could be found within the boundaries of great multi-ethnic empires, and thus birthplace said little about ethnicity. In addition, the boundaries of eastern Europe have been radically recast three times in a century, and European immigrants and their children could be properly confused as to the country of their birth. What was the birthplace of a person born in Bukowina? If the census asks, "what country were you born in?" there are at least four reasonable candidates. Most of today's immigrants, in contrast, come from countries whose boundaries have been stable for a century or more, and their birthplaces and those of their parents permit us to make reasonable judgments as to their ethnic group.

This, I argued, was all that was needed in place of the present questions on race, Hispanicity, and ancestry. These two questions would provide less detailed data but more accurate data. They would also be more responsive to what America was like, and what it was becoming.

I knew the proposal was politically naive, but I was not aware of how powerful and steady were the forces that created the present unsatisfactory situation until I went further into the history of the creation of the present categories (Skerry 2000; Nobles 2000; Anderson and Fienberg 1999; Bryant and Dunn 1995; Mitroff, Mason, and Barabba 1983). This research underlines the somewhat utopian character of my proposals today.

The experts seem to agree that when it comes to the census, the political outweighs the scientific, and this is a reality we have to live with. The word "political" can, of course, refer to many things, from the more to the less noble. What we have today in the census is political in all these senses.

Some of it is, in part, the result of major civil rights legislation, which, to my mind, falls on the noble side. That legislation had to be interpreted by the courts and by the administrative agencies, however, under the pressure of ethnic groups. As we follow this process further into the details that shaped the form of the census questions, the element of nobility in the political process declines. I am not sure the legislation itself, which was concerned with the right to vote, required what the census has done in its effort to respond to the demand for small-area data on Hispanics and Asian Americans. One could make a case that questions on birthplace and parental birthplace alone and the language question could give us the data to satisfy the legislation. But it would not give us the data in a form that satisfies proponents of distinct group interests and activists.

There are also the less noble political interventions. The census questions, whatever we think of their incongruity and irrationality, are the direct result of powerful pressures from the ethnic groups concerned, from Congress, and from the Executive Office of the President. These are political, alas, not only in the sense that political actors are involved but also in the narrower and less respectable sense that they are often motivated by narrow partisan political considerations.

Thus, Peter Skerry informs us, the unfortunate "ancestry" question was "criticized by social scientists for being vague and uninformative" in comparison with the question on birthplace of respondent's parents that it replaced. The Census Bureau also opposed it. "So why did the ancestry question end up on the questionnaire?" Skerry asks. "According to former deputy census director Louis Kincannon, who was working at the Statistical Policy Division of OMB when the decision was made, 'the ethnic desk' in the [Carter] White House insisted that the ancestry question go on the census. . . . It is evident that in the period leading up to the 1980 Presidential campaign, politics overrode the objections of both the OMB and the Census Bureau" (Skerry 2000, 37).

Democrats are understandably more responsive than Republicans to ethnic-group pressures, but Skerry tells us that Republican administrations have been no help, either. Concerning the origins of the Hispanic question, he notes that:

> the finalized questionnaires for the 1970 census were already at the printers when a Mexican American member of the U.S. Interagency Committee on Mexican American Affairs demanded that a specific Hispanic-origin question be included. . . . Over the opposition of Census Bureau officials, who argued against inclusion of an untested question so late in the process, Nixon ordered the secretary of commerce and the census director to add the question. . . . So it was hastily added to the long form. As former bureau official Conrad Taeuber recalls, "The order came down that we were to ask a direct

question, have the people identify themselves as Hispanic." (Skerry 2000, 37–38)

The pressures initially come from the ethnic groups involved or their leaders. Although there is only an uncertain relation between the numbers and the benefits that members of a group might get from one affirmative action program or another, undoubtedly the notion that one will in some way benefit from being counted as a distinct group plays a role in these pressures. At one time, Asian Indians were divided as to whether they should be "Caucasian" or yet another Asian race. Melissa Nobles reports on the discussion in the 1970s of the Federal Interagency Committee on Education on devising racial and ethnic categories for various federal programs. "The committee debated whether persons from India should be categorized under the 'Asian and Pacific Islander' category or under the 'White/Caucasian' category. . . . In the trial directive, they were classified as Caucasian, but they were reclassified as Asian in the final version (most likely in response to Asian Indian lobbying to ensure racial minority status)" (Nobles 2000, 79).

At the time, many in the Asian Indian community, taking into account their relatively high educational and economic position in the United States, rejected the idea that they should be eligible for benefits. Alas, the possibility of getting preferences for Indians under affirmative action programs for government contracts outweighed other considerations, and Indians—or at least some leadership groups—decided it was best to join the Chinese, Japanese, Koreans, and the rest as an "Asian race." I recall a report in an Indian newspaper that President Ronald Reagan's Small Business Administration (SBA) director had announced to an Indian conference that the SBA had decided to include South Asians among the groups that were considered qualified for preference in bidding for government contracts—this despite the fact that President Reagan was publicly an opponent of affirmative action programs. No doubt the administration hoped to garner a few Indian contributions or votes.

Congressional intervention can go into a level of detail that boggles the mind. Congress intervened in the wording of the 1990 race question when the Census Bureau shortened it to include only seven categories. Representative Robert Matsui introduced legislation "in which the formatting of the . . . race question was spelled out, even to the point of stipulating that 'Taiwanese' be one of the subgroups." Both houses passed it. "It was only President Reagan's pocket veto that blocked this extraordinary degree of congressional involvement in what is ordinarily considered the technical side of questionnaire design" (Skerry 2000, 41).

Social scientists deal with levels of irrationality—irrationality, that is, from the point of view of social science—that cannot be much affected by reasoned argument. Stanley Lieberson describes what happened when he attended a conference preparatory to the 1990 census. "I naively suggested that there was no reason to have a Hispanic question separate from the ethnic ancestry question since the former—as a far as I could tell—could be classified as a subpart of the latter. Several participants from prominent Hispanic organizations were furious with such a proposal. They were furious, by the way, not at me (just a naive academic), rather it was in the form of a warning to census personnel of the consequences that would follow were this proposal to be taken seriously" (Lieberson 1993, 30).

So, what else is new? Undoubtedly the degree of political intervention, however we understand the term "political," is now at a peak, and to propose changes in the race, Hispanicity, and ancestry questions is probably an exercise in futility. (I wonder whether Reynolds Farley's excellent suggestion that the three questions be combined into one—"What is this person's primary identity?"—followed by the five "official" group designations, with write-ins permitted under each, has ever gotten any public discussion.)

In the longer view, we know that politics has always played a significant role in the census. Melissa Nobles tells us the fascinating history of the use of "mulatto" in the census—a term that was included in censuses from 1850 until 1920 (Nobles 2000). It was originally introduced to support slaveholders' arguments that freedom and intermixture was bad for blacks. The abolition of slavery did not end the use of the category—it could still be used, its proponents believed, to argue that races were best off separated and that intermixture produced an inferior human being. In 1888, a member of Congress from Alabama, having decided that it was necessary to go into more detail on this thesis, introduced legislation—which passed both houses and became law—directing the census to "take such steps as may be necessary to ascertain . . . the birth rate and death rate among pure whites, and among negroes, Chinamen, Indians, and half-breeds or hybrids of any description . . . as well as of mulattoes, quadroons, and octoroons" (quoted in Nobles 2000, 56). Indeed, so directed, the census did have categories for quadroons and octoroons in the 1890 census—however useless may have been the results.

The mulattoes, quadroons, and octoroons are gone. What are the long-term prospects for that astonishing list of races in the census and that equally astonishing list of "Hispanics"? Will the lists get longer in the future, or shorter, and what factors might affect their future?

This is an interesting exercise in forecasting and prediction. It is possible that the pressures that derive from affirmative action and the hope for benefits from it, for example, will decline as affirmative action itself is restricted. It has already been banned, by public referendum, judicial action, or administrative action, in the public colleges and universities of four states. One effect of this ban has been an increase in the number of students giving no racial or ethnic identity to university authorities. There has been a substantial increase in the number of such students at the University of California at Berkeley. Why identify oneself if there is no longer a benefit in doing so? Is there an incipient revolt one can detect against the degree of racial and ethnic categorization that has been institutionalized, a revolt that will reduce further the reliability of these questions?

Much of the institutionalization of these categories in the census can be traced to the Voting Rights Act, and the ill-advised extension of this act in 1975 to "language minorities," persons of Spanish heritage, American Indians, and Asian Americans. I do not know what evidence there was, even in 1975, that these groups were prevented from voting because of lack of knowledge of English. This act requires hundreds of jurisdictions to produce voting materials in various languages—itself an irritation in various parts of the country. I wonder whether there is any evidence this has increased voting among members of these groups. (I would guess there is not.) These provisions require the census to tabulate and distribute census small-area data on the groups protected in the Voting Rights Act very rapidly after a census has been taken.

There is an inherent contradiction between the assumptions of this act and the requirement that one know English to be naturalized as a citizen. When a large number of Jewish immigrants spoke Yiddish and read only Yiddish-language newspapers, they had no trouble voting in substantial numbers equivalent to their English-speaking neighbors—even electing Socialist legislators. Are matters very different for current immigrants speaking foreign languages? Will these provisions survive, even to the census of 2010? Note that whenever a measure to declare English the "official language" gets on the ballot, as it has in a number of states, it passes. This suggests a popular hostility to these Voting Rights Act provisions. How long would they survive if submitted to a popular vote? The original point of the act was to overcome barriers to voting by blacks in the South, which were indeed great, were enforced by white officials, and had little to do with knowledge of English. The bilingual voting assistance provisions come up for renewal in 2007. Is it possible that some bold member of Congress will suggest that they are no longer needed?

All this suggests that the present distribution of political forces is not eternal, and the time may come when the questions now used for race and Hispanicity will seem as outlandish as the 1890 attempt to count quadroons and octoroons. The powerful assimilatory forces in American life are at work—working more slowly, it is true, for blacks than for other groups but still working to an end that will change how the census asks about race, Hispanicity, and ancestry. I hope that change comes about not because of some xenophobic revolt against this excessive census involvement in racial and ethnic categorization but because the members of the groups so marked out themselves no longer see any reason for the U.S. government to inquire officially into an ever murkier and indeterminate racial and ethnic identity.

Notes

1. My proposal is most easily found in Hartman 1997. It originally appeared in *Poverty and Race,* the newsletter of the Poverty and Race Research Action Council.

2. On the mix of ethnicities, see the impressive demonstration in Perlmann 2000. It is also evident in the analysis of responses to the ancestry question presented in Lieberson and Waters 1998.

References

Anderson, Margo J., and Stephen E. Fienberg. 1999. *Who Counts? The Politics of Census-Taking in Contemporary America.* New York: Russell Sage Foundation.

Bryant, Barbara Everitt, and William Dunn. 1995. *Moving Power and Money: The Politics of Census Taking.* Ithaca, N.Y.: New Strategist Publications.

Hartman, Chester, ed. 1997. *Double Exposure: Poverty and Race in America.* Armonk, N.Y.: M. E. Sharpe.

Lieberson, Stanley. 1993. "The Enumeration of Ethnic and Racial Groups in the Census: Some Devilish Principles." In *Challenges of Measuring an Ethnic World.* Proceedings of the Joint Canada–United States Conference on the Measurement of Ethnicity. Washington: U.S. Department of Commerce, U.S. Bureau of the Census.

Lieberson, Stanley, and Mary Waters. 1988. *From Many Strands.* New York, N.Y.: Russell Sage Foundation.

Mitroff, Ian I., Richard O. Mason, and Vincent P. Barabba. 1983. *The 1980 Census: Policymaking Amid Turbulence.* Lexington, Mass.: Lexington Books.

Nobles, Melissa. 2000. *Shades of Citizenship.* Stanford, Calif.: Stanford University Press.

Perlmann, Joel. 2000. "Demographic Outcomes of Ethnic Intermarriage in American History: Italian-Americans Through Four Generations." Working Paper 312. Annandale-on-Hudson, N.Y.: Jerome Levy Economics Institute.

Skerry, Peter. 2000. *Counting on the Census: Race, Group Identity, and the Evasion of Politics.* Washington, D.C.: Brookings Institution.

16

MULTIRACIALISM AND THE ADMINISTRATIVE STATE

Peter Skerry

T HE 2000 census was the first in U.S. history to offer respondents the option of identifying themselves as belonging to more than one race. This multiracial option was considered a necessary adaptation to the demographic and cultural changes that the United States has been experiencing. The civil rights lobby, which resisted this change, has by and large been fighting a rearguard action. Yet at the same time, the provenance of the multiracial option was an unlikely alliance between multiracial advocates and conservative Republicans, two groups whose understandings of race in contemporary American society seem, in spite of their obvious differences, equally shortsighted. Not surprisingly, the multiracial option poses daunting challenges that should give us all pause.

The multiracial option draws attention to the fundamentally political nature of the census generally and its racial and ethnic categories specifically. These are not issues that we Americans are eager to confront. Nor will they just disappear from public discourse, since the multiracial option reflects an ongoing collision between the powerful and still evolving forces of identity politics and the authoritative and enduring needs of the administrative state. Up to now, awareness of this dynamic has been confined to elites. Once out of the bottle, however, this genie threatens to erode public confidence in and support for racial and ethnic statistics.

In this sense, conservatives who supported the multiracial option as the wedge that would bring down the entire edifice of "counting by race" might be proved correct. Yet regardless of the wisdom of race-conscious policies, race consciousness antedates them and will not soon disappear. In any event, we Americans, however regrettably, continue to have but one way of talking about social and economic disadvantage—in terms of race. Until we have some alternative categories for addressing such issues, we need to be careful about what we wish for.

The Politics of the Multiracial Option

The process by which the multiracial option came to be implemented illustrates the fundamentally political nature of the census. More specifically, it demonstrates how a small number of political novices were able to get the Office of Management and Budget (OMB) in a Democratic administration to rule against the clear wishes of civil rights organizations.

In censuses before 2000, respondents were not supposed to check more than one racial category. If they did identify as belonging to more than one race (as about 0.5 percent did on the 1990 census), their answers were recoded for one race (OMB 1997, 36897). In recent years a growing number of multiracial individuals and parents of mixed-race children opposed this one-race restriction—on the grounds that it forced individuals, in particular children, to deny parts of their racial heritage, thereby adversely affecting their self-esteem, psychological well-being, and sense of pride in family (Graham 1994; Perlmann 1997; Williams 2000). In the early 1990s, in response to such criticism, the OMB began exploring the implications of a move to a new census item that would allow individuals to identify themselves as members of more than one race (Skerry 1996).

Those implications turned out to be ambiguous. On the one hand, extensive test surveys demonstrated that an extremely small segment of Americans—fewer than 2 percent—identified as "multiracial" when offered the explicit opportunity (OMB 1997, 36903). Yet those surveys also revealed significant impacts of a multiracial question on specific groups. A multiracial option reduced the number of people identifying as American Indian or Alaska Native and as Asian or Pacific Islander. At the same time, there was little impact on the numbers reporting their ancestry as white or black (OMB 1997, 36907).

The response to these findings was striking and somewhat surprising. Many American Indian tribal governments expressed concern about a multiracial question (Edmonston et al. 1996, 39). Some Hispanic leaders also raised objections. The most vocal and sustained disagreement, however, was voiced by African American leaders and organizations, who, to judge by the test results, had the least to lose from the proposed change. Whatever the results showed now, these leaders argued, a multiracial question would eventually reduce the numbers of those identifying as black and, more to the point, would potentially blur the categories upon which hard-won antidiscrimination and affirmative action programs are based. Long-time allies of these leaders, including civil rights enforcement agencies of the federal government, also argued against any change in the existing racial classification scheme (Linda Matthews, "More Than Identity Rides on a New Racial Category," *New York Times*, July 6, 1996; Nobles 2000, 129–45).

In the face of such opposition, the OMB decided in the fall of 1997 against the creation of a new, separate multiracial category or question on the 2000 census. Instead, the agency opted for a compromise that would permit individuals to check off more than one of the existing racial categories listed on the census form—a compromise that has come to be known as the multiracial option (Stephen Holmes, "People Can Claim More Than One Race on Federal Forms," *New York Times*, October 30, 1997). The crucial decision about how such multiracial responses would be tabulated was postponed until later.

If the OMB's decision to implement the multiracial option demonstrates anything, it is that the federal statistical system is not as institutionally conservative as has been widely suggested (Starr 1987, 52–55). On the contrary, instead of clinging to established procedures for the sake of data continuity, the system appears quite capable of responding to outside pressures by changing its policies dramatically and abruptly. This was the case during the 1990s, when policy makers were clearly prepared to adjust the census statistically to make up for persistent minority undercounts, and again in 1997, when they ruled in favor of the multiracial option (Skerry 2000, 121–77).

This decision also highlights the federal statistical system's responsiveness to a genuinely grassroots but politically inexperienced and marginal constituency. Indeed, in July 1996, at the peak of the battle for a multiracial question on the census, multiracial advocates were able to turn out only two hundred people for their Multiracial Solidarity March on Washington (Nobles 2000, 143). Even in a political system such as ours, in which determined minorities often get their way, the success of the multiracial movement is stunning.

Moreover, as Joel Perlmann has observed, multiracial advocates are motivated "more [by] recognition of multiraciality than [by] any specific political or economic advantage for multiracials. The advocates do not want to deny a part of their own or their children's origins." Unlike those pushing for census adjustment as a remedy for minority undercounts, multiracial advocates are driven not so much by group interests as by personal identity concerns (Perlmann 1997, 10; Williams 2000). This makes their achievement all the more remarkable—and worrisome.

To be sure, the multiracial movement received a boost from conservative Republicans in Congress, who see multiracialism as a way to weaken or undermine what House Speaker Newt Gingrich called "artificial" racial and ethnic categories (Barbara Vobejda, "Hill Reassured on Racial Check-off Plan for Census," *Washington Post,* July 26, 1997). Yet one should not exaggerate the importance of such conservative support. After all, it was President Bill Clinton's OMB that opted for the multiracial option. The Clinton administration could conceivably have rebuffed the multiracial advocates in the name of civil rights—a position strongly urged by the civil rights lobby, to whom the administration was clearly attentive.

Blatant and Brazen

The responsiveness of the OMB to the multiracial movement is an apparently benign example of how politics shapes the racial and ethnic categories used by the census. Indeed, this case is so benign—an instance of the little guy winning—that few would regard it as politics at work. By contrast, there are much more blatant examples of political pressure being brought to bear on the census. One of the most vivid is the Hispanic-origin question, added to the census questionnaire in 1970. A clear victory for Hispanics, this was also one of the Nixon administration's more brazen intrusions upon the prerogatives of the Census Bureau.

The episode even involved a bit of drama. The finalized questionnaires for the 1970 census were already at the printers when a member of the U.S. Interagency Committee on Mexican-American Affairs demanded that a specific Hispanic-origin question be included. The same White House that had recently inaugurated Hispanic Heritage Week was quick to respond (Petersen 1997, 120–21). Over the opposition of Census Bureau officials, who argued against inclusion of an untested question so late in the process, Nixon ordered the secretary of commerce and the census director to add the question. But the short form was already in production, so the Hispanic question was hastily added to the long form (Choldin 1986). As a former bureau official, Conrad Taeuber, recalls, "The order came down that we were to ask a direct question, have the people identify themselves as Hispanics. . . . The 5-percent schedule had barely started at the printers when we pulled it back and threw in the question which hadn't been tested in the field—under orders" (Taeuber n.d., 9).

In 1980 the Hispanic-origin question was moved onto the census short form (the form mailed to every household). In 1978, when these changes were announced, demographers and statisticians denounced them as "political." The headline on the front page of the *New York Times* declared, "Census Questions on Race Assailed As Political by Population Experts" (Robert Reinhold, *New York Times*, May 14, 1978). Our memory of such matters is short, however. Now deemed integral to the census, the separate Hispanic-origin question is no longer understood to be the result of lobbying efforts, much less the machinations of the Nixon White House. On the contrary, proposals to eliminate the question, or merely to amend it, are today denounced as "political" intrusions on the scientific prerogatives of Census Bureau professionals.

From Low Politics to High Politics

Countless such episodes are well known to census specialists, if not to the general public (Skerry 2000, 9–79). The experts universally acknowledge that the census is enmeshed in politics; but they also claim that social science has important and distinct contributions to make to the census. This perspective was evident in the debate over statistical adjustment that raged for much of the 1990s, when statisticians and demographers insisted that their expertise equipped them to transcend politics by providing scientific solutions to the persistent problem of minority undercounts. In essence, experts argue that though the census is indeed impacted by politics, the areas with which they themselves deal are immune.

My own view is that politics pervades even the scientific dimensions of the census. When it comes to the census, no meaningful distinction can be drawn between "the scientific" and "the political." To the fundamentally political questions that inevitably confront the census, whether minority undercounts or the multiracial option, science has no definitive answers. As Melissa Nobles puts it, "Census bureaus are not innocent bystanders in the arena of politics; census data are never merely demographic data" (Nobles 2000, x). In true technocratic fashion, however, social scientists tend to believe that they are equipped to deal with the means, while leaving the actual ends in the hands of politicians. Yet in politics, as in life, it is seldom possible to separate ends from means. Moreover, the ends typically shape the means, and vice versa (Skerry 2000, 101–20).

This perspective applies a fortiori to census efforts to collect racial and ethnic data. The history of these efforts reveals that the census is political not only in the low, self-interested sense but also in a higher, much loftier sense.

The census is not just a nose count—which could be accomplished by adding up administrative data from birth records, death certificates, and the like. Rather, a census is an effort to situate the population in three dimensions: geographical, temporal, and social. None of these dimensions has any natural units. All are calibrated according to certain conventions derived from and agreed on through politics.

One such calibration is the boundary that the census must draw around the nation. The Census Bureau must decide, for example, whether Americans living abroad, including diplomats or military personnel, are to be included in the census and, if so, where they are to be situated geographically (Zitter 1988; Hollmann 1988). Then, too, the census is necessarily a snapshot in time, and the bureau has to decide when its snapshot is best taken (Habermann 1995). Again, there is no scientific answer to this question, and different decisions impact varied interests differently. Finally, there are the social boundaries that the census must draw. Many of these— between men and women, for example, or among age categories—are taken for granted and barely noted. More visible and controversial have been the boundaries between ethnic and especially racial groups (Petersen 1987).

Thus the essential, defining characteristic of any census is the drawing of boundaries. Understood in this light, the census is an inherently political exercise, in the Aristotelian sense of the proper ordering and maintenance of the diverse parts that make up the whole. Whereas Plato sought to unify the polis by eliminating the categories and distinctions that he saw pulling it apart (such as those between men and women, family and polis, young and old, private and public), Aristotle took such competing and partial claims of justice as inevitable and regarded the statesman's role as responding to and balancing those claims. In that task, the creation of categories and the drawing of boundaries were fundamental.

Yet Aristotle also understood that these activities of the statesman are fraught with difficulty. Precisely because nature provides no definitive guide, boundaries and categories are invariably subject to challenge. The political theorist Arlene Saxonhouse explains that "because we ourselves, as a composite of a multiplicity of characteristics, vary along so many dimensions, the political regime is forced to establish boundaries and select criteria to define the order of its polity, but always those boundaries are subject to dispute and to counterclaims" (Saxonhouse 1992, 227). Aristotle would not be surprised to see the modern census engulfed by political contention.

Neither would the framers of the United States Constitution, who grasped as fully as anyone the inherently political nature of the census. This is not to say that the framers abandoned the census to sheer power politics. Rather, as was their wont, they embedded it in a structure that would balance one set of political interests against another. Thus, in Article I, section 2, of the Constitution, they made the census the basis for apportioning among the states both representatives and direct taxes—the former causing states to maximize their population totals, the latter to minimize them.

To be sure, such direct taxes were rarely levied on the states and were eventually obviated by income taxes levied on individuals. That does not change the framers' understanding of the census as an explicitly political tool that was part carrot and part stick. Rather than keeping politics at bay, the framers relied on politics—not science—as the mechanism by which an impartial result would be achieved.

An Instrument of State Authority

Politics inheres in the census in yet another way. As is evident, the census is inextricably bound up with the administrative needs of the contemporary welfare state. Census data are critical in the determination and distribution of myriad governmental benefits, from income supports to minority voting districts. In the scramble for these benefits, politics comes to be seen as the articulation and satisfaction of needs rather than the pursuit of the power needed to amass the resources to meet those needs. In other words, we tend to overlook that the census is an instrument of state authority for the purpose of political rule. As James Scott reminds us, however, in *Seeing Like a State*, "The categories used by state agents are not merely meant to make their environment legible; they are an authoritative tune to which most of the population must dance" (Scott 1998, 83).

This aspect of census taking is less apparent in the modern era than it was in antiquity. In classical Rome, the *census* was the official list of the Roman people, compiled for purposes of military service and taxation. It was maintained by the *censors*, two magistrates who wielded enormous authority: if for any reason both censors indicated their official disapproval of a citizen's conduct, the censured individual could be removed from his tribe and consequently lose the right to vote. This specific authority is clearly cognate with our term "censorship," though the connection with the census is almost never made today.

This authoritative, even coercive aspect of the census is particularly difficult for Americans to grasp. It is no accident that we invariably overlook the framers' conception of the census as a mechanism to levy taxes as well as to apportion representation. We prefer to focus on that aspect of the census that ministers to our needs and aspirations. Thus, in a pathbreaking essay on the sociology of official statistics, Paul Starr likens modern statistical systems to laws and constitutions—sets of agreed-upon, impersonal rules that restrain power and enlarge liberty (Starr 1987, 57). Similarly, former census director Kenneth Prewitt contrasts the contemporary U.S. census favorably with its ancient antecedents:

> Our census is different from those historical censuses. Our census is the very first census, in recorded history, which is used to bring power back to the people, not to take something away from the people. . . . The historic reasons for a census were . . . military conscription or taxation. That is, what could you take from the people? Whereas, our census is about allocating power back to the people and now allocating resources, as we just said— federal moneys—back to the people. (Prewitt 2000, 4)

Both Starr and Prewitt are certainly correct to emphasize the role of our census in bolstering American liberties. But their neglect of the census's concurrent reliance on the authority, power, and ultimately coercion of the state is telling.

A Virtual Regime Principle

When race is involved, Americans have an even more difficult time recognizing the census as an instrument of state authority. After all, the preferred means of categorizing individuals racially or ethnically on the census is self-identification, which is premised on "respect for individual dignity" (OMB 1995, 44692) and on the principle that the federal government "does *not* tell an individual who he or she is, or specify how an individual should classify himself or herself" (OMB 1997, 36874).

Whatever one's opinion of the merits of the multiracial option, it undeniably jibes with the letter and spirit of self-identification undergirding today's census. There are many methodological and practical reasons for relying on self-identification, but in the American context, self-identification of race and ethnicity is sustained by more than convenience to bureaucrats or social scientists. It accords with strongly held beliefs in individual choice and liberty. Most Americans feel uneasy when a person is assigned to a racial or ethnic category by the government. To the extent that we regard such categories as legitimate, we tend to think that the individual should decide where he or she belongs. As an OMB official once put it to me, "We don't classify individuals around here!" (quoted in Skerry 2000, 46).

One reason Americans dislike the idea of a government agency assigning individuals to racial or ethnic categories is the nation's past failures to apply its individualistic values to various racial minorities. Slavery, Jim Crow laws, the mistreatment of Indians, and the wartime internment of Japanese civilians are just the first examples that come to mind. Because of this historical gap between our values and our deeds, self-identification of race and ethnicity has now emerged as a virtual regime principle (Mann 1979, 86–96).

Further entwining self-identification with individualism are evolving American conceptions of race and ethnicity. The OMB accepts the received academic wisdom that race and ethnicity are not biological categories but social constructs. Yet before the ink was dry on its 1978 regulations, race and ethnicity were being transformed by the wider culture. The historian David Hollinger suggests that, under the influence of multiculturalism, ethnicity has subtly shifted its meaning from a social concept denoting affiliation to one or more groups to a psychological concept denoting identity (Hollinger 1995, 6–7). Similarly, a report on the census published by the National Academy of Sciences emphasizes "the increasing recognition that race and ethnicity are subjective, personal characteristics" (Edmonston et al. 1996, 18). Thus the social historian Stephan Thernstrom notes with concern that ethnicity in the census has become "a matter of choice, a state of mind rather than a matter for genealogists to determine: 'It doesn't matter if you don't think I look Chinese. I feel Chinese; ergo I am Chinese'" (Thernstrom 1992, 97).

Yet however powerfully embedded the idea of choosing one's own race and ethnicity may be in our individualistic political culture, the realities of public policy eventually intrude and require that the government impose order. Self-identification results in such a profusion of facially incorrect or merely idiosyncratic responses (and nonresponses) that sooner or later federal bureaucrats must violate their commitment to self-identification and force the data into usable categories—namely, those established by the OMB in 1978 (OMB 1978, 19269). In spite of its own declared aversion to doing so, our liberal regime has no choice but to exercise authority in this realm. From the policy maker's perspective, the plain fact is that racial and ethnic identity are too important to be left completely to the preferences of individuals.

The specific challenges facing the Census Bureau here are enormous. As race and ethnicity have become more subjective and psychological categories, they have also become more imprecise and volatile. At the same time, they are more critical than ever to public policy. The more the census tries to count identities, the more difficult it finds its task. These changes go to the heart of the bureau's traditional view of its mission. As Stanley Lieberson has noted, there is "a general disposition of censuses to avoid asking attitudinal questions or other 'subjective' questions" (Lieberson 1993, 32). This is why the Census Bureau has long described itself as "the fact-finder for the nation." Precisely because the uses to which these numbers are put are so controversial and politically explosive, the bureau must cling ever more tightly to its mantle of objectivity. As it wades into increasingly subjective, attitudinal phenomena, this self-conscious mission becomes imperiled.

Torn between the regime principle of self-identification and the bureaucratic requirements of the contemporary administrative state, the OMB and the Census Bureau have up to now maneuvered quite successfully. But their clear exercise of governmental authority in a realm viewed as private is a delicate balancing act that most Americans, if fully apprised, would regard with uneasiness, even outrage. It is no accident that OMB officials typically avoid using the word "race" when discussing their classification scheme, opting for the seemingly neutral term "population group" (OMB 1997). There should be no doubt that these agencies are negotiating a political minefield of misapprehension and distrust—among minorities and the general public alike—of the government's ability to deal fairly with racial and ethnic matters.

Of course, government officials understand the tension between the vagaries of personal identity and the demands of bureaucratic rationality. And they know that to resolve this tension, authority must be exercised. They are also acutely aware, however, of the need to act with discretion. At the OMB, standing as it does at the center of a decentralized statistical system within which myriad federal agencies jealously guard their prerogatives, officials are ever at pains not to appear to overstep their institutional prerogatives.

This balancing act is hardly an isolated example. On the contrary, it is typical of how authority more generally is wielded in the contemporary American administrative state. In what some have called "the new American political system," substantive policy goals are pursued less through conventional political and legislative means than through arcane legal and administrative channels that leave many ordinary Americans feeling bewildered and excluded (King 1990). This regime has emerged for a variety of technical and political reasons, but as Theodore Lowi observes, at its center is liberalism's aversion to acknowledging the authority and power that the contemporary state does—and must—exercise (Lowi 1979).

Implications for Multiracialism

According to a National Academy of Sciences study, "If self-identification is taken as a basic principle, there are no grounds for recoding a multirace person to a single race" (Edmonston et al. 1996, 38). Yet this is precisely what federal executive agencies have required in the aftermath of the 2000 census. Thus, to implement the Voting Rights Act, the Justice Department has issued a guidance for reducing multiple-race responses to the 2000 census to the original mutually exclusive, single-race categories established in 1978 by OMB Directive 15 (U.S. Department of Justice 2001). This violation of the self-identification principle does not appear to have provoked much criticism from multiracial advocates, though one wonders how long the silence will last.

Of still greater concern is the public scrutiny that will eventually be focused on the tabulation of these multiple-race responses. The census has long relied on various tabulation methods to make sense of idiosyncratic, inconsistent, and incorrect responses (and nonresponses) to its conventional questions (Skerry 2000, 51–79). Moreover, though the choices involved in these tabulations were always "political," in the sense that they affected outcomes for various groups and interests, they occurred behind a veil of administrative discretion and went largely unexamined. Now such tabulations will increasingly be politicized. Alternatively, one could say that these procedures will be increasingly democratized. Either way, they will come under much greater scrutiny than ever before. Alluding to the old adage about politics resembling sausage making, the demographer Josh Goldstein cautions, "We're going to be looking at more and more of the sausage."

As with sausages, the result will not be pretty. There may now be a consensus among intellectual and policy elites that race and ethnicity are socially constructed, but this perspective has only just begun to penetrate the public mind. When it becomes apparent that race and ethnicity are also politically constructed, such data will appear all the more arbitrary and artificial. Public disaffection with them can only grow.

Of course, this is fine with conservatives who have supported multi-racialism as a means of undermining the entire post-civil-rights regime of affirmative action and group rights—in the words of the commentator James K. Glassman, the multiracial agenda means "the beginning of the end for the whole delicate and ridiculous architecture of race-counting" ("Is America Finally Going Color-Blind?" *Washington Post*, June 3, 1997). From this perspective, census questions about race and ethnicity are one of the ways in which the state has been propping up distinctions that would otherwise long since have melted away. The prescription is clear. Citizens should feel no obligation to answer racial and ethnic questions, along with other "invasive" items, on the census. So declared conservative activists and Republican politicians while the Census Bureau was conducting its 2000 enumeration (D'Vera Cohn, "Census Too Nosy? Don't Answer Invasive Questions, GOP Suggests," *Washington Post*, March 30.).

Like the multiracialists preoccupied with issues of personal identity, these conservatives are so caught up in their own wishful scenario that they fail to see the larger implications of the multiracial agenda. Public disaffection with race-conscious policies is as great as it has ever been, and this disaffection has now spread to the collection of racial and ethnic data on the census. Yet however understandable, even justified, these negative reactions may be, it is simply not the case that the elimination of racial and ethnic data will have the effect of eliminating race consciousness in the broader society. It is encouraging to see an increasing number of Americans come to feel that their racial identity is a matter of individual choice. The fact remains, however, that for many more Americans, racial identity (whether their own or that of other groups) is not merely subjective and malleable. Thus it is all the more curious—and troubling—to see the federal statistical system respond with such exquisite sensitivity to a small group of activists whose demands are hardly representative or typical.

This is not a brief for either side of the debate over race-conscious policies. To be sure, our efforts to count racial and ethnic groups are highly imperfect and becoming more so. The need for such data is not about to disappear, however. For better or worse, race is the only way we have of talking about social and economic disadvantage in the United States today (Skerry 1999). Precisely for this reason, racial and ethnic data will continue to be crucial, not only for the governmental and nongovernmental entities that implement race-based policies but also for those who would criticize or even condemn such policies.

Because of the multiracial option, contemporary public policy is now at a precarious juncture. Perhaps the most revealing indication of this is the degree to which the multiracial option has put minority leaders on the defensive. Of greatest concern should be the response of African Americans. As Joel Perlmann and Mary Waters emphasize in the introduction to this volume, African Americans are the minority group with the sharpest boundary and the least out-marriage. They have also been the loudest opponents of the multiracial option. In an era when blacks are already struggling with the demographic and political competition of immigrants and other minorities, especially Hispanics, the multiracial option can only exacerbate their defensiveness. Because political and policy outcomes involving census data are highly unpredictable, the multiracial option will only add to the anxiety felt by black civil rights organizations. Regardless of one's position on multiracialism, it is important to recognize that for African Americans this is a highly volatile and emotional issue.

Multiracialism may well be the silver bullet that finishes off the affirmative action regime. If so, however, this outcome will not bring the nation to a state of colorblind innocence. Moreover, what began as understandable assertions of American individualism against the prerogatives of the administrative state—on the part of either multiracialists or their conservative supporters—will end up contributing to confusion and cynicism among the general populace and to anxiety and defensiveness among minorities. Especially in the short and medium terms, multiracialism will do more harm than good.

References

Choldin, Harvey M. 1986. "Statistics and Politics: The 'Hispanic Issue' in the 1980 Census." *Demography* 23(August): 403–18.

Edmonston, Barry, Joshua Goldstein, and Juanita Tamayo Lott. 1996. *Spotlight on Heterogeneity*. Washington, D.C.: National Academy Press.

Graham, Susan. 1994. Presentation before the National Research Council Workshop on Race and Ethnicity Classification, Washington, D.C. (February).

Habermann, Hermann. 1995. "The Census: A Cornerstone in the Construction of a Nation." Paper presented at the Central Statistical Service. Pretoria, South Africa (November 17).

Hollinger, David A. 1995. *Postethnic America: Beyond Multiculturalism*. New York: Basic Books.

Hollmann, Walter P. 1988. "Applying Residence Rules to the Military." *Society* 25(March–April): 54–55.

King, Anthony. 1990. *The New American Political System*. 2d ed. Washington, D.C.: AEI Press.

Lieberson, Stanley. 1993. "The Enumeration of Racial and Ethnic Groups in the Census." In *Challenges of Measuring the Ethnic World: Science, Politics, and Reality*. Washington: U.S. Bureau of the Census.

Lowi, Theodore J. 1979. *The End of Liberalism: The Second Republic of the United States*. New York: W. W. Norton.

Mann, Arthur. 1979. *The One and the Many: Reflections on the American Identity*. Chicago: University of Chicago Press.

Nobles, Melissa. 2000. *Shades of Citizenship*. Stanford, Calif.: Stanford University Press.

Office of Management and Budget (OMB), Executive Office of the President. 1978. "Directive 15: Race and Ethnic Standards for Federal Statistics and Administrative Reporting." *Federal Register* 43(May 4).

———. 1995. "Standards for the Classification of Federal Data on Race and Ethnicity." *Federal Register* 60(August 28).

———. 1997. "Recommendations from the Interagency Committee for the Review of the Racial and Ethnic Standards to the Office of Management and Budget Concerning Changes to the Standards for the Classification of Federal Data on Race and Ethnicity." *Federal Register* 62(July 9).

Perlmann, Joel. 1997. *Reflecting the Changing Face of America: Multiracials, Racial Classification, and American Intermarriage*. Public Policy Brief 35. Annandale-on-Hudson, N.Y.: Jerome Levy Economics Institute.

Petersen, William. 1987. "Politics and the Measurement of Ethnicity." In *The Politics of Numbers,* edited by William Alonso and Paul Starr. New York: Russell Sage Foundation.

———. 1997. *Ethnicity Counts*. New Brunswick, N.J.: Transaction Books.

Prewitt, Kenneth. 2000. Transcript of "Talk of the Nation." National Public Radio. March 21.

Saxonhouse, Arlene W. 1992. *Fear of Diversity: The Birth of Political Science in Ancient Greek Thought*. Chicago: University of Chicago Press.

Scott, James C. 1998. *Seeing Like a State: How Certain Schemes to Improve the Human Condition Have Failed*. New Haven, Conn.: Yale University Press.

Skerry, Peter. 1996. "Many American Dilemmas: The Statistical Politics of Counting by Race and Ethnicity." *Brookings Review* 14(summer): 36–39.

———. 1999. "The Racialization of Immigration Policy." In *Taking Stock: American Government in the Twentieth Century,* edited by Morton Keller and R. Shep Melnick. New York: Cambridge University Press.

———. 2000. *Counting on the Census? Race, Group Identity, and the Evasion of Politics*. Washington, D.C.: Brookings Institution.

Starr, Paul. 1987. "The Sociology of Official Statistics." In *The Politics of Numbers,* edited by William Alonso and Paul Starr. New York: Russell Sage Foundation.

Taeuber, Conrad. N.d. "Conrad Taeuber: Oral History." Washington: Bureau of the Census, History Staff.

Thernstrom, Stephan. 1992. "American Ethnic Statistics." In *Immigrants in Two Democracies: French and American Experience,* edited by Donald L. Horowitz and Gerard Noiriel. New York: New York University Press.

U.S. Department of Justice. 2001. *Guidance Concerning Redistricting and Retrogression Under Section 5 of the Voting Rights Act*. Washington (January 18).

Williams, Kim. 2000. "Boxed In: The United States Multiracial Movement." Ph.D. diss., Department of Government, Cornell University.

Zitter, Meyer. 1988. "Enumerating Americans Living Abroad." *Society* 25(March–April): 56–60.

17

MULTIPLE RACIAL IDENTIFIERS IN THE 2000 CENSUS, AND THEN WHAT?

Jennifer L. Hochschild

This is the beginning of the end of the overwhelming role of race in our public life.
　　　　　　　—Martha Farnsworth Riche, Census Bureau director from 1994 to 1998

When [Census 2000's] history is written, the issues surrounding sampling and other aspects of measurement theory will be a footnote . . . to the real story of this count: multiracial identity. With "Question 8: What is this person's race? Mark one or more," we turned a corner about how we think about race in this country.
　　　　　　　—Kenneth Prewitt, Census Bureau director from 1998 to 2001

L ED, IRONICALLY, by the Census Bureau, which used to be seen as a stodgy data collector, the United States is embarking on a dramatic experiment that will change the way our government counts races and recognizes multiracials. This experiment will have repercussions on a wide range of attitudes and activities, from individual self-identification through corporate advertising budgets to allocations of billions of taxpayers' dollars and millions of people into voting districts. We do not know how it will turn out, and we do not have a clear goal or set of goals at which we are aiming. It is an extraordinary, fascinating, and difficult moment in an extremely sensitive political arena. Certainty about any of it, empirically and normatively, seems misplaced.

Confessions

To begin with, I must confess to uncertainty over the outcome of this innovation. I do not know where or how far the new structure permitting multiracial identification will go—and neither does anyone else. Based on an array of evidence including smaller surveys in 1996 and 1998, demographers expected that 2 or 3 percent of previously identified African Americans would choose more than one race in the 2000 census; the actual figure was almost 5 percent.[1] Claudette Bennett, the chief of the racial statistics branch at the Census Bureau, remarked, "We really didn't expect that number. . . . We just don't really have a good handle on it right now" (quoted in Eric Schmitt, "Multiracial Identification Might Affect Programs," *New York Times,* March 14, 2001). That seems exactly the right initial response to a phenomenon that is newly conceptualized, newly measured, and rapidly changing at the same time that it is being conceptualized and measured—perhaps partly *because* it is being conceptualized and measured.[2] If statisticians could not predict what people would choose even a few years after the initial surveys, how much less can they predict the trajectory of choices into the future, especially given that those choices themselves will be deeply affected by the interpretation and consequences of previous choices, not yet made? As the OMB puts it, the percentage of the population giving multiple responses to the census questions on race and ethnicity "may increase as those who identify with more than one racial heritage become aware of the opportunity to report more than one race" (OMB 2001, 7). Moreover, the political and policy implications of these unpredictable choices are themselves unpredictable, mainly because they too will rest on interpretations not yet developed and choices not yet framed.

If my first confession is really recognition of the fluidity of multiracial identification, a second is recognition of the normative complexity underlying racial and ethnic identity. I do not know what the optimal outcome of this process might be. Should we strive to use multiracial identification as the entering wedge of a move toward a twenty-first-century version of Israel Zangwill's "melting pot," or Michel (J. Hector St. John) de Crèvecoeur's "American, this new man"? Would doing so water down the commitment to civil rights enforcement and to redistricting to ensure equitable representation of people of color in governance? Should we interpret the increasing number of people who claim to be part American Indian or Alaska Native as the final death rattle of whites' previous views of Indians as savages to be exterminated? Or will doing so dilute the culture, traditions, and meaning of being Native American until Indian identity becomes analogous to drinking green beer on St. Patrick's Day?

In short, should we celebrate multiracial self-identification as the best indicator of the social constructedness of race or deplore it as a thin disguise over a continuing structure of racial domination? I am not in a position to answer these questions, nor do I believe, more contentiously, that anyone else has grounds for moral certainty, either. Here also, too much depends on choices not yet made, interpretations not yet conceived, policies not yet implemented, leaders and social movements not yet materialized.

Questions

The uncertainties revealed by these confessions suggest that Americans need to consider, even if we cannot resolve, a set of more specific questions raised by the Census Bureau's initiative and our responses to it. If one could answer these questions satisfactorily, we would move closer to a clear normative goal and a set of political and policy prescriptions for pursuing it.

First, how should multiraciality itself be interpreted? In one view, multiraciality indicates the artificiality of—and thereby can hasten the abolition of—the old racial identities that have caused so much misery and unwarranted hierarchy. Some proponents endorse multiracialism because "classification . . . [is] the nemesis of mankind, a reflection of intellectual empty-headedness." We must reject "any . . . doctrine that would subordinate the will and aspirations of the individual to that of an artificial grouping," and we must work to prevent future generations from being "indoctrinated in collectivist, identity politics dogma" (Charles Michael Byrd, "Census 2000 Protest: Check American Indian!" January 1, 1998. Accessed May 18, 2002 at: *www.webcom.com/~intvoice/protest.html*).

In another view, multiracialism is itself a new identity to be added to the traditional ones. The stated goal of the Association of MultiEthnic Americans is:

> to educate and advocate on behalf of multiethnic individuals and families. . . . Every person who is multiethnic/multiracial has the same right as any other person to assert a personal identity that embraces the fullness and integrity of their actual ancestry. . . . A positive awareness of interracial and multicultural identity is one of the essential keys to unlocking America's, and also the world's, profound difficulty with the issues of race and interethnic relations. (Accessed May 16, 2002 at: *www.ameasite.org/abtamea.html*)

Finally, particular forms of multiracial identity may actually expand membership in traditional racial and ethnic categories. The clearest case here is that of Native Americans; if everyone who claims and can prove some Indian ancestry gets incorporated into the population of Native Americans, then that group will be several times larger than it was a few decades ago, when people with mixed ancestry opted out or were pushed out. "The number of American Indians and Alaska natives who defined themselves by only that category grew by 26 percent in the past decade to 2.5 million. But when the number of people who said they were part Indian [was] added, the total ballooned to 4.1 million, a 110 percent increase since 1990" (Eric Schmitt, "For 7 Million People in Census, One Race Category Isn't Enough," *New York Times,* March 13, 2001). In this case, that is, a multiracial identifier may strengthen an established single-race identifier.[3]

A second question grows out of the statistical nightmare that the new census categories have produced. Every demographer has warned of the difficulties in comparing the 2000 census with earlier censuses, and every collector of data in schools, universities, police departments, hospitals, survey research firms, advertising agencies, and so on has expressed the same concern. The issue is, of course, not just statistical, because the allocation of individuals to categories will deeply affect decisions about whether voting districts dilute minority electoral power, whether corporations discriminate in hiring and promotions, and whether programmatic funding for particular locations should be increased or decreased.

The Office of Management and the Budget (OMB) partly responded to these concerns in its *Guidance on Aggregation and Allocation of Data on Race for Use in Civil Rights Enforcement and Monitoring,* issued in March 2000 (known as Bulletin 00-02). Its rules include the following: "Responses that combine one minority race and white are allocated to the minority race. Responses that include two or more minority races are allocated as follows: If the enforcement action is in response to a complaint, allocate to the race that the complainant alleges the discrimination was based on. If the enforcement action requires assessing disparate impact or discriminatory patterns, analyze the patterns based on alternative allocations to each of the minority groups" (OMB 2000, 61–62).

How should we view these allocation rules? To proponents of multiracialism, the first two reify the stigma implied by the phrase "one drop of blood" and retreat from the conceptual leap represented by the possibility of multiple identifications:

All of a sudden to finally be given the opportunity to choose more than one race, and then seemingly have that taken away seems a little suspect. Besides, it would be wrong to say that I would only be discriminated against because I am Korean or Asian American. I used to bus tables, and people used to think I was Mexican. The reality is that I might be discriminated against because someone thinks I am Native American or Latino or Asian American. And sometimes people are discriminating against others just because they are multiracial—not because they are perceived to be one thing or another. (Matt Kelley, quoted in Solomon Moore, "Census' Multiracial Option Overturns Traditional Views," *Los Angeles Times,* March 5, 2001)

Conversely, some see Bulletin 00-02 to be implicit acknowledgment of the flaws of multiracialism (or the political strength of its opponents), because the first allocation rule reduces the possibility that multiracial identifiers will dilute the political strength of the African American population in civil rights contests. There are other possibilities; the new allocation rules could even strengthen the claims of small racial groups, such as American Indians or Native Hawaiians, by adding to their numbers those with some white ancestry. The third allocation rule implies, in stiff bureaucratic language, that OMB has no idea how the new allocation rules will or should be used in the most important cases.

More subtle questions also arise. People who are both American Indian and white have, on average, a higher socioeconomic status than people who are only American Indian. Therefore as the reported population of American Indians rises as a result of the rule set down in Bulletin 00-02, the average socioeconomic status of American Indians will rise statistically, although, of course, not actually. Might this apparent change be used politically to claim, for example, that the condition of American Indians is improving and they therefore need less federal support?

These are all political as well as substantive and normative questions, so a further question about process immediately arises: who should decide on any or all of this? Members of advocacy groups, whether for a particular race or for multiracialism, have the strongest commitment, the most knowledge, and the deepest feelings about these issues. They therefore have strong grounds for claiming a right to participate in, if not to make, decisions on rules of allocation and on interpretations of new data. Their very status as advocacy groups, however, also undermines their legitimacy, because they cannot be expected to act in the broad public interest (whatever that is) and they cannot necessarily make trustworthy claims about representing their entire group.

Experts within the relevant agencies or brought in as consultants have equal and opposite virtues and defects compared with advocates. Experts are in a better position than advocates to weigh arguments—whether statistical, political, moral, or organizational—against one another; they might have a longer and deeper historical perspective; and their predictions about the future might be more plausible or at least less biased. However, they lack the legitimacy of being an insider in this most intensely personal set of issues; they may falsely believe that they can find technical or statistical resolutions to what are inherently political choices; and their own biases and interests may play a larger role than they intend or perceive.

Given that these issues are inherently political, perhaps the actors with the greatest democratic accountability—that is, legislators—should decide how to allocate and use the new census data. One's response to that possibility depends on how one views democratic decision making on controversial and delicate issues. As some see it, lawmaking is too likely to be distorted by politicians' electoral incentives, special interest groups bearing campaign contributions, noisy minorities (in the arithmetic sense), and public ignorance or apathy. Conversely, after all of the sound and fury, perhaps elected legislators are best suited to respond to an array of legitimate interests through sensible compromises that push the resolution of problems as far as—but no further than—it can appropriately go at a given moment.

After all, as Winston Churchill reputedly observed, democracy is the worst form of government—except for all of the others.

Another arena for deciding how to use the information in the 2000 census might be the courts. Here, too, there are virtues and defects. Judges are insulated from short-term electoral incentives and interest group pressure, and they are trained to consider the deep constitutional implications of decisions involving race and ethnicity. However, they are to some degree captives of the cases brought to them, precedents, and lawyers' efforts to shape the meaning of a claim of discrimination or harm. Most Americans trust the courts more than other political institutions (*Public Perspective* 1997), but we hear a constant refrain about the United States being an overly litigious society. Transforming recognition of multiracials into a full-employment policy for attorneys, though inevitable to some degree, might not be in society's best interests.

Let us assume, as I believe is reasonable, that advocacy groups will play an important role in any likely arena of decision making. It is not clear what members of advocacy groups for nonwhite or multiracial identities ought to seek. The starting rule of thumb is that larger numbers produce more clout in the public arena; that was presumably a central motivation in the first allocation rule of Bulletin 00-02. But what if a particular group has a fixed set of resources to distribute among its members—say, residence on an Indian reservation or revenues from oil production for Alaska Natives? In that case, members of a group might not want to increase their numbers, especially with people who are partly nonmembers and who are likely to have a higher economic status and thus a normatively weaker claim to the group's resources. Advocates for Native Americans or Alaska Natives might well find themselves at odds with advocates for blacks or Hispanics in setting an allocation rule for people with multiple identifications.

Another complexity lies in the relation between race and ethnicity—that is, between the census question asking if the respondent is Hispanic or Latino and the question asking about the respondent's racial identification. The logic of the questions requires both an ethnic and a racial response, and the Census Bureau points out that the sixty-three possible racial responses are doubled when one adds the ethnic choice to the racial choices. Membership in some of those possible 126 groups will be vanishingly small (such as Hispanic black Native Hawaiians or Hispanic black Asian whites).[4] Difficult questions arise, however, when one considers the relatively large number of Hispanics who do not identify with any census-defined race.

The OMB estimated that up to 30 percent of Hispanics would not choose a race in the subsequent question, and it portrayed "confusion regarding the distinction of Hispanic or Latino origin from race" in pre-test interviews. Respondents made such comments as, "Race I guess means the color somebody is. Or their cultural heritage," or "If Hispanic had been offered as a race then I would have chosen that," or "The race question is difficult because it doesn't have enough categories, it's too restrictive. . . . It doesn't specify anything about Central or South American descent" (OMB 2001, 16–17, 70). The OMB's predictions were borne out; almost all of the 15.4 million people who chose "some other race" rather than any of the five races defined on the census form were Hispanic (Schmitt, "For 7 Million People in Census, One Race Category Isn't Enough").[5]

Should we concur that what the OMB observed is best identified as "confusion"? Perhaps, instead, its interview respondents were expressing an intuitive understanding of the social construction of race or simply a perception that the whole concept of clear racial lines is incoherent, especially for people from Latin America. In that case, Hispanics might provide another wedge into a twenty-first-century version of the melting pot. A third possibility is that many Hispanics are insisting that, whatever they are, they are not white, nor black, nor American Indian—despite a history in which all of those groups contributed to shaping the current population of Latin America. In that case, rather than an incipient melting pot we have an indication of identity-based separatism in which a substantial portion of Hispanics seek clear lines of "racial" demarcation away from the standard racially identified groups. That would bode ill for coalitions among people of color as well as for assimilationist hopes.

The tension between many Hispanics' desire to elide the lines between race and ethnicity and data collectors' need for complete and symmetrical information makes interpretation of the 2000 census results empirically difficult and politically fraught. The Department of Education, for which the imperative to categorize Hispanics is most pressing because of the rapidly increasing number of Hispanic school-aged children, has so far thrown up its hands.[6] As the OMB puts it, "Once the Department of Education reviews the results of Census 2000, the Department will reach a final decision on what data will be collected on the racial identification of Hispanic/ Latino individuals." Just how these results will produce an allocational decision rule, the department leaves up to the reader's imagination (OMB 2001, 70).[7]

Both major political parties will have to grapple with the questions raised by the multiple identifier option, but its impact on the two parties will be different. Because the Republican Party controls one house of Congress (and is almost tied for the other) and the presidency while precedent-setting decisions must be made, it can expect to be the brunt of intense and conflicting advocacy. Decisions will be controversial, difficult, uninformed by experience, and necessary—a circumstance that politicians and their appointees abhor. In the end, however, wrestling with the questions I am posing will probably present a more serious problem for the Democratic Party. The politics of racial identification are more like the politics of the death penalty than the politics of abortion—that is, a relatively small number of people care passionately about the issue, and they disagree profoundly, but most Americans have little knowledge of or interest in the problem. Those who do care are disproportionately non-Anglo and disproportionately Democratic. They are inclined to oppose the Republican Party for a variety of reasons, so how the Republican administration chooses on this issue will not make much difference in their overall level of support. A disproportionate share of Republicans, conversely, are Anglos, the vast majority of whom will be indifferent to this issue. In short, Republican leaders must choose but have a lot of political freedom about what to choose; Democratic leaders may not choose but will remain under a lot of pressure from important constituencies to take a position, and the constituencies will disagree on what position the party should take. On the whole, in this domain it will be more comfortable to be a Republican than a Democrat over the next few years.

A Thought Experiment

One way to devise a coherent response to the questions and uncertainties I pose would be to develop a thought experiment. It begins with an observation by Kenneth Prewitt, who was the director of the Census Bureau while the 2000 census was being developed and administered: "Once you have opened up the census in this revolutionary fashion there's really no natural limit, no natural boundaries between the races" (quoted in Solomon Moore, "Census' Multiracial Option Overturns Traditional Views," Los Angeles Times, March 5). What would be lost, and what gained, if the racial and ethnic census categories fell of their own weight and were abandoned?

This prospect is implausible but not impossible. Other complex and deeply embedded policies have been abandoned through federal legislation—most of the federal tax code in 1986, most airline and trucking regulation in 1978 and 1983, respectively, and Aid to Families with Dependent Children (AFDC) in 1996. Political scientists increasingly argue that policy change does not always follow an incremental or path-dependent route; in situations that are roughly predictable (or at least explainable with hindsight), policy makers overthrow established laws and routines and substitute new ones, or nothing, for them (Carmines and Stimson 1989; Baumgartner and Jones 1993).

Why might such an overthrow occur in this case? First, despite all of the disputes, every analyst and advocate agrees on one thing; the categories and procedures of the 2000 census are unsatisfactory. On the one hand, there are too many possibilities. No civil rights enforcement agency, school superintendent, or advertising executive can work with 126 mutually exclusive groups, or even half or a third of that number, if some were combined.

On the other hand, there are too few categories. Some people still cannot find an appropriate location in the census: " 'I define myself as a Muslim,' says one interview subject who speaks for many more than herself. 'To me that's what dominates my life' " (Eric Schmitt, "Broader Palette Allows for Subtler Census Portrait," *New York Times,* March 12, 2001). Jews are as much an ethnicity as a religion; Muslims may refuse to make racial or ethnic distinctions among fellow Muslims; Americans whose ancestors came from the subcontinent of India may not identify as Asians; people from Spain or Brazil may not be comfortable calling themselves Hispanic or Latino. The lobby to add a Middle Eastern or Arab ethnic category did not succeed for the 2000 census, but it might in the future; long before September 11, the OMB recommended "further research . . . to determine the best way to improve data on this population group" (OMB 1997, 11–12). An Internet document claiming that "Census 2000 is biased against multi-ethnic and white citizens" lists seventeen examples of "the rich ethnic heritage of *white* émigrés to this great country" that are "excluded" from the census and complains, "I am not 'white'! I am German-Irish-American, but there is no space on the Census 2000 form for me" ("Census 2000 is Biased Against Multi-Ethnic and White Citizens!" Accessed May 18, 2002 at: *www.adversity.net/special/census2000—a.htm.*) A typology with both too many and too few categories is not stable.

Second, Americans increasingly recognize, or insist, that race and even ethnicity is a social construction. Demography meets deconstruction, and the census's encouragement of increasingly complex self-identification helps the deconstructive instinct along. "When you combine what their mother's side brings and what I bring, tell me what they get? It's all a personal perception," or "I had to think twice about it and call a few friends to see what they put down" (Schmitt, "Broader Palette Allows for Subtler Census Portrait"). Young blacks were four times as likely as older blacks to choose more than one racial category on the census form.[8] Adolescents are twice as likely to identify as mixed race when they are interviewed at school as when they are interviewed at home (Harris and Sim 2000). Interracial and interethnic unions are increasing very rapidly, and presumably so is the number of interracial and multiethnic children.[9] A relatively small increase in the number of interracial and interethnic marriages and children leads to a very large increase in the number of Americans with at least one family member who is of another race or ethnicity.[10] That arithmetic fact is likely to have the important political consequence of further undermining a belief that racial boundaries are "real" and fixed, whether biologically or socially.

A third reason to think that the census's current racial and ethnic classification scheme may fall of its own weight is political. No strong constituency is determined to maintain this particular system, and a variety of groups find one or another aspect of it deeply problematic. Many Republicans would arguably prefer to abandon all racial and ethnic classifications, whether out of a principled belief in colorblindness or a strategic judgment that civil-rights-based and related pressures would be much less effective absent data. Many Democrats seek to maintain these classifications, whether out of a principled belief in the politics of identity or the same strategic judgment. But Democrats disagree on what data to collect and how to measure and use them; arguably, disagreements over the 2000 census will exacerbate already severe tensions among advocacy groups in the roughly defined "civil rights coalition." Advocates for multiracialism, whether they see it as a new identity or as the dissolution of all old racial identities, are not satisfied with the current system. A policy that has no powerful friends and many powerful enemies is not stable.

Finally, the American public may be increasingly impatient with "hard" racial classifications, while they embrace "soft" ones. For example, public opinion surveys show that a majority of Americans reject those forms of affirmative action that seem to imply reverse discrimination or racial preference but endorse those forms that seem to imply special efforts, outreach, extra training, and so on (Steeh and Krysan 1996; Bobo 2000). Corporations now promote "diversity," at least verbally, while resisting "quotas."[11] Similarly, the "Cherokee grandmother" ploy now provides social standing that would have been unthinkable a century or even a few decades ago. Two-thirds of Americans now think that it would be "good for the country" if more people "think of themselves as multiracial rather than as belonging to a single race"; that is a substantial majority and a considerable change from only a few years ago (Gallup Organization, Cable News Network, and *U.S.A. Today* 2001; Princeton Survey Research Associates, *Newsweek* poll, February 1–3, 1995; see also *Washington Post*, Kaiser Family Foundation, and Harvard University School of Public Health 2001). Systematic studies show that most public policies in the long run follow the contours of changes in public opinion (Page and Shapiro 1992; Sharp 1999; Monroe 1998). It is thus conceivable that the census will respond to the growing public preference by moving toward recognition of multiple racial or ethnic ancestries but away from sharply differentiated racial or ethnic categorizations.

If this thought experiment is sufficiently persuasive to take us to the next step, then we need to ask the final, crucial question: what would be gained, and what might be lost, by moving, for example, to a question asking about ancestry, allowing for multiple responses but not asking for a racial and ethnic self-identification? In policy terms, the most important response would have to address civil rights concerns. Whatever else it does with the census, the government must be able to monitor and successfully challenge employment discrimination, voting dilution, school segregation, and the possible undercount of the census itself. Thus any move to eliminate the race categories would be inappropriate unless there were some clear alternative way to accomplish that task. Perhaps reporting one or more ancestors from Africa (or Latin America) could suffice to put the respondent into a protected group for civil rights enforcement purposes.[12]

In normative terms, the most important issue would be whether it is desirable to have such a strong governmental signal that race and ethnicity should be played down in the public realm. Race may be a social construction, but no one can deny that it matters; as Lawrence Bobo of Harvard University says, ask Vincent Chin or James Byrd whether race is only a social construction.[13] Thus any move to eliminate race categories would also be inappropriate unless there was some clear alternative way for the government to signal that it would continue to take race into account in making budgetary, statutory, and regulatory decisions. It is hard to see how that might be done.

There would, then, be real, and in my view unacceptable, costs to eliminating some form of racial categorization in the U.S. census. The government has policy responsibilities and sends political messages that cannot be ignored. Nevertheless, it is not possible to put the genie back in the bottle; the multiracial identifier, with all that it implies about complexity and fuzzy boundaries, is unlikely to be abolished. Nor should it be; if we are somehow to incorporate racial identity into Americans' long-standing commitment to individualism and self-definition, the first step is to enable people to choose their own racial identities.

Perhaps the most imaginative suggestion comes from David Hollinger, who proposes that two questions be asked on the census. The first would provide the data needed to combat discrimination and would read, "Do you have the physical characteristics that render you at risk of discrimination, and if so, do those characteristics make you black, red, yellow, or brown?" The second would register cultural identity, and would ask something like this: "Do you consider yourself to be a member of any of the following ethnoracially defined cultural groups?" (Hollinger 2000, 179–82). Hollinger's questions obviously need to be reformulated, but his instinct to separate the legal and political from the emotional components of "race" may be the right route for resolving the dilemmas discussed in this chapter. Another possibility would be to drastically reduce the racial and ethnic typology to only two choices: black and non-black. That would take the U.S. back to the original purpose of the civil rights law of the 1860s, 1870s, and 1960s: to overcome the heritage of black slavery. That choice clearly implies major assumptions about the assimilation of nonblack immigrants and indigenous peoples and about black exceptionalism. It would be highly controversial, to put it mildly.

It may be a deep irony that the Census Bureau is introducing the

United States to a whole new way of thinking about race in the twenty-first century. But so it is; there is no point in resisting Americans' desire to check more than one box. The task of researchers and policy makers is to understand that desire and to use it "to promote the general Welfare." That is, after all, what the same Constitution that created the census also created the federal government to do.

Notes

1. The release of initial data from the 2000 census indicates also that 6 percent of Hispanics, 14 percent of Asians, and 2.5 percent of Anglos chose more than one race. That sums to 2.4 percent of the American population, or 6.8 million people. (Eric Schmitt, "For 7 Million People in Census, One Race Category Isn't Enough," New York Times, March 13, 2001.)

2. This may be the social science analogue to Heisenberg's uncertainty principle, the theory in quantum mechanics holding that one cannot simultaneously measure a particle's location and its momentum.

3. In operational terms, users of the census data can "report the total selecting each particular race, whether alone or in combination with other races. These totals would represent upper bounds on the size of the population who identified with each of the racial categories" (OMB 2001, 8, quoting from its 1997 *Federal Register* notice mandating the multiple identifiers).

4. However, 823 people checked all six race categories in the 2000 census (Martin Kasindorf and Haya Nasser, "Impact of Census' Race Data Debated," *USA Today,* August 13, 2001).

5. Based on this Schmitt article, I calculate that 42 percent of Hispanics chose "some other race."

6. "Thirty-five percent of Latinos are younger than 18, compared with 24 percent of non-Latinos." (Eric Schmitt, "For 7 Million People in Census, One Race Category Isn't Enough," New York Times, March 13, 2001.)

7. It may be that the Department of Education is simply being more forthright than the other agencies that monitor and enforce civil rights. The OMB's *Provisional Guidance* just notes the presence of Hispanics in its discussion of voting rights, employment discrimination, Title VI enforcement, vital records keeping, and crime reporting (OMB 2001).

8. More precisely, 8.1 percent of blacks aged seventeen and younger identified with more than one race, compared with 2.3 percent of blacks aged fifty and older. The interracial choice increased proportionally in intervening age groups (Eric Schmitt, "New Census Shows Hispanics Are Even with Blacks in the United States," *New York Times,* March 8, 2001). These results presumably reflect both an actual increase in interracial parentage among young people and an increasing willingness to acknowledge white or other nonblack ancestry.

9. U.S. Bureau of the Census, "Interracial Tables," table 4 and 5. Accessed May 18, 2002 at: *www.census.gov/population/www/socdemo/interrace.html.*

10. According to Joshua Goldstein, "Despite an intermarriage rate of about 1%, about 20% of Americans count someone from a different racial group among their kin." Interracial kinship increases with education for all but whites (Goldstein 1999, 405). Goldstein does not consider Hispanic ethnicity; if it were added to the model, the intermarriage rate would be higher, and the kinship connection with someone of a different race or ethnicity would be dramatically higher.

11. Two examples: the president and CEO of DuPont Corporation is featured in a Conference Board publication saying that "we have proof [that] diversity improves our business performance. . . . Diversity in our company is itself a business imperative vital to our ongoing renewal and our competitiveness into the 21st century" (Hart 1997, 5). In the late 1990s, IBM widely distributed an advertisement with a rainbow coalition of happy workers consulting around a table beneath the banner, "Diversity works." Above the picture, the text proclaims, "It has long made sense to us at IBM to welcome and value individual differences. . . . In our diverse marketplace, that's always good business" (published, among other places, in *Atlantic Magazine*, June 1998, 43).

12. This is, in part, an empirical and testable question: would too many whites whose forebears came from Africa be inappropriately included, or too many blacks who think of themselves as descendants of Jamaicans or Mexicans be inappropriately excluded? That leads into, of course, a discussion of how many is "too many" and what it means to be white or black in this context. A similar set of questions could be raised about Hispanics, but their situation is in any case more complicated with regard to civil rights laws and voting rights enforcement.

13. Vincent Chin was a Chinese American beaten to death in 1982 by two autoworkers in Detroit who blamed him for the crisis in the auto industry induced by Americans' move to Japanese-built cars. James Byrd was an African American dragged to his death behind a truck in Jasper, Texas, in 1998 by three white supremacists.

References

Baumgartner, Frank, and Bryan Jones. 1993. *Agendas and Instability in American Politics.* Chicago: University of Chicago Press.

Bobo, Lawrence. 2000. "Race and Beliefs About Affirmative Action." In *Racialized Politics: The Debate About Racism in America,* edited by David Sears, Jim Sidanius, and Lawrence Bobo. Chicago: University of Chicago Press.

Carmines, Edward, and James Stimson. 1989. *Issue Evolution: Race and the Transformation of American Politics.* Princeton, N.J.: Princeton University Press.

Gallup Organization, Cable News Network, and *U.S.A. Today*. 2001. Gallup/ CNN/*USA Today* Poll, conducted March 9–11.

Goldstein, Joshua. 1999. "Kinship Networks That Cross Racial Lines: The Exception or the Rule?" *Demography* 36(3): 399–407.

Harris, David, and Jeremiah Sim. 2000. *An Empirical Look at the Social Construction of Race: The Case of Mixed-Race Adolescents*. Research Report 00–452. Ann Arbor, Mich.: Population Studies Center, University of Michigan.

Hart, Margaret. 1997. *Managing Diversity for a Sustained Competitiveness*. 1195– 97–CH. New York, N.Y.: Conference Board.

Hollinger, David. 2000. *Postethnic America: Beyond Multiculturalism*. New York: Basic Books.

Office of Management and Budget (OMB), Executive Office of the President. 1997. *Revisions to the Standards for the Classification of Federal Data on Race and Ethnicity*. *Federal Register* 62(October 30): 58782–90.

———. 2000. *Guidance on Aggregation and Allocation of Data on Race for Use in Civil Rights Monitoring and Enforcement*. Accessed May 18, 2002 at: *www.whitehouse.gov/omb/bulletins/b00-02*.

———. 2001. *Provisional Guidance on the Implementation of the 1997 Standards for Federal Data on Race and Ethnicity*. *Federal Register* 66(January 20): 3829–31.

Monroe, Alan. 1998. "Public Opinion and Public Policy, 1980–1993." *Public Opinion Quarterly* 62(1): 6–28.

Page, Benjamin, and Robert Shapiro. 1992. *The Rational Public: Fifty Years of Trends in American Policy Preferences*. Chicago: University of Chicago Press.

Public Perspective. 1997. "The NORC Series on Confidence in Leaders of National Institutions." *Public Perspective* 8 (February–March): 2–5.

Sharp, Elaine. 1999. *The Sometime Connection: Public Opinion and Social Policy*. Albany: State University of New York Press.

Steeh, Charlotte, and Maria Krysan. 1996. "The Polls–Trends: Affirmative Action and the Public, 1970–1995." *Public Opinion Quarterly* 60(1): 128–58.

Washington Post, Kaiser Family Foundation, and Harvard University School of Public Health. 2001. *Survey of Biracial Couples*. Washington, D.C.: *Washington Post*.

18

RACE IN THE 2000 CENSUS: A TURNING POINT

Kenneth Prewitt

I MAGINE yourself in 2050, writing a history of Census 2000. What issues would be prominent? Here is a plausible list:

- the fierce partisan debate focused on whether dual-system estimation (statistical sampling) should be used to adjust for census coverage errors
- the resulting extraordinary level of oversight exercised by both the legislative and executive branches and the resort to litigation to influence census methodology
- the design and impact of the first-ever paid advertising campaign, coupled with an unprecedented effort by the Census Bureau to form partnerships with groups and organizations positioned to assist the bureau in motivating the public to cooperate with the census
- the resulting reversal of a three-decades-long decline in the rate at which households mail back the census forms
- the higher-than-expected levels of census coverage as measured by the reduction in the net undercount and the corresponding reduction in differential undercounts across racial groups
- the technical innovations that helped Census 2000 improve coverage and overall data accuracy, such as data capture, which for the first time used intelligent character recognition.

These are important issues, to be sure, but they do not match the historical significance of the multiple-race response option. I base this chapter, then, on one strong premise: when Census 2000 is interpreted from the vantage point of history, it will not be partisan politics or civic mobilization or coverage improvements or technical innovations that will command the most attention. It will be the multiple-race question on the census form.

It will take some time for the significance of the multiple-race option to be widely appreciated. The national level of multiple-race responses is and for some time will remain relatively low. Moreover, despite geographic clustering and higher rates of multiple-race identification in younger age groups, the multiple-race characteristic is overall too small to command major public attention.

In the early years, media coverage of the multiple-race patterns will focus on how to bridge from the 2000 to the 1990 and earlier census data so as to chart trends and analyze broad changes in the nation's racial demography. There will continue to be scattered human interest stories, but generally the multiple-race responses are being collapsed for ease of journalistic reporting. Scholars will provide more nuanced analysis, but it will be many years before the full impact of this work finds its way into public discourse and public policy.

If public attention is initially muted, this follows, in part, from the way government agencies that enforce nondiscriminatory laws and public policies based on racial classification have accommodated the expanding number of racial categories. They have negotiated collapsing rules. How long this will last is, of course, a major question addressed in this volume and a topic to which I return later in this chapter.

There is a third reason why the significance of the multiple-race item is not immediately apparent. The Office of the Chief Statistician in the Office of Management and Budget (OMB), which managed the process that led to the multiple-race option in federal statistics, opted not for a single multiple-race category but for the "mark one or more boxes" format. This matters. A single multiple-race category would have had more sociological traction, and perhaps more political salience, than the scattering of multiple-race answers across dozens of discrete categories. There exist organized advocacy groups focused on multiracialness, whereas there are no such organizations of, for instance, persons who are black–American Indian or Asian-white or any of the dozens of groupings generated by the "mark more than one box" option. Having scattered the multiple-race respondents across so many groupings, it is not likely that there will now be a single multiracial identity pulling them all together. The Hawaiian daughter of a Japanese father and a native Pacific Islander mother will not see herself as linked, sociologically or politically, with the Virginian offspring of a black-white marriage.

Though the long-term prospects for racial identity in the national consciousness, and the influence of the multiple-race option in our measurement system on these identities, are questions beyond the analytic reach of today's social sciences, we can engage in informed speculation. I see four trends in the intermediate future: pressure to expand the number of racial categories; growing scientific doubts about the reliability of racial measurement; increasing public discomfort with racial classification; and greater difficulties reconciling how race is measured with how the resulting classification is used in lawmaking and public policy.

Although the four trends are interdependent, they are not all moving in the same direction. The pressure to expand the number of racial categories is motivated in part by race-based social policy. These pressures also intensify scientific concerns and public discomfort, however, which in turn complicate race-based policy making in a manner that lessens its legitimacy.

Before turning to these trends, a disclaimer: that I served for two years as director of the Census Bureau does not give me special insight into the issues on which I here comment. The OMB decision to allow multiple-race responses preceded my directorship. Although I closely observed the application of the multiple-race item in Census 2000 operations, so did many others—including, especially, the specialists writing for this volume. My views derive from the careful scholarship reported in this volume and elsewhere in the social science literature.

Pressure to Expand the Number of Racial Categories

It is, of course, no accident that the past half-century has witnessed the expansion of the racial classification system, for political reasons well documented elsewhere in this volume. Even in the 2000 census there was pressure from Asian Pacific Islanders not just to be independently counted, which they were for the first time, but to be given their own line on the census form rather than appearing as a category along with other Asian groups. Though Arab Americans accepted, reluctantly, that they would not be separately counted in the 2000 census, there is strong interest in including an Arab racial response category in 2010.

Proliferation begets proliferation, and nothing so strongly signaled proliferation as the multiple-race option, with its legitimization of sixty-three combinations of what had been a handful of separate, nonoverlapping race groups. On what grounds might the federal statistical system declare that enough is enough? There are no scientific grounds; there are no political grounds. To have gradually moved from three to four, five, six, and then, radically, to sixty-three measured groups (even accepting that the sixty-three will be collapsed to fewer than a dozen for most purposes) is to acknowledge that there is no natural limit.

The pressure to proliferate is given emphasis by the government's position that one's race is what one believes it to be. This is to underscore and legitimate identity politics, again as so well described elsewhere in this volume. Identity politics is inherently self-proliferating, as more and more subgroups come to believe there to be political advantage in a separate group identity. Scholars have described the way the drive for social and political recognition has changed the American political landscape, and the census classification is central to the politics of recognition. If these politics are now taken up by new immigrant groups—for example, the recent immigrants from Africa who do not see themselves as African Americans— more and more discrete categories will be demanded.

If history is our guide, the pressure to proliferate will be accommodated by those who manage the measurement system. Political leaders will go to great lengths to avoid the charge that they are showing race favoritism, and the line of least resistance will be to proliferate categories and combinations.

Growing Scientific Doubts About Racial Measurement

Race is less well grounded in science than any other population characteristic measured by the nation's statistical agencies. Continuous change in race measurement across two hundred years of census taking makes the point eloquently. No such changes have tracked the way we measure age or gender. Classifications that have scientific grounding are not radically altered by prevailing political currents.

From a scientific perspective, the multiple-race option in Census 2000 and the official acknowledgment that one's race is subjective, that it is what one wants it to be, lead to doubts about racial measurement. As scientists continue to document their concerns (in part by analyzing Census 2000 data), policy makers and public alike will become more confused. Scientific doubts will complicate technical decisions at the Census Bureau and throughout the statistical system. In its technical and operational choices, the bureau depends heavily on views of the scientific community. It will not wish to be seen as making unscientific choices. However, it also invites and acts upon advice from a large number of stakeholders other than the scientific community, especially for a decennial. Included among these stakeholders are advocates for more detailed racial measurement. In the mid-1990s there were sharp differences about racial measurement, but these differences faded during the actual census operations. By the time Census 2000 was being fielded, community stakeholders and scientific organizations had focused attention on Census Bureau efforts to minimize the differential undercount, and on this issue there was general agreement. Earlier differences will resurface as research (already under way in this volume and elsewhere) documents serious problems of reliability and validity in racial measurement, putting the Census Bureau in the difficult position of balancing best science practice with responsiveness to stakeholder needs.

The multiple-race item and racial measurement more generally underscore the dual nature of the decennial and the fuzzy boundary separating politics and science in census taking. The decennial was political in its inception, charged with the task of redistributing power as America's restless population moved westward. To this earliest, constitutionally grounded political task have been added many others, not the least of which is the central role of census data in enforcement of one person, one vote law, the Voting Rights Act, and many laws and policies enforcing nondiscrimination. To these can also be added the use of census data in federal formula spending. The decennial census carries heavy political duties and has successfully done so by steadily improving the quality of the science applied in the design and operation of the census.

The exception has always been in the measurement of race. Take note, for example, of the flawed census science used to justify racial hierarchies in the nineteenth and early twentieth centuries. Since the middle of the twentieth century, census-measured race has had the goal of eliminating rather than justifying discriminatory social practices. Nevertheless, the multiple-race option opens again the issue of whether the measurement system is scientifically robust enough to carry the social policy weight being placed on it. The Census Bureau and its sister statistical agencies are obligated to provide data for legitimate political purposes, but not if doing so puts accepted scientific standards at risk.

Increasing Public Discomfort with Racial Measurement

Although no reliable baseline exists, informed observers and anecdotal evidence suggest that public discomfort with the race item in Census 2000 was unusually high. The Census Bureau might have inadvertently stimulated this discomfort.

A combination of factors drew sustained public attention to the fact that census undercounts are unevenly distributed across different racial groups—more specifically, that whites tend to be well counted (perhaps, in selected subgroups, even overcounted), whereas racial minorities tend to be undercounted.[1] These racial differentials in census coverage were widely discussed in the media and became the focus of intense partisan debate over the use of dual-system estimation to improve census accuracy. Civil rights groups and their spokespersons in Congress saw Census 2000 as the civil rights issue of the decade.

The Census Bureau mounted an extraordinary public effort to reach the hard-to-count minority groups. Paid advertising, community mobilization, partnership programs, and related public service messages stressed the importance of census participation among inner-city minorities, immigrant farmworkers, the rural poor, Native Americans, and undocumented workers. Because the public face of the census was disproportionately about reaching those who traditionally have been missed in the census, it was easy to think of the census as something for and about race.

The census form itself may have further contributed to this public view. In preparing for the 2000 decennial, issues of respondent burden and form simplification were important to the Census Bureau. The short form was the shortest in census history. Marital status as well as several housing items that had been on the 1990 short form were moved in 2000 to the long form, given to only one in six households.

What remained on the short form were primarily items for which block-level data are required: age, race, ethnicity, gender, and number of people in the housing unit. These items are used in redistricting and to enforce voting rights laws.[2] The ethnicity and race items were particularly complicated and thereby lengthy, with multiple categories for the Asian and Hispanic categories. If you simply inspected the short form it would not be unreasonable to conclude that the purpose of the census was to collect racial information. This occurs at a historical moment in which race-based social policies are under political attack, with litigation and referendums being used to dismantle quota programs and selected affirmative action practices.

A plausible assumption is that the multiple-race item further stimulates public sentiment about the awkwardness and possible inappropriateness of government-sponsored racial classification. Sensitivity about government use, or misuse, of census racial data was in a minor way aggravated during Census 2000 by a sudden flare-up about Census Bureau cooperation in the 1941 internment of Japanese American citizens. Talk-show hosts complaining about the census as a violation of citizen privacy were delighted to have the internment as a case in point.

In the absence of carefully designed public opinion surveys we cannot be definitive about public sentiment toward the government's measurement of and classification by race. It is likely, however, that the first two trends noted—pressure to proliferate categories and scientific doubts—contribute to a public uneasiness with the expanding scope and complexity of racial measurement.

Reconciling How Race Is Measured with How the Resulting Classification Is Used in Lawmaking and Public Policy

Race, along with gender and age, has been included in every decennial since the first in 1790. The census has mirrored and facilitated the centrality of race in America's political and social history. Other contributors to this volume document in rich detail how the measurement of race is never very far from the political purposes to which it has been put, whether the issue is defining citizenship, justifying notions of racial superiority, establishing (or dismantling) discriminatory laws, relocating Native Americans, applying racial criteria in immigration controls, introducing equal opportunity programs, experimenting with affirmative action, fighting racial profiling, or ensuring such basic rights as access to the voting booth.

The nation's long linkage of racial measurement and race-focused policies has rested on a comparatively small number of discrete racial categories. Across a 210-year history, there has been a reasonably close fit between what the policies set out to do to, or for, race groups and the way in which race is measured. This has been particularly so following the civil rights movement of the 1960s, which led to the widespread use of statistical proportionality in public policy.

The multiple-race item on the 2000 census form, and its spread across all federal statistics, represents a sharp break in this historical pattern. None of the race-conscious laws or policies in the middle to late twentieth century were designed with 126 or sixty-three or even a dozen categories in mind. The Census Bureau made a firm decision to report the full array of responses to the multiple-race option. Government agencies responsible for administering race-sensitive laws have done the best they can to align their tasks with this new reality.

To assess how well this alignment will work, whether it will withstand legal challenge and what future adjustments will be necessary, is not the task of these reflections. I make a simple, obvious point: the racial measurement system is now vastly more complicated and multidimensional than anything preceding it, and there is currently no prospect of returning to something simpler. The number of categories is too few to accommodate identity politics but too many to fit with law and legislation as currently designed. The situation is politically unstable, and something will have to give. Either statistical proportionality in race-based policy making will become much more multidimensional in ways hard to imagine, or the policies will confront a growing disconnection from the racial classification on which they have so long depended. The political choice might then be to move away from race-based policy.

To present the nation with this choice is what I have in mind in calling Census 2000 and its measurement of race a "turning point." One outcome, as some fervently hope, is that the arrival of the multiple-race option in the census classification will so blur racial distinctions in the political and legal spheres and perhaps also in public consciousness that race classification will gradually disappear. On the other hand, it may be that the proliferation will lead to more refined categorization to be seized upon by new groups intent on the benefits associated with the politics of recognition.

Notes

1. Any serious observer of a decennial census, starting in 1790, knows that the final count is only an approximation of the true count, and that in all likelihood the true count has always been higher than the reported count. That is, every census has two major coverage errors: persons missed and persons erroneously included. Historically it has been assumed that the one source of error, missed persons, is higher than the other. Censuses have net undercounts. The first systematic measure of the undercount occurred in the early 1940s, when the government initiated mandatory, universal selective service registration as part of the war effort. Though obviously not its intention, this universal registration provided statisticians with two independent counts of males between ages twenty-one and thirty-five—the count recorded in the 1940 census and the count of those registered for military service. Comparing these counts provided the first reliable measure of how many persons, at least in this demographic group, had been missed in the census. It was quickly discovered that African American males of draft age had been missed in the census at much higher rates than white males. Thus the differential undercount first emerges as a racial classification, an artifact of available vital statistics. That is, had there been two independent measures of social isolation (having a phone in 1940) it might have predicted coverage error more strongly than race. And this artifact persists, for the differential undercount has historically been measured by comparing demographic analysis using vital statistics with census counts. Vital statistics have always distinguished black from non-black, making that population distinction particularly convenient. Now, of course, the undercount is also measured through dual system estimation, which uses questions from the short form. Because the short-form includes race and ethnic data (these traits are needed at the block level for administering the Voting Rights Act) the public discussion of differential undercounts continues to be framed around race. This is not incorrect so much as partial, and is true only because race is a surrogate for variables that if available might be more strongly predictive of census coverage errors—social isolation, civic indifference, fear of government, irregular housing, immigrant status, illiteracy, et cetera.

2. Name, phone number, and household relationships remained on the short form to assist the Census Bureau in its many quality control operations. One other item, whether the unit is owned or rented, has such a high predictive value for census coverage that it was retained for the short form as a factor for constructing post-strata groups in dual system estimation.

Appendix

19

COMPARING CENSUS RACE DATA UNDER THE OLD AND NEW STANDARDS

Clyde Tucker, Steve Miller, and Jennifer Parker

D ATA users who are interested in time trends for economic, social, and health characteristics by racial and ethnic groups may need to consider bridging methods for understanding the census data collected under the new standard. The "bridging estimate" predicts how the responses would have been collected and coded under the old standard. It is designed for use in analyzing historical trends in data series.

It should not be assumed that bridging is useful or required in every situation. Users should carefully consider whether they need bridging estimates. Bridging estimates may not be needed if the user can tolerate a "break" in data series or if comparison to another data series provides enough information about the change. Bridge estimates serve at least two purposes: they help users understand the relation between the old and new data series, and they provide consistent numerators and denominators for the transition period, before all data are available in the new format. This chapter is intended to inform users about the statistical characteristics of selected bridging methods.

The analyses presented here make use of survey data in which the same respondent provided racial information in response both to a question structured under the old standard and to questions similar to those that might be structured under the new standard. The results discussed represent the work of a group of statistical and policy analysts drawn from federal statistical agencies that use and produce data on race and ethnicity. The results of the research conducted on several methods for creating bridges are presented. An "other" race category appears in much of the analysis because it is included in the decennial census and some other surveys.

All of these methods involve the use of individual-level records. Analysis is limited to data collected using the separate questions for race and Hispanic origin. Under the new standards, when reporting is based on self-identification, the two-question format is to be used; even in the case of observer identification, this is the preferred format. It is expected that some users will bridge to a distribution that uses the combined format for the question on race and ethnicity. Thus, bridging both to the old racial distribution arising from the use of two questions and one based on a combined, single question are analyzed. The latter analyses required the creation of a combined distribution from data collected using the two-question format. It should be clearly understood that this is a "manufactured" distribution and may be different from one obtained when actually using a combined question format. Based on the research, the strengths and weaknesses of each bridging method are discussed. The last two sections of this chapter discuss weighting data collected under the 1997 standards to 1990-based population controls and suggested bridging strategies for users of the new race and ethnicity data.

The primary criterion for choosing a bridging method, and the one examined here, is the ability to measure true demographic change over time (see OMB 2000, appendix D, for a discussion of the other criteria). This will be accomplished if the effects of the change in methodology can be eliminated. Thus, the ideal bridging method would be one that matches how the respondent would have responded under the 1977 standards, had that been possible. In the ideal situation, differences between the new distribution and the old would only reflect true change in the distribution itself. Furthermore, this bridging method should assign an individual's response under the new standards to the proper single category under the old standards.

Methods for Bridging

The framework for bridge tabulation methods is given as a matrix in table 19.1. Each method focuses on the assignment of the responses from individuals who identify with more than one racial group. Responses from individuals who identify with only a single racial group under the new standards are assumed to have been the same under the old standards. The response "Native Hawaiian or Pacific Islander" is assigned to the old racial category of "Asian or Pacific Islander."

Deterministic whole assignment methods (upper left quadrant in table 19.1) use deterministic rules for assigning multiple responses back to one and only one of the racial categories from the old standards. Four alternatives are examined.

The first assigns multiple responses that include white and one other race to that other race category, but when the responses include two or

TABLE 19.1   *Overview of Framework for Historical Bridge*
             Tabulation Methods

	Assignment Method	
Category Assignment	Deterministic (Following a Set of Predetermined Rules)	Probabilistic (Based on a Probability Distribution)
Whole assignment (person assigned completely to one category)	Smallest group Largest group other than white Largest group Plurality	Equal fractions NHIS fractions
Fractional assignment (person assigned partially to each selected category)	Equal fractions NHIS fractions	

Source: Authors' configuration.

more racial groups other than white, assignment is made to the race with the lowest single-race count among the races other than white. The second assigns responses that include white with one other racial group to that other race, but when the responses include two or more racial groups other than white, assignment is made to the race with the highest single-race count among the races other than white. The third assigns multiple responses to the race (including white) with the highest single-race count. In this case, any combination with white is assigned to the white category, and combinations that do not include white are assigned to the group with the largest single-race count. The fourth alternative, identified in the table as the plurality method, assigns responses based on data from the National Health Interview Survey (NHIS). For a number of years, the NHIS has permitted respondents to select more than one race, with only the first two responses captured. However, respondents reporting more than one race were given a follow-up question asking them to select the one race with which they most closely identify. For these respondents, the proportion choosing each of the two possibilities as their main race was calculated. Using the plurality method, responses for those in a particular multiple-race category are assigned to the one race with the highest proportion of individuals selecting it as their main race on the follow-up question.

Deterministic fractional assignment methods (lower left quadrant in table 19.1) also use deterministic rules for fractional weighting of multiple-race responses, assigning a fraction of the weight to each one of the individual racial categories that are identified. These fractions must sum to one. Two alternatives are examined. The first assigns each of the multiple responses in equal fractions to each race identified. Thus, responses with two racial groups are assigned one-half to each group; those with three groups are assigned one-third to each, and so on. The second alternative assigns responses by fractions to each racial group identified, with the fractions drawn from empirical results from the NHIS. For example, if 60 percent of the respondents selecting both white and black chose black as their main race and the other 40 percent chose white, multiple responses of black and white would be assigned at a weight of 0.6 to the black count and 0.4 to the white count.

Probabilistic whole assignment methods (upper right quadrant in table 19.1) use probabilistic rules for assigning multiple-race responses back to one and only one of the previous racial categories. There are two alternatives, which parallel the two alternatives for deterministic fractional assignment except that here, for a given set of fractions, the response is assigned to only one racial category. The fractions specify the probabilities used to select a particular category. The first alternative uses equal selection probabilities, the second uses the NHIS fractions where possible and equal fractions when no information is available from NHIS. Using the example given earlier, a multiple response of black and white would have a 60 percent chance of being assigned to black and a 40 percent chance of being assigned to white. Probabilistic whole assignment will yield nearly, on average, the same population counts as deterministic fractional assignment. Only the results from deterministic fractional assignment are presented in this chapter. In practice, there would be a difference between deterministic fractional assignment and probabilistic whole assignment when computing variances for tabulated estimates, and the two methods will yield relatively small differences in distributions for respondent characteristics.

The final tabulation method considered in this chapter is termed the all-inclusive method (not presented in table 19.1). Under this method, all responses are used. Responses are assigned to each of the categories that an individual selects, and thus the sum of the categories totals more than 100 percent.

Data Sources

The data used in the tabulations in this chapter come from three sources. The National Health Interview Survey is a continuing nationwide sample survey designed to measure the health status of residents of the United States (Adams and Marano 1995; Massey et al. 1989). The May 1995 Supplement on Race and Ethnicity to the Current Population Survey was one in a series of studies conducted for the federal agencies' review of the standards for data on race and ethnicity. The 1998 Washington State Population Survey, designed to provide information on Washington residents between decennial censuses, collected data on employment, income, education, and health, along with basic demographic information.

National Health Interview Survey

The analysis here uses NHIS data from an analytic file that contains three years of data (1993, 1994, and 1995). For each of these years about forty-five thousand households were interviewed, resulting in slightly more than 100,000 individuals each year. The total sample for the bridge analysis is 323,080 (5,237 respondents did not provide data on race).

Since 1976, the NHIS has allowed respondents to choose more than one racial category. As the respondent is handed a card with numbered racial categories, the interviewer asks, "What is the number of the group or groups that represent your race?" If a respondent selects more than one category, the interviewer then asks, "Which of those groups would you say best describes your race?"

For this analysis, a variable called "detailed race" was created from responses to the first question, which allowed identification with more than one racial group. This information is not included in the public-use data files of the NHIS. However, in internal files, the first two race groups mentioned are recorded for each observation. Even if a respondent selected more than two groups, only two were recorded on the intermediate (internal) file. From the two recorded racial responses, detailed race was coded into five single-race groups (white, black, American Indian or Alaska Native [AIAN], Asian or other Pacific Islander [API], and other) and eleven multiple-race groups (white-black, white-AIAN, white-API, white-other, black-AIAN, black-API, black-other, AIAN-API, AIAN-other, and API-other).

The variable for main race, used as a reference point representing the racial distribution under the old standards, is primarily derived from the detailed-race response and the responses to the second question, which asks the respondent for the group that best describes his or her race (Adams and Marano 1995). For respondents who selected one detailed-race group, the main race is the same as the detailed race. For respondents who selected more than one racial group, the main race is the one group reported as best describing their race. Some respondents who had chosen more than one race for the question on detailed race responded as "multiple race" or "other" to the main-race question. For this analysis, these responses were combined into the "other" category. Categories for main race were white, black, AIAN, API, and other.

The combined race and ethnicity variable, referred to here as "combined main race," uses the respondent's answer to a question on Hispanic origin to reassign the respondent to the Hispanic category. While asking the respondent whether any of the following groups were of his or her national origin or ancestry, the interviewer hands the respondent a card listing Hispanic groups as categories: Puerto Rican, Mexican, Cuban, Mexican American, Chicano, other Latin American, and other Spanish. For this report, whites, blacks, others, and those reporting more than one race who identified with any of the Hispanic groups were categorized as Hispanic and not according to their race. Asians, American Indians, and Alaska Natives were not reclassified. A respondent who did not answer the Hispanic-origin question was assumed to be non-Hispanic.

Supplement on Race and Ethnicity

The May 1995 Supplement on Race and Ethnicity to the Current Population Survey (CPS) was designed to address the following issues: the effect of having a "multiracial" category among the list of races; the effect of adding "Hispanic" to the list of racial categories; and the preferences for alternative names for racial and ethnic categories (for example, African American for black, Latino for Hispanic). The supplement was organized into four panels representing a two-by-two experimental design for studying the first and second of these issues. Each panel was given to one-fourth of the sample, or about fifteen thousand households (about thirty thousand individuals). All respondents in a household received the same set of questions; household members aged fifteen years and older were asked to respond for themselves, and parents answered for children under the age of fifteen.

Only two of the panels in the CPS supplement permitted respondents to report in a multiracial category (panels 2 and 4), and only one panel had separate race and Hispanic-origin questions (panel 2) as ultimately recommended in the new standards. Therefore, panel 2 data were used to analyze the effects of the different tabulation methods for the two-question format. The new Hispanic question, preceding the race question, simply asked whether or not the respondent was Hispanic. The smaller sample (about thirty thousand observations) hampers analysis and generalizations when the focus is on the small portion of the sample (about 1 percent) who identified themselves as multiracial.

There are additional limitations to these data for evaluating the bridging methods. The option respondents were given to identify multiple races in the CPS supplement was a multiracial category with a follow-up question asking respondents to indicate all the racial groups with which they identified. The new standards allow people to identify directly with all the racial groups they choose and do not include a "multiracial" category. Furthermore, a large percentage of individuals who chose the multiracial category in panel 2 of the supplement did not specify more than one racial group (see Tucker et al. 1996). For purposes of this evaluation, individuals were classified as belonging to the specific racial categories they identified.

Those who identified as being multiracial but then did not give two or more specific racial groups were reclassified in the one racial category they gave. Thus, the distribution of the CPS supplement data reported here differs from that published in earlier reports, which classified as multiracial any person who identified with the multiracial category, even if he or she specified only one racial group. This new distribution is referred to here as the edited distribution.

This edited distribution was used with the various tabulation methods. As in the NHIS tabulations, the resulting distributions were compared with a reference distribution based on the respondents' original answers (in the first CPS interview) to the race question that followed the old standards.

The combined race and ethnicity format, still referred to as the reference distribution in the relevant tables, uses the respondent's answer to the Hispanic-origin question to reassign the respondent to the Hispanic category. For this report, whites, blacks, others, and those reporting more than one race who identified with any of the Hispanic groups were categorized as Hispanic and not according to their race. Asians, American Indians, and Alaska Natives were not reclassified. A respondent who did not answer the Hispanic-origin question was assumed to be non-Hispanic.

Washington State Population Survey

The 1998 Washington State Population Survey (WSPS) was conducted by telephone and included 7,279 households with telephones. Blacks, Asians, Hispanics, and American Indians were oversampled. The designated respondent was the individual with the greatest knowledge about the household. The respondent weights reflect this oversampling; thus, results are representative of the Washington population as a whole. The response rate for the entire sample was between 50 and 60 percent.

Information about the race of the respondent was collected twice during the course of the interview. At the beginning of the survey, the respondent was asked, "Are you of Hispanic origin?" The respondent was then asked, "What is your race?" The categories were the ones appearing under the old standards, but the order was as follows: black; American Indian, Aleut, or Eskimo; Asian or Pacific Islander; and white. An "other" category also was allowed, and the interviewer recorded the verbatim response on a "specify" line. Near the end of the survey, the respondent was asked race questions conforming to the new standards. In addition to the same Hispanic-origin question, the respondent was asked to specify country of origin. For race, the respondent was asked to select one or more categories. This time the categories were ordered as follows: white, black or African American (or Haitian or Negro), American Indian or Alaska Native, Native Hawaiian or other Pacific Islander, Asian. Again, an "other" category was provided. Asian respondents were also asked, in a follow-up question, to specify country of origin. The results from the race question at the end of the survey were used with the tabulation methods. The reference distribution came from the answers to the original race question. A combined race and ethnicity format was not created from the WSPS data, because unedited information from the race question using the 1977 format was unavailable.

Results of Statistical Analyses

Statistical analyses were performed using each allocation method. The race distributions based on the reported proportions of multiple-race responses, misclassification rates, race distributions assuming an increase in the multiple-race response, and the effects of each method on outcome measures were analyzed.

Analysis of Race Distributions, Using Reported Proportions of Multiple-Race Responses

For the first phase of the analysis, the distributions of race using each bridging method were compared with the reference distribution in each data set. At the time, it was unknown what percentage of people in the United States would identify with more than one racial group in Census 2000 and in subsequent surveys. For purposes of illustrating the effects of a greater proportion of individuals identifying with more than one racial background, analyses also were conducted increasing the proportion of multiple-race responses by factors of two, four, six, and eight. Of necessity, these tabulations assume that the increases are the same across the different combinations of more than one race.

National Health Interview Survey Information about how respondents who selected two racial groups might identify if there were only the option to select a single racial group can be obtained from the NHIS by looking at a comparison of detailed-race and main-race classifications. For individuals in multiple-race combinations that had sufficient sample size, the main-race designation was compared with the detailed-race response. The distribution of race was calculated using the detailed-race variable, the main-race variable, and the different tabulation alternatives in which responses from individuals of more than one race are allocated to a single racial group. For the most part, the distribution from the main-race variable was used as a reference in comparisons with the distributions produced by the different tabulation methods.

With fewer than 2 percent reporting more than one race over these three years, the race distributions appeared very similar under different tabulation methods (see table 19.2). The estimated distribution from the NHIS fractional assignment method was closest to the reference distribution for all race groups. The largest-group whole assignment and the plurality methods also led to distributions close to the reference distribution. The whole allocation assignments for smallest group and largest group other than white produced distributions similar to one another. These two whole allocation methods greatly overestimated the number of AIAN respondents relative to the reference distribution. Equal fractional assignment overestimated the numbers in the AIAN group but not nearly as much as the whole allocation methods for smallest group and largest group other than white. The all-inclusive allocation method, by definition, leads to a higher proportion of respondents in each racial group, relative to the reference distribution; however, the increase for the AIAN group is considerably larger than for the other racial groups. The sum total for the all-inclusive method is greater than 100 percent, reflecting the duplicate assignment of the multiple-race respondents.

The goodness-of-fit measures lead to similar conclusions; the NHIS fractional allocation method had the smallest goodness-of-fit value (that is, the best overall fit), followed by the largest-group whole allocation method. Whole allocations for the smallest group and the largest group other than white had the largest goodness-of-fit values, indicating a poorer overall fit than the other methods. When bridging to the combined question format ("combined main race"), the NHIS fractional allocation and plurality methods had the closest correspondence to the reference distribution as measured by the goodness-of-fit statistic (data not shown).

Supplement on Race and Ethnicity   A smaller proportion reported more than one race in the CPS supplement survey compared with the NHIS. This is largely the result of recoding in the supplement two-race responses involving "other" to the single-race category of the other race mentioned. As can be seen in table 19.3, the all-inclusive allocation method and whole allocation methods for the smallest group and the largest group other than white have the poorest fit to the reference distribution, based on the race question in the initial CPS questionnaire. The NHIS fractional method provides a relatively close fit. The largest-group whole allocation method and the plurality method give the closest fits. These observations are largely confirmed by the goodness-of-fit measures. For the combined format (data not shown), the largest-group whole allocation method and the plurality method perform the best. The NHIS fractional method also provides a reasonable fit.

Washington State Population Survey   The analysis of the Washington State Population Survey data includes only data from the household

TABLE 19.2 Distribution of Race for Bridge Tabulation Methods, National Health Interview Survey, 1993 to 1995 (Percentage)

Race group	Reference Distribution[a]	Deterministic Whole Assignment					Deterministic Fractional Assignment	
		All Inclusive	Smallest Group	Largest Group Other Than White	Largest Group	Plurality	Equal Fractions	NHIS Fractions
White	80.29 (.71)	80.82	79.39	79.39	80.82	80.57	80.10	80.29
Black	12.74 (.62)	12.91	12.74	12.91	12.67	12.90	12.70	12.74
American Indian or Alaska Native	0.93 (.07)	1.78	1.77	1.63	0.81	0.82	1.29	.93
Asian or Pacific Islander	3.54 (.36)	3.76	3.73	3.72	3.44	3.44	3.58	3.54
Other	2.50 (.27)	2.39	2.38	2.35	2.27	2.27	2.32	2.50
Total	100.00	101.65	100.00	100.00	100.00	100.00	100.00	100.00
Goodness of fit[b]			.00255	.00194	.00025	.00022	.00062	.00001

Source: Centers for Disease Control, National Center for Health Statistics. Authors' compilation based on data from National Health Interview Survey, 1993 to 1995.

Note: All percentages weighted to be nationally representative; 5,237 observations were missing race and are not tabulated.

[a] Reference distribution is main race. Standard error in parentheses.

[b] Goodness of fit = multiple of likelihood-ratio chi-squared statistic, G2 (Agresti 1990, 48).

TABLE 19.3   Distribution of Race for Bridge Tabulation Methods, May 1995 Current Population Survey Supplement on Race and Ethnicity (Percentage)

Race group	Reference Distribution[a]	Deterministic Whole Assignment					Deterministic Fractional Assignment	
		All Inclusive	Smallest Group	Largest Group Other Than White	Largest Group	Plurality	Equal Fractions	NHIS Fractions
White	82.35 (0.51)	80.96	80.42	80.42	80.96	80.74	80.68	80.72
Black	11.11 (0.37)	11.14	11.02	11.14	10.92	11.13	10.99	11.00
American Indian or Alaska Native	0.68 (0.10)	1.15	1.15	1.03	0.80	0.80	0.96	0.86
Asian or Pacific Islander	3.29 (0.23)	3.41	3.39	3.39	3.33	3.30	3.35	3.34
Other	2.58 (0.22)	4.11	4.02	4.02	4.02	4.03	4.02	4.09
Total	100.00	100.77	100.00	100.00	100.00	100.00	100.00	100.00
Goodness of fit[b]		0.00451	0.00431	0.00387	0.00320	0.00323	0.00359	0.00355

Source: Bureau of Labor Statistics. Authors' compilation of data from the May 1995 Current Population Survey (CPS) Supplement on Race and Ethnicity, data from panel 2 only.
Note: All percentages weighted to adjust for sample design and nonresponse; however, estimates are not nationally representative.
[a]Reference distribution is from the original CPS race question conforming to the old standard. Standard error in parentheses.
[b]Goodness of fit = multiple of likelihood-ratio chi-squared statistic, G2 (Agresti 1990, 48).

respondent. Thus, children are not likely to be represented. Because the racial characteristics of the population in Washington State differ substantially from those of the nation as a whole, the results of the analysis of these data offer a contrast to those for both the NHIS and the CPS supplement. Only 2 to 3 percent of the state's population is black. Although whites reporting a single race make up more than 86 percent of the population, the Asian Pacific Islander group still represents about 3 percent of the population (as in the nation as a whole), and Alaska Natives and American Indians (alone or in combination with white) about 3 percent of the state's population. In the reference distribution (table 19.4), AIAN is 1.3 percent of the population. Those reporting more than one race make up more than 4 percent of the state's population.

As can be seen in table 19.4, the all-inclusive, the smallest-group, and the largest-group-other-than-white methods provide the poorest fit to the reference distribution, especially for the AIAN category. The largest-group and the plurality methods understate the proportion in the AIAN category, and the equal-fraction method overstates it. Their goodness-of-fit measures, however, are approximately equivalent. The NHIS fractions method clearly provides the closest fit.

Analysis of Misclassification Rates

In addition to the overall racial distributions produced by the tabulation methods, the misclassification of individuals also needs to be examined. These misclassification rates were formed by comparing individuals' answers to the race question under the old standards with the assigned category of their responses to the race question under the new standards, using each of the tabulation methods. The misclassification rate and its standard error for each race by tabulation method were produced.

National Health Interview Survey The misclassification rates (table 19.5) for the "other" race category are relatively large (and significantly different from zero) in all tabulation methods. The smallest-group method and the largest-group-other-than-white method perform the best for both the AIAN and API categories. Note, however, that these two methods have the highest overall misclassification rates because of the weight given to the white category, which is large relative to the other categories. The largest-group, plurality, and NHIS fractions methods produce substantial misclassification rates for the AIAN category.

Similarly, for methods bridging to the combined format, the "other" race category had the highest misclassification rates. The size of this category, however, is much smaller now that the Hispanics have been removed.

TABLE 19.4   Distribution of Race for Bridge Tabulation Methods, Washington State Population Survey (Percentage)

Race group	Reference Distribution[a]	All Inclusive	Deterministic Whole Assignment				Deterministic Fractional Assignment	
			Smallest Group	Largest Group Other Than White	Largest Group	Plurality	Equal Fractions	NHIS Fractions
White	88.97 (0.31)	90.06	86.19	86.19	90.06	89.66	88.08	88.63
Black	2.27 (0.17)	2.84	2.44	2.84	2.44	2.82	2.49	2.56
American Indian or Alaska Native	1.29 (0.08)	3.21	3.21	2.84	0.88	0.88	2.02	1.19
Asian or Pacific Islander	3.04 (0.16)	3.20	3.19	3.15	2.94	2.94	3.06	3.03
Other	4.44 (0.31)	5.07	4.98	4.99	3.68	3.71	4.35	4.59
Total	100.00	104.38	100.00	100.00	100.00	100.00	100.00	100.00
Goodness of fit[b]		0.00770	0.00833	0.00676	0.00170	0.00211	0.00167	0.00024

Source: State of Washington, Office of Financial Management. Authors' compilation based on data from the Washington State Population Survey, 1998.
Note: All percentages weighted to adjust for sample design and nonresponse; however, estimates are not nationally representative.
[a] Reference distribution is from the original CPS race question conforming to the old standard. Standard error in parentheses.
[b] Goodness of fit = multiple of likelihood-ratio chi-squared statistic, G2 (Agresti 1990, 48).

TABLE 19.5   Multiple-Race Respondents Misclassified by Bridge Tabulation Methods, National Health Interview Survey 1993 to 1995 (Percentage)

Main Race	Deterministic Whole Assignment				Deterministic Fractional Assignment	
	Smallest Group	Largest Group Other Than White	Largest Group	Plurality	Equal Fractions	NHIS Fractions
White	1.12 (.08)	1.12 (.08)	0.00 (.00)	0.07 (.01)	0.56 (.04)	0.32 (.02)
Black	1.00 (.10)	0.00 (.00)	0.89 (.08)	0.00 (.00)	0.94 (.08)	1.24 (.10)
American Indian or Alaska Native	0.00 (.00)	2.26 (.46)	13.25 (1.26)	12.27 (1.19)	6.62 (.63)	11.39 (1.09)
Asian or Pacific Islander	0.44 (.10)	0.24 (.07)	3.12 (.47)	2.95 (.44)	1.71 (.24)	2.31 (.32)
Other	7.89 (1.01)	8.25 (1.07)	9.67 (1.45)	9.67 (1.15)	5.08 (.60)	8.17 (.98)
Total	1.24 (.07)	1.14 (.07)	0.59 (.03)	0.52 (.03)	0.82 (.04)	0.81 (.04)

Source: Centers for Disease Control, National Center for Health Statistics. Authors' compilation based on data from National Health Interview Survey, 1993 to 1995.

Note: Standard error in parentheses.

Supplement on Race and Ethnicity Table 19.6 gives the misclassification rates for the CPS supplement. Misclassification is much greater here compared with the NHIS. The rates for the AIAN and "other" categories are extremely large, and the results differ little from one tabulation method to another. When the combined format was examined, the conclusions were the same (data not shown).

Washington State Population Survey The results from the WSPS, presented in table 19.7, fall in between those for NHIS and the CPS supplement. Although the smallest-group method and the largest-group-other-than-white method have substantial misclassification rates for both AIAN and "other" categories, these rates are not nearly as large as the ones for the other tabulation methods. Misclassification in the API category is much the same for all methods. Given the size of the white category and the somewhat greater misclassification rates for this category using the smallest-group and largest-group-other-than-white methods, these two methods again have the highest overall misclassification rates.

Comparisons of the Race Distributions, Assuming an Increase in Multiple-Race Responses

The effects of increasing the proportion of the population reporting more than one race (data not shown) are quite similar for the three data sources. As the proportion increases, the size of the AIAN category under the various bridging methods diverges more and more from the reference distribution. This is particularly true for the all-inclusive, smallest-group, and largest-group-other-than-white methods, in which the size of the AIAN category can be four to five times larger than in the reference distribution when the number reporting more than one race increases eightfold. The API category is affected in the same way but to a lesser extent. Because of their relatively larger size, black and white groups are less affected than the smaller groups; however, even those estimates increasingly differ as the number of multiple-race respondents increases. The largest-group, plurality, and NHIS fractional methods continue to perform best in all three analyses. These conclusions are much the same when looking at the combined race and ethnicity format.

Effects of Methods on Outcome Measures

Because changes in the reporting or assignment of race affects which individuals get classified under which category, the characteristics of particular racial groups could be altered. For example, the proportion in a racial category reporting crime victimization, a particular economic status, or the incidence of a disease can vary depending on which bridging method is used.

TABLE 19.6   Respondents Misclassified by Bridge Tabulation Methods, Current Population Survey (Percentage)

Main Race	Deterministic Whole Assignment				Deterministic Fractional Assignment	
	Smallest Group	Largest Group Other Than White	Largest Group	Plurality	Equal Fractions	NHIS Fractions
White	3.62 (0.23)	3.62 (0.23)	3.26 (0.22)	3.32 (0.22)	3.44 (0.23)	3.38 (0.23)
Black	4.38 (0.70)	3.86 (0.63)	4.67 (0.65)	3.86 (0.63)	4.43 (0.66)	4.34 (0.65)
American Indian or Alaska Native	37.11 (6.32)	37.20 (6.34)	39.58 (6.31)	39.58 (6.31)	38.34 (6.28)	39.28 (6.30)
Asian or Pacific Islander	5.90 (1.32)	5.78 (1.28)	6.41 (1.37)	6.56 (1.41)	6.12 (1.33)	6.21 (1.34)
Other	40.64 (4.06)	40.64 (4.06)	40.64 (4.06)	40.64 (4.06)	40.64 (4.06)	40.09 (4.06)
Total	4.97 (0.26)	4.90 (0.25)	4.73 (0.25)	4.70 (0.25)	4.84 (0.25)	4.77 (0.25)

Source: Bureau of Labor Statistics. Authors' compilation of data from the May 1995 Current Population Survey (CPS) Supplement on Race and Ethnicity, data from panel 2 only.
Note: Standard error in parentheses.

TABLE 19.7 Respondents Misclassified by Bridge Tabulation Methods, Washington State Population Survey (Percentage)

Main Race	Deterministic Whole Assignment				Deterministic Fractional Assignment	
	Smallest Group	Largest Group Other Than White	Largest Group	Plurality	Equal Fractions	NHIS Fractions
White	3.19 (0.29)	3.19 (0.29)	0.59 (0.13)	0.79 (0.15)	1.90 (0.18)	1.44 (0.16)
Black	9.39 (2.84)	0.71 (0.24)	2.32 (0.74)	1.85 (0.70)	5.44 (1.48)	2.74 (0.62)
American Indian or Alaska Native	11.49 (2.46)	14.20 (2.47)	32.52 (3.80)	32.23 (3.83)	22.19 (2.77)	29.39 (3.55)
Asian or Pacific Islander	6.17 (2.96)	6.26 (2.96)	7.01 (2.94)	6.93 (2.94)	6.59 (2.95)	6.70 (2.94)
Other	10.37 (1.77)	11.15 (1.75)	26.70 (3.26)	26.74 (3.26)	18.37 (2.09)	17.66 (1.99)
Total	3.84 (0.28)	3.72 (0.26)	2.40 (0.26)	2.55 (0.24)	3.12 (0.23)	2.71 (0.20)

Source: State of Washington, Office of Financial Management. Authors' compilation based on data from the Washington State Population Survey, 1998.
Note: Standard error in parentheses.

In the last phase of the analysis, the impact of multiple-race reporting on outcome measures was assessed. Five outcome measures were examined: three from the NHIS and two from the CPS supplement. From the NHIS, three routine health outcomes were calculated: percentage of respondents in poor or fair health, percentage of children living with a single mother (a proxy for restricted access to resources for, among other things, health care), and percentage of respondents with no health insurance. From the CPS supplement, the proportions of respondents who were unemployed and the labor force participation rates for different racial groups were calculated. These estimates based on the bridging alternatives are not meant to be precise measures of these factors but are used to demonstrate the possible impact that reporting of multiple races and the tabulation methods may have on these and similar estimates.

Sensitivity of Three Health Indexes to Multiple-Race Reporting

Turning to the measures of outcomes, table 19.8 presents the results for three indexes of health. The health indexes for single-race groups did not appear to change much under any of the tabulation methods. In particular, the largest single-race groups (white and black) are mostly unaffected by additions or subtractions of multiple-race respondents, primarily owing to their size relative to the proportion multiple race, even when estimates for the multiple-race groups are distinctly different from their single-race counterparts. In some cases (all-inclusive, smallest-group, largest-group-other-than-white, and equal-fractions methods), the AIAN group has a smaller percentage uninsured. These differences derive from the large difference in percentage uninsured between the single-race AIAN and the multiple-race AIAN-white group, accompanied by the fact that a relatively large proportion of AIAN-white respondents is included as AIAN under the allocation methods. The number reporting poor or fair health is unaffected by the bridging method chosen. The percentage of children living with a single mother is different for the single-race and the multiple-race groups, yet the differences are not evident in the allocation methods. Only in the case of the AIAN group is there a possible effect, with the percentage dropping when the all-inclusive, smallest-group, and largest-group-other-than-white methods are used.

The sensitivity of these health measures is similar when the combined race and ethnicity format is used. For Hispanics, the choice of allocation method has little effect on the health measures.

Sensitivity of Economic Indicators to Multiple-Race Reporting

Looking at table 19.9, it appears that all of the methods produce a large increase in the unemployment rate for the AIAN category, and the largest-group, plurality, and NHIS fractional methods produce the largest changes.

These increases, however, are not statistically significant. Only in the case of labor force participation rates in the AIAN category are there any statistically significant differences compared with the reference distribution. The participation rates are larger when the all-inclusive and smallest-group methods are used.

The sensitivity of these economic indicators are much the same under the combined race and ethnicity format. The only significant differences involve the AIAN labor force participation rates, paralleling those reported earlier. Hispanics are unaffected by allocation method.

Discussion

These results should be viewed with caution. Many assumptions had to be made in these studies. It is unclear how people will respond to the new racial question in the future, and these responses could differ by mode of data collection and with the subject of the survey. Furthermore, most of this work on developing bridging methods relied on sample data, and small samples at that.

As stated earlier, an ideal bridging method in this case will be one that not only accurately recreates the population distribution under the old standards, such that the only difference remaining is a function of true change over time, but also assigns an individual's response to the old category that would have been chosen. The methodology used in these studies allows users, within limits, to see how well the bridging methods using racial data collected under the new standards can match data from the same respondents collected (at about the same time) under the old standards. To the extent that there is a match, any change that would occur from this point forward would indicate true change. If the match is poor, it is not possible to isolate the true change.

When comparing the different methods to their reference distributions (whether using only the race question or the combined format), the racial categories that were most sensitive to method chosen were the numerically small ones, particularly the AIAN category. Although different data sets were used in each study and the racial questions were not the same, the studies indicate that the largest-group deterministic whole assignment method, the plurality method, and the two deterministic fractional assignment methods produce distributions closer to the reference distributions than do the other deterministic whole assignment methods and the all-inclusive method.

One reason the largest-group assignment method results are so close is that the method has little effect on the smaller races, because most assignments are made to black or white, and the percentages for these two races are so large that the relatively small increase they receive is not noticeable. The plurality method produces a good fit because it makes assignments at

TABLE 19.8 Sensitivity of Selected Health Survey Variables to Multiple-Race Reporting and Bridge Tabulation Methods (Percentage)

				Deterministic Whole Assignment				Deterministic Fractional Assignment	
Race Group	Detailed Race[a]	Main Race[b]	All Inclusive	Smallest Group	Largest Group Other Than White	Largest Group	Plurality	Equal Fractions	NHIS Fractions
No health insurance[c]									
White	13.4 (.3)	13.5	13.5	13.4	13.4	13.5	13.5	13.5	13.5
Black	18.1 (.5)	18.0	18.0	18.0	18.0	18.0	18.0	18.0	18.0
AIAN	32.2 (2.1)	32.3	26.7	26.7	27.5	32.2	32.1	27.9	31.0
API	18.9 (1.3)	18.5	18.2	18.2	18.3	18.9	18.9	18.6	18.7
Other	32.5 (1.1)	31.1[e]	32.0	32.1	32.1	32.5	32.5	32.3	30.9
White-black	15.6 (2.3)								
White-AIAN	22.9 (1.4)								
White-API	11.2 (1.9)								
Other combinations	19.0 (2.1)								
Poor or fair health[c]									
White	9.5 (.1)	9.6	9.6	9.6	9.6	9.6	9.6	9.6	9.6
Black	14.5 (.4)	14.6	14.6	14.5	14.5	14.7	14.6	14.6	14.6
AIAN	14.1 (.9)	14.3	13.8	13.8	13.4	14.1	14.2	14.0	14.2
API	8.0 (.4)	8.0	7.8	7.8	7.8	8.0	8.0	7.9	7.9
Other	11.7 (.5)	11.8[e]	11.7	11.8	11.7	11.7	11.8	11.8	11.7

White-black	6.4	(1.0)								
White-AIAN	12.5	(.7)								
White-API	5.5	(1.0)								
Other combinations	14.1	(1.7)								

Children living with single mothers[d]

White	14.6	(.3)	14.7	14.9	14.6	14.6	14.9	14.7	14.7	14.7
Black	54.7	(1.1)	54.4	54.1	54.2	54.1	54.5	54.1	54.3	54.3
AIAN	32.1	(3.6)	31.6	28.0	28.0	26.6	31.2	32.2	30.1	32.2
API	11.7	(1.0)	12.2	12.4	12.4	12.5	11.7	11.7	12.3	11.9
Other	26.3	(1.9)	26.0[e]	26.4	26.3	26.1	26.3	26.3	26.5	27.0
White-black	40.9	(3.1)								
White-AIAN	21.1	(2.3)								
White-API	16.7	(2.9)								
Other combinations	34.3	(3.6)								

Source: Centers for Disease Control, National Center for Health Statistics. Authors' compilation based on data from National Health Interview Survey, 1993 to 1995.

Note: All percentages weighted to be nationally representative. Data on race missing for 5,237 observations (1.6 percent) and are not tabulated.

[a] Detailed race is response to question, "Which group or groups best describe your race?" Standard error in parentheses.

[b] Main race is response to question, "With which race do you most closely identify?"

[c] N = 251,196. Health insurance data obtained for only half of 1993.

[d] N = 86,941.

[e] Includes multiracial.

TABLE 19.9 Weighted Estimates of the Unemployment Rate and Labor Force Participation Rate Under the Basic CPS and the Bridging Methods Computed from the Race and Ethnicity Supplement to CPS

Labor Measure and Race Category	Basic CPS	All Inclusive	Deterministic Whole Assignment				Deterministic Fractional Assignment	
			Smallest Group	Largest Group Other Than White	Largest Group	Plurality	Equal Fractions	NHIS Fractions
Unemployment rate								
White	4.82 (0.24)	4.73	4.71	4.71	4.73	4.71	4.72	4.72
Black	9.29 (0.90)	9.39	9.22	9.39	9.28	9.31	9.31	9.31
AIAN	9.76 (3.66)	11.84	11.84	10.67	12.51	12.71	11.87	12.71
API	4.85 (1.12)	4.39	4.41	4.39	4.40	4.40	4.40	4.40
Other	6.74 (1.62)	7.73	7.88	7.88	7.88	7.83	7.88	7.83
Labor force participation rate								
White	66.30 (0.42)	66.25	66.23	66.23	66.25	66.25	66.24	66.24
Black	62.53 (1.01)	62.78	62.70	62.78	62.68	62.78	62.72	62.72
AIAN	57.66 (3.75)	65.75	65.75	64.49	63.47	63.60	64.57	64.19
API	66.53 (2.22)	65.60	65.45	65.66	65.41	65.38	65.46	65.46
Other	68.73 (2.46)	68.45	68.38	68.38	68.38	68.38	68.39	68.39

Source: Bureau of Labor Statistics. Authors' compilation of data from the May 1995 Current Population Survey (CPS) Supplement on Race and Ethnicity, data from panel 2 only.

Note: Estimates weighted to adjust for nonresponse and survey design but are not nationally representative. Standard error in parentheses.

the level of specific racial combinations. The performance of the NHIS fractional assignment method can be discounted to a degree in the NHIS study because the analysis is somewhat circular; however, the results from the CPS supplement and the Washington State Population Survey show this method yields a relatively close match. The equal fractional assignment method produces a reasonable match in these studies. The primary reason that the other two whole assignment methods and the all-inclusive method do not perform as well is that they alter the white percentage to some extent and substantially increase the percentage in the AIAN category.

In the case of misclassification rates, some contradictory results emerge, both when using the race question alone and when using the combined format. Although the AIAN and "other" categories have high misclassification rates across all tabulation methods in the CPS supplement, the same is not true for the other two surveys. The smallest-group and largest-group-other-than-white whole assignment methods produce the most comparable results for the AIAN category in both surveys and for the "other" category in the WSPS; however, these methods have higher overall misclassification rates. Both the CPS supplement and the WSPS have large misclassification rates for these two categories when using many of the tabulation methods.

When the distributions of the outcome variables are examined, all methods produce comparable and relatively close matches for all health outcomes. For the AIAN unemployment rate, the largest-group whole assignment method and the NHIS fractional assignment method appear to produce the least comparable results, but none of the differences are significant. There are significant differences in the AIAN labor force participation rates for several of the tabulation methods. It is likely that which method is best at matching a reference distribution for outcome measures will depend on the outcome being examined.

Weighting When Appropriate Population Controls Are Unavailable

For those using the new racial categories in surveys conducted before the release of new population controls from the 2000 census (expected in 2003), a method is needed to allow the use of the updated 1990 controls. The following advice is provided for researchers who find themselves in this situation:

- Choose a whole allocation bridging method.
- Create a bridged distribution using the chosen method.
- Weight this bridged distribution to match the 1990-based controls.

- Use the final weight from this process when reporting distributions for the new racial categories, including the multiple-race combinations.
- Provide the following caveats to data users: weighting was not done using controls based on the new definitions, and the bridged distribution is not necessarily the same as would have been obtained using the old race question.

Choosing a whole allocation bridging method will simplify the task. Data producers should select the bridging method that they judge to be the most appropriate for their data users. Provide any available information to evaluate the likely discrepancies between the bridged distribution and the distribution that would have been obtained using the old race question. Reweighting to the new controls, once they become available, is strongly recommended.

Strategies for Users

Based on the foregoing analyses, we suggest certain strategies for bridging that depend on the user's needs. In providing these strategies, two assumptions are made. The first is that the user is interested in the analysis of a historical data series. The second follows from the first: the bridging methods are most effective for users who are not simply doing cross-sectional estimates of the current counts in the racial categories or the present and future characteristics of these populations. It should be noted that all of the bridging methods would require, to some extent, prior knowledge of population characteristics when working at the local level.

If the user wants to examine change across the whole racial distribution, the plurality method or one of the fractional allocation methods will most likely provide the best approximations to the distributions from the past. They actually are based on information concerning how the respondents would have answered the question on race under the previous standards. Although the new distribution should reflect only the growth in the racial categories owing to population change and not that owing to methodological change, most of the other methods produce a substantial increase in the size of the American Indian and Alaska Native population not attributable to change over time. Accompanying the increase in this category is a corresponding decrease in the white category. Other distortions could occur as the size of the population identifying with more than one race grows.

If the user is interested in a particular racial category, the method chosen will depend on whether the user wants to err on the side of inclusion or exclusion, especially for the smaller racial groups. Use of the smallest-group method or the largest-group-other-than-white method will include a substantial number of individuals that might have identified with the larger racial group in the past. The characteristics of the group might change simply as a result of their inclusion. This is particularly the case for the AIAN category, and the differences between methods with respect to inclusion or exclusion will be greatest in areas having a large AIAN population, such as the state of Washington. On the other hand, these methods do not exclude anyone who can claim a racial heritage other than white.

Analysis of the combined race and ethnicity format indicates that the choice of tabulation method has little effect on Hispanics. Keep in mind, however, that these results are based on the use of a "manufactured" variable and may not truly represent what would have occurred if an actual combined format had been used in the past. It is also the case that the AIAN category is still affected by the choice of bridging method when using the combined format.

The choice of bridging method also could depend on the substantive characteristics of interest. Some characteristics may not be affected by the particular bridging method chosen. Others will show more change with one method or another. In these cases, the bridging method chosen will depend upon what the user is trying to discover. As we have already noted, health outcomes appear not to be affected by the choice of bridging method, but economic outcomes are.

Geographic characteristics also could affect the choice of bridging method. The user may have knowledge of local populations that would dictate which method should be used. For instance, the user might know that in a particular area those who identify as white are likely to identify as American Indian also when given the opportunity, but if forced to select a single race, they would almost certainly choose white. This knowledge might lead the user to use a bridging method that minimizes assignment to the American Indian and Alaska Native category.

The fact that the smallest-group and the largest-group-other-than-white methods give larger counts for the smaller racial groups might favor their selection in some circumstances. Reliability and confidentiality standards normally would restrict the analysis of these categories. Even though these bridging methods may produce less-than-ideal comparisons with the past, the larger size of the categories resulting from using these methods could increase analytical power enough to allow conclusions to be drawn.

Although the selection of a bridging method should be made for substantive or methodological reasons, simplicity cannot be discounted altogether. Users must have both the substantive knowledge and methodological skill to use the more complicated methods. They also must be able to explain and defend them.

References

Agresti, Alan. 1990. *Categorical Data Analysis*. New York: Wiley.

Adams, Patricia, and Marle Marano. 1995. "Current Estimates from the National Health Interview Survey, 1994." *Vital Health Statistics* 10(193).

Massey, James T., Thomas F. Moore, Van L. Parsons, and William Tadros. 1989. "Design and Estimation for the National Health Interview Survey, 1985–1994." *Vital Health Statistics* 2(110).

Office of Management and Budget (OMB), Executive Office of the President. 2000. *Provisional Guidance on the Implementation of the 1997 Standards for Federal Data on Race and Ethnicity*. Washington: OMB Office of Information and Regulatory Affairs (December 15).

Tucker, Clyde, Ruth McKay, Brian Kojetin, Roderick Harrison, Manuel de la Puente, Linda Stinson, and Edward Robison. 1996. "Testing Methods of Collecting Racial and Ethnic Information: Results of the Current Population Survey Supplement on Race and Ethnicity." *Bureau of Labor Statistics Statistical Notes* 40.

Index

Boldface numbers refer to figures and tables.

ACS. *See* American Community Survey

Add Health. *See* National Longitudinal Study of Adolescent Health

affirmative action: compliance with requirements of, 162, 168–71; narrowing of, 288; official minority designation, origin and development of, 289, 292–98; politics of, 323–25; public opinion regarding, 349

African Americans: blood quantum, classification by, 204–5; in California (*see* California); fractional assignment and, 205–6; in the Glazer proposal, 320–21; history of counting by race, 284–85; intermarriage rate, 6–7, 232, 240; multiracial identification, percentage in 2000, 341; official minority, designation as, 290–98; one-drop rule (*see* one-drop rule); opposition to multiracial reporting, 328, 337–38; population growth of, 216–17, 243–45; proportion of nonwhites, 6; slavery (*see* slavery); youth (*see* multiracial youth)

Agassiz, Louis, 280

Alba, Richard, 239, 320

AMEA. *See* Association of MultiEthnic Americans

American Community Survey (ACS), 141–46

American Indian Child Welfare Act, 199

American Indian Policy Review Commission, 191, 195–96

American Indians: accessibility of for census, 192; blood quantum, classification through, 190–95, 198–99; descent principles compared to other ethnic minorities, 203–4; full bloods, mixed bloods, and blood not reported, 1910 and 1930, **193;** intermarriage rate, 6, 239; projections by blood quantum, **194–95;** racial classification by race and ancestry, **201;** racial classification of, 5, 189–90, 212–13; reallocation guidelines, problems posed by, 140–48; self-identification, classification through, 199–203; self-identification and increase in, 34; tribal membership, classification through, 195–99; tribal membership by blood quantum, requirements for, **199;** youth (*see* multiracial youth)

ancestry: blood quantum and, 190–95, 198–99, 204–7; Census Bureau questions regarding, 8–9, 59; Current Population Survey questions regarding, 9–10; the Glazer proposal and, 320–21; hypodescent *vs.* hyperdescent, 203–4; one-drop rule (*see* one-drop rule); politics behind the census question on, 322–23; problems with using to identify multiracials, 66; responses to the new race question and, 14

Anderson, Margo, 23, 25

A Place for Us (APFU), 35

apportionment. *See* reapportionment/redistricting

Aristotle, 332

Asians and/or Asian Americans: intermarriage rate, 232, 239–40; Italian immi-

Asians and/or Asian Americans (*cont.*)
grant experience, differences from,
225*n*3; modeling population growth of,
216–17, 223; population growth projections, 244–45; reallocation guidelines,
problems posed by, 140–48; self-identification of, 210
Association of MultiEthnic Americans
(AMEA), 34–37, 342
Azevedo, Fernando de, 308

Bakke, Regents of the University of California v., 183*n*10
Barth, Fredrik, 199
Bazile, Leon M., 265
Bennett, Claudette, 341
BIA. *See* Indian Affairs, Bureau of
Black No More (Schuyler), 260
blacks. *See* African Americans
Bobo, Lawrence, 350
Brazil: censuses from 1872–1919, 305–7;
censuses from 1920–1950, 307–8; censuses from 1960–2000, 308–10; census
results: color and inequality, 310–13;
color composition of population, **306;**
the color question in censuses, 304–5;
multiracial counting in census, comparison with U.S., 300–301, 303, 313–14;
multiracialism, implications of confronting, 313–15; multiracialism and national
identity, 302; race, class, and poverty,
303–4; racial identification, measurement
effects in, 68
Brazilian Institute of Geography and Statistics (IBGE), 300–301, 307–10, 312–13
Brennan, William, 183*n*10
bridging methods, 365–66; data sources,
368–72; discussion of results, 383–87;
distribution of race for tabulation
methods, **374–75, 377;** framework for,
366–68; multiple-race respondents misclassified by tabulation methods, **378,
380–81;** need for, 138–39, 141; overview of framework for tabulations, **367;**
results of statistical analyses, 372–83;
sensitivity of health survey variables,

384–85; strategies for users, 388–89;
weighted estimates of labor variables,
386; weighting when population controls
are unavailable, 387–88. *See also* reallocation guidelines (OMB Bulletin
00-02)
Burr, Aaron, 272
Butler, Arthur, 282
Byrd, James, 350

California: African American mothers, odds
of monoracial-monoethnic birth to native-born, **110;** births to native-born and
foreign-born mothers, **106;** controversies
over services for and successes of minorities, 288; demographic transformation
of, 102–3; Hispanic mothers, odds of
monoracial-monoethnic birth to native-
born, **112;** multiple-race reporting in,
50–52, 111–13; multiracial-multiethnic
births, **104–5, 107, 109;** multiracial-multiethnic births, impact of maternal age
and education, 108–11; multiracial-multiethnic births, trends in, 103–7; racial
and ethnic data, 103; Watts riot, 292;
white mothers, odds of monoracial-
monoethnic birth to native-born, **111**
Carter, Lawrence, 237
Castaneda v. Partida, 166–67
Census Bureau, U.S.: "check all that apply"
option, operationalizing for 2000, 40–45;
Current Population Survey (*see* Current
Population Survey); presentation of racial data for 2000, 56–57; projections,
racial and ethnic (*see* projections, racial
and ethnic); race and Hispanic origin
questions, 1990 and 2000, **42–43;** results
from the Census of 2000 (*see* Census of
2000)
Census of 2000: African Americans, previously identified choosing more than one
race, 341; "check all that apply" option
(*see* "check all that apply" option); comparing data with previous censuses (*see*
bridging methods); distribution of multiple-race population, **47;** frequency of re-

porting multiple-race ancestry, **46;** geography of multiple race reporting, 50–52; maximum and minimum counts of races, 48–49; multiple-race population by state and county, **128;** multiple-race reporting by county, **54;** multiple-race reporting by metropolitan statistical area, **53;** multiple-race reporting by state, **51;** population by number of races reported, **46;** race groups, comparison of minimum and maximum counts, **49;** reallocation of multiple-race results, **127**

"check all that apply" option: adoption of, 328–29; complexity of racial data produced by, 52, 55–57; consideration and adoption of, 36–37; OMB guidelines, 39–40; operationalizing for 2000, 40–45; respondent use of in 2000, 45–48; significance of, 355. *See also* reallocation guidelines (OMB Bulletin 00-02)

Chin, Vincent, 350

Civil Rights Act of 1964, 289–90

civil rights law: compliance with desegregation and affirmative action, 168–71; defined, 29*n*17; discriminatory impact, 161–62, 165–68; ethnic fraud and racial discrimination, 208–9; impact of OMB allocation rules, 15–17, 124–25, 133–34, 141–52, 159, 162, 176–79; legal status required by regulations, 11; multiracial census, implications of, 13, 161–63, 165, 180–81; redistricting and voting rights, 171–75; when multiraciality matters, 163–65. *See also* multiple-race data and single-race laws

Clinton, Bill, 37, 329

compliance with desegregation and affirmative action, 162, 168–71, 291–98

Congressional Black Caucus, 18, 206

Cook, Thomas, 64–65

Corrin, William, 64–65

CPS. *See* Current Population Survey

Crèvecoeur, J. Hector St. John de, 3

Current Population Survey (CPS): data for population projections, 235–37; ethnic origin questions, 9; parental birthplace questions, 8; population estimates, origin of, 216; Supplement on Race and Ethnicity, 36, 140, 368, 370–71, 373, 375, 379–80

Dayton, William, 282

del Pinal, Jorge, 240

desegregation, school, 162, 168–69

discriminatory impact litigation, 161–62, 165–68

Du Bois, W. E. B., 63

DuPont Corporation, 352*n*11

Dwight, Sereno Edwards, 273

Edmonston, Barry, 22, 26

Education Department, U.S., 346

EEOC. *See* Equal Employment Opportunity Commission

Eisenhower, Dwight, 289, 291

Equal Employment Opportunity Commission (EEOC), 289, 292–93, 295–97

ethnic fraud, 208–9

ethnicity: data collection on, 2, 7–10 (*see also* multiracial reporting or classification; racial classification); race and, 3–4

ethnic switching, 201

Fair Employment Practices Committee (FEPC), 289

family structure, self-identification as multiracial and, 71–72, 75, 79, 87

Farley, Reynolds, 16, 19, 25–26, 324

FEPC. *See* Fair Employment Practices Committee

Fernandez, Carlos, 34

Fernandez, Marilyn, 240

fertility, assumptions regarding for population projections, 235–37

Fitzpatrick, Joseph, 240

Fong, Hiram L., 292

fractional assignment, 205–6, 264

Freyre, Gilberto, 302

Gans, Herbert, 121

Garrison, William Lloyd, 277

gender, self-identification as multiracial and, 74–75, 84, 86

Gingles, Thornburgh v., 172, 184*n*15–16

Gingrich, Newt, 25, 36, 329

Glassman, James K., 337

Glazer, Nathan, 23, 26, 261–62

Golden, Reid, 239

Goldstein, Joshua, 12, 20, 25–26, 66, 336, 352*n*10

Gonzales, Henry, 292

Goyette, Kimberly, 64, 121

Graham, Hugh Davis, 23, 25

Graham, Susan, 34–36, 122

Griggs v. Duke Power, 166, 182*n*6, 293

Gurak, Douglas, 240

Harris, David, 19

Harrison, Roderick, 16, 20–21, 25–26, 36

Hasenbalg, Carlos, 311–12

Hemphill, Joseph, 275

Hirabayashi, Gordon, 265

Hispanics: in California (*see* California); Census Bureau questions, 8–9, 12–14, 36, 57–58; Census Bureau questions, 1990 and 2000, 41–44; Census Bureau questions, politics of, 330; classification of, 5–6, 345–46; identification as, OMB guidelines for, 121–22; intermarriage rate, 232, 240; Italian immigrant experience, differences from, 225*n*3; modeling population growth of, 216–17, 223, 231; official minority, designation as, 291–92; population growth projections, 244, 248; race question and, 345–46

history of racial classification: administering the census, 271–72; census of 1820, expansion of data, 276–77; colonial proposals, 269–70; the Constitution, 270–71; controversy and change throughout the, 33–34; early conflict over apportionment, 272–74; immigration and, 227; intermarriage and, 3–7; Missouri Compromise, conflict leading to, 274–76; official minority designation, origins and development of, 288–98; official statistics, use of, 138; postbellum recon-struction, 284–85; sectional conflict and census reform for 1850, 277–84; slave state strength and power, **278;** the state and the lengthy history of race counting, 259–60

Hochschild, Jennifer, 23

Hollinger, David A., 266, 297, 334, 350

Hutchinson, George, 265

IBGE. *See* Brazilian Institute of Geography and Statistics

IBM, 352*n*11

immigrants: assumptions regarding migration, 238–39; Italians (*see* Italian immigrants); population projections of, 227–31, 242–43; race and, 224, 227; restrictions on, racial concerns and arguments for, 3; sources of, 227–28

Indian Affairs, Bureau of (BIA), 191–92, 194, 197–99, 207

Indian Health Service, 191

Inouye, Daniel K., 292

intermarriage: African Americans, 6–7, 232, 240; American Indians, 6, 212, 239; Asians and/or Asian Americans, 232, 239–40; assumptions for population projections, 241–42; data on, 38–39; defined, 231; estimates of by race and sex, **39;** growing prevalence and recognition of, 1–2; Hispanics, 232, 240; history of racial classification and, 3–7; Italian immigrants and population projections, 219–23; population projections and, 228, 230–31, 233–34, 244–48; prevalence of ethnic in American history, 3; racial/ethnic projection models and, 215; rates of, 232–33, 239–41; reasons for, 107; significance of, 229; studies of, 64. *See also* family structure

international migration, assumptions regarding for population projections, 238–39

Interracial Family Alliance, 35

Interracial Lifestyle Connection, 35

interracial marriage. *See* intermarriage

Italian immigrants: ethnic origins among immigrants and descendants, **220;** marriage patterns and population projections, 219–23; origins of third generation immigrants, **222;** time from first to fourth generation immigrants, **221**

Jacobson, Matthew, 22, 25
Jefferson, Thomas, 272, 274
Johnson, Lyndon, 289, 293, 297
Justice Department, U.S., 27, 174–75, 336

Kalmijn, Matthijs, 232
Kao, Grace, 64–66
Kennedy, John, 289, 291–93, 297
Kennedy, Randall, 267n3
King, William, 281–82
Korematsu, Fred Toyoaburo, 265

Landrith, James A., Jr., 122
La Raza Unida, 297
Latin America: multiracialism in, 301–3; poverty and inequality in, 303
Leadership Conference on Civil Rights, 37
Lee, Ronald, 237
Lee, Sharon, 22, 26, 240
Lee, Shawn, 240
Levy Economics Institute, 2, 18
Lieberson, Stanley, 324, 335
Liebler, Carolyn, 202–3
Lim, Nelson, 68
Lincoln, Abraham, 284
Lind, Michael, 121
Lott, Trent, 337
Lovell, Peggy, 311–12
Loving v. Virginia, 35, 265
Lowi, Theodore, 336

Macon, Nathaniel, 276
Mann, David, 291–92
marriage, interracial. *See* intermarriage
Matsui, Robert, 41, 323
McKinney, Nampeo, 35
methodology: comparing 2000 data with previous censuses (*see* bridging methods); measurement effects, 68; multiracial youth, study of, 69–71; racial measurement, scientific doubts about,

357–58; response variability, 211; undercounts, 361n1
Miller, Steve, 21
minority designation, origins and development of official, 288–98
Minority Rights Revolution, The (Skrentny), 291
Montoya, Joseph, 292
moral imperatives of race counting, 259–62
Morgan, Lewis Henry, 190
Morning, Ann, 12, 20, 25–26, 66
mortality, assumptions regarding for population projections, 237
multiple-race data and single-race laws: estimates of reallocation, 126–31; implications of reallocation, 14–17, 122–26; OMB reallocation guidelines (*see* reallocation guidelines (OMB Bulletin 00-02)); political and administrative problems of, 2, 11–14, 24–25, 333–36; problems of reallocation, 132–34; reallocation of 2000 Census multiple-race results, **127;** socioeconomic characteristics by race, 1990 Census and OMB reallocation, **130;** unresolved issues of reallocation, 125–26. *See also* civil rights law
Multiracial Activist, 122
multiracial population: in California (*see* California); existence of multiple, 68; socioeconomic characteristics, **132;** studies of, 63–68; youth (*see* multiracial youth)
multiracial reporting or classification: adoption of, 13–14, 34–37; age and, 58; in Brazil (*see* Brazil); classification schemes and, 62–63, 66–68, 97; frequency of, 45–48, 58; geography of, 50–52, 58; history and legacy of, 264–66; litigation, implications for (*see* civil rights law); options for, 350; politics of (*see* politics of the census); public discomfort regarding, 358–59; questions about, 342–47; redistricting and, 58; scientific doubts about, 357–58; significance of, 1–2, 354–56, 359–60; uncertainties about, 340–41. *See also*

multiracial reporting or classification (*cont.*)

ethnicity, data collection on; reallocation guidelines (OMB Bulletin 00-02)

multiracial youth: descriptive statistics for self-identified, **73–74;** descriptive statistics for white-American Indian subgroup, **85–86, 88–89;** descriptive statistics for white-Asian subgroup, **91–92, 94–95;** descriptive statistics for white-black subgroup, **80–83;** identifying, 66–68; methodology for study of, 69–71; National Longitudinal Study of Adolescent Health data, 69; racial classification schemes and, 63, 96–97; racial composition of sample, **72, 78;** results of study of, 71–77; studies of, 64–65; white-American Indian subgroup, 84–90; white-Asian subgroup, 90–96; white-black subgroup, 77–84. *See also* youth

National Academy of Sciences, 334, 336
National Association for the Advancement of Colored People (NAACP), 297
National Center for Health Statistics, 239–40
National Education Longitudinal Study, 66
National Health Interview Survey (NHIS), 140, 147, 367–70, 372–74, 376, 378
National Longitudinal Study of Adolescent Health (Add Health), 69
Native Americans. *See* American Indians
NHIS. *See* National Health Interview Survey
Nixon, Richard, 330
Nobles, Melissa, 4–5, 23, 25, 323–24, 331
Nott, Josiah Clark, 264, 280–81, 284

O'Connor, Sandra Day, 27
OFCC. *See* Office of Federal Contract Compliance
Office of Federal Contract Compliance (OFCC), 293–95
Office of Management and Budget (OMB): changing the race question, 13, 328–29; "check all that apply" option (*see* "check all that apply" option); definition of race and ethnicity, 113*n*1; Directive 15, 4, 11–12, 36, 189, 200, 297; Hispanics, classification of, 5–6, 345–46 (*see also* Hispanics); multiple-race data, guidelines for use of (*see* reallocation guidelines (OMB Bulletin 00-02)); recommendations for presentation of racial data, 55–57; self-identification and administrative requirements, tension between, 334–35
OMB. *See* Office of Management and Budget
one-drop rule: civil rights considerations and, 16; as exception in racial fractional determinations, 264; modern *vs.* traditional use of, 120; offspring of intermarriage, classification of, 1, 4; *vs.* hyperdescent in determining group membership, 203–5

Park, Robert Ezra, 63, 79
Parker, Jennifer, 21
Passel, Jeffrey, 22, 26
Perlmann, Joel, 22, 25–26, 265, 329, 337
Persily, Nathaniel, 16, 25–27
Petri, Thomas, 37
Philadelphia Negro, The (Du Bois), 63
politics of the census, 327–29, 336–38; the Constitution and, 332; Hispanic-origin question, 330; multiracial counting, opposition to, 13, 35–37, 67; multiracial counting, support for, 11–13, 17–18, 34–37, 298; multiracial option and, 327–29, 336–38; national interests, intertwining with, 25–27; OMB allocation plan and, 120 (*see also* reallocation guidelines (OMB Bulletin 00-02)); one-drop rule and civil rights, 16 (*see also* one-drop rule); policy instability, 348–49; politically-motivated interventions, 321–26; public discomfort regarding racial classification, 358–59; racial categories, pressure to expand number of, 356–57; Republicans and Democrats, 18, 346–47; science and, 330–32; self-identification and administrative requirements, tension between, 333–36; state authority mani-

fested in, 332–33; use of new census data and, 344–45

population growth, modeling of, 216–17. *See also* projections, racial and ethnic

Powell, Lewis, 183*n*10

President's Committee on Civil Rights (Truman Committee), 290

Prewitt, Kenneth, 1, 23, 333, 340, 347

projections, racial and ethnic: approaches for the future, 250–51; considerations for and uses of, 228–29; data and assumptions, 235–42; fertility assumptions, **236**; growth of race-ethnicity groups, 242–44; intermarriage and, 215, 230–34, 244–48; intermarriage assumptions, **241**; international migration assumptions, **238–39;** Italians, 219–23; justifications for, 216, 218, 224–25; mortality assumptions, **237;** multiple-origin population, implications of growth of, 248–50; origins of, 216–18; population by racial group, **243, 246–47;** population projection model, 229–30, 233–35; single- and multiple-origin base population, **236;** uses of, 234

Project RACE. *See* Reclassify All Children Equally

race: black-white divide, primacy in America, 6; concept and legacy of, 263–67; ethnicity and, 3–4; history of intermingling in America, 3–7 (*see also* history of racial classification); as social construction, 68, 157, 260, 336, 348

Race and Ethnic Targeted Test (RAETT), 152–53

racial classification: abandonment of, thinking about, 347–51; "check all that apply" option (*see* "check all that apply" option); the Glazer proposal, 318–21; history of (*see* history of racial classification); irony of choosing only one option, 11; morality of, 259–62; multiracial reporting (*see* multiracial reporting or classification); need for, 215; one-drop rule (*see* one-drop rule); politics of (*see* politics of the census); primary single

race chosen by respondents with multiple-race ancestry, **129;** self-identification (*see* self-identification); through blood quantum, 190–95, 198–99, 204–7; through community recognition, 195–99, 207–9. *See also* ethnicity, data collection on

racial intermarriage. *See* intermarriage

racism, 211–12

RAETT. *See* Race and Ethnic Targeted Test

Reagan, Ronald, 323

reallocation guidelines (OMB Bulletin 00-02): areas requiring further research, 139–40; challenges of, 120–21, 131–34; "civil rights" allocation, **142;** civil rights laws and, 2, 15–17, 124–25, 133–34, 141–52, 159, 162, 176–79, 223; discrepancies with past counts, problems regarding, 139–48; ethnic fraud and, 208–9; inadequacies of, 137–39, 158–59; need for, 119; operationalizing and meaning of the data, problem of, 149–58; political environment of, 298 (*see also* politics of the census); the procedure, 121–22; questions regarding, 343–44; race combinations, determination of, 185*n*22. *See also* bridging methods; "check all that apply" option; multiple-race data and single-race laws

reapportionment and/or redistricting: democratization of voting and, 285*n;* early conflict over apportionment, 272–74; impact of multiracial reporting, 58; as justification for census, 56; OMB reallocation guidelines and, 140; racial categories, need for, 113*n*2; Voting Rights Act of 1965 and, 123–24, 133, 162, 171–75

Reclassify All Children Equally (Project RACE), 34–35, 122, 154–55

Riche, Martha Farnsworth, 340

Roosevelt, Franklin, 289

Roybal, Edward, 292

Sawyer, Thomas, 35

Saxonhouse, Arlene, 332

SBA. *See* Small Business Administration

school desegregation, 162, 168–69

Schuyler, George S., 260, 264

Schwarcz, Lilia Moritz, 306

Schwartzmann, Simon, 312–13

science: making "race" and, 261; racial measurement, doubts about, 357–58

Scott, James, 333

Seeing Like a State (Scott), 333

self-identification: of American Indians, 199–203, 209–10; Census Bureau embrace of, 10–11, 163; change to in 1970, 34; ideological attraction and administrative problem of, 333–36; of Italian immigrants, 223; problems of, 67, 209–12; reallocation guidelines and, 120, 149–58, 189

Seward, William, 281–82, 284

Shaw v. Reno, 123–24

Sim, Jeremiah, 67–68

Simpson, Kenneth, 35

Singer, Audrey, 240

Skerry, Peter, 23, 25, 322–23

Skrentny, John, 291–92

slavery: early census counting and, 269–85; reparations, 206–7

Small Business Administration (SBA), 294–95, 323

Snipp, Matthew, 5, 21, 23

Sollors, Werner, 22–23, 25

Starr, Paul, 333

state, the: authority of and the census, 332–33; making "race" and, 261–62. *See also* politics of the census

Stolcke, Verena, 263

Stonequist, Everett, 63

Tabah, Leon, 251

tabulation. *See* reallocation guidelines (OMB Bulletin 00-02)

Taeuber, Conrad, 330

Tafoya, Sonya, 20

Talmadge, James, 274

Taylor, John W., 275

Telles, Edward, 68

Thernstrom, Stephan, 334

Tidwell, Billy, 35–36

Time, "browning of America" article, 217–18

Toomer, Jean, 263

To Secure These Rights (Truman Committee), 290

Truman, Harry, 289–90

Tucker, Clyde, 21, 137

Tuljapurkar, Shripad, 237

undercounts, 1, 361n1

Underwood, Joseph, 281–82

U.S. Commission on Civil Rights, 290

Vasconcelos, José, 302

Vianna, Oliveira, 307

Voting Rights Act of 1965, 123–24, 133, 162, 171–75, 325

Wallman, Katherine, 37

Ward's Cove Packing Co., Inc. v. Atonio, 182n5

Washington State Population Survey, 140, 368, 371–73, 376–77, 379, 381

Waters, Mary, 320, 337

Wood, Charles, 311–12

Woods, Tiger, 37, 218, 298

World Bank, 309–10

Xie, Yu, 64, 121

Yamanaka, Keiko, 240

youth: descriptive statistics for multiracial and monoracial, **76–77**; descriptive statistics for white-American Indian, white, and American Indian self-identified, **88–89**; descriptive statistics for white-Asian, white, and Asian self-identified, **94–95**; descriptive statistics for white-black, white, and black self-identified, **82–83**; multiracial (*see* multiracial youth)

Yulee, David, 282